HEMINGWAY IN SPAIN

Hemingway in Spain

A PERSONAL REMINISCENCE OF HEMINGWAY'S
YEARS IN SPAIN BY HIS FRIEND

JOSÉ LUIS CASTILLO-PUCHE

Translated from the Spanish by Helen R. Lane

DOUBLEDAY & COMPANY, INC.
Garden City, New York   1974

ISBN: 0-385-08337-8
Library of Congress Catalog Card Number 73–22150
Translation Copyright © 1974 by Doubleday & Company, Inc.
All Rights Reserved
Printed in the United States of America
First Edition

LIST OF ILLUSTRATIONS

"Courage is
a headlong escape forward."

PREFACE

Many people have wondered how I came to be friends with Ernest Hemingway. This is how it happened.

In 1954 Ernesto appeared in the dusty arena of Madrid, for the second time since the Spanish Civil War. He had come to Spain in 1953, but had stayed only a short while, like a partridge alighting and then suddenly taking wing again; still, this brief visit in 1953 had been something of an event, for it was his first in fifteen years. He had solemnly promised himself that he would never set foot in Madrid, the "capital of the world," as he called it, as long as any of his Spanish friends were still behind prison bars. And he had kept his promise.

During all the years that he had stayed away, he had wandered far and wide. He had turned up in Europe, where as a raw youth he had first come under fire as an ambulance driver during the First World War; in Africa, that continent that exhilarated him and kept him from feeling bored and restless for a time; on the shores of the Caribbean, where he labored at writing; and even in his own country, which delighted him but often threatened to become a painful irritant. During all that time, he had felt, in his own words, more or less a prisoner wherever he was, and the most miserable kind of prisoner to boot—one outside prison, which is far worse than being one inside. And he had been a prisoner outside the bars in another way too, for he had been on the losing side in Spain, the country that next to his own was closest to his heart. It was not until 1954 that he felt he could come back to Madrid. Like a bull in the ring, the first thing he did was head straight for his *querencia*—his turf, the haunts he loved best.

When he arrived, a reporter from the daily paper *Informaciones* came to see him in the Hotel Palace and found him reading a novel while he was being massaged, getting his hair and fingernails cut, and having his calluses pared; he'd just come back from his famous safari in Africa, during which he'd been in a plane accident and been given up for dead. He greeted the man from *Informaciones*, book in hand, and the reporter asked him, "May I ask what you're reading?"

"A friend of mine who's a matador gave me this novel and I haven't been able to put it down," he replied. "I didn't know anybody in Spain was writing such powerful and such spontaneous stuff."

The book this great author was praising was my novel *With Death on My Back*.

Hemingway gave the reporter permission to take his photograph with the book in his hand and again praised it highly, as he was also to do later in Paris, New York, and Havana—a gesture that reminded me of a magnanimous *presidente* of a bullfight who on a sunny afternoon with no wind awards two ears and a tail to a brash *novillero* appearing in the ring for the first time.

And that was how I became friends with Ernesto Hemingway.

Though this was how our friendship of many years began, it came to be much more than gratitude toward a revered master on my part and mere politeness on his. He was interested in my most intimate problems as a writer—and publicly celebrated the publication of my book *The Avenger* with the words, "From now on we're going to be close friends," even though we had long since called each other by the intimate *tú*. I was fortunate—and unfortunate—enough to see and hear him in moments of weakness, anger, or some other passing mood exactly as he really was, though it was never easy to discover the real man beneath his booming laughter.

As I say, we were friends and there were no pretenses between us, just an enormous frankness and sincerity on both our parts from the very first. He was the one who made it possible for me to come see him at his home in Havana and to visit the United States for the first time; with all due modesty, I believe he did so out of a feeling that was more than mere gratitude to me for having stood by him through thick and thin, in moments of confusion and moments of triumph. I was his friend when people were beginning to avoid him and when he was the lionized Nobel Prize winner, his friend the day of his accident in Burgos and the day the unfortunate rumor went the rounds in Madrid that he had died at "La Cónsula," in Málaga. I moved heaven and earth to ensure that articles and essays on him that might interest Spaniards got into print, and out of personal affection for him and enormous admiration for his art, I gave lectures about him in universities, literary societies, high schools, and so on, even though I was quite aware that I was not an accomplished public speaker. I simply tried to decipher the great enigma: an author whose works were praised to the skies but also unread, a man who enjoyed enormous popular acclaim but almost never showed his real self.

There are many things about Hemingway's affable, insecure, pathetic personality that have never come to light however, for though his status as a master of the art of storytelling is recognized more and more by highly respected critics, his human qualities are still, if I may be pardoned an unflattering adjective he would not like at all, more or less virgin territory.

In any event, every time he came to Spain, he got in touch with me and we went on many unforgettable trips together. I must add that it was not as easy to get to see Ernesto as might be supposed. And if just getting to see him was difficult, getting to talk with him or spend time with him was a heroic undertaking, and usually people gave up. When he was in Madrid or the Escorial or Málaga or Valencia, he could often be seen stealing down the service stairs of his hotel to escape the crowd of writers, reporters, and photographers lying in wait for him in the lobby or at the front entrance. What is more, even on the rare occasions when he finally granted someone an interview, I could see that usually no sort of real communication or genuine dialogue ever began between Ernesto and the interviewer. And what generally appeared in print later was one more facile, slick, surprising profile, full of the sort of cynical elusive repartee, the leg-pulling at which Ernesto was such a master. Interviews such as this never more than scratched the surface of his personality; he was extremely clever at hiding his real self.

Like a number of others who considered themselves to be on more or less intimate terms with Ernesto, I often noticed how cagey and wary he was—both a pathetically lonely and a pathologically devious man. Still I believe I managed to gain his confidence to some degree, above and beyond the literary concerns we shared. I tried my best never to pry, and on more than one occasion I was able to prove my loyalty to him. I have wondered countless times why his behavior toward me was quite unlike his behavior toward others, and I have come to think that it was because he thought of himself as the protector of the literary vocation of a writer he believed in and I for my part was fascinated by a man who was a living legend.

But I believe there was also something else; a sort of natural affinity, a striking similarity of temperament, certain identical turns of mind were responsible for our mutual friendship. Many times, we found we understood each other perfectly without having to say a word. I still insist that the title of my first novel, *With Death on My Back*, must have struck a chord in Ernesto, who often had sudden intuitions and liked or disliked things instantly—though later the book of mine he thought most highly of was *El Vengador.* The protagonist of *With Death on My Back* is obsessed throughout the book by the idea that he may die at any moment, so Death might be considered the main character. This undoubtedly attracted and impressed him, for Ernesto was not a man who had death riding on his back; he bore it much deeper within himself, in his guts, a continually bleeding wound.

His obsession with death is the only explanation for his almost mystical attraction to bullfighting. Many people have mistakenly thought that Ernesto fervently loved bullfighting because he relished the violent sensations aroused in the spectator by the gratuitous bloodshed of the bullring. But this was not so. The crowded stands in the arena, the barricades, the bull chute were an almost metaphysical revelation to him; they allowed him to transcend completely the much-publicized sensationalism of the bullring, like a horse in the arena trampling its own entrails underfoot. In bullfighting he sought—and managed to find—something profoundly tragic, a mirroring of the dilemma and the drama of his own tormented spirit, something at once cruel and majestic, a symbol of the human condition illuminated with sudden flashes of beauty and art. The sudden gleam of light on the yellow sand. The sight of blood streaming down the animal's back as he bellows in anticipation of death. The steel of the sword held on high, foreshadowing the moment of truth. And a lone man facing the bull.

But let us leave all this until later, because it in fact was the beginning of the end. People the world over who have always thought of Hemingway as a man blessed by fortune and privy to every secret of the Muses and the Graces, those who have always regarded Hemingway as a vital, triumphant, pleasure-loving, invincible figure must prepare to adjust their sights and view him from a very different angle. As I caught glimpses of his inner emptiness, his emotional chaos, the constant danger he exposed himself to, I realized what a phenomenal fiasco his life had come to be, and how certain words that seemed mere surface decoration were a perfect reflection of his inner defeat, as for instance when he refers to the heart and the emotions as the red cape that excites the bull, and to the world as one vast bullring. Since, in the bullring Ernesto hoped to find not only the grace note of art that embellishes life, but also the breath of immortality that would enable him to tolerate the nothingness of existence, the bullring came to be the one path of escape Ernesto attempted to follow.

Our affection for each other remained as genuine as ever during the final years of Ernesto's life, when his fame reached its peak and then declined, marking not only his eclipse as a writer but also his end as a man. He came and went, he worked feverishly at times, he faithfully promised to do this or that and really believed he would keep his promises. But Ernesto had gone beyond the point even of vast self-delusion; he was now a living ghost, a wreck of a man, or rather a man who had made a wreck of himself. It was not the terrors of the outside world but his inner fears and cowardice that had sapped his greatness. Many people have spoken of Ernesto's mask, but to say that he always wore one reveals only half the truth, as is always the case with masks. I for my part believe that the clowning, the evasiveness, the flagrant exhibitionism he constantly hid behind were a self-mortifying mask, a façade to conceal his shyness. All this, too, was necessary in order to be able to go on living at this crucial turning point in his life's journey, in order to appear to be a great success at the very moment in his career when utter physical and spiritual weariness had made him the victim of an overwhelming, deadly depression.

And so, even though just two months before his death I received a letter from him that sounded very cheerful and said, "We'll be seeing each other soon and have a great time together," as I read it I had a feeling, or rather a premonition, that the time might soon come when I would receive another letter, with news of his death. How could I have had such a strong presentiment of what was about to happen that the news that he had killed himself came as no surprise to me, but seemed instead a confirmation of something I had long feared?

Several years have now gone by since that macabre rifle shot rang out in the peace and quiet of Ketchum, Idaho, splattering Ernesto's brain tissue all over the room. The world was stunned, and still has not recovered from the shock.

Studies that are the product of arduous and patient research, subtle essays, sensational documents having to do with Hemingway's life and work are slowly beginning to appear. We are beginning to learn a great deal more about his basic themes, his technique as a novelist, his incomparably beautiful style, his development as a writer. The explorations of Ernesto's personality, on the other hand, have as yet failed to give us a clear and adequate picture of him. The various views advanced regarding his outlook on life and his sensibilities are fragmentary ones. A man as fabulous as Ernesto was bound to be the subject of a whole gallery of portraits, both harmless ones painted by his intimates and outrageous ones painted by prejudiced commentators who have endeavored to unravel the almost impenetrable mystery of the man.

I believe that Spain owes Ernest Hemingway a book that is a sincere testimonial, one that will go deeper and further than a coldly factual, scrupulously documented biography. That sort of study will come soon enough, and critics and scholars will be eager to get their hands on it. I am convinced, however, that there is need for a book that is almost the precise opposite of such a biography: a deeply felt, passionate, intuitive, personal book that without being unfaithful to his memory would serve as a fervent reminder to Spain that Hemingway was the most outstanding observer of our country in the modern era. Morever, because along with a chorus of deeply grateful and loyal admirers Ernest Hemingway has had a number of vicious detractors, resentful men with axes to grind, and bitter critics, it is only fitting and proper that a Spanish friend should offer him the homage he so greatly deserves from this country he loved so dearly.

I wanted to repay my friend Ernesto the man and Hemingway the writer the debt I feel I owe them by writing a quite unconventional book. Instead of amassing a pile of scholarly notes on neat little cards, I have tried to recall our real-life experiences together; instead of searching through the literature on Hemingway for apt quotations, I have tried to bury myself in nostalgic memories; instead of underlining phrases in books that already belong to the history of literature, I have tried to fall in step with Ernesto once again, and walk about and talk with him again, as we so often did in the streets of Madrid and along the roads in the Spanish countryside. By doing so, I may have deprived him of the noble composure, chiseled in marble, of a Nobel laureate, but perhaps he will seem a more intimate, more human figure. I am not a Hemingway scholar; I was his friend.

I am certain Ernesto would find it terribly funny if I wrote a book full of pat facts, the sort of book whose first sentence would read, "Ernest Hemingway was born in Oak Park, Illinois. . . ." I can hear him laughing now!

But I purposely began at the end, because what I have written is not a scholarly biography to be read by college students, but a chaotic, hasty, Hemingwayesque confession. Since Ernesto hasn't had a street in Madrid or a square in Pamplona named for him yet, I hope the publication of this book will serve as the first stone for the monument we must someday erect in his memory. This is a book from the heart, the way Ernesto liked things to be, both in art and in life.

The reader must not expect this to be a mellow book full of sentimental anecdotes. Though Ernesto, writing of his experiences in our country in peace and war, of our bulls and the banks of our trout streams, made Spain fashionable, he was doing something more than grinding out a sort of colorful travel brochure. If Spanish places and people figured in his novels and short stories, it was a way of honoring them by capturing their very essence, for his real subject was not simply the landscape or superficial customs, but a life-style and a very special set of values. Spanish local color in Hemingway is in a class all by itself.

This is in no sense, either, an "official" biography or an effort to praise Hemingway to the skies. To a certain extent, I have shattered the conventional mold he has been cast in, but I have done so neither out of self-interest nor out of caprice, but rather because I thoroughly dislike pious images and because I believe that free interpretation of the facts is a perfectly legitimate practice for a writer. I leave it to authorized biographers and learned professors to write more careful, less impressionistic books about Ernesto.

My little stone for his monument awaits the reader.

—J. L. CASTILLO-PUCHE

Madrid, summer 1967.

HEMINGWAY IN SPAIN

1   I was spending the summer of 1961 with my family in Benicasim. What was it exactly that made me turn on my transistor radio on
July 2, since ordinarily I can't stand listening to it?

All I heard was the words: "Mrs. Hemingway stated that her husband
had accidentally killed himself while cleaning a rifle at six-thirty this
morning."

"So he's committed suicide," I said.

What made me say that? Anyone, even an expert hunter, can "accidentally kill himself" handling his favorite gun. But the only question in
my mind at that moment was which shotgun or rifle he had killed himself with. Ernesto had gotten his first rifle at the age of ten, and was
allowed to shoot three cartridges a day. But I was sure he hadn't shot
himself with that first rifle. Nor with the one his father had used to
blow his brains out one Thursday in December around the year 1928.
Ernesto had chosen a Sunday morning—he'd always rather disliked
Sundays, ever since the days, perhaps, when his mother had dragged
him off to church on Sunday to sing in the choir. Could it have been
one of the beautiful shotguns that Ernesto had brought back with him
from Spain on his last trip, thereby causing a great commotion among
the customs inspectors, who had finally decided that all they could do
was let them go through, pretending to be not only blind and deaf but
a little crazy as well? It couldn't have been either one of those two superb Eibars, though. It must have been one of his favorite rifles, one of
the ones specially made for him that never missed, as he had proved by
shooting many a lion or bear or rhinoceros. An absolutely dependable
automatic rifle, without a telescopic sight, naturally, for since the shot

had been aimed backward and the target was the hunter himself, there was no need of one. Ernesto, I was sure, had gone straight to the mirror the moment he had got out of bed (I had seen him obsessively peering into the mirror in his hotel room with an anxious look on his face time and again during his last visit to Spain), and for that very reason there was no need of a telescopic sight.

He must have said to himself: "Enough of this! Why complicate things any more?" And almost like a sleepwalker, like a magic bull-fighter, he had begun the final *suerte*. Surely he was quite conscious of what he was doing, in complete control of every movement of his body, the absolute master of the terrain, knowing exactly what the bull he was facing was like . . . or rather the bull inside the double-barreled rifle, its two horns . . . the final thrust . . .

Why did the death of others—the very word—make his hair stand on end, while he bore his own death about him as reverently as though it were a holy tabernacle? Doubtless he had long been haunted by this death at the end of a rifle barrel, had planned it, pondered it, decided the moment had come and done the deed in his mind countless times.

I couldn't be wrong. I had smelled his death—yes, smelled it, the way he had often jokingly said he smelled the death of bullfighters—like a juicy joint of meat we are counting on enjoying at a gay picnic, but when we slice into it, it gives off the first faint spoiled smell, the almost imperceptible yet unmistakable odor of certain, imminent death.

Hadn't he feared it and even had vivid dreams about it? He'd dreamed for instance that he'd died in the Hotel Suecia and was standing watching his body being taken out the back door, the one he used to make his secret getaways, on its way to the morgue for an autopsy. Hadn't there been an especially macabre glint in his eye when he told me how the wheel of his car had fallen off just as he was coming into Burgos one day? Burgos—what a perfect place to rest in peace for all eternity, like a gleaming marble statue of a great military captain! And then, seeing that his story had upset me, he had taken out his money clip—the same one that was swiped from him in Murcia—and said to me, "This is what saved our lives." He pointed to the Saint Christopher engraved on it. And then he drew closer and said in my ear, "I knew it would work. Patrick gave it to me. You haven't met him yet, have you? You will. He's a little bit thick between the ears, but a good kid anyway. What you people call a *pedazo de pan*."

It had been exactly six-thirty in the morning, a good time of day for an expert hunter. As he picked up the rifle and loaded it, the church bells may well have been ringing for early mass at the chapel of Our Lady of the Snows, and Ernesto may even have said to himself, "Hear that, Ernest? The bells are tolling for thee." What was it that led me to think that the night before, he'd stood staring up at the sky with a glass of whisky in his hand that he never did finish drinking, which was quite unlike him, and that he'd been a little brusque with Mary?

There was no doubt about it. He'd killed himself. "Fortune's darling," as people who scarcely knew him called him, had come to the end of the road: no more drinking, no more hunting, no more trips to visit the Europe he loved (and visit his secret love, Spain), no more marvelous feasts, no more writing, no more bulls, no more caressing and being caressed by women, no more fucking. And I was certain he had picked up the rifle as he might have picked up his pen. Quite willing to sign his autograph, for the very last time, with a bold flourish. For violent death was his unmistakable signature.

I began dazedly stuffing things into my suitcase.

The news of his death had upset me terribly. I couldn't help suddenly remembering his hearty "damns" and "hells"—his usual reaction when something didn't suit him or didn't go right. Before pulling the double trigger, he may well have exclaimed, "What shit" or "What a fucking world" or "This is revolting"—his usual outbursts when something went wrong. And now not just "something," but everything, had gone wrong.

I couldn't finish my dinner. A little while later I had a phone call from Madrid telling me the same thing I'd heard on the radio. The people calling didn't know any more about it than I did, except that the private funeral wouldn't be until Friday (during the fiesta of San Fermín in Pamplona—what a cruel joke!), because they were waiting there in Idaho for Ernesto's son Patrick to get there from wherever he was, Africa or India.

I wanted to go straight to Madrid, but the best I could do was take an absurdly slow train that got me into Valencia early in the morning; that was the only way I could make connections with the Iberia plane for Madrid. I remember that during the long wait, after asking myself all the usual stupid, childish questions: "Why did he do a thing like that?" "Why did he kill himself just when we were expecting him for the fiesta of San Fermín?" all sorts of thoughts about what had gone on in Ernesto's body and mind and soul over the past few years kept running through my head. Suicide is seldom a sudden, completely unpredictable act, but rather an inescapable conclusion, arrived at consciously, or more often unconsciously, an inner logic pursued relentlessly, stubbornly, from the basic premises to the final, irremediable, violent solution. The cocked and loaded rifle that his own life had always represented had to track accurately and zero in on the proper target: the death of the desperate hunter himself.

It was a foregone conclusion that Ernesto would die with a gun in his hand.

3

So as I packed my suitcase, I kept remembering things, the words I had written about him in 1954 for instance: "His favorite toy is a rifle, a delicate plaything." And in a talk at a university: "Ernesto's life will end with a big bang." And that was precisely what had happened. The shot had not only gone straight through that noble head, the head of a blasphemous prophet or a wicked pirate, but had also set the pulse of the entire English-speaking world racing in terror. His death was a perfect reflection of his life-style, but also of his literary style. But which had he asked more of, life or art? His answer to that question had been two bullets.

Once more, he had been true to himself, sincerely living out an inner drama, for knowing Ernesto as I did, I knew that his public image as the "champ" no matter what he did—fighting wars, collecting scars, fishing, hunting, carousing—hadn't entered into it at all.

The mystery of the *beyond* was more than terrifying to him. Nothingness absolutely fascinated him. The role he played in public, that of a footloose vagabond, a prophet with no mystery to preach, or a missionary disguised as a tourist on a non-stop spree, fooled many people. And then there were his other favorite roles: the soldier under fire in the front lines, the peerless, perfect sportsman. But all this was only his outermost, his most obvious shell. That was why some people thought of him as a great gentleman of the Renaissance and others saw in him a street beggar who might swipe your wallet if you weren't careful. Everything about him was a bit confusing and hard to put your finger on. Hemingway's great booming laugh was famous, but few people had seen him in one of his more private moods: remote and withdrawn, as if lost in a world of his own, assuming the pose of a disappointed, mistrustful, frightened child. A number of critics in fact have said that Hemingway never grew up, that his disenchantment with the world was a typically adolescent trait. I readily confess that I more or less watched for signs of this, and from the very first saw and felt that he was very vulnerable. Even though I'd seen him beat his chest like a Hercules and dive naked into an ice-cold river in Navarre, I was always afraid for him. His inner helplessness always made me feel that he was in mortal danger, for he seemed utterly defenseless, utterly without protection, even against himself.

And so while others saw Hemingway as a great hulk of a man, brimming over with high spirits and vitality, prodigal with his money and everything else, a celebrity who partook heartily of the banquet of life and, most important of all, came out on top in every battle with it, I for my part saw a Hemingway who was an extremely pessimistic, broodingly romantic figure. Ernest Hemingway was a man torn to pieces, flayed alive, a fake tough guy, as James Joyce had called him.

As I waited for hours in that absurd railroad station, pacing up and down, afraid that the train might not stop for me, I began thinking about Ernesto's life, his work, and his death. I tried to relate little remarks he'd made on his last visit to things he'd written in his last letters to me, and trace symbols in his works back to real experiences he'd shared with people he was fond of. It wasn't easy: I had a vision of him blown to bits, like a lion shot point-blank, and at the same time I remembered how he used to open the door of his hotel room, cock his fists like a prize fighter, and say: "O.K., on your toes now!" and give me an affectionate little fake uppercut to the jaw. I tried to think about some of his books, and realized that there was more death—in the singular—in them than there were dead people, that plural that can give rise to obsessive thoughts about your own death. And of course his works were much more a reflection of his own personal drama than creations of his imagination. Because his philosophy had been reduced to one basic question ("How can we live, seeing we have to die?"), it had ended up being the most deadly of philosophies.

"I was trying to learn to write, commencing with the simplest things"; "one of the simplest things of all and the most fundamental is violent death," he had said. Is it true, though, that death is one of the simplest things to write about, as though it were an old friend? If so, why did the most complex and anguished characters he created skirt the subject?

Ernesto was obviously a good, kind man underneath, but he couldn't possibly have helped playing the fool. Why shouldn't the herculean gladiator step into the circus arena with the firm intention of enjoying the spectacle too, since he's bound to end up the loser some day? That was the philosophy that Ernesto embraced with all his heart, very early in his life, once and for all. And even more importantly: he refused to make a spectacle of himself. By that I mean that he, the real Ernesto, refused to display his most intimate self to others. So the only thing to do was make a false spectacle of himself. But when the hour of truth draws near—old age, infirmity, death—who of us can play the clown? And that was the hour that had been at hand.

He would have to have been blind not to see that. The cord may have been strong, but it was bound to break. And the cord had long since been almost worn through. Things hadn't been going at all well for Ernesto, even though he seemed to all of us to be at the peak of his success and in the very best of form.

Though we had failed to realize it, perhaps the most telling and fateful sign of the change in Ernesto was that writing had become an enormous struggle that left him anxiety-ridden and depressed as he confronted the blank pages before him.

5

He couldn't take it any more. How strange! Writing of death in "Fathers and Sons," he had said:

> He had died in a trap that he had helped only a little to set, and they had all betrayed him in their various ways before he died.

What trap? And what trap had he, Ernesto, fallen into—not at the age of fifty-seven but at the age of sixty-one. The one he had set for himself. Few writers have said so much about themselves in so few words:

> I shall never forget how sick it made me the first time I knew he was a *cobarde*. (Bell)

Wasn't Ernesto's suicide foreshadowed by Jake Barnes's castrated manhood in *The Sun Also Rises?* And by the morbid self-destruction of the hero of "The Snows of Kilimanjaro"? Wasn't his whole life an inexorable, systematic process of killing himself? Most likely, Ernesto had condemned his father's suicide as an act of cowardice in order to anticipate the critics who were bound to do so in his name. Probably he had also done so in order to escape their judgment by implicitly condemning his own cowardly suicide before the fact.

Killing himself had been a passive act. He had been violently propelled by the sheer force of moral inertia into the arms of nothingness, his great beloved, his terrible jealous mistress.

What a confused, complicated drama Ernesto's life had been, but at the same time what a stark and cruel one! Hadn't his ultimate hero been the matador, that godlike figure who may both kill and be killed? And why not kill yourself when you find yourself cornered like a bull?

As I paced up and down the train track, I kept mulling over absurd syllogisms in my mind, like a stubborn scholastic, and my premises kept leading to the same conclusion. I said to myself: he only did what he could, because he only did what he knew how to, and therefore he did what he wanted to. . . . Had there been any way for him not to kill himself?

But perhaps it was quite unfair to say: "He died the way he lived, like a pagan, like an agnostic, like a nihilist, like a brooding romantic, like an absolute fool." No, that was not all there was to it.

Why kill yourself if you give others, when they are with you, the feeling that they are living beyond the limits of the normal, that they are intensely, radiantly, passionately alive? What blind demon had contrived to unsettle Ernesto's brain at the end, when he had always believed he had a guardian angel at his side? And above all, did he think that he had died a hero's death by killing himself? What was heroic

6

about that? It was true, of course, that killing himself was more heroic than patiently waiting for the next injection or the next ridiculous, repellent suppository. Ernesto had always felt an instinctive repugnance for the lingering death of old people, wasting away in their beds. He refused to die in bed. To be stinking carrion in a downy, foul-smelling bed. It was obvious that in his mind the great slab on which the bull is butchered was a far better end than a comfortable home for the aged.

It had been a Sunday, and in Benicasim the townspeoples' dancing and carousing had gone on long past nightfall. Even at this late hour the fun was still not quite over on the terraces, in the pine groves, and down on the beach. There was a brothel near the train station, and now and again I heard a deep sigh, a feeble moan, the sound of laughter. I could hear youngsters singing on the beach, and at times their voices mingled with the music blaring out of a record player on one of the terraces. From time to time a car or a truck went by on the highway angling up the hill.

The truth was inescapable: Hemingway had killed himself the way he liked to do everything: deliberately and cleanly, following his instincts. Without any possibility of backing down at the last moment. The wire services and radio stations all over the world were doubtless still lamenting the fact that Hemingway the expert hunter had been careless or clumsy. But how could he be accused of being clumsy with a gun, when only a year or so ago he had expertly shot a cigarette out of the lips of Ordóñez, the matador? Unfortunately, it had been a predictable "accident," one just waiting to happen for some time. Ernesto obviously had not wanted anybody to see that he was in a state of total collapse, a wreck of a man. It had not been a clear, quiet night the evening before, I decided. It had been a gloomy night, one of those nights when fences and stones exchange unforgettable confidences. A deathly still night, with an implacable moon casting its cold light.

But it didn't matter now. I suddenly remembered Ernesto's closest friend—aside from Mary, of course, his fourth and last wife, an extraordinary woman who doubtless understood him better than anyone else in the world. Hemingway's boon companion was his cat Colón—Spanish for Columbus—a handsome tom that ate off Ernesto's plate at the table and had certain unusual responsibilities. If Colón decided that a visitor was not to be trusted, he would run away and hide, and Hemingway governed himself accordingly. To Ernesto, Colón was not just a proud, imperious creature. He was privy to unfathomable secrets.

"You know," Ernesto once said to me, "that Spanish proverb about cats having seven lives is really true."

What had Ernesto's pampered, spoiled tomcat done when he heard

7

the shotgun blast? Had Colón been there purring at Ernesto's feet or perched on his shoulder, as I had often seen him? That was the sort of thought that kept running through my head. I had to occupy my mind somehow, and I had lots of time on my hands. The train wouldn't arrive for another hour. But I couldn't stand being home, or anywhere else. From time to time a sentence from one of his books or a conversation would come to me. Many of his words had long weighed on my mind, as heavy as paving stones, the way phrases must ring in a matador's ears as he works with the *muleta*: "Closer, you coward!" "Come on, you ridiculous clown, get in closer!" "This isn't what you're being paid thousands of *duros* for, as if they were orange-seeds!" "Another sissy who's living on his family fortune!" But the phrases of Hemingway's that I was remembering just then were very different, phrases only he could have said or written: "A man can be destroyed, but not defeated" (*The Old Man and the Sea*); "I was trying to learn to write, commencing with the simplest things, and one of the simplest things of all and the most fundamental is violent death" (*Death in the Afternoon*); "An old man is a disgusting thing" ("A Clean, Well-Lighted Place"); " 'Is dying hard, Daddy?' 'No, I think it's pretty easy, Nick. It all depends.' " ("Indian Camp"); "One thing he had always dreaded was the pain" ("The Snows of Kilimanjaro"); "And just then it occurred to him that he was going to die. It came with a rush; not as a rush of water or of wind, but of a sudden evil-smelling emptiness" ("The Snows of Kilimanjaro"); "All he felt now was a great tiredness and anger that this was the end of it. For this, that now was coming, he had very little curiosity. For years it had obsessed him; but now it meant nothing in itself. It was strange how easy being tired enough made it" ("The Snows of Kilimanjaro").

"Don't be silly," I had heard him say to Mary in a voice that seemed to come from far away, giving her a hug and then drawing closer to me and whispering in my ear: "She'll be taken care of when I'm gone and won't have to worry about money. . . . Everything that hasn't been published yet is in the bank vault, and it's for her"; and then another day when I naïvely asked him: "What does life mean to you?" he had replied: "What does life mean? Life's a stinking whore." And then I'd said: "What about death?" He had answered very gravely, with an edge of anger in his voice: "You mean the Bald Lady? She's the worst whore of all!" And then later that same day in the elevator: "José Luis, the very worst thing in the world is losing your mind and making a spectacle of yourself. That's the very last thing I'd want to happen to me."

I could hear the barking of working dogs on farms and spoiled lapdogs in town above the chirping of the crickets. A skyrocket took off into the sky from a nearby chalet, leaving only a faint trail of sparks, as

8

though the powder had been wet. There was no sign of the train yet. There was still a long half hour to wait.

It suddenly occurred to me that there had been an even clearer indication of what was about to happen. On Ernesto's last visit to Madrid, I had gone with him to the office of a doctor who was a good personal friend of his and whose professional opinion he trusted a great deal. When he came out after seeing the doctor he said:

"Bad news."

"What's the trouble?" I asked.

"Nothing. He just suddenly had a very sober look on his face and brought up the same old things again—my liver, my blood pressure, my drinking. . . . I still think that pissing alcohol is a lot better than pissing blood, don't you? But he was so damned serious about the whole thing . . . more serious than I was. . . ."

Ernesto was silent for quite a while, and then, speaking of Dr. Medinaveitia, he said. "But he's one of the best, he's a real champ"— and got out a flask of vodka and took a big swig.

We had lunch together that day, and as we were eating he suddenly said, in a casual tone of voice, without being dramatic about it at all: "I'm not doing bad at all, really. . . . I'm almost sixty. Who would ever have bet I'd live this long? Not me, certainly, and I do lots of heavy betting on long shots! Don't drink, don't travel, don't eat, don't fuck, don't live! It's as though they were handing you death on a platter!" He was in a bad mood by the end of the afternoon, and I noticed that for several days after that he diluted his shots of whisky with the juice of almost half a lemon.

Yes, it was all over and done with now. And I still couldn't believe it: Ernesto was dead, stone cold dead. And his fear of dying was the cause of what Dr. Medinaveitia had called a dangerous slide downhill. Ernesto had held out five years longer than his father, exactly half a decade. . . . "Who would ever have bet I'd live this long?" Not Ernesto, certainly. And perhaps I wouldn't have either, though at the time I had no reason to think he wouldn't make it. I suddenly recalled my last article about him.

In the last days of the "dangerous summer" of 1960, a news story from Sweden, reporting in great detail how Ernesto had died at "La Cónsula" (his friend Bill Davis's estate near Málaga) had immediately traveled around the globe. Ernesto was used to this sort of thing. This was not the first time he'd seen headlines reporting his own death in all the newspapers. But this time he didn't joke about reading his own obituary, the way he had when he'd been in two bad plane crashes in the bush in Africa. At that time his only comment had been: "These stories about my kicking off are getting to be a pretty dull joke."

And when people kept pressing him about how he'd felt when he'd read the reports of his own death this time, he had added: "I had to make a transatlantic phone call to Mary, who was thousands of miles away. She still hasn't gotten over the shock."

People kept making jokes about it, and I teased him a little too: "What's it like to lie in state?"

"Dying is much more important for the survivors than it is for the stiff," he answered—the sort of sarcastic quip concealing his real feelings that was so typical of him.

I laughed that day in 1960—my fears had been needless—and wrote an article for my paper entitled "Seven Lives Like. . . ." Ernesto had liked it a lot, even though his reaction to being reported dead hadn't been at all the same as in 1953. Back then, he'd laughed when he recounted his version of the big to-do the news of his death had caused. According to him, the English had wanted to know how much money he'd left in the bank; the Italians had wanted to know how many unpublished or unfinished manuscripts were lying around; the French had drawn up a fairly accurate list of his marriages and love affairs; and the Spanish—ah, the Spanish!—had gotten down on their knees and fervently prayed God to forgive him the fit of insanity that had brought him to Madrid one day to fight on the Republican side. . . . How he laughed when he read my article! In it I had written:

> As I got off the train this morning, I was greeted with a piece of news that will astound you, Ernesto: I was told you were dead; a "stiff," as you'd put it. I know what a sense of humor you have. Some bore, some boob, some imbecile who didn't know his ass from his elbow had passed on the news of your death to Marino, who was terribly upset and phoned me immediately. Absurd. No doubt somebody had waked you up trying to get you to give him an interview—one of the countless ones you resign yourself to giving rather than making a fuss, and all you get for your trouble is hearing miserable celebrity-chasers claim you're a publicity hound. . . . Well, anyway, your little joke (you doubtless sent word: "Tell him I'm dead," or maybe you played dead there in your bed—I've seen you pull tricks like that) put everybody in a state of shock, and they called me and told me you were dead. I confess I didn't believe a word of it. I find it impossible to believe you could be dead, and once again it turned out that you weren't. The impossible simply can't happen. And if it does happen, it won't be in such a ridiculous way as that. . . .

But why was it that back then I had been certain that Ernesto had been playing a practical joke, just as I was certain now that he had shot himself? I remember that I had gone on writing my article that day

(August 8, 1960), paying no attention to the big headlines in the paper: RADIO STOCKHOLM REPORTS HEMINGWAY DEAD IN SPAIN.

> You're tough and strong, despite the fact that you mistreat yourself and are more reckless than almost anybody else. I refused to believe it, and went to the newspaper office with the photograph I'd taken of you one day in Havana (Havana's beginning to be a bit of a bother and a bore these days), a very intimate photograph, showing you fondling the symbol of your life, the sly cat with seven lives who goes by the telltale Spanish name of a great globe-trotter, Colón, and who either comes to you or runs away— it all depends—when you call it. No, it's not time yet. There's more thread to spin, more wood to split, many more bulls to fight. But meanwhile, Ernesto, please be careful, because one day you may really die, and those of us who are fondest of you will be tricked into laughing like crazy, not believing it. . . .

That hadn't been too far from the truth. Only this time there wouldn't be any reprieve. When a man's finger squeezes the trigger of an automatic shotgun . . .

Everything was different this time, because after the blast from the shotgun there had been no booming laughter, no swig of vodka to celebrate being still alive and kicking. Ernesto wouldn't beat his chest this time and say, "I'm not immortal yet. . . ." But perhaps the moment had come when he would begin to be. The precise moment when his head crashed through the wall separating him from the Great Mystery.

All at once I forgot everything, the train, Benicasim, my family. . . . I had a sudden blinding image of Ernesto, like a flash of lightning, and could recall perfectly the husky note in his voice as he said to me, apropos of the false rumor that he had died, "Me die in *Spain*? What a laugh! There have been lots of times I've fucked up and almost kicked the bucket, but not in Spain. . . . Spain's not a country you *die* in, it's a country you *live* in."

What were his very last words that night? What was on his mind just before he pulled the trigger? If he had gotten up in the middle of the night to get a drink of water to wash down one of the pills he was always taking, what had he said to Mary, what were the last words he ever spoke to her, without either of them realizing that they were his last farewell? And what was the final thought that crossed his mind when he got up in the morning and saw the sun rise and heard the birds noisily awakening in the trees?

I was beginning to understand something else now. "Spain's a country you live in," he had said, and he had come to Spain like a thirsty cloud soaking up moisture so as to end a terrible drought, so as to com-

11

bat a mortal tedium. Spain was the abundant, perpetually flowing spring he required to quench his tremendous thirst, the great gust of wind he needed to fill the terrible vacuum.

Only a few weeks before, he had written me: "We'll be seeing each other soon. You can expect me any day now."

We'd have a great time together, naturally. The year 1959, which he had said was the happiest twelve months in his whole life, seemed like only yesterday. But now the fiesta of San Fermín was about to begin, and there would not be another "dangerous summer." How could I doubt what his last thoughts had been early that July morning?

The first of January, the second of February, the third of March, . . . they say in Pamplona, counting the months till fiesta time.

Spain was an obsession, an insatiable need, the most precious part of Hemingway's art perhaps and the key to his style. I could see him arriving now, like a bull that unexpectedly finds the gate to the ring open, advancing with the sheer weight of a mountain avalanche, with the curved tips of the moon showing above the crestline, with the blind force of a falling star hurtling earthward as if terra firma were something more than its final destination.

"We're eagerly awaiting your arrival, as always," I had written back.

There was only one way of warding off fatigue, idleness, despair, loneliness, emptiness, suicide. If Ernesto had been in Spain, he probably would not have killed himself; he would not have had the courage to commit suicide. It would have seemed a great blasphemy to him. I suddenly remembered his confession in *The Dangerous Summer:*

> I prayed for all those I had in hock to Fortune, for all friends with cancer, for all girls, living or dead, and that Antonio would have good bulls that afternoon.

No words could be simpler than that, or more revealing. In Spain he probably would not have had the courage to kill himself, or rather, he would not have allowed his weakness to overcome him. "In Spain pain is regarded as merely something a man has to bear," he had said once. I remember very well how he had lowered his voice then and said in a whisper:

"You Spaniards are inured to pain."

"That's not true."

"Well, you embrace it as though it were your *beloved* then."

"Yes, it's been the *querida* of many of our mystics."

"But an ugly, hideous *querida.*"

"One always comes to hate every *beloved* in the end. . . ."

Spain had not only given him certain metaphysical roots (in so far as a man like Ernesto, a ravenous devourer of the passing instant, could ever have roots, or embrace a metaphysic). He had also found in Spain a pinnacle from which he could project an even more sublime image of himself. That was why he had wanted to come, even when the doctors told him he wouldn't be able to. I was virtually certain he would never have killed himself in Spain.

I suddenly exclaimed aloud: "Ernesto, what an idiot, what a beast, what an absolute madman you are!" And then I added: "Yes, you were an utter madman, a thoroughbred, an untamable wild beast. Ernesto, you shouldn't have picked up that shotgun or examined it to see if it was loaded or looked down the barrel or fingered the trigger. . . . When you got out of bed, you should have gone to your monk's desk and picked up a pencil and begun to write words down, the first ones that came to you, even if they made no sense whatsoever. Or you should have grabbed an ax and taken your feelings out on some old oak tree there around your house; or started kicking a tin can around, the way you're doing in a photograph I have of you taken on a snowy day. If only you'd worked your depression off skinning a lamb, or eating a pheasant, or roping a colt or a steer on some nearby ranch! Anything but what you did, anything but that. That was really a dirty trick you pulled on us."

He knew very well that we were expecting him. I am almost certain that in his last moment of utter despair, Ernesto thought not only of the unfinished and unrevised manuscripts he was leaving behind, but also of the trip to Spain he would never take now. Hemingway the world-famous writer had become Hemingway the subject of gossip at cocktail parties all over the globe, and there was only one remedy for the loathing he felt: return to the mother lode, drink again from the perpetually flowing spring, surrender to the bullring as to a passionate mistress.

He would thus have returned to the crater of the volcano, to the devouring code of the bullring that was his canon for every imaginable sport, because it was the very symbol of his life. He would be radiant, because he would be returning to the country of his heart, to his arena, to his seat in the *plaza de toros* or to the matadors' passageway, the road of hope stretching out endlessly before him.

He *had* to come, because when he was in Spain, he was more like one of us and more like himself, more his own master and more the slave of his art. Boredom and despair could not touch him here. Here he would discover the truth, *his* truth. And why not come right out and say it? he would find his salvation here.

Spain had become something more than a drug or strong spirits to Ernesto. Spain was more than a healthy stimulus, a delightful support to lean on. It was also a spiritual handhold for a shipwrecked man who had been floundering about for years in a valiant, vain attempt to fight off the terror of death.

He would be coming. . . . It was a macabre transposition to project the vivid image of Ernesto, alive and laughing, in high spirits, on the wall of nothingness when he was a corpse with its head blown to bits. No, Ernesto would not be coming; he would never be coming again.

A young boy with a sweater draped over his shoulder arrived at the station. The lanterns of the fishing boats offshore were bobbing up and down on the water.

It hurt to think about the way Ernesto had died. He had always tried to have his characters die a dignified, Spartan death; he had hung out in our lowliest taverns and above all in the *callejón*—the passageway for the matadors behind the wooden fence—seeking to learn the secret of Spanish stoicism.

Why couldn't you just die once and for all instead of going through all the bothersome business of living on and on, like a novel you can't find the right ending for? And what is life in the end? An absurd game in which you always lose something, and not "Winner Take Nothing," the title of one of his short stories, but rather as in the famous passage in "A Clean, Well-Lighted Place":

> It was not fear or dread. It was a nothing that he knew too well.
> It was all a nothing and a man was nothing too. It was only that
> and light was all it needed and a certain cleanness and order.
> Some lived in it and never felt it but he knew it all was nada y
> pues nada y nada y pues nada. Our nada who art in nada, nada
> be thy name thy kingdom nada they will be nada in nada as it is
> in nada. Give us this nada our daily nada and nada us our nada
> as we nada our nadas and nada us not into nada but deliver us
> from nada; pues nada. Hail nothing full of nothing, nothing is
> with thee.

A cruel mysticism!

I heard the train whistle first, and then the chugging of the locomotive. What awful things they were going to write about Ernesto in Madrid! There was lots of material, too much material, so it was bound to attract the vultures, as usual. The ravenous vultures, repulsive fat black birds with long, bare, craning necks and bald heads, who could never understand Ernesto or appreciate what he stood for, would pick his most glorious dreams to pieces. "I didn't take life seriously. Other people's lives, yes, but not my own. . . ."

"Here's an empty compartment. You can snore all the way to Valencia," the conductor said.

There had been signs for some time that Ernesto was becoming more and more demoralized. Something was gnawing away at him from inside, something was worrying him terribly. But hadn't that been true of him all his life? From the moment he first enters literature, or rather, enters life, walking up a Michigan hillside from the lakeshore with his father, Ernesto is a creature trapped between life and death, a being already on the most intimate terms with the drama of personal destruction. In those early days did he sometimes manage to forget, to escape the horror of life, the awareness, that is, that death is inevitable? I don't believe he ever did. Jouncing about there in the dark in the wooden train compartment, I began to have a clearer picture of the life of this great mystic whose God was forever absent, of his disturbed personality, outwardly cruel and aggressive, but possessed of a profound inner drive toward a peace that was forever out of reach, toward a serenity that was forever unattainable. Was there a single passage in the work of this most famous of contemporary novelists that was idyllic or peaceful or optimistic? I thought back over all his novels and short stories, all his titles, and could not recall even one such sentence. All his characters are ripped apart by the teeth or the claws of a wife or a mistress; these gaping wounds are his own, and few writers have been as fascinated by their own pain. The pain he suffered was not a testimony to human endurance however, but rather something that may appear to be more selfish: Hemingway the author decided to make himself a living victim, in his very flesh, of the clash between the ideal and the real, the tragic bridge between the swaggering optimism of a life lived to the hilt and a sinister, wearisome, fatal nihilism. Ernest Hemingway had experienced in his very heart and soul this perilous, maddening battle whose outcome was his destruction of himself. I remembered how we'd said good-by on his last night in Spain. He hated winding up an evening—yet another sign of his growing panic at being left by himself, of the terror he felt at bedtime. He made lots of good-humored jokes about not liking it in bed for the first time in his life, but it was plain that to him lying there alone in the dark was like draining the last bitter dregs of his defeat, a defeat he had foreseen, dreaded, fled, and morbidly sought his whole life long.

The train had pulled into a station—Castellón no doubt, because we couldn't be in Sagunto already. Day laborers were walking up and down the corridors, harvesters probably. Or maybe they were soldiers or sailors. In any event, they had country accents, the metallic ring of the Valencian dialect.

Was it because something was missing in Ernesto's life that he had reached absolute bottom and felt that there was nothing else to do but blow his head off? He had everything any ordinary mortal could wish for: combat decorations; the Nobel Prize; a perfectly charming wife; world fame; money pouring in from his publishers; friends, good friends, all over the world. What sort of illness was he suffering from exactly, besides his bad liver, his high blood pressure, his diabetes, and above all the blotch covering half his face, which he did his best to conceal by growing a heavy beard, the blotch that sometimes turned an angry red and started peeling off in peculiar-looking flakes, the telltale patch that constantly drove him to the mirror to look at his face and stroke it with his hand, as if it might be . . . ?

He had told his biographer, Kurt Singer, that he would fight against himself, to make himself accept death as something beautiful.

What did he mean by saying that he would fight against himself? When and where was it that we had talked about his health or death? When Ordóñez had been gored probably, or perhaps when we were waiting in his doctor's office. He had told Singer that if he ever got sick he wanted to go fast.

And he had "gone" like a sudden explosion—powder, smoke, flames, an earsplitting blast, and then total, dead silence.

There was a mystery about his life, but it was not all that impenetrable. Had his death had the aura of grandeur Ernesto wanted it to have? There was no way now of changing his billing on the bullfight posters.

I had to seek the answer to many more questions. I had to trace the stream back to its source. There are no secrets in the lives of rough-and-ready, down-to-earth men like Ernesto. Or if there are, the key to them must be one that is both hidden and in plain sight. Little by little my mind went back over the most famous passages in Hemingway's work, and what finally seemed to me to shed a clear, bright light on the ultimate secret was not any single passage, but rather the whole of one of his works, the first story, "Indian Camp," in his book *In Our Time*. This collection of short stories was first published in 1925, soon after Ernesto had gone back to France and visited Spain. He thus already knew what the literary world was like, and already was fascinated by bullfighting and the world of the bullring, the "circle of death." But this particular story had its source in a trauma dating from an earlier period, one that haunted him all his life and one that he returns to again and again in his works. The young hero of the story, Nick Adams, is obviously Ernesto, and the most impressive thing about the story is the little boy's sudden, brutal, cruel meeting of death face to face for the first time. While out hunting in the Michigan woods, Dr. Adams, Nick's father, is summoned to attend an Indian woman in childbirth. Things go badly, and the doctor is obliged to perform a Caesarian on the woman with a jacknife, without an anaesthetic. The woman's husband, who has injured his foot very badly with an ax, is lying all this time in the upper

tory over death; nobody has ever tried so hard to be the absolute master of his destiny. Ernesto's entire moral code as a man of action and every line of his writing are spurs to drive himself on to win the fight, battle stripes to remind him of his courage. And sometimes, many times, he was quite sure that he was now a combat-hardened veteran, that he had mastered the situation; but the battle continually began all over again. Was it not true, however, that he was able to confront the death of others with a certain stoicism? I remembered at that point how he had borne up under the tragic sight of the bodies of the Key West veterans who had drowned in a hurricane, close to the spot on the beach where they had swum for recreation, just as he had earlier borne up under the sight of dead bodies on the battlefield. But one more quotation that shed light on the great enigma flashed through my mind, the unusual self-revelation of a passage in *Across the River and into the Trees:* "Yes, ecstasy is what you might have had and instead you draw sleep's other brother." I was sure now that the gun he had used had been his favorite rifle, the Mannlicher 6.5.

His moments of exhilaration, his delirious frenzies, his frenetic joys, his exhausting "vacations," the fears that had haunted him, his dangerous obsessions were now over forever. He had suffered a great deal and no one had noticed, and he had been incapable of facing up to the inevitable solemn confrontation with his old *compañera,* with the beloved who made shivers run up his spine. He had not done what he had done out of skepticism, or even out of pride, but out of weakness, out of bone-deep weariness, out of a sickness unto death of describing himself as a man entirely willing to face the "great whore," but knowing all the while that he was not certain in his heart of hearts how he was going to respond. It was all quite clear to me. After practicing all his life, his aim couldn't help but be perfect.

The train was pulling into Valencia, and we were bathed in that Mediterranean light that in the early morning is like splashing yourself with orange-blossom cologne. The train was jerking to a stop, and trucks loaded with bricks or bananas were crossing the tracks. We had arrived at last. I took a taxi to the Calle de la Paz, but unfortunately the bus for the airport had already left. I hailed a taxi. You can't let it get you down when things go wrong, I reminded myself. I remembered then that Ernesto had begun *The Sun Also Rises,* his first great work, in this very city.

I was anxious to get to Madrid to talk to his close friends, to Ordóñez and to Quintana, the man who had first introduced him to the world of bullfighting, and to Mary, whom I would telephone, even though the call would leave me broke for some time.

I kept urging the taxi driver to drive faster, but when we got to the airport the plane for Madrid had already taken off. I was upset at having missed it, but as it happened I fell into conversation with an airport official in the bar who told me that if I got a move on and went to see the colonel at the military base, I might be able to hitch a ride on an Army plane leaving for Madrid that morning, though I wasn't to tell anybody who had sent me there.

I went out to the base, and by a stroke of luck ran into a couple of pilots whom I'd met the year before on a junket around Spain. They were quite willing to give me a ride, expecially when they learned what had happened. "Poor Ernesto!" one of them said. "He must have been a sour old bastard," another said. "He was a fantastic guy," one of the others said. Ernesto was no longer a fascinating figure to people in Spain; he had become a sort of joke, in fact. "Why does he always wear checkered shirts and a cap with a visor?" they wondered. But these men still had more or less of a soft spot in their hearts for him. They had heard that he knew every swearword ever invented and had said that Manolete faked it in the bullring and that his money clip had been swiped in Murcia and that he was a guy with real balls who had doubtless spent money like water to get all that publicity, but now he'd up and killed himself, and was it true that he drank like a Cossack all day long and had a whole harem of good-looking tarts? "Poor guy, he won't be kicking up his heels any more now," they said. There was less talk about his works, except that one man said that *For Whom the Bell Tolls* was a phony book, and I didn't dare contradict him, since he was the co-pilot of the plane and might have left me behind.

I couldn't get my mind off the last days of Ernesto's life. We friends in Spain knew that he had been in the Mayo Clinic for fifty-three days and that the doctors had ordered complete bed rest. His diabetes had gotten worse, he had a raging case of infectious hepatitis, and his blood pressure had had an alarming tendency to shoot up and up. But he had been better when he left the hospital, and had lost forty pounds, which was all to the good. I vaguely remembered that the name of the hospital he had been in was Saint Mary's, and that had cheered me; he'd gone there under the false name of George Saviers, a doctor friend of his, so that reporters wouldn't bother him.

How had Mary broken the news to Ernesto that his beloved friend Gary Cooper, who had proved to have a cancerous tumor as big as a house, had died a good Christian death a short time before? This must have been a terrible blow to Ernesto, because more than once he had said to me: "I'd let myself be skinned alive for any of my real friends, like Gary Cooper." Now both of them had "gone back to the barn," as Gary Cooper's widow had said in her telegram. Ernesto had passed on, had crashed through the wall of nothingness, without being able to tell even his great good friend Gary Cooper what lay beyond.

Apparently Ernesto had felt better after leaving the clinic, but he was nonetheless a hollow shell of his former self. And there was still the tell-tale mirror to show him that he was an old man, not the affectionate "Papa" he had been before, but a man who'd grown old before his time, an elderly man whose memories had turned to ashes. Old age was a stark defeat, and Ernesto was unwilling to endure the humiliating sight of himself wasting away to skin and bones, slipping into what goes by the name of senility. He did not realize that his health had already begun to fail in such a pitiful way. But that was why he had returned to Ketchum, to Sun Valley, drawn there by the irresistible impulse that makes the dying tiger hide in the bush, or the dying bear seek out a dark cave. But it was not only his health; some force more powerful than the feeble logic of a sick man had driven him to suicide.

As I stood there talking with the pilots, my mind kept going back to the disconcerting moments that had led up to this suicide that might well be described as "fascinating," in the sense that a serpent fascinates its prey. How many years ago was it that Ernesto's father had committed suicide? It had been just thirty-three years ago, because that was how old Ernesto's son Patrick was; he had been born by Caesarian section, like the Indian woman's baby that same year. So Ernesto was just about to turn sixty-two. The thought suddenly surprised me, because even at that fairly ripe age and even though he looked like an old man, there was nonetheless something timeless about Ernesto; he gave you the feeling that he was a living classic, now that all his romantic dreams had burned to ashes. When you are a veritable force of nature and feel an irresistible drive to create and your art is driving you to frantic despair, there is no possible solution. Authentic despair is never a pointless theme in a novel. If an author begins to project his own genuine despair onto his characters, a sort of indissoluble bond is gradually established between them; and if the characters the author loves most die with the word *nothingness* on their lips, the author, too, will envelop himself in nothingness, making it his only secret, his only message—a writer like Hemingway especially, in view of the fact that his style and his works were created out of his own flesh and blood. I remembered what Philip Young had written: "In Hemingway's world things do not grow and bear fruit; but explode, break, decompose, or are eaten away."

No, resignation was foreign to Ernesto's temperament. He had given up all hope, for himself or for anything else. Whenever you talked to him about the future, about the bright new beginning that tomorrow represents for every writer who is inured to the ups and downs of his critical reputation, he would reply very vaguely: "What's fated to be will be." Write more? What for? His periods of spiritual aridity were becoming more and more prolonged. That was why he spoke of the works he had stored away in bank vaults with much the same self-satisfaction as a rich miser gloating over his accumulated treasures. Was he losing his acute sense of curiosity as a writer? His memory was no longer completely reliable, and his powers of concentration were failing. Little by little he was allowing his creative gifts to go down the drain. Life had been extremely generous toward him, but the time had come now to settle the bill it had presented him: an exorbitant bill, to be paid in pain and suffering, a bill he would be unable to pay unless he had a sizable balance on hand in his spiritual bank account.

After the clinic, there was only one way to end the series of disasters that had befallen him: breaking out one of his favorite guns, one of the ones made especially for him, perhaps the 12-gauge double-barreled shotgun with silver insets that he had kept hidden, wrapped in rags, under his mattress in his house in Cuba in the days of the Batista regime. He had taken great delight in showing it to me, along with several other firearms. Because if one of them missed, there was still this one, and this one . . .

What would Ordóñez, the matador, think of this "accident"? The same thing I did, perhaps. I would go to see him as soon as I got to Madrid, or rather as soon as I'd written my article about Ernesto. Because the first thing I was going to do was go to the newspaper office, the only one Ernesto had ever visited in Spain.

Ordóñez had been planning to meet Ernesto at the fiesta of San Fermín, in Pamplona, and now he would go on waiting forever, as if for a *corrida* that would never begin, though *corridas* always start on the dot. Niño de la Palma, Ordóñez's father, a bullfighter who had his ups and downs, had been the *torero* who had inspired Ernesto to become a novelist. And if Ernesto wanted to remain a master of the genre, all he needed to do was return to his original source of inspiration and rekindle within himself the bright glow surrounding his first idol, because Romero, the matador of *The Sun Also Rises*, modeled on Niño de la Palma, was still a figure who was essential, indispensable, irreplaceable for his art. But Ernesto had stood Niño de la Palma up too.

Why were bulls and bullfighters the very first and the very last thing he had celebrated in his writing? If I thought about it, the answer might lie in a passage from *Death in the Afternoon:*

Now the essence of the greatest emotional appeal of bullfighting is the feeling of immortality that the bullfighter feels in the middle of a great faena and that he gives to the spectators. He is performing a work of art and he is playing with death, bringing it closer, closer, closer, to himself, a death that you know is in the horns because you have the canvas-covered bodies of the horses on the sand to prove it. He gives the feeling of his immortality, and, as you watch it, it becomes yours.

That was it exactly. Closer, closer, closer, as close as possible. That was the great fascination. Later, referring to the glorious 1959 season, Ernesto had written: "It would have been tragic to miss it and it was tragic to watch it." And this time, the last time, the time that perhaps would have made it possible for him to be with us a few years more, he had failed to show up as he'd promised.

I wondered where Ordóñez was, right then. Perhaps in Madrid or on his estate in Málaga; but wherever he was he was waiting for "Papa," his beloved friend, to arrive. Whoever the *presidente* of the first *corrida* might be, Ordóñez was naturally planning to dedicate the first bull to Ernesto. Or he might have heard about Ernesto's death and already be on his way to Idaho. That was the least he could do for "Papa." "Papa" deserved everything. Ordóñez was surely already aboard a plane, on his way to Ketchum, I decided. If I'd had the money, I would have been on my way there too, that very minute . . .

We were in a little bar, and since it was a very hot day, we ordered beer. I was about to drink mine, and suddenly remembered what Ernesto had said to me in the bar of the Hotel Felipe II: "Don't drink that horse piss."

Beer turned his stomach. It seems to me that that was when I asked him why he was so hard on people sometimes and at other times so patient with them. A serious look came over his face, and he said, rather gravely: "I'm a judge who thinks too much about what the sentence should be," and tapped his forehead with his finger.

"That's pretty bad," I answered.

"Yes, but then it's my heart that hands the sentence down," he said, putting his hand on his chest.

"Does that seem better to you?"

"I don't know. I just know that I'm the judge I'd like to appear before after I'm dead."

As the pilots jabbered on about a recent soccer match, I thought about this remark of Ernesto's. The word *judge* especially. Ernesto sitting as a judge of himself, coldly analyzing himself, and then finally mercifully pardoning himself? Never.

One thought led to another. One day I'd said to him: "People say lots of bad things about you and nobody knows that you have certain very Christian feelings."

"You don't know me very well either."

"But who do you think knows you any better?"

He appeared to be lost in thought for a moment, and I was quite certain that he was about to utter the word God; but he realized that that was what I was expecting him to say, so as he often did he turned the whole thing into a joke and said, "My cat."

Ernesto instinctively refused to engage in any sort of speculation as regards the Absolute. He felt its dizzying attraction, however, and to escape it he immediately flung himself into the furious embrace of momentary pleasures. Perhaps it was because he was determined to be the anti-pedant *par excellence* that he avoided speculation about more serious subjects in his writings as well. He would have felt hobbled had he embraced any of the dogmas with which exquisitely sensitive, over-civilized people cluttered up to their lives, watering them down for their own convenience; he preferred to play the role of the noble savage, living a life without *whys*, his heart riveted to the present, to each moment as it came. His philosophy was the exaltation of the instant, draining the cup of life to the last drop.

I had a couple more drinks with the pilots in the bar at the airfield. My spirits revived a little, and perhaps in order to relieve my inner tension, I began telling them some war stories about Ernesto.

One was the tale of how he had dealt with certain tenderhearted souls who had come to Madrid from Geneva back in 1938, hoping they could do something to mitigate the horrors of the Spanish Civil War. These solemn-faced pacifists turned up at the Hotel Florida (the headquarters for the leaders of the Republican cause, for foreign newsmen, and for the horde of commissars and politicians attached to the International Brigades) seeking an interview with the famous war correspondent Ernest Hemingway. Ernesto invited them up to his room for a drink and they gave him a long lecture on non-violence, the need to "humanize" the war, and the necessity of drawing careful distinctions between the cause of freedom and useless bloodshed. Ernesto sat quietly listening to them, like a lamb being led to the slaughter. But finally he'd had enough; he pointed to a package wrapped in paper on top of his big standing wardrobe. "Look what I have here!" he said to them. "What is it?" they asked. "Look, can't you see what it is?" They went over to the wardrobe to have a closer look, and drew back in horror. "That's the body of the latest Fascist I've done in. I shot him just last night. A youngster as frail as a branch of almond blossoms. Come on, have a look!" The whole bunch of pious pacifists, distinguished lawyers and doctors, ran down the stairs as if the devil himself were at their heels; they were still gagging when they reached the lobby. The package actually contained big hunks of bloody buffalo meat someone had sent Ernesto from Chicago! He was keeping it on ice in his room so he could invite friends in to have a slice or two with him. Wars aren't quite so bad if you have bread and wine and a little fresh meat to go with them.

We were aboard the plane now, and would be in Madrid in no time. It was a bit windy and the plane kept bouncing up and down. If I arrived early enough, I would write an article for one of the afternoon papers bidding farewell to my beloved friend and admired master. As we flew through fleecy-white clouds, I remembered the days when Ernesto and I had first become friends.

He had stopped suddenly in the doorway of a bookstore one day and said to me, "Tell me what you really think: did I kill anybody in the Spanish War or didn't I?"

I took his question seriously, and had the impression he was about to let me in on some sort of secret. He made a little clucking noise with his tongue and added:

"They killed me first though. Do you know what I mean?"

When we came out of the bookstore he fell into the same mood again, as though trying to rid himself of some secret burden. But all he said was: "You should have seen Madrid when there were shells falling and sharpshooters on the rooftops. . . . The people blossomed anew every morning; it was simply amazing. I'll never forget it; I swear it's the greatest thing I've ever seen in my life. . . ."

He walked on for a moment, then stopped and said: "But I've also seen the filthiest, the most miserable, the most disgusting things here. It was in Madrid that I discovered what a man is really like in his three fundamental parts: his head, his heart, and his balls. . . ."

Below us, all of La Mancha looked like an old, patched mat of esparto grass. From the air the little villages looked like herds of newly shorn sheep. From time to time I caught sight of a car driving down one of the little back roads.

We had become increasingly intimate friends, and nothing, nobody ever came between us, for Ernesto was an iconoclast about everything except his affection for the people he chose as close friends. Literature alone would not have made us such fast friends, despite my profound admiration for his work. He did not believe in uplifting social messages or in politics (however progressive and revolutionary they might be), and he had even less faith in any kind of aesthetic ties to others; or at any rate the only time he was ever willing to discuss his work or the work of other writers was when he felt the need to explain something about his books or unburden himself about his problems as a writer. If the critics could only have heard him when, among friends, he really got going about the business of being a writer! But he always insisted that a writer shouldn't say very much about his own work or his own

25

personality, he should talk only about other things, because you have to throw a few scraps to the buzzards occasionally.

What would I write about this complicated man who had apparently killed himself because he no longer had any faith or hope in anything? A passage from one of his works kept running through my mind. But would I manage to make myself understood? Would I be understood by the buzzards who devour the corpses of others, mouthing that holy word, *charity*, a word whose mystery God alone understands?

In Ernesto's short story "Today Is Friday," one of the three Roman legionnaires who have been present at Christ's crucifixion says, "Why didn't he come down off the cross?" And another soldier, standing on the threshold of the Mystery, answers, "He didn't want to come down off the cross." The first soldier, who undoubtedly has stood beneath many crosses, replies in disbelief, "Show me a guy who doesn't want to come down off the cross." But the soldier who has divined the Mystery of the Crucifixion adds, with impressive sincerity, "I thought he was pretty good in there today." In other words, Christ at least had not been the cornered beast who becomes panic-stricken at the supreme moment and flees the embrace of death. A man may learn to stand his ground, like the torero implacably facing the bull's blind charge.

But all this might seem too subtle, and at critical moments such as this, the best thing to do is to be as simple as possible. It was not time yet to explain the aridity, the disgust, the rootlessness, the inertia of Ernesto's last years as I had seen them. Beneath all his energy there had been weariness; beneath his frivolity there had been boredom; beneath the outward triumph there had been unbearable, mortal tedium.

It was foggy when we landed, and I was superstitiously inclined to be more fearful than usual that day. The officers who had been on the plane wanted me to have another drink with them in the bar, but I didn't have time. It was almost noon already. I hurried off to the *Pueblo* office. What a long walk it seemed today! I felt even worse when I sat down at a typewriter. Would I be able to write even one line? I sat there trembling in the strangest way, unable to decide what to write, my mind a perfect blank. Not one word came to me, and at one point I almost burst into tears. How sentimental a person can sometimes be!

"Is your copy ready yet?" they kept asking me.

Finally I began banging the typewriter and out came "Oaks Also Fall," more a lament than an obituary, more an elegy than a paean of praise. I wrote:

> This was the way it had to be. This way and no other.
> More than once, God knows, a strange shiver ran up my spine
> when I saw you lovingly stroke a rifle with your great paw, petting

it as though it were a puppy, with more affection, I'm certain, than when you stroked the pelts of the panthers and lions hanging on your walls. Certain premonitions are infallible. I'm quite sure the weapon you killed yourself with was the gleaming rifle you kept under your mattress in the days of Batista.

"I always keep this one around," you said with that booming laugh of yours and that grin that was like an enormous slice of watermelon.

You couldn't have died in bed.

The pack on your back had grown too heavy. You might have put more things in it. But it wasn't worth the trouble. Writing was now a thing of the past. The chips were down. Literature had given you all it could.

It had to be this way and no other. Just as people would use a silly word, a banal but terribly tragic word, the word *accident*, to describe the fall of a great fighter. But the bullfight was over now, and you had made the final passes with the best of them.

When I heard the news last night, why did I suddenly remember the day that I learned, to my astonishment, that you could still recite the Lord's Prayer?

As I write this, I remember something you said:

"Death? Just another faceless nobody."

But few men have been as haunted by death, as obsessed with death, as you, though death appeared to be the exact opposite of everything you stood for—people saw only your outer shell. You kept death safely hidden, carefully set aside especially for you inside a cartridge, in the smell of gunpowder that always exhilarated you, in the dark chamber of your powerful rifle, in that stupid, diabolical, toylike object, the trigger of a gun. . . . The most expert, the most skilled hand may falter. Even if it is the hand of an expert marksman. Even if it is the hand of a genius. What a clumsy tremor in a once perfectly steady trigger finger!

You have lived life to the hilt. You had to die in that way and no other. You couldn't possibly have died in bed. It was quite obvious that you had to enter the dark wood of the awesome Mystery with a firm step, smelling of gunpowder, with your brain smashed to a bloody pulp, as though trampled by an elephant.

That was the way it had to be. Oaks also fall.

There was no doubt that Hemingway had been a sturdy oak, and had always wanted to be one, though at times he had been a felled oak, a sight not without a beauty all its own. He had wanted to be struck by death's thunderbolt in a country where oaks grow, for there are many of them around Ketchum, if memory serves me correctly; there are a number of them around the green expanses of the cemetery, where this one particular oak felled by a rifle shot awaits our charity—a little prayer for the man and all possible fervor for his work. Ernesto was to be buried beneath oak trees, in a spot the malevolent buzzards had never reached. And they never would, now.

What had Ernesto left behind, above and beyond the riddle of his life? A great deal, really.

He had not left a large body of work. Six novels; approximately fifty short stories, some of them fantastic successes and others irritating disappointments; the best interpretation of the world of bullfighting ever published by a non-Spaniard; a handful of subtle, carefully documented articles on hunting or fishing; a rather bad play; many pieces of journalism, some of them absolutely first-rate, others at least solidly crafted; a collection of letters that were more or less puzzling and full of nonsense. Was that all? No, come to think of it, he had also left us a few modest, curious poems.

But this was still not all; there was more. Because at the precise point where his work left off, his humanity began: a man who had lived a life so full of restless wanderings and thrilling escapes that he was world-famous, a romantic genius, when that species was dying out, who became a classic through his determination to create a distinguished body of writing; a biography that was incomplete, and would remain so, precisely because of the colorful adventures that masked his real personality; a destiny divided between peace and war as few others have been, for Ernesto was a peace-loving warrior who mysteriously lost hope.

He had often experienced writers' block at crucial moments, held back by a desire to keep his own life private or social cowardice or whatever one cares to call it; but when it came time to do away with himself, the rifle had not jammed.

He was no longer even a friend, because from now on my memories of him would be worth little or nothing. Only Hemingway the writer counted now, the closed book of a life fervently devoted to art, an existence literally riveted to the earth, the sea, the air. But the warrior, the fisherman, the hunter, and the artist too, had been treacherously betrayed by a single enemy: the man himself. That same morning, I had heard on the radio that Ernesto's mortal remains would be removed from his house like the dead body of a bull dragged out of the bullring, and placed in a lead coffin.

My one answer to everyone's questions was, "Men like Ernesto never die."

But Ernesto had died. I made my way homeward like a sleepwalker, and when I got to the bar on the corner by my apartment, I stopped in for a drink. I was so upset thinking about Ernesto that I started out the door without paying, and the waiter, who was new there, shouted after me, "Hey, friend! You with the long hair!"

"What's the matter?"

"You forgot to pay."

"Bring me another short one."

I paid for both drinks and left. When I arrived at the building where I lived, the concierge's wife took one look at me and said, "Is anything wrong?"

Was anything wrong! I had no idea. It struck me as very odd, though, that nobody else seemed to feel that anything was wrong.

The paper would be coming off the presses right about now, with the usual headline. No, it wouldn't be the usual headline. It would be one in bold type, and there would be photos on the front page. Ernesto's death would sell a lot of papers. Like the appearance of one of those erratic, mysterious comets.

I shut myself up in my apartment, where all the furniture was shrouded in dust covers for the summer, opened the door onto the balcony, and lowered the blinds. It was a sweltering day.

The concierge came up to tell me that one of my pet birds had died and another had gotten loose.

"Never mind. There's nothing we can do about it," I told him.

As I sat there, I noticed Ernesto's photograph, the one taken when he came to visit Don Pío Baroja, he is wearing, incredibly, a dark tie with polka dots, sitting like a schoolboy, with his feet together, leaning forward a little, in quite a formal pose. There was an intimate photograph of Mary too, with an affectionate dedication she had written on the day we had said good-by: "Love to José Luis, from Mary." Ernesto had always signed photographs of himself more formally. His read: "To José Luis, from his friend Ernesto Hemingway."

But these were only relics. What was preying on my mind at that moment was Mary's reaction when she'd found Ernesto with his head blown off. Apparently she had been asleep upstairs when the two shots rang out. It had been very early in the morning, one of the favorite hours of the huntsman. Ernesto had killed himself in the downstairs hallway, dressed in his pajamas and slippers. He had gone straight from his bed to one of the chairs down there, thought things over for a moment, grabbed his most trusty and most beautiful shotgun, and thought no more.

Had he left any sort of farewell note, any special message, with or without some key? What other key was there except his work, his life?

I telephoned Ordóñez's house. He wasn't there, but would be back the next day at the latest. His wife, María del Carmen, was terribly distraught and depressed. She didn't know what had happened. Strangely enough, all Ernesto's closest friends could not accept the fact that he had killed himself, even though they were quite sure that that was what had happened, and all they could talk about was his bad luck and the hand of fate.

I spent some time going through papers and photos looking for letters from my dead friend. I greatly regretted not having kept a detailed diary of all our meetings and outings. We had spent moments together that we would never share again, and my memories could never recapture them in all their intimate detail. But does anyone in midstream believe himself capable of capturing the water's mad dance?

"You'll be coming back soon," I had said to Ernesto.

"I'll always come back," he had answered.

And then, drawing Mary aside after dinner at La Brasa, I had said to her, "You must take good care of him."

And she had answered, "He's like a little kid. But he's okay. Lots better than when he first came."

The sort of life Ernesto had led in Spain the year before had been sheer madness, enough to kill a horse. Rushing here, there, and everywhere, going to bed in the wee hours of the morning, getting up very early, drinking practically limitless quantities of alcohol, eating as much as he pleased, trying to write, patiently and laboriously, when there was nothing else going on, crossing out whole paragraphs, rewriting, correcting, filling up page after page . . . During his last days in Madrid, I had seen how nervous and distant he was as he labored to simplify his text. His editors in the United States were pressing him to boil down the article they had commissioned to a few thousand words, and he had been doing his very best to comply.

I had his letters in front of me. What struck me most at that moment were the half-joking phrases about his state of health that invariably appeared in all his letters. There were very few of them that failed to mention his blood count or his weight.

"Mary has a hemoglobin count of 4,600,000, better than Samson's before his hair got cut off, and she's got no excuse. I've gotten a good report too. I'm down to 200 pounds. . . . I'm not in a rut at all . . . work's going very well. . . ."

This was in 1959. One of Ernesto's last letters to Juanito Quintana, his old friend and confidant in Pamplona, dated June 1960, a letter that Juanito had sent on to me, said: "I don't know when I'll be able to get to Spain this year. I've been working like a dog, I've written more than 100,000 words since the end of January, and that's a lot for me. Valerie and Mary are typing the whole thing now, and then I'll have to make corrections."

The tone of this letter was very strange. Ernesto's spoken Spanish was much more fluent and precise than his written Spanish. It was plain to see that he had doubts and misgivings when he wrote in Spanish, and he usually fell into a much more formal sort of diction and made grammatical errors. His spoken Spanish was much clearer, much more spicy and picturesque.

I put the letters aside and picked up one of his books, *For Whom the Bell Tolls,* in Olga Sanz's dreadful Argentinian translation. The epigraph of this passionate depiction of recent Spanish history was taken from a sermon by a daring Renaissance adventurer, John Donne, a resounding bit of rhetoric calculated to appeal both to Catholics and to Ernesto:

> No man is an *Iland,* intire of it selfe; every man is a peece of the *Continent,* a part of the *maine;* if a *Clod* bee washed away by the *Sea, Europe* is the lesse, as well as if a *Promontorie* were, as well as if a *Mannor* of thy *friends* or of *thine owne* were; any mans *death* diminishes me, because I am involved in *Mankinde:* And therefore never send to know for whom the *bell* tolls; It tolls for *thee."*

If Ernesto used this paragraph (taken from Donne's sermon "The Pain of Death," delivered on April 3, 1625, before Charles I) as an epigraph, he did not do so merely to justify the title of his book. The idea that every tolling of the death knell involved his own death had long haunted him. And with the Spanish Civil War the idea had taken on a much deeper significance.

I opened the book and began to read.

What a lot of sheer nonsense has been written about this book! And how much more nonsense was to be written after Ernesto's death. The old Spanish proverb "Nobody's rabid after the dog dies" just isn't true, especially when it is not a dog, but a lion, that dies.

I went to Tetuán to send Mary a cable, but the whole business was very complicated, and I never found out exactly how much it would cost to send it or whether it would ever arrive. I went downtown then to the main office of Transradio and didn't have quite such a hard time getting it sent off. But I wouldn't be able to attend the funeral; if I'd had enough money for even a one-way ticket, I would have bought one instead of sending a cable. The message I sent cost me a lot, even though it was very short. And despite the fact that they charged me two thousand pesetas, the cable never did arrive, and my money was never refunded. Mary Hemingway couldn't understand why she'd had no word from me. If I had written everything I had on my mind in that cable, it would have cost me a fortune.

I had a bite to eat and lay down for a while, knowing that people were bound to start calling soon to ask me about Ernesto. Then I listened to a dull radio broadcast on "Ernesto Hemingway, the bullfight *aficionado*." Just as I was going out the door, the telephone rang.

"Are you sure he committed suicide?"

"I've had a feeling he'd kill himself."

"And how do you know that's what happened?"

"How can I be sure? I don't have any certain knowledge, but there's no doubt in my mind that he killed himself."

This was neither the first nor the last telephone call about Ernesto's death I received. And I noticed that a number of people seemed rather pleased when the news reports kept pouring in confirming that he had died by his own hand. Spanish publishers in particular seemed very excited at the news of his death.

"It's going to be much easier to get permission from his widow for a Spanish edition now."

"We must get there ahead of everybody else."

This wasn't the first time publishers had tried to get the Spanish rights to Ernesto's works, though they were even more insistent now. I was more obsessed than ever by the image of buzzards hovering over some colossal prey. More than once, publishers had asked me to intercede with Hemingway to secure them publication rights, but I had never been willing to broach the subject directly, especially when this or that candidate had subtly hinted that I wouldn't be forgotten if I put in a good word in his behalf. But they had underestimated me. If you were friends with Ernesto, you couldn't turn into a buzzard too, not even a relatively harmless one. He had often spoken to me of how disgusted he was at the bad Spanish translations of his work, and how anxious he was to remedy this lamentable state of affairs; for that very reason, I had carefully kept my distance, even though he was the one who had brought the subject up and even suggested that I review the entire matter. But, at the same time, he had left everything up in the air and gone on to discuss other things. My impression was that he didn't want any kind of trouble with his New York agent, who was a sort of literary executor. And in all truth, more often than not the offers from Spanish publishers had been so small as to border on the ridiculous; they wouldn't even have paid for Ernesto's snacks on a trip to Paris or Pamplona.

In the years just past, Ernesto's income had varied from year to year, but he probably averaged something like $400,000 or $450,000 a year. His U.S. taxes were very steep, of course, and took a good chunk out of that sum. His last letters were full of the two things that preyed most on his mind: his health and his taxes. "We're in the midst of making out our income tax, trying to keep some of the money we made in 1959 and justifying our legitimate expenses," he wrote to his friend Quintana in June 1960. Financially speaking, he could consider himself one of the world's most highly rewarded authors. But he seldom boasted about his earnings, and complained bitterly about his taxes and expenses. Although he pretended that money didn't mean very much to him, and spent almost every penny of it the minute he earned it, he worried about it a great deal during his lifetime. He earned huge sums when he was at the peak of his fame, but money slipped through his fingers, and despite his apparent lack of concern about finances, he was very much afraid of being hard up and not being able to maintain his high standard of living. I had known him to be quite tightfisted in the oddest of circumstances. But, at the same time, he felt obliged to put up a splendid front. I have known a number of famous writers, and a number of writers without much of a reputation but a lot of money, and I have never seen one of them who made such a point of being generous and free with his money. Ernesto's pride and his need to be independent undoubtedly had a great deal to do with his generosity. He often used to say: "Nobody ever picks up the check when I'm around."

"Listen, there must have been a time or two when somebody else paid for you," I once answered.

"Well, a couple of times maybe. But only when I let them. I'd always rather pay myself."

"You're lucky you've got the money."

"Yes, I'd always rather pay the tab myself, for me and for everybody else. It's better that way."

And he always *had* paid, at least as long as I'd known him. The night before he left Spain on his last visit, he'd taken me aside and shown me a check made out to one of my colleagues on the newspaper.

"Do you think this is okay?" he asked me.

"The check or the amount?" I answered laughingly.

"It's just a token. The guy went out of his way to be nice to a friend of ours. It's only right to show we appreciate it."

"He'll be very grateful, especially since he's pretty hard up right now."

The check was worth a lot, I thought to myself, not only because it was for a generous sum, but because it had Ernesto's signature on it. Even if you were broke, it would be worth your while not to cash it at the bank.

Ernesto regarded money as the symbol of his freedom. He didn't like gifts, he refused to let other people pay for him, he had everything his way. When Camorra, a Spanish friend of his, found out that Ernesto had been robbed of nine thousand pesetas in Murcia, he tried to reimburse him, as a friendly gesture. Ernesto got very angry and his only answer was, "Who do you take me for, anyway?"

He was accused more than once of being a tightwad. I had a violent argument, in fact, with a reporter in Havana who had claimed that Ernesto was rather a skinflint. The truth of the matter was that his great shyness, his lack of self-confidence made him very ill at ease when he wasn't the one who was paying the bill or doing the inviting. He wouldn't have given up the code that allowed him absolute freedom, the freedom of the noble savage amid the corrupting luxuries of civilization, for anything in the world. No, he was not a penny pincher or a selfish man. But the fact of the matter was that paying for his independence had cost him a lot, and at times, toward the end especially, he was afraid he might not be able to continue to play the role of a person who scorned money and what it would buy. Ernesto's values were simple and straightforward, in good times and in bad. But I could understand why he might have appeared to outsiders to be a bit selfish. He didn't care to have any intimate friendships, any ties that would restrict him, any honors—other than those he himself freely chose; he was deathly afraid of being dependent on anything or anybody, and therefore, like a miser, or a jungle savage, he made sure that he would have the wealth, the power, and the self-sufficiency that would allow him to accept or reject any claims that society or fame might make on him. In the last days of his final visit to Spain, however, I noticed that he seemed to be a bit worried about money. But there was good reason for this; he had been traveling for many months and had had heavy expenses. He would be very irritated when he wrote something that didn't come out right, and even more irritated when his accounts didn't balance. But in the end he would always say, in a confidential tone of voice: "Those guys from the Internal Revenue Service get almost everything I make anyway. They're the ones you're working for, and they dog your every footstep . . . they're worse than rats. . . ."

Like everybody else, Ernesto was quite different when things were going his way, from when they weren't. When the wind was favorable and there was smooth sailing ahead, his motto was "Doing what I want to do, going where I want to go, being with the people I want to be with —that's what I want."

A marvelous philosophy—providing, of course, that you have the means to make it a pleasant, elegant way of life.

One day when I was with him, a journalist asked him, "What would Hemingway's own description of himself be?"

"That's very simple," he replied. "He'd describe himself as a person who could do anything, once he'd made up his mind to do it."

Among the many descriptions of Ernesto that various people have come up with since his death, I was struck by Ingrid Bergman's thumbnail portrait of him: "More than a man, Hemingway was a style of life." That was exactly what he was, a style of life that was the exact opposite of everything around him.

While he tapped his own personality on every page of his fiction in order to create more or less believable characters, it seems to me that he left us the most complete picture of himself in *The Old Man and the*

Sea, although this may well be his most self-effacing work. This book was very difficult for him to write, and though the story of the old fisherman was a transposition of his own experience, it is nonetheless Ernesto himself who confronts all the voracious predators in this work. If the death of the great fish in *The Old Man and the Sea* ultimately foreshadows Ernesto's own death, it is also a symbol of the resignation, if not the optimism, he tried to distill from his own lonely life, above and beyond his four marriages, his battles, his phenomenal adventures. What is saddest about this story is that despite Ernesto's efforts to dig down to the very roots of serenity, he himself never managed to attain this sort of peace.

As these thoughts occupied my mind, I realized that there was more, much more, to Ernesto than what I had glimpsed and vaguely expressed when I had described him as a pathetic, extremely sensitive person. His exuberant, booming, contagious laugh had most often been a cover-up for an incomprehensible feeling of failure and defeat. Often, he had deliberately assumed the cynical pose of a man who had given up every hope of happiness, but even at such times he seemed a vulnerable man whom life had betrayed, a man tearing away the blindfold of illusion from his eyes.

Perhaps he had always been such a person, long before that tragic morning when he made up his mind to put an end to a singularly successful life. There had always been just a trace of carefully repressed bitterness in the very set of his lips.

That was why I used to ask myself, whenever I said good-by to him: "Why, why does he always leave me with the feeling that he's falling apart inside? How can such a vital man lose all his faith, even faith in life itself?" Contrary to what many people believed, Ernesto did not trust life at all. "How can we live, seeing we have to die?" How sad it was that he had found no answer to that question.

Nothing was easy to explain. He had faced a machine gun bravely; withstood the onslaughts of sharks; allowed a leopard to approach within ten yards before firing a shot straight to its heart; run in front of bulls like a heedless young boy; swum against the current in an icy river; lain in ambush for German submarines in the Caribbean in a boat he had converted into a veritable floating bomb; gone through the front lines four or five times during the Spanish War, once or twice in a light tank; eaten and drunk like a latter-day Heliogabalus; billed and cooed and made love to a young girl like a shy cadet. . . . What inner mechanism had failed? At what point had the fatal crack occurred?

His works might shed more light on the question. Not only would his characters give me a strange, sad, lonely feeling; following in his footsteps, I would be able to trace his effort to develop a cheerful stoicism, his struggle against becoming totally demoralized, his desperate attempt to ward off skepticism and impotence by clinging to things that were warm, happy, and hopeful. But how powerless the drug of momentary pleasures and exciting adventures had been against an inescapable decline of the spirit!

I remembered him—and from now on always would remember him—standing there singing, with the glass of wine in his hand, staring as if hypnotized while the matador picked up the sword for the kill. This image was so vivid and powerful that it blotted out my memory of the aimless, anxiety-ridden human being I had more than once glimpsed when there was nothing much doing and he was depressed. Usually, however, he flung himself into the adventure of living with more apparent self-confidence and more sheer gusto than anybody else. Though his face seemed at times to have deliberately assumed the mask of a happy man, there was still nothing strained or artificial about it. Though Ernesto himself may not have felt full of life and in high spirits, those around him did, just looking at his radiant face.

Suddenly I had a disturbing, crystal-clear recollection of the angry red streak running from his nose to his cheek, the rash of little whitish pustules that sloughed off like dandruff, the ghastly-looking skin infection that he had tried so hard to conceal by growing a luxuriant beard. Could that have been why he killed himself? It had certainly begun to worry him, and it preyed on his mind even more because he either would not or could not admit the possibility that this skin disease might be malignant. Was this what finally broke his spirit—looking at himself in a pitiless mirror? Bullfighters may be courageous throughout their careers and then suddenly one day fall to their knees in front of the bull and tremble like reeds shaken by the wind. A house of cards may be quite steady until suddenly one card bends a little and all of them start to tumble down. There are battles that are nearly won, and then one flank retreats and everything falls to pieces. This is how the once-invincible man is brought low—and also how the weak man who has had successes and triumphs but has caught a glimpse of what a hollow façade they may be comes to be like other men and earns their compassion. Dying is very easy, and killing oneself may be a new beginning, for to die is to learn.

Nonetheless I could not forget that his harshest words, both spoken and written, and his greatest scorn had been reserved for cowards. Can there be anything more cruel than his description of a man who was once his idol? "If you see Niño de la Palma, the chances are you will see cowardice in its least attractive form," he had written in *Death in the Afternoon*. How can anyone forget Ernesto's contempt for the bull-fighter who loses his courage when he faces the bull, his repugnance for the craven general who permits his troops to be pointlessly slaughtered, his savage ridicule of the man who commits suicide?

And all this time the most inane sort of chatter about Ernesto's travels, his divorces, his adventures, his acts of bravery, his triumphs kept pouring out of the radio. I paced back and forth, feeling as if I had been badly betrayed. Was his pessimism so deeply rooted that not even the possibility of losing himself in his art and the prospect of the coming festival of San Fermín could have rid him of his apathy? What right did he have to do what he had done when his friends in Spain were expecting him?

This was part of the mystery. He was always laughing and joking and allowed no one to see his inner pain. Had he revealed it as freely and as openly as he did his infectious pleasure in life, he would have depressed everyone around him.

"I'll be seeing you soon," he had said as he put his arm around me and bade me farewell, still giving me advice: "Leave journalism." Doubtless he was already withdrawing from life. But since his retreat had to be an honorable one, he forced himself to be as imperturbable as a philosopher. This farewell to life had to be a lonely one, the stealing away of a wounded giant. Had he deliberately carried his secret to the grave with him? And did a hearty peal of laughter, the very last of his life, mingle with the sound of the exploding bullet? Or had he done the deed like the careful hunter he had been all his life?

His art had always been a salvation and a defense for him, a source of energy and a life buoy to cling to. But the sad truth was that his work, too, was teetering on the edge of an abyss.

The presentiments I had had about him were becoming clearer and clearer now. Suicide in Ernesto's case was something more than a literary theme. Precisely because it was a subject he had both stubbornly pursued, and carefully avoided, both ridiculed and feared, I realized now that he had been deeply obsessed with the thought of his own finger on the trigger. His depression had become a burden that there was no point in carrying any longer. Looking back, I could see this more plainly now.

"You've got an eye for good titles, José Luis," he had said to me one day. 'With Death on My Back' is a fine one, a great one."

Without quite knowing why or how, you had the feeling that he had sacrificed his life for his art. The something that would be left behind on the printed page might be more important than anything he had experienced in his life. His death might be a way of balancing the books, and not only in the sense that they would put an end to the financial troubles people said were preying on his mind. Everyday truths would count up to one hard truth; the passing beauty of the moment, a gloriously ephemeral beauty, would add up to his definition of himself, a definition that would be possible only after he had destroyed himself. Yet his words kept ringing in my ears.

"Don't let anybody tame you or domesticate you, José Luis," he had said.

"You know I'm doing my best to see that that won't happen," I answered.

"That's right—not even death. The great whore may be able to do that, but it should only happen on the other side."

"I don't follow you."

But now I was beginning to understand.

I was dead tired. Not even the babies bawling their heads off in the next apartment could keep me from getting drowsier and drowsier.

I had Ernesto's last letter in my hand, with a tentative travel schedule. With my eyes half closed I read:

". . . And my health is much improved."

". . . work's going very well. . . ."

And then I fell asleep.

2   I was starved when I woke up, and had a terrible headache. I opened all the windows and began pacing up and down the terrace. The plants in the flowerpots needed watering, so I watered them.

The first thing I would do would be to call Ernesto's doctor friend who had treated him during his last trip to Spain. He could provide me with the most accurate information on the last days of Ernesto's life.

But I was not able to get in touch with Dr. Medinaveitia. I would have to wait until later.

I dropped in at a couple of neighborhood bars where they often put out free lunches. But nothing appealed to me. I had a couple of beers and a few fried potatoes and left. But once outside on the street again, I realized I was still terribly thirsty.

I began to write a letter to Mary, but I never got beyond the fifth line, and tore up all my drafts. All of them seemed superficial. I was incapable of writing one line that expressed genuine feeling or sorrow.

I got all of Ernesto's books down off the shelves then and piled them on the floor. Where should I begin? Reading a bit of *The Old Man and the Sea* would be the most satisfying, for that book was always comforting reading, despite the old fisherman's bad luck. The moral to be drawn from it is the same lesson taught by certain great mystics or by those awesome ascetics who in the end are won over to a spirit of charity and indulgence. But the thought occurred to me that basing my solitary tribute on a single novella might seem frivolous, even though it is one of those tricky, apparently superficial narratives that can catch you up like a sudden whirlwind. Beginning with a novella might appear to be too facile. Nor was it the moment to immerse myself in the world of bullfighting, because even though the *corrida* was the alpha and omega of Ernesto's writing, I was not in a mood for *encierros* and *broncas*—the running of the bulls through the streets and hoots from the crowds in the stands at the bullring. At that very moment Pamplona was in a mad whirl of activity, in excited anticipation of the great annual fiesta. Just a year ago in the Plaza del Castillo I had asked Ernesto: "What is it you like most about the San Fermín fiesta?"

"What I like most is the way it begins. I don't like the way it ends as well."

I picked up *For Whom the Bell Tolls*, because it has always seemed to me that this work has been greatly misunderstood and even vilified in Spain. You could never talk about Ernesto or his work in this country without somebody mentioning this novel, which to my mind is much more than a complacent utopia, and much more than a bitter portrait of a very special sort of political infighting.

Anyone who studies Ernesto's work would be obliged to conclude that Hemingway the writer was a liberal, not because of any programs or dogmas he espoused, but because of his personality and his habits. But since the word *liberal*, all by itself, might not be an adequate description of Ernesto's geographical and spiritual itinerary during his lifetime, the Hemingway scholar would be obliged to add that Ernesto was profoundly democratic, a man led by his temperament, rather than by what he had learned from books, to be a defender of the principles of freedom. He was a democratic man, though not in the sense of the easygoing, comfortable conformism that that word implies for many people. Others have come to Spain for pleasure or profit, but Ernesto came to our country to suffer and to bear witness to his suffering.

This novel had caused scandal and bitter controversy in Spain. It would be many years before our country would view this book rationally, and lovingly heed its real message and meaning, because *For Whom the Bell Tolls* is a work that is above parties and ideologies and the usual sort of political propaganda.

For Hemingway the ideal of freedom was a call to battle, a thoroughly revolutionary ideal. We must prove worthy of our freedom and conquer it, fighting tooth and nail for it if necessary. It was not only that the very cornerstone of Ernesto's view of life was freedom for all; attaining this goal necessarily presupposed making changes that may well have seemed anarchical to a number of people, but basically they were aimed at a more just and more humane social order. There was always something of the reformer in him, and it might be claimed with some justification that no other writer of his time had as clear a conception of what the future had in store as Hemingway in his zeal to smash every idol erected by convention, hypocrisy, and fraud, both in society and in politics.

And this was what brought Ernesto closer and closer to Christianity in its purest and most radical form. Wherever I opened the book, the revealing phrases leaped to my eye. When they are planning to blow up the bridge, for example:

> "No," said Robert Jordan, "I do not like to kill animals."
> "With me it is the opposite," the old man said. "I do not like to kill men."
> "Nobody does except those who are disturbed in the head," Robert Jordan said, "but I feel nothing against it when it is necessary. When it is for the cause."

Ernesto, or rather Robert Jordan, agrees with the Spanish partisan and these lofty reasons for participating in the endeavor. Yet in Spain Ernesto is most often regarded as a more or less hard-bitten, bloodthirsty adventurer, a soulless, pitiless spectator. How little Spaniards knew him!

Ernesto's conduct during the Spanish Civil War was most honorable and completely responsible, and his sympathies lay with the side that in his mind and heart he was convinced was defending truth and justice. He was the exact opposite of a mercenary. He was one of the few *romantics* who came to Spain to participate in our Civil War.

He hated Fascism with a passion, and thought that there was a serious possibility that what to him was a monstrous idea might spread like a plague among a people such as the Spanish, whom he had loved for many years. As a correspondent, he had seen the depredations of Fascism on its native soil in Italy, and he believed it necessary to stamp it out at all costs in Spain, a country with a dangerous tradition of messianical fanaticism.

The phone rang. It was Finita. How had she found out that I was in town? No, I didn't want to go out with her. I didn't have one extra cent in my pocket, but I didn't let on to her that I was almost flat broke. She had heard about Ernesto, and wanted to comfort me, or wanted me to comfort her.

But I wanted to go on with what I was doing, paying my lonely tribute to Ernesto.

As the Spanish War was entering its most critical phase and the outcome was still uncertain, Ernesto was convinced that the Republican cause was lost, yet he nonetheless gave a speech in Carnegie Hall on June 4, 1937, before the anti-Fascist League of American Writers, in which he said that Fascism is a lie told by bullies.

That had always impressed me. Because before I knew Ernesto as a person and Hemingway as a writer, it had seemed to me that when a man becomes a propaganda instrument for either side in a war, the truth of this man and his legacy—not only his message but his very stature as a man—risk being distorted. It is most regrettable that there were propaganda organs, recruiting centers, intelligence services on both sides during the Civil War, exactly similar instances of the same fundamental mechanism.

I went down to the bar on the corner and got a siphon of soda water that cost me ten duros. They didn't have any mineral water. I also bought some rat poison in the drugstore. My apartment smelled dreadful.

Wars that are lost not out of miscalculation but out of an excess of fervor and moral sincerity give rise to more violent emotions than those won out of an instinct for self-preservation. Victory often brings more problems than defeat.

I had been on the winning side. Ernesto had been on the losing side. But he hadn't altogether lost the war, any more than I had decisively won it, since a new symbol confronted both of us: a Spain that had not proved to be what it should have been, after having defeated a Spain that was not to be, and the Spain that had won would never be what it should be if it neglected the Spain that had been defeated.

The proof of Ernesto's inviolable spirit of independence and his absolute integrity with regard to the conflict is the fact that when he came back to Spain in later years, no one could ever claim that he supported this or that group, nor did he ever answer any of the appeals occasionally addressed to him, steadfastly refusing both to humble himself for having been on the losing side and to be co-opted by any political faction. The war was over, he felt, and he firmly intended to remain absolutely neutral; and with admirable steadfastness, that was exactly what he did. Many temptations came his way, but his inviolable code always saved him. His views in private were something else entirely, but even in the company of close friends he never allowed himself to go beyond the sort of joking remarks that any Spaniard with a critical turn of mind and a healthy sense of humor might make.

I was sure there were rats in my apartment. I hadn't seen any, but there was an awful smell and tracks all over. I decided to call Benicasim long distance, and wished I hadn't. In Spain you don't simply place a long-distance call, you "celebrate" it, a solemn verb that would not be necessary if the telephone service were modern and efficient. These "celebrations" take hours, though the whole business is so exhausting you don't feel much like "celebrating" when you finally get your party. I tried to get through two or three times, and finally canceled the call, after having come close to insulting the telephone operators. I didn't say *al carajo*—"to bloody hell with you"—one of Ernesto's favorite expletives, but I was tempted to.

As I waited, I went on leafing through *For Whom the Bell Tolls*, and it was an eye opener to me. I know that it will be many years before Spaniards realize what a noble-spirited, impartial novel this is. Stubbornly refusing to recognize the great power and depth of this book, many Spaniards have attempted to dismiss it as "fake journalism." By pinning the label of "just another reporter" on Ernesto, they have tried to minimize his importance as a most unusual eyewitness. He was not a combatant; he was something more than that. And *For Whom the Bell Tolls* can be understood only in the light of his passionate love for Spain on the one hand, and his thoroughgoing aversion for both Fascism and Communism on the other.

Even though he himself had not borne arms, he had been a front-line correspondent, and even though he had not personally thrown hand grenades at advancing tanks, in spirit he had been a soldier in the vanguard. He had tried to rise above the battle and get a clear picture of the two contending ideologies, and at the same time he had sided against the political commissars and spies who were standing in the way of victory for the Republican cause. The witness he bore was quite simple: his sympathies were with the common people he loved, and he embraced what he took to be the people's cause.

He was unwilling to discuss the subject any further, claiming that the whole Civil War was past history now. His conduct was absolutely above reproach.

"That I am a foreigner is not my fault. I would rather have been born here," his hero Robert Jordan says.

From the very first, Ernesto was aware of the extraordinary importance of the Spanish Civil War, for he was quite certain that the outcome of the Battle of Madrid would have a profound effect on the future course of history.

Ernesto—like Pío Baroja, for one example—had no ironclad, definite ideology. He had ideals, which are not the same thing, and he had been interested in certain areas of philosophy. He had fought courageously for ideals he thought would make man's lot more just.

Ernesto had deliberately played the hero in the Spanish War, (in a way that came close to being childish) more out of an overwhelming desire to be a heroic figure than because of the necessities of the situation. All the risks he took, all the disputes in which he intervened, all the dreams of valor that he forged were like strong spirits he had distilled out of needs stemming from his own personality. The other wars he had fought in or covered as a correspondent had involved more general problems, had been more abstract duels, so to speak; the Spanish War, however, was a direct confrontation between two radically different, fanatical, totally irreconcilable antagonists who had sworn to destroy each other. The issues were black and white; what was at stake was a whole style of life, a world view, the acceptance or the rejection of all human history. This was not a war fought in the front lines according to tactical plans drawn up by general staffs; it was a battle fought in the streets and the countryside according to the instincts of the people, a total destruction of the enemy improvised from moment to moment. Not only were there grimacing corpses on the battlefields; civilians, too, died dramatic deaths. Above and beyond the horror of soldiers whose dead bodies were riddled with machine-gun bullets, there was the brutal, inhuman slaughter of non-combatants, a collective sadism, senseless cruelty.

Wasn't bloodshed what you wanted to see, Ernesto? Didn't you want to see with your own eyes what Goya had painted, what had haunted Quevedo in his dreams, what a people stretched on the rack between life and death, crucified between heaven and earth, are capable of?

More than once when Ernesto entered a room, there were Spaniards who still glared at him accusingly, as if he were an opportunist without a conscience, a blithe survivor of the hecatomb. These fierce glances hurt Ernesto, and he fled from them.

And more than once when Ernesto entered a room, I saw people stare at him as though he were a tamed animal on exhibit; the tension was unbearable until somebody made some trivial gesture to save the situation.

It was best not to remind Ernesto of the Spanish War. If he wanted to talk about it, he would do so; if he wanted to be by himself and silently brood about the past, we let him. That way he would feel more or less at ease.

"I won't feel happy about the whole business until I see a certain thing happen."

"What's that?" I asked.

"I can't tell you, but you can guess."

Sometimes as he was walking down the street, someone would come up to him, respectfully shake his hand, and say in a very deliberate tone of voice, "Greetings, *comrade*."

And Ernesto would reply, almost automatically, "Greetings."

But only when he was quite sure that the person was really loyal to the cause would he add the Republican slogan "No pasarán" or "Viva la República."

One time, near the headquarters of the Falange, I saw him stop and stare at a Falangist wearing a full-dress uniform. The expression on

Ernesto's face was a poem in and of itself, and what was most noticeable about it was the strange look of pity in his eyes.

Planes kept flying over my block, and I would have given anything to be on one, headed for Ketchum. But I couldn't possibly go. As usual, the nasty problem of money was standing in my way.

Ernesto's loyalties to the Republican side were partly sentimental, but something else, something more important, was also involved. And therefore the bridge in *For Whom the Bell Tolls*, one more bridge to be blown up in yet another war, is also an allegory, and smashing it to smithereens becomes a symbol, something that goes beyond propaganda to become an inspiring, constructive lesson.

Neither "Reds" nor "Whites"—nor "Blues" nor "Purples" nor any other faction—had ever managed to reach the same lofty heights as Ernesto when he took pen in hand and wrote about the Spanish War. His book was far superior to a chronicle of martyrdom or an incendiary pamphlet. For Ernesto the task at hand was not to try to describe and illustrate a dogma or a program, but rather to show men how to behave decently and honestly—by his own personal example first of all.

Ernesto didn't like thinking about the war, and tried to keep his mind off it. But when he couldn't help brooding about it, he'd start reminiscing in a sad tone of voice and often end up in a rage. I knew how the conversation would go before he even opened his mouth:

"I was never a turncoat, José Luis."

"I'm sure you weren't, Ernesto."

"I swear I always went wherever I thought I was needed."

"I'm sure you did."

"If anybody can prove to me that I betrayed the cause, he has every right to spit in my face, and I wouldn't lift a finger to defend myself."

"I know what you mean, Ernesto."

"I'm the number-one loser."

"I know."

"You know me very well, and you know I wouldn't swear to a thing if it wasn't true."

"I know you've always tried to be an honorable man, and you always have been."

"Well, I swear I tried my damnedest not to do anything to damage the cause."

"I understand perfectly."

"The war was lost because . . ." and at that point he would get very angry and start swearing like a trooper. After a while he'd say, in a distracted, testy tone of voice: "I'll never change." Then he'd add despairingly: "What a bitch not to have gotten killed during the retreat. . . ."

Nonetheless Ernesto never made speeches and never took part in plots or transmitted secret messages or railed against the Franco regime. He faced up to the facts fatalistically, kept his thoughts to himself, and respected the code of the loser to the letter. He had no faith in political parties or conspiracies. The one thing that sometimes revived his hopes a little was the morale of the Spanish man in the street, who appeared to have boundless powers of recuperation.

But when Ernesto left Spain in 1939 he took with him not only the taste of defeat but also a passionate, unremitting hatred for Communism, not only as an ideology but as a disgraceful political system. "The Commies acted like a bunch of filthy swine in Spain," he used to growl angrily. His differences with the Communists were irreconcilable, and when I read in the papers that he had received invitations to visit the Soviet Union, I was certain he would not accept them. Neither the Communist system nor its methods were to his liking. By temperament Ernesto was incapable of following a party line. The only discipline he could accept was the self-imposed discipline a man abides by out of fervent enthusiasm for a cause or because he has a dream. As a man who in the final analysis was sentimental and tenderhearted, he was repelled by extremism and political murder. An ardent partisan of Fidel Castro's in the beginning, he grimaced in disgust when he saw the Cuban Revolution taking the wrong turn and exclaimed, "What a bloody shame—a marvelous opportunity gone down the drain!"

At times the highhanded ways of certain Spaniards appalled him, but since he knew the realities of the situation he had no illusions. Spain for him was not the triumph of a dubious cause, but a long and deeply painful purgatory that in the end would become a more noble, more human struggle for justice.

Very few people have understood the role he played in our war. If he came to fight in Spain, it was for more profound motives than simple solidarity with the Republican cause. He knew Spain well and was well aware of its class discrimination, its cultural backwardness, its social injustice, its feudal structure. I have seldom witnessed a more deep-rooted sense of justice in a writer; Ernesto did not have to express it in odes or manifestoes: it was inborn. And few writers, it seems to me, have had such an inviolable sense of honor, in something close to the Spanish meaning of the word. All this made him feel very sympathetic toward the Spanish people, almost a part of them, and, as he saw it, they were threatened by foreign powers.

I returned again and again to the key text, to the words of Ernesto's that explained everything, to the most transparent phrase of all: "Man

is not made for defeat. . . . A man can be destroyed but not defeated."
(*The Old Man and the Sea*)

One day Ernesto had had a less guarded conversation with me about our war and had been very outspoken about certain comrades on the Madrid front.

"He acted like an armchair general."

"Who did?"

"He was always a fake guerrilla, sitting in the lobby of the hotel writing page after page of war stories."

"Who was that?"

"Who do you suppose? Malraux, that's who, the phantom of the Madrid front!"

Then, going on in the same vein, he said: "And then there was Arturo Barea, that little leprechaun who spent all his time in the basement of the Telephone Building. . . ."

But he had nothing against either of them as writers, and immediately added, as though he realized he'd been too rough on them: "But they behaved okay. I wish I could say the same about certain other people."

For Whom the Bell Tolls was still there in front of me. On whatever page you open this novel, you see immediately that it is a generous, romantic, subjective outpouring. This hymn to action for action's sake centers on the blowing up of a bridge that is no ordinary bridge. In order to mark Robert Jordan's exploit with his own authentic stamp (apart from showing him in the midst of a passionate, unexpected love affair), Hemingway has made Jordan keenly aware of the great danger involved in blowing up the bridge and at the same time quite certain that his sacrifice of himself will in no way change the outcome of the battle in his sector.

Even the title of his novel has confused people, although Ernesto's intention is quite obvious. The bell does not toll either for the persecuted and defeated "Reds" or for the victorious and vindictive "Whites" or "Blues." The death knell rings out for each and all, for the protagonist and for the most humble "volunteer" in all the brigades, for every soldier who died in the trenches on either side, for every man whose life was snuffed out anywhere in Spain. The bell tolls because Ernesto's beloved spiritual homeland is dead.

The hero of *For Whom the Bell Tolls* is not a Spaniard belonging to any of the extremist parties; he is a universal "stranger," a man with illusions, a dreamer, a demolitions expert whose specialty is blowing up railroad tracks and bridges, who comes to Spain to aid the Republican cause wholeheartedly, but who also is waging another war within himself, a more terrible conflict than the one for which the bells are tolling, because it is a battle against a loss of faith and confidence in everything, including, perhaps, himself. Even though he shares a few moments of tenderness with María and experiences the joy of love, his attitude whenever he is with the guerrillas is an epitome of Hemingway's own epic spirit, the story of a man who stands forever apart despite his constant efforts to forge bonds of solidarity with his fellows.

"What was your main reason for coming to Madrid when it was under siege?" I asked Ernesto one day.

"I couldn't be happy in my own country. As soon as the war began, I regarded myself as just one more soldier called to the colors," he replied.

I suddenly made up my mind to call Bill Davis. If anybody knew anything more than what had been reported in the papers, it would be Davis. He lived just outside Málaga, on an estate called La Cónsula, the place where Ernesto had been staying when the Swedish news service had falsely reported him dead a little less than a year before. What if this latest report of his death was false too? It would be the fourth time he had been reported dead. I would be very interested to know what Mr. Davis thought about the whole thing.

But there was no way of contacting him. I knew that there was no telephone at La Cónsula, one of the things Ernesto liked most about the place when he'd stayed there, especially during his lengthy visit there in 1959, while he'd been working so hard on *The Dangerous Summer*. Ernesto always introduced Bill to people as "my nigger, my slave." Antonio Ordóñez had once jokingly accused Ernesto of getting Davis to write all his books for him, and from then on Ernesto had called Bill Davis his "darky." But Davis wasn't dark at all; he was very fair-haired, rather fair-skinned, and stout. He looked like a farmer or a diviner looking for hidden treasure. Bill never said much, but he could size up a person or a situation instantly. Ernesto trusted him implicitly, and Davis was both a sort of protective wall and an excellent sounding device for Ernesto during his last visits to Spain. Davis wasn't exactly a man you took an immediate liking to, but he was always extremely courteous and kept his nose out of other people's business.

I got off to a bad start with the telephone operators and things got worse and worse. I would have liked to leave word for Davis to call me the next day. But the hours went by, I smoked one cigarette after another, and nobody seemed to be able to find out how I could get word to him at La Cónsula. He might not even be in Spain. Could he have flown to Idaho? He had plenty of money, or at any rate appeared to be very well off.

Davis had lived in Spain for more than ten years, had been all over the country, and had a fair knowledge of Spanish politics and the workings of Spanish society. He was a practical sort, and he had been a great help to Ernesto in rewriting and revising *The Dangerous Summer*, giving him particularly sound advice about eliminating certain names or personal references that might get him in trouble. When Ernesto and Davis got into complicated arguments or needed some point or other cleared up, I would get a call from Ernesto, and sometimes one from Davis too; but when it came to the final decision, Bill was right there at Ernesto's elbow, ruddy-faced and slow-moving and very quiet. At times Davis was that way because he'd had too much to drink and was in a sort of vague state halfway between laconic wisdom and Buddhist indifference. In short, Davis not only provided Ernesto with a pleasant, safe retreat at La Cónsula, but was also as faithful as a bird dog to him and may even have seemed like a sort of bodyguard at times. He never appeared to care much about art and literature, but it is quite possible that he deliberately fostered that impression.

I went on with my reading, following Ernesto about in Madrid as it was in those days, a period we Spaniards know very little about, despite all the propaganda put out by both sides. In more than one article that appeared in the press, Ernesto was described as a sort of outlaw who wandered all over Madrid during the time it was being besieged and bombarded, stirring up the people and urging them to "sack" the city. Nothing could be further from the truth. Hemingway had come to Barcelona from Paris in 1937, at a time when he no longer felt the least desire to kill. He had come to Spain out of an inner need to play the hero, at a time in his career when his creative energies were temporarily at a low point. He went from Barcelona to Valencia and Alicante, and finally arrived in Madrid, the city he had long ago called "the capital of the world"; he now called it "the front-line trench of the world" and made it his headquarters. It was where he belonged.

He had not come with empty hands, for he had more than forty thousand dollars of his own money with him, and wanted to use it to equip a fleet of ambulances. It was money he had saved up over the years, and more than once he told me how happy it had made him to be able to make such a generous gesture.

He hadn't come to write manifestoes or to organize a battalion of intellectuals; from the very first, his principal concern was to try to reconcile the various factions squabbling over the command of the Republican forces and co-ordinate their efforts. His role was partly that of a strategist and partly that of a missionary, a military adviser nobody listened to, and above all else a compassionate comrade sharing a humiliating defeat.

The impact of Madrid on Ernesto was so great that he did more than have a quick look around and then sit down to write. He traveled back and forth between Spain and America a number of times, trying to muster support for the Republican cause, trying to reconcile the warring factions, sharing the crushing burden of imminent defeat with his European and Spanish comrades. He was never a combatant, with a fierce hatred of the enemy; he was, rather, a witness who had fervently embraced a cause. Even though he had been personally involved in the furious battle for the city, as in the attack on Carabancheles, or during the nights when the city was shelled, or in the attacks on the Casa de Campo or the Ciudad Universitaria, and constantly urged the Republicans to remain on the offensive, he never considered himself a leader, much less a field marshal. He was merely another comrade who leaped into the breach when danger threatened. And being in the front lines became something more or less divorced from the real, concrete circumstances: for him it was a kind of personal holocaust.

"I often went hungry in Madrid, José Luis. I discovered what it's like to go for days without a bite to eat. I helped search for dead bodies many a time, and buried peasants and women and children . . ."

"I know you did, Ernesto."

"The Spanish people were very close to my heart, and they still are; I was at their side in their hours of agony. Nobody can ever take that away from me."

Few people have realized that there may be a fundamental parallel between *For Whom the Bell Tolls* and *The Old Man and the Sea*. In both cases there is the same inner loneliness as a heroic battle is being fought, the same sort of epic defeat, and the message of both books is an appeal to hope amid disaster.

I put *For Whom the Bell Tolls* back down on the floor several times. It required an enormous effort to translate this Argentinian dialect into Castilian Spanish. (The English original must be marvelous!) At any rate, Ernesto had written this book in white-hot fervor. He had begun writing early in 1939, in the terrifying shadow of the final defeat of the Republican cause, and had finished it in June 1946. This novel is the product both of enormous passion and great perseverance. The depiction of historic episodes that other narrators on both sides had dealt with in a propagandistic or narrowly sectarian way, as chapters in an epic struggle, was not anywhere near as important to Ernesto as the task of bearing fervent personal witness to what he had seen.

Out of a sense of misgiving and a sense of caution, I had questioned Ernesto closely about the material he had used, in particular the models for the Spanish characters. According to Ernesto, these characters had been more or less drawn from life. When he decided in 1953 that it would be all right for him to return to Spain, he had discovered that Pilar was still alive in Galicia. When I asked him: "What about El Sordo?"

"El Sordo died," he answered. "But not the way he did in the novel."

"Was he shot by a firing squad?"

"No, he was killed on the Guadalajara front."

Anyone who believes that Ernesto came to Spain to watch the battles of the Spanish War like a sensation-seeking tourist is quite mistaken. The Spanish Civil War affected him deeply. The enthusiasm and devotion with which he flung himself into the filming of *The Spanish Earth*, serving as its assistant director, its narrator, and more or less its protagonist, is ample evidence of this. A pathetic, dense, joyous film, it has scenes full of fervor and action, and others that are a model of sober restraint and quiet lyricism.

One day (when he was feeling very happy because they hadn't searched his luggage when he entered Spain or left it, and both the carabineros and the Guardia Civil had treated him with the greatest deference), he showed me, with a conspiratorial air, a photograph of himself dressed in a Basque hunting cap and big high boots and said to me, in a very nostalgic tone of voice, "I was a *man* in those days."

Ernesto had written me dedications in a number of his books. They are as precious as gold pieces now. But one day when I handed him a copy of *The Fifth Column* and asked him to autograph it, he said, very curtly, "I'm not going to sign that miserable book."

To make the best of an awkward moment, I said, "You're right. It's a very bad translation."

"No, it's not that. That book is crap."

How much was Ernesto influenced by what the critics wrote about his work? I myself had thought that this particular book seemed hastily written, confused, complicated, and propagandistic. But I was hoping that Ernesto would stand up for it. But he didn't even have a good word to say about the subject he had been attempting to deal with—another evidence of his deep-rooted sincerity. If *For Whom the Bell Tolls* became a classic, it would be because of its searing humanity, whereas *The Fifth Column* had an involved plot centering on a conflict of groups and parties that Ernesto had not only handled awkwardly in his play but also hadn't really altogether understood. The difference was that between a clear, uncompromising book and a tasteless piece of special pleading.

Beyond all else, the Spanish Civil War for Ernesto had been a problem of the proper emotional response, a test of his honor as a writer. He had once said that it was a writer's job to tell the truth.

So I had to go back to *For Whom the Bell Tolls*, because this was the book that he would be remembered for in Spain, or rather, the one that would set Spaniards to ringing his death knell. What would the papers say about him this afternoon and tomorrow morning? The bells would begin to toll, but what would they be saying?

51

What mattered to Ernesto was that the Spanish people had gone on living; that fact was more important to him than all his painful memories of what had happened at Teruel, Brunete, Guadalajara . . . For many people, both inside the country and out, the war had eventually died out, so to speak, like a devastating plague.

A Portuguese journalist had recently gone aboard the *Francesca Morosini*, approached Ernesto, and asked him point-blank, like a prosecuting attorney, "Isn't it true that you fought with the Reds during the Battle of Madrid?"

"So they say I was in Spain during the Civil War, do they? I haven't the slightest idea—I don't remember, and it doesn't interest me in the least. But if they say I was there, okay. There are three things I don't like to talk about: wars, books I'm planning to write, and physical ailments."

And that was true. It was also true that he had been trying for years to get rid of all the vultures. He made fun of them, he shocked them, he cursed them, he spat on them—or simply tossed them a hunk of meat. But they nonetheless managed at times to tear a bit of living flesh out of him. The Spanish Civil War—they had been attacking him on that flank for years. He was therefore obliged to be a bit devious about it, and even to fool himself, speaking in half-truths, making enigmatic gestures, shutting up altogether, playing the fool, or giving crafty, cagey explanations. They had all tried to pin him to the wall, some of them in sly, underhanded ways, and others quite openly, with cruel criticism and ugly maneuvers. Fortunately none of them had succeeded.

Instead of sadly, eloquently, impetuously repeating the commentary he had written for *The Spanish Earth*, the only thing Ernesto had done to defend himself in recent years was say a few reluctant words, which I am certain at times made him sick to his stomach. Polite, evasive words were his only possible answer to violent attacks and underhanded maneuvers. Few people were aware of how deeply hurt Ernesto had been when he visited Spain. People would sidle up to him in a bar or a train station or at the gate of a bullring and whisper a few nasty words in his ear, or shout some insult at him. He never once turned a hair. But when he'd finally join me, he'd say: "Man, you sure have to do a lot of cape and sword work in this country!"

He would not have denied his past, but it made him almost physically ill when people brought up the subject of the Spanish War. Not because he was afraid, although he was often quite uneasy and took precautions, but rather because he had deliberately and respectfully retreated to a neutral corner, and didn't want to break his implicit promise not to take sides publicly. For Ernesto, his so-called "Spanish adventure" had been something sacred, something intangible, something supremely important in his life. The war had shown him people's true faces: criminals, mercenaries, opportunists, idealists, tacticians, hired thugs, loyal volunteers, parasites, martyrs.

I went down to get the afternoon paper but it hadn't arrived at the newsstand yet. I walked slowly on toward the Plaza de Castilla. I couldn't get Robert Jordan out of my mind. In a moment of ecstasy— Hemingway had always been a master at capturing these fleeting moments of great exaltation—this would-be hero says, very simply:

> Dying was nothing and he had no picture of it nor fear of it in his mind. But living was a field of grain blowing in the wind on the side of a hill.

The Plaza de Castilla looked like a print of an urban eclogue. There were many workers and a few women and children waiting in line for streetcars and buses. They didn't seem at all out of sorts; they looked happy, and a number of them were leafing through the title pages and tables of contents of new and used books piled on a little bookseller's cart. Several families were picking their way through flowerpots, terra cotta jars, and earthenware pots at a stand selling cheap pottery. I noticed that some of the vessels were half full of rain water. The woman at the stall was chanting, "Ashtrays, salad bowls, genuine fountains from Talavera and Puente del Arzobispo," over and over, in a monotonous, singsong voice.

It was depressing. The articles about Ernesto in the majority of the afternoon papers were hardly earth-shaking: a few commonplaces about the dangers of violence, a quotation or two from his works on death in the bullring, a few lines about his style, which was said to have gone from exuberant self-expression to laconic understatement due to the direct influence of Gertrude Stein, and other such drivel. There was also mention of the telegram canceling Hemingway's hotel reservations in Pamplona for the fiesta, and a few words mentioning that he had remained faithful to his calling as a journalist.

I took a streetcar home even though it was only a short walk back. The ride gave me time to read the article on Ernesto by Martínez Berganza, the young journalist who had received the first Hemingway Prize.

Back home again, the thought came to me that *For Whom the Bell Tolls* is eloquent proof of the dictum that imagined truth is more real than reality as seen through eyes other than those of a great novelist. From the very first pages of Ernesto's book it is clear that the style of writing is an absolutely perfect expression of the horror of the events being narrated. There is no discrepancy between matter and manner anywhere in the book. Hemingway undoubtedly had a great deal of material, mountains of material, for this novel at hand, for he had arrived in Madrid at a time both of great courage and great terror, and he knew how to listen. But he very wisely toned down or eliminated many scenes of sheer horror, decanting their essence rather than showing them in naked detail, for he was the very opposite of the writer who deliberately tries to make your hair stand on end. What carefully calculated effects, what a sense of restraint and balance, what serenity of spirit he arrived at in this book in order that his testimony might have lasting value, above and beyond political contingencies of the moment! That is precisely what constitutes a work of art.

Very early one morning, just after dawn, that hour when you don't feel like talking about anything serious but want to keep the conversation going, I once remarked to Ernesto, half jokingly, "When the Italians, the French, and the Spanish talk about you, they always mention the word death."

"Well, death either creeps up on you from inside or from outside," he replied. "If it comes from outside, you can describe it—more or less—in your writing. But if it comes from inside, it will always remain a mystery. . . ."

That was what death had always been to Ernesto, a mystery, and what it always would remain. After a few moments' silence, he said, almost fiercely, "Death keeps crooking its finger at me. But I go on banging my typewriter anyway. When I go, I want to go fast."

"Fast?"

"When I say fast, I mean *with style,* too," he said.

I felt a shiver run up my spine and decided to drop the subject of death. When Ernesto started hinting darkly at things, it was best to leave him alone and not press him. The minute he suspected you were curious, he became very evasive.

He was very reluctant to discuss either the Civil War or *For Whom the Bell Tolls.* He was not only thoroughly disgusted by the Spanish translation, but also had the feeling that Spaniards would find it a difficult book to understand. He would discuss it only on those rare occasions when he felt he could be absolutely frank about it. Ernesto had seen the Spanish War at first hand only at certain periods, but he had lived those periods intensely. For Ernesto, Madrid under siege was full of drama, but also full of local color, vibrant life, and even humor. He had never been this close to the pulsing flow of life and death, of violence and pleasure. He never forgot it. And the streets in Madrid that he chose to wander through in the last years of his life were the same ones he had explored long before. The more elegant and luxurious sections of the city that had been built up later did not interest him at all, and he made his way through them like a blind man, indifferently and almost scornfully.

Wherever you opened his book, there were blinding flashes of insight.

54

Throughout the novel there were paragraphs that explained everything, or at least played a very important part in the over-all picture.

But all this also reminded me that Ernesto Hemingway was not yet in his grave, although the authorities had apparently given up the idea of performing an autopsy. I tried to imagine him with a hole through his head. Doubtless his face, in particular that part of it that had suffered the most severe ravages of time—his chin, his nose, his jaw, his beard—had been blown to bits. Ernesto would not have liked to think of himself as a shattered corpse slowly decaying.

Since it was summertime, people had their windows wide open, and you could hear radios and record players turned up full blast. I couldn't imagine why people said Madrid was deserted in the summer months!

Wherever you opened this novel, revealing passages leaped to your eye:

> "We killed a pair of guardia civil," he said. . . . "Daddy's big game."

A passage such as that pinned down a feeling that deserved examination, because even though the Guardia Civil is highly respected in Spain, it sometimes becomes a much-despised target of people's hatred. Ernesto never claimed to be a sociologist or a philosopher, but he often pointed to other people's problems just as accurately as he put his finger on his own:

> "And this foreigner with the rare name, how did he die?"
> "He was captured and he killed himself."
> "How did that happen?"
> "He was wounded and he did not wish to be a prisoner."

This is a novelistic transposition of one of Ernesto's own thoughts, which he had long pondered.

> "He killed more people than the cholera," the gypsy said. "At the start of the movement Pablo killed more people than the typhoid fever."
> "But since a long time he is *muy flojo*," Anselmo said. "He is very flaccid. He is very much afraid to die."
> "It is possible that it is because he has killed so many at the beginning," the gypsy said philosophically. "Pablo killed more than the bubonic plague."

This passage is a perfect expression of the temper of the times, because the description of Pablo as a person who sent more people to their deaths than a devastating plague is an accurate reflection of popular opinion at the time. Many people in Spain were convinced that passages like this represented Ernesto's own personal beliefs, but what they really reflect is his deep aversion to the whole struggle—the war of brother against brother, the endless lies, the lofty preaching, the appeals for vengeance that aroused Spaniards' hatred and made them deaf to the need for a society based on human justice.

Precisely because he was on intimate, almost familiar terms with death, Ernesto endeavored to keep it at a distance, at the very moment when the "Great Bald Lady" was blindly and capriciously setting up the pins, as though it were all a trivial game.

I got up from the table, poured myself a big slug of whisky, lit a cigarette, turned out the lights, and collapsed in my armchair. I looked at my bookshelves, with dozens of books on the Civil War, some upside down and others ranged neatly row on row like cadets. What a lot of trash, what lies, what bombastic apologetics, what overpriced merchandise, what cynicism, what cruelty, what sacrilege!

I closed Ernesto's book in anger when I reached the paragraph that read:

> "We will take her after the bridge," Robert Jordan said. "If we are alive after the bridge, we will take her."
> "I do not like to hear you speak in that manner. That manner of speaking never brings luck."

This was one of the most characteristic sides of Ernesto's temperament, of his morbid sensibility, a superstition of his that bordered on the ridiculous. What letter, what encounter, what dream, what memory had cut off his view of the horizon as he journeyed from the Mayo Clinic to his house in Ketchum? Ernesto was terribly superstitious, and remained so to the very end.

In *The Dangerous Summer*, when Juanito Quintana mentions the danger that Antonio Ordóñez deliberately confronts every day and says, "Antonio's had eleven bad wounds now and after each one he's better," Ernesto immediately tries to ward off possible bad luck:

> "I knocked three times on the trunk of the big pine tree we were standing by in the garden."

He was right to do so, even though he was a bit hysterical about it and tried to pass the whole thing off as a joke. But deep down he took this sort of thing very seriously. The wrong move or unlucky omens, the "good fortune" foretold by gypsies and other such superstitions were very important to Ernesto. When he mentions the girl hurt in an accident outside the bullring in Aranjuez whom he takes to the hospital, he says:

> "I was afraid she had a fracture at the base of her skull. She was bleeding sluggishly. But there was no hemorrhage and I was very careful to carry her gently and carefully and at the same time not get blood on my suit."

56

But then he adds:

"I did not care about the suit but what had happened to the girl was a bad enough omen without taking evidence of it into the first row of seats at the bullring."

How had he come by this respect for superstition and this fear of Lady Luck? Most likely it was something he had picked up in the world of bullfighters and the motley crowd surrounding them, that world that inspires an almost sacred respect in many people, including Ernesto, though it is a world that on close examination proves to be trivial and ridiculous, a world in which only the matador is worthy of respect. Nonetheless Ernesto was convinced, in his mind and heart, that all these absurd signs, from the lines in the palm of one's hand to the way the fortuneteller's cards fall, were very important. He even believed that the attraction or repulsion a woman feels for you, your domestic life, or your financial success can be foretold by an insignificant detail, a face, a word, a fatal coincidence or a fatal absence.

As there was no ice in the apartment and whisky with warm water tasted awful, I phoned the store next door to try to get some ice cubes. But nobody answered.

Then I began to read the interview Ordóñez had granted the bullfight critic Gonzalo Carvajal, which the latter had entitled "Papa Ernesto Is Dead and Gone." Carvajal told how shocked Ordóñez had been when he left the ring after killing his second bull and had heard that Ernesto had "stolen a march on him" and gotten to meet the "Great Bald Lady" before he did by putting a twenty-gram bullet through his head. Ordóñez also mentioned the time when he had been badly gored by a bull in Aranjuez; the first face he had seen in the operating room was Ernesto's. His great friend was standing there right next to the surgeon. The great matador had ended the interview with the sad words:

"We will never see each other again till we meet in the beyond. I still can't believe it, because those who die on us as suddenly as a flash of lightning (a reference to a poem by Miguel Hernández)—and I have known since eight-thirty last night how suddenly that is—'kill those of us who are left in this world,' one of the many things Papa said when reporters put out a false bulletin that he was dead."

It is sad but true that bullfighters always have a chorus of tenors or baritones around them, keeping them company both at funerals and at drinking parties. In this respect they resemble kings, who keep a well-paid entourage of jesters and solemn mourners at their courts, ready to celebrate with laughter or tears, as the occasion demands.

One thing was certain: Ernesto was very important to Ordóñez, because Ernesto had celebrated him as the hero of a sort of universal struggle. But I am not sure whether Ordóñez realized how indispensable his person and his art were to Ernesto. I believe that Ernesto's feelings toward Ordóñez were much nobler and much more unusual. I was certain that Ordóñez's grief stemmed in part from the realization that in a way he was even more important to Ernesto than Mary; he was the only person who could possibly have revived Ernesto's interest in living after his two visits to the Mayo Clinic. But Ordóñez's affection for Ernesto was a recent thing, and more apparent than real. The older man, however, regarded their friendship as a fathomless sea, far removed from the world of superficial emotions.

I picked up my glass again, because apart from the cry to "Papa" wrung from my heart earlier, whisky was my only tie to Ernesto just then. It was as though the very word literature had suddenly ceased to exist. Ernesto's death had been too literary, leading us to suspect that he had not confronted it as masterfully and as expertly as the matador facing the bull.

But I had to be careful not to forget certain small details that now seemed especially significant, in retrospect. I remembered, for instance, that one day when I had gone up to Ernesto's hotel room with him, I had noticed that he immediately went over to look at himself in the mirror, and I watched him intently.

"What are you staring at?" he asked me.

"Nothing, nothing—your beard," I answered.

"Well, you can look as long as you like."

He didn't usually speak in that testy tone of voice, but he had become very touchy lately. After a moment, he said: "What are people saying about this thing on my face?"

"What are they saying?"

"Yes, that's what I asked you."

"Nobody's even mentioned it. What is there to say?"

He turned around then and eyed me intently. Then he said, "I'm sure they're saying something. Something particularly nasty . . ."

"Nobody's said a word to me about it. They're all jealous of your beard."

"Well, I want you to know it isn't syphilis or anything like that."

After that, I took special pains not to appear to be staring at those blotches that plagued him so. I confess they had worried me—and Ernesto had noticed. I would often pretend not to notice things, especially when he was nervous or upset. It made me very uncomfortable to see him get all worked up about something when his almost demoniacal pride was hurt.

I had retreated to the window after his rather sharp words to me. A few moments later he was his usual, goodhearted self again, and he walked over to me and gave me a big affectionate bear hug, which startled me almost more than his fit of temper had. Maybe that was why he had made an effort to be conciliatory and warmly confidential in his last letter to me:

"Things are going very well otherwise. I weigh 197 pounds—8 less than last year—and I'm being very careful about how much I drink and so on."

Even Ernesto probably didn't believe that last part.

I got into the shower, and as I was soaping myself, I began to go over titles of novels dealing with the Spanish Civil War. I was convinced that very few of them would prove to have enduring literary value. Ernesto knew what he was talking about when he said, "War is one of the great subjects, and beyond any doubt one of the most difficult to deal with sincerely."

Just as I was going out the door, the phone rang. One of the morning papers wanted me to write an article on Hemingway. I couldn't do it; I just wasn't up to it. I was still so overwhelmed by the tragedy that anything I wrote would be inappropriate. How many people were trying to drown the guilt they felt deep down inside in a sea of adjectives. Let them write of theology and charisma, let them try to forget by continuing to live their stupid, frivolous lives. And *they* were the ones who called *Ernesto* an atheist! Yes, an atheist. In all their detailed descriptions of the bloody deed, how few of them had had the courage and the nobility of spirit to find a source of wisdom in that mountain of torn, bleeding flesh. No, Ernesto had not killed himself in a spirit of blasphemy, nor because he thought he was a man accursed, nor because he wanted to leave others with the impression that he was a strong, invincible man. He had done away with himself because he saw no other way out, in a moment of total emptiness, a moment of something more than despair, a moment of agonizing, inescapable, endless weariness of spirit.

He could find nothing to cling to, either within himself or without, either close at hand or far away. He had become obsessed with the thought that he would die a lingering death, that his muscles and nerves would slowly waste away. And his hand had begun to tremble as though he had already committed the crime against himself. . . . No, he had flung himself into the abyss, the abyss he had gazed down into so many times and fled in terror, the abyss that had boxed him in a corner and made him a writer, that had made art something more to him than an amusement or a pastime or a profitable sport. . . .

I was terribly restless. I couldn't sit still, and I couldn't concentrate. I paced up and down, leafing through various books of Ernesto's, murmuring disjointed phrases, pounding my fist on the wall. I'd be better off going out for a while. Because I now had in front of me an article written by a woman reporter, a colleague of mine, that had made me furious. The article that said: "Our war . . . which he did not understand. . . ." And then went on to rake up all the usual filth, out of the usual envy and rancor:

"Spanish blood! Mr. Hemingway liked seeing it spilled—he practically smacked his lips over it in his books, catering to the vulgar tastes of international readers. And he made lots of money out of it. It was a point in his favor in the Nobel Prize competition."

Could there be a more vicious slander of an idealistic freedom-fighter, of a noble, sincere, irrepressible revolutionary passion? I had these incredible words before my eyes, written about a man who had loved Spain more than any other country save his own native land and given ample proof of his love.

This same sort of viciousness was undoubtedly what had led a spiritually deaf journalist to write: "If Spain admired Ernesto, it was because of his reputation as a tough guy."

The most grotesque thing about words such as those was seeing who had written them and where they had appeared. I was enraged, and felt like cursing.

A reporter had once snidely asked him, "Why don't you wear your war medals, Don Ernesto?"

"Because they may have been awarded me by mistake," he had answered drily.

Ernesto was lying with his head blown off on the other shore of the river, near a grove of oak trees. And the bold, evil vultures were wheeling overhead, waiting to swoop down on his dead body. Fortunately he would not feel the pecking of these treacherous, ravenous creatures, nor would these blind, impotent birds be able to fly up to that verdant hillside just below the snowline.

There was no reason to be concerned. Ernesto was beyond their reach. He was above the sort of facile classification that divides people into "rightists" and "leftists"; he was above the zealous apologetics hailing his every line as a contribution to peace. He was worthy now of the honor that comes to a man only when he gives up everything and takes up the noble but crushing burden of being totally misunderstood.

I suddenly couldn't stand it another minute, ran downstairs to the street, and hopped on a bus without waiting for it to stop for me.

One of the articles about Ernesto had said: "The facts have not yet come to light, but it is horrifying to know, yes, to *know* that certain cases may well be excluded from the holy mystery of Pity. May God have mercy on Ernesto Hemingway, who lived well and died badly."

It seemed to me that I would be obliged to write another article, one less lyrical and a little more forceful. I began to compose it right there on the bus. It would read something like this:

Death is a mystery to which God alone has the key. Who has conferred on us mortals the right to judge our fellows? Even though his death was unfortunate—and his life, too, in many ways—Hemingway will always be an ideal in the life of every writer for two important reasons: his unfailing goodness, and his unwavering sincerity, even when shells were falling. Incapable himself of toadying or self-abasement, what he despised most in others was hypocrisy and the pretense of morality on the one hand, and the parading of amorality and vice on the other. Those who could criticize Ernesto for the sort of life he led—which was doubtless a much simpler and cleaner life than it has been made out to be in the press and at cocktail parties where his name is dropped—ought to have led very decent and dignified lives themselves.

The very thing that made Ernesto so popular and so engaging was his modesty and his air of an innocent, willful, sad child who never grew up.

We shall leave it to God to determine his fate for all eternity. Let us concern ourselves with what he has left us, those satisfying crumbs of his art. As Spanish writers, let us dedicate ourselves—beyond the question of war and peace, the horns of bulls, and the barbed wire of the trenches—to unraveling the profound reasons for his deep ties to Spain. Whether we like it or not, we Spanish writers are as intimately related to his work as rivers are related to the sea.

3   There was a terrible traffic jam in the Calle de San Mateo. Car horns were honking and drivers were hurling insults at each other. If I had had a desk and a pad of paper, I would have had more than enough time to draw up a deposition. I had suddenly been seized with an overwhelming urge to defend Spain's warm, fast friend, Ernesto Hemingway, against all his enemies.

The bus had stopped in the little grillwork station on the Avenida de José Antonio. I walked down the Gran Vía toward the Plaza de Callao. It was the time of day when hunters with licences, and poachers too, were out in full force. The street was full of men waiting for women they were meeting. They had a thoughtful look on their faces, as though they were going through that sort of mental casuistry that almost always ends either in furtive pleasure or in guilt-ridden self-reproach.

When I reached the Plaza de Callao, I suddenly found myself on the steps of the Hotel Florida, almost without realizing what I was doing, as though I were obeying some inner imperative. I halted in my tracks and said to myself, "Why didn't you go to the Callejón de la Ternera?"

The clerks at the desk must have thought I was a guest, and even the bellboys standing by the elevator greeted me as though I were a familiar face. But since I simply stood there staring, I must have alarmed them or aroused their suspicion. In any event, one of the sharper-eyed clerks at the reception desk walked over to me as I stood there at the bottom of the stairway and said very politely:

"Was there something you wanted? Can I help you?"

"No," I answered, and added, in the tone of voice of somebody on an important errand determined to let nothing stand in his way, "I just want to have a look around upstairs."

"Which room is it you're looking for? Are you trying to find somebody?"

"I'm just going upstairs, if you don't mind. I merely want to look around for a moment."

The clerk just stood there, rooted to the spot, not knowing whether he should bar the way or offer me his hand. Was I a police officer or some oddball guest? I went on up, climbing the stairs instead of taking the elevator. I had gotten no farther than the second floor when the door of the elevator opened and a plump little old curly-haired man dressed in the Florida uniform stepped out. He recognized me immediately; he had not only often seen me with Ernesto, but had once told me in the bar that he "liked my writing very much."

"Is there anything in particular you wanted?" he said to me very politely.

"I just wanted to look around."

"Go right ahead—you can stay as long as you like."

"I just wanted to have a look around for old times' sake."

"I understand. It's because he's dead."

"Yes, because he's dead."

"The moment I saw you I said to myself: he's come back because Ernesto's died. For old times' sake—the days when he used to stay here and would go upstairs with you and then come down to the bar and have a couple of snorts with you. And you used to keep right up with him, I remember. . . . I'll go up with you if you like," he said obsequiously.

"Tell me, why did he kill himself?" he asked me.

"Do you think *he* knew why?" I replied.

"Sure, he was the only one who did."

"Who knows? Maybe he didn't have any idea why."

We went upstairs.

"I think he must have killed himself on account of all that bullfighter business. It must have upset him terribly," he said.

"To hell with it."

"You're right: to hell with it."

"That's what I kept telling him. When I visited him in Havana, he was busy writing. I said to him, 'Ernesto, what are you doing?' 'You can see what I'm doing—writing a bunch of crap,' he answered, very seriously."

We went up the stairs, with the plump little man leading the way, bowing and scraping. Just before we got to Ernesto's floor, he turned and said to me, "You look quite a bit fatter these days."

"I haven't put on much weight."

63

"You look like you have. Quite a lot. And now that you've let your hair grow, you look more and more like *him*."

"I don't think that's true."

"You shouldn't comb it over the top of your head like he did though. You should let it alone, let it grow the way it wants to, like a quail's nest. Right?"

He stopped outside one of the doors along the hall and said, "This was the room he had first, but they tell me he didn't like the people in the adjoining rooms. We can't go in, because there's somebody in there, a newlywed couple from Albacete. We may have to go in eventually for an autopsy though. Because the only thing they've ordered from room service is orangeade. Gallons of it! Orangeade's got lots of vitamins in it, I know, but even so . . ." He turned away with a sort of pirouette and motioned to me to follow him.

When we got back to the stairway, he climbed up several more flights, to the fifth floor, not waiting for the elevator, motioning to me to follow him.

"He stayed up here, too," he said. "I'm not sure whether it was before or after he had that room down below. All I know is that he kept watching which direction the shells were coming from, and kept moving to rooms farther and farther inside the hotel . . ."

He opened a door. It was only a hotel room, not a prison cell, but both in this room and in others, in hotels and other places, and even in his own house, Ernesto had had nightmares and severe attacks of anxiety. Madrid during the war had been a great "test of courage" for Ernesto, because he liked to sleep with the light on at night, and since that wasn't permitted, he would cover his bedlamp with a shirt. But what had happened when the lights went out? The Ernesto they remembered at the Florida wasn't just the Ernesto who drank like a fish and bawled songs and kicked up his heels. The last time I had come here with Ernesto, I had expected this old man to say to him, "Oh yes, you're the fellow who used to invite girls and guitar players to your room," but as a matter of fact what he had said was: "Oh yes, I remember you very well . . . when time dragged, you used to sit quietly reading a book." His room looked almost forbiddingly quiet now. There were big stains on the wall, but there was no way of telling if they were from glasses of whisky flung on nights of wild abandon.

"Can we go up to the terrace on the roof?" I asked my guide.

"Certainly. Maybe it'll be a nice night," he answered.

Even though he was very tired, he hurried up the stairs, obliging me to follow him two steps at a time.

It turned out to be a beautiful night, and a good chance to see all of Madrid spread out below. But it was not a Hemingway Madrid, because there were bright neon signs everywhere. And in that harsh light my guide looked even more pasty-faced than he had before. He was also a bit more obsequious.

"Let's go back downstairs," I said to him.

"Have you seen everything you wanted to see?"

"I'm very grateful to you," I said, putting my hand in my pocket to offer him a tip. But as I reached into my pocket this pale-cheeked old man with the shameless smile stopped me and said, "No, I wouldn't think of it."

As we went down the stairs, I thought to myself: that little man may seem to be a buzzard, but he really isn't one. The very worst sort of people were the ones who looked as harmless as sparrows but were capable of devouring their own father's very bowels, washed down with Rioja wine.

We went down to the lobby in the elevator, and apparently the clerks at the desk were still curious as to why I had gone upstairs. But I had lost all my nerve. I would have liked to examine all the hotel records, including Ernesto's old bills, but I didn't dare ask to see them. They had probably thrown them away anyway. So all I did was order beer from the bar downstairs and ask the clerks to join me, but they said they weren't allowed to.

I tried to imagine that stuffy, bourgeois hotel lobby as it had once been: a center for bad news, because not only the speeches calling on the besieged Madrileños to resist, but also the inevitable reports of the victorious advance of the "Rebels," as the Loyalists called the other side, had filtered up to the Florida, like a stone fortress on a steep hillside.

Middle-class families were going in and out, some with aching feet and others sweating like gypsies. There were also a few bored-looking foreigners sitting in the lobby in their shirtsleeves reading newspapers or novels.

I said good-by to the clerks, thanking them profusely so as to pave the way for myself in case I wanted information later, and went out on the street. The Plaza de Callao was like an oven in the summer heat, and like the floodgate of a reservoir as well. There were swarms of people, and above all the noise I could hear laughter and greetings being exchanged.

I walked down toward Preciados. At the corner, I stopped and tried to remember: what year was it that Ernesto's father had committed suicide? I had forgotten, even though I had written it down that very afternoon. When someone once asked Ernesto why his father had killed himself, he had answered, half seriously and half jokingly: "Nobody understood him."

Had anyone understood Ernesto? I am very much afraid that even the women who had been closest to him had brushed against a shroud

65

when they thought they were fingering the warm shawl of love. What they had touched was not flesh but bark.

I turned off on the street leading to the Callejón de la Ternera, Ernesto's favorite haunt in Madrid, where an expression often came over his face that seemed to indicate that he was satisfied with life for the moment.

Had Ernesto ever been really happy at any time in his life? I often felt a cold shiver run down my spine because of the way he treated Mary; even though he was as deeply attached to her as a kid in love for the first time, he was noticeably cold and distant and indifferent to her at times, as though he were a stranger living at her side. He made excuses for not making love to her—*corridas* he simply had to see, the trouble his writing was giving him, the trips he wanted to take with friends all of a sudden, the difficulty of getting away from other people—but the truth of the matter was that Ernesto seemed to have become the mere shadow of his former self. More than once he'd said, half jokingly, that he'd still be making love when he was eighty-five, but I had seen him get all flustered and nervous and excessively talkative with captivating young girls just beginning to blossom. His hand could still tell what was flesh and what was cloth, but his mind could no longer differentiate between a physical decline that was medically explainable and a wasting away of the spirit.

We had stopped on this very corner and gone in this very door many a time. We had eaten here the day he had gone to see Dr. Medinaveitia.

I went inside. Every table was taken, unfortunately. At Ernesto's table there were several men with beards, but not beautiful full ones, and a couple of young men who looked like a cross between fags without a lover and bards without their instruments. As for the women at the table, they could be either prostitutes or blue-blooded *marquesas*.

On the wall, in a very nice frame, was a photograph and a text about Ernesto, the famous trencherman who had so often been a guest of the house. But it wasn't really Ernesto in the photograph—it was simply a publicity shot. Nobody was reading the text or noticing how splendid his beard was, the beard of a cheerful Hamlet or the skipper of a boat with no mates aboard.

I stood there in the doorway of the restaurant for a moment.

I went back to the hustle and bustle of the Gran Vía.

A thought was taking shape in my mind, almost like a chunk of marble. Had it ever occurred to me that there was a good chance that Ernesto might die of cirrhosis of the liver, of arteriosclerosis, of coronary thrombosis, of pneumonia? Such a possibility had never once crossed my mind. Nor had I ever thought that his skin disease, that carefully concealed, oozing blotch on his face, might kill him. To me Ernesto was a life-machine. If something went wrong with the machine I was certain it would explode. And it had. His life couldn't have ended any other way.

Why hadn't he lost his life in Italy as he played at being a hero? Why hadn't he been killed liberating Paris, at the hands of his mortal enemies the Germans? Why hadn't he been trampled to death by an elephant, fatally gored by a rhinoceros, torn to bits by a lion in Africa? Why hadn't he been mortally wounded at Teruel or Brunete or Asturias or on the Ebra? If he had been, he wouldn't have written *A Moveable Feast* or *For Whom the Bell Tolls* or *The Old Man and the Sea*, of course.

I was standing in front of the show window of a gunshop on the Calle de Preciados now. I glanced idly at the fishing rods and then suddenly found myself staring in fascination at the deadly rifles in the window. Which of his guns had Ernesto used? Had I held the death weapon in my own hands?

I would have been willing to bet a thousand to one that Ernesto wouldn't die in bed. Powerful personalities, for whom fame is the spur, can't stand the thought of being pitied, of people weeping and wailing at their bedsides. And when a man's mind will not entertain that possibility, his will, too, will falter in the face of such a fate.

I looked up at the big windows of the Hotel Florida; there were lights on in most of the rooms. As many lights as in a house where a wake is being held. I was reminded of a line from one of Ernesto's short stories, "Now I Lay Me."

> But some nights I could not fish, and on those nights I was
> cold-awake and said my prayers over and over and tried to pray
> for all the people I had ever known.

He had left us something apart from his works, apart from this endless dying in the midst of life that had made San Juan de la Cruz pray:

> Ven muerte tan escondida
> que no te sienta venir. . . .
>
> Death, steal over me so quietly
> That I don't hear you coming. . . .

Apart from his fear of the emptiness of the beyond, which he kept under tight rein, and the savor of his "Our Fathers" whenever I heard them, he had left us something more, something like the cheerful murmur of a freely running stream, a prose as swift as the flight of ducks, as mysterious as the couplings of fishes. He had also left us, of course, the almost mythical story of the migrations of the *Neoreminthe Hemingway*, a species of porpoise discovered by ichthyologists who had gone out with him on the *Pilar*, a strange creature which curiously enough has no dorsal fin. But this creature that has survived for so many eons will continue to traverse the cold ocean depths, a symbol bearing Ernesto's name that is as imperishable as the sea itself. . . .

The lights suddenly went off in the inviting display window with its brand-new rifles and its virgin fishhooks, and I walked on.

In order to kill yourself, all you have to do is close your eyes, and then *bang*. . . . The suicide victim doesn't even realize that *the deed has been done*. But you must close your eyes. Or maybe you shouldn't close them; maybe what you should do is open them as wide as possible. Your hands shouldn't tremble, though. Ernesto's hands had been quite unsteady for some time, however, and his voice had begun to tremble a little, too. I had noticed it when we said good-by in 1960. . . .

There were many things I would still have to search for. Because even though suicides almost always leave a brief note for the authorities, Ernesto hadn't. The only place we would find a farewell note from him was in his books.

Some very solemn thoughts must have crossed Ernesto's mind as he wrote of the old fisherman's great duel with the marlin in *The Old Man and the Sea*, for writing it meant reliving all his dreams and failures. A number of phrases in the book still had a live heartbeat, as though just laid bare by the surgeon's scalpel:

> He took all his pain and what was left of his strength and his
> long gone pride and he put it against the fish's agony. . . .

Extraordinary things had happened on the old fisherman's boat. The reader was free to interpret them as he liked, and draw whatever conclusions he cared to. The luckless old fisherman is something more than an arcane symbol. And what about the great fish? It is possible, and even probable, that the agony of the fish which finds redemption through its mortal struggle is just as meaningful an allegory.

If the great fish, tied to the boat as the bull is cornered in the ring, could speak in its agony, its ideal might prove to be the Hemingway metaphysic. As I entered the Puerta del Sol, I remembered the very words Ernesto had said to me there, in a hoarse voice and perfect idiomatic Spanish, "You should have seen what happened to me here when I got a stretcher for a broad who'd been thrown to the ground by an exploding shell and was lying there dripping with blood. Do you know what she did when I picked her up? She kicked me! And do you know what she said? 'Why don't you leave me alone, you disgusting old goat?' That was what she said. And she was bleeding like a bull. . . ." Then he added, in a nostalgic tone of voice: "It was too beautiful a spirit to win out."

The old man says almost the same thing after the sharks get the fish:

"It was too good to last."

When ideals were at stake, Ernesto was always inclined to be pessimistic, and would suddenly become very skeptical. The blood of martyrs was no more highly prized than mordant irony in Ernesto's scale of values.

I would have to read his books very carefully. If I read them the right way, I would discover where the truth lay, and his work would turn out to be all of a piece. Precisely because he was a very fragile, very simple, very innocent man, a man of great feeling, a passionate romantic and idealist through and through. As when he wrote of the Fifth Regiment of the International Brigades:

. . . you felt that you were taking part in a crusade.

This was the truth as he saw it, *his* truth. But when Ernesto used the word *crusade*, he did not mean it in any grandiloquent, theological sense; he meant by it a heroic fight for a noble idea, and wrote it with a capital letter. Anything that involved subtle, closely reasoned intellectual argument seemed fraudulent to him, and even though he had a brilliant mind, he was always wary of the powers of intellect. His strong point was human feeling, carefully veiled.

It was not easy, therefore, to determine the ruling principle underlying his ideology. He reacted negatively to anything that was systematic or methodical or a potential threat to human freedom in the long run. Although he was accused of being indecisive, he deliberately chose to take his stand in a rather vague emotional terrain, one almost outside of time and space, even when he was fighting for a cause. The moment he actively subscribed to an idea, or became enthusiastic about a man, he immediately felt the sere wind of skepticism rise within him. I would have to sit down and for the first time carefully read every line he had ever written, taking notes as I went along.

I began to think about all the things we had never gotten around to doing together. We had planned to visit a town in Teruel where they run huge, fierce bulls in the streets, a tradition going back many years. They run them at night, as I remember, with little balls of burning pitch on their horns. Everybody gets half drunk and runs round and round the bulls, and if the little ball burns down too far, one of the bulls will often gore some strapping local lad and leave him shivering in the chill embrace of death. We had also been invited to go duck hunting in the Albufera de Valencia, on one of those autumn mornings when the ducks fall on the wet rice fields like aerial bombs. I was also planning a visit to my home town, La Yecla, the scene of Boroja's *La Voluntad*, a place haunted by legions of evil demons, according to Don Pío.

I recalled the night we had been at the Casa Valentín. Walking around afterward, when we got to the Puerta del Sol, Ernesto had flung his arms out and shouted, "No *pasarán!*" (the Loyalist watchword) in a cavernous voice, in memory of the past.

People halted in their tracks. Standing there with his arms outstretched, shouting in that great booming voice of his, Ernesto looked as though he could barricade the entire Puerta del Sol all by himself. Then he repeated, "They shall not pass!" in German, English, French, Italian, and Russian. People shook their heads and said, "That guy's really plastered! He can't even stand up."

But he could—and did. He started laughing then and stood there ramrod straight, distracting a bull with an imaginary muleta or letting it thunder past him to its doom in the imaginary abyss.

"That foreigner's really tied one on!"

"Me, a foreigner? You bastards!" Ernesto roared.

It had been one of his last nights in Spain. I could understand very well now how this man who had shouted, "No *pasarán!*" at the top of his lungs could have been so afraid of serious illness, of becoming physically repulsive and wasting away. Not that he had felt he was seriously ill; he had simply felt completely burned out.

I went into a dive on the corner of Carretas that as far as I could remember I had never been in before, more a cheap café than a bar. To the stupefaction of everyone in the place, I ordered a Pernod, which is what I had often seen Ernesto drink in taverns where people stared at him in stony silence when he walked in. And I said to myself, "Was Lord Byron any more fascinating? Was Tolstoy any more human?" They searched for the Pernod bottle for a long time, and then asked me if I wanted it in a tall glass, and whether they should heat it in the espresso machine. They finally put the glass with the yellow liquid in front of me and added a few drops of water; what had looked like urine suddenly turned to milk.

I tasted it, and a favorite phrase of Ernesto's suddenly came not so much to my mind as to my palate: "Ah, alcohol . . . the great giant killer."

Ernesto was a giant, and even his death had been that of a Goliath felled by a little pebble striking him in the temple. I sniffed at the Pernod and sipped it, and more than memories, it brought back remembrance, shared moments, the lived experience itself. I felt the same shiver run down my back that Robert Jordan had felt in the cave near

Segovia when he took out his canteen and began slowly pouring absinthe into his cup.

It was very late, but they let me in at L'Hardy even though they were just about to close. The shiny dark wooden paneling hadn't exactly burst into flower; in fact the place seemed more gloomy than ever. Two married couples, friends of the owners, were having a party that was on its last legs. I asked for some consommé, as people often do there, but for some reason they gave me a very odd look. One of the ladies, a pretty woman with very white skin, was sitting with her thighs and legs apart, like a Flemish triptych as though presenting herself to you as a kind of offering. The little short man in the party said:

"Well, I see he cashed in his chips."

"This time he really did," the woman with her legs generously parted chimed in.

"Every last one of them," said the little short man in the carefully pressed plaid suit.

It wasn't surprising that they were all talking about Ernesto, because the newspaper was lying on the marble counter next to the pastry tray. I felt like going over to their table and telling them that Ernesto had cashed in his chips some time ago and thus air my own personal theory for the first time, but I didn't have the nerve. I left the place and went out into the street again.

I had to weigh things carefully. Ernesto had not fallen to his knees like a badly killed bull about to receive the *coup de grâce* with the dagger. No. Ernesto was the matador, but a matador who doesn't want to see the dead animal dragged out of the ring, because he has also identified with the bull. I walked on, lost in thought.

"No. He is dead."

"Can one ask how he died?"

"He shot himself."

"To avoid being tortured?" the woman asked.

"Yes," Robert Jordan said. "To avoid being tortured."

I went into the Cervecería Alemana and nothing happened. That is to say, it was just as quiet in there as it would have been if Ernesto had walked in the door, shaking hands all around or giving everybody a bear hug, swearing a blue streak, or simply slowly walking over to a corner table without saying a word and sitting there with his ears pricked up and his eyes wide open, constantly on his guard and never missing a thing—his usual way of making his presence felt.

The shrimp was marvelous and so was the crayfish. But the people at the bar weren't talking about bulls; they were talking about soccer. That seemed very ironic, even though Ernesto had apparently been a fairly good football player in high school, before he took up boxing. But sooner or later there would be talk of Hemingway and bullfighting in the Cervecería that night, for a great many *aficionados* and supposedly inspired guides to the bullfighting world hung out there. The latter are almost all the same type, or rather the same subtype, of writer, producers of yards of elegant, old-fashioned prose about bulls; but since bulls can't pay them for these warm tributes, some two-legged animal pays for them—in bills slipped to these critics in an envelope. Somebody always pays. Ernesto had a pretty good idea of how it went. Whenever he was traveling with *toreros,* whether rich ones or just "small fry" in the bullfighting world, he always dutifully kicked in his share.

Behind the column where the bootblack usually sat, right next to the telephone, a skinny man with little round glasses, like the sacristan of a monastery, was reading something to another man in an emphatic tone of voice. I began to eavesdrop, circumspectly at first and then making no attempt to conceal my interest in what he was reading. Ernesto's name had been mentioned. It was not surprising that he would be remembered tonight in this tavern that had been one of his favorite haunts. The skinny, sad-faced man with the glasses was reading a passage aloud to a stout man with very curly hair so long it touched his shirt collar:

> The spectacle of death attracts him. He foresees death, he anticipates it, he chases after it; he wants to be closer to it, to see its face; he comes down from the stands to the *burladero,* walks around in the *callejón,* and trails along to the infirmary. He seems to be tracking death in the bullring. I don't know if he loves it or fears it, scorns it or worships it, beckons to it or flees it. He plays with it as though he carried it around constantly with him. He speaks of it as though it were his inseparable companion. Men who are full of life seem to be the ones who talk most about death, as though it were something a long way away. Who knows how close or how far away death is! It is not the sublime concept of "Nearer, my God, to Thee," of "dying because I do not die." Nor is it Saint Francis's reverent wish "that death overtake us as we are obeying the will of the Lord." Apparently it is something quite the opposite. . . .

I was standing so close now I could have read the words myself. There was a whole crowd of us in front of the bar, all talking to each other in the familiar form as though we had known each other all our lives.

"That's quite a sermon, my friends!" I said.

"I hope you don't mind my reading it," the man with the glasses replied.

"Don't you like it, my friend?" the perspiring fat man with the long curly hair asked.

"I was wondering who it was preaching that sermon," I said.

"It's by Corrochano, Don Gregorio."

"Oh, I see."

"Don't you like it?" the sweat-drenched fat man asked again.

"Were you perhaps a friend of the *deceased?*" the man with the glasses asked with a smile.

I suddenly remembered other commentaries Corrochano had written, in particular the ones during the great to-do in Spain when *The Dangerous Summer* came out. When Ernesto used the words "cheap tricks" in reference to Manolete, the *aficionados*—and many other people—were terribly offended. It was something like an insult to the whole country, throwing down the gauntlet to challenge every last Spaniard. The newspapers and magazines had taken out on Ernesto all their resentment for things that had happened long before. His worst sin wasn't what he had written about bullfighting; they naturally brought up again his whole role in the Civil War. As a matter of fact, what Ernesto had said about Manolete was an open secret, that is to say, a number of bullfight critics and *toreros* who were loyal admirers of the Cordovan matador had said more or less the same thing. I remembered the article in which Don Gregorio Corrochano had dared to speak of "literary tricks," referring to Ernesto. And one day on the radio he had refused to grant that Ernesto was a figure of world stature in the realm of letters; he had questioned whether Ernesto deserved the Nobel Prize, claiming that he had won it simply because of all the publicity he had gotten. And unlike other dull, conceited poseurs who write utter trash in the bullfight columns, Corrochano has an excellent reputation as a sharp-witted critic! Don Gregorio's finest hour had been when he took it upon himself to criticize, in italic type, "Hemingway's grammatical errors," citing as an example the sentence: "Antonio imparted death at least twice a day." According to this astute critic, what Ernesto had really meant to say was, "Ordóñez *confronted* death at least twice a day."

A model of critical interpretation! But as the men there in the bar went on reading Corrochano aloud like simpletons, I thought about this sentence; like many that Ernesto wrote, it doubtless had a much profounder meaning than was apparent at first. Ordóñez obviously faced death twice each afternoon as he fought his two bulls, although strictly speaking, the first one might kill him some afternoon so he'd only have faced death once. But the plaster saint of the bullring had gone on to say: "I presume that Hemingway doesn't mean that Antonio *shared* death, which is what the word *impart* implies, but that he *risked* death. It's a Nobel sort of misuse of language."

When Ernesto used the word "impart," he meant exactly what he said. He was not referring to the fact that Ordóñez risked death every time he faced a bull, but that as he fought the bull he communicated, transmitted, shared, in a word *imparted* death to all those present, because all the spectators participate in his possible death, just as the priest *imparts* the benediction, in God's name, to each and every worshiper, beginning with His minister at the altar who invokes it and through his holy office sends it out to the four points of the compass. The priest does not bless himself, he shares and imparts the benediction as a depositary of the holy charism. When he gives the benediction, he shares a sacred treasure that has been entrusted to his keeping.

Isn't that obvious? Yes, the matador is like the celebrant of a sort of sacred rite, to use Hemingway's definition, or the depositary of a sacred treasure, to use an irreverent but similar figure of speech. The *torero* is death's intermediary: he has the power to both give it and receive it. And on approaching the mystery of death, it is not only his own death, but a death that belongs to all those in the *plaza de toros* who are willing and able to receive it.

It is quite clear from Ernesto's writings that he saw, better than any other writer, better certainly than Don Gregorio ever could, that in the *corrida* there are vestiges of a sacred pagan rite.

"Even if you saw him killed it would not be you who would be killed, it would be more like the death of the gods," he had written in *Death in the Afternoon*. Let us note that he does not say, it would be *the death of a god*, but *the death of the gods*, because each and every spectator participates in this death, the death *imparted* by the *torero-*officiant. This verb thus expresses the meaning exactly. It is surprising that an expert such as Don Gregorio Corrochano couldn't see any farther than his nose and had accused Ernesto of a misuse of language.

I will not go so far as to say that Ernesto provided as clear or as detailed an explanation of the evolution of bullfighting from a rite to a sport as that advanced by my much-admired late-lamented friend Ángel Álvarez Miranda, in his impressive, rigorously documented study of "the efficacious transmission of the power of the bull at the precise moment of death." But how can this be understood by people who flock to the bullring merely to see another thrilling spectacle? Ernesto wasn't looking for excitement in the bullring, though many people have accused him of this too. He had said himself that he came away from the *plaza de toros* a better, more peaceful, terribly sad but uplifted man.

The point is worth emphasizing. It is obvious that at the moment of greatest danger in the *corrida*, at the moments of greatest tension in the combat between the man and the bull, those present at this ceremony are before an altar, so to speak, and actively participating, not only physically but spiritually, in this death being celebrated by each and all. Is that blasphemy? I do not believe so. The death that the bull can inflict on the *torero* is shared by the crowd as a whole and by each of the faithful individually.

This is not the feeling of the *torero*, but rather that of the spectator, because the *torero* is concentrating so hard on killing the bull that he does not have time to perceive any such thing. It is the spectators who come back from another world when the sound of applause fills the bullring.

> Now the essence of the greatest emotional appeal of bullfighting is the feeling of immortality that the bullfighter feels in the middle of a great faena and that he gives to the spectators.

There is no doubt that the bullfight is a holdover of the sacred, despite its stark cruelty at certain moments and its balletlike configurations at others. To cite Álvarez de Miranda's authoritative study: "The phenomenon of the *corrida*, from the historico-religious point of view, appears to be yet another instance of a religious rite that has become an entertainment, as happened so frequently in the world of antiquity—this was the evolution, for instance, of Greek tragedy and Roman games, and perhaps also Cretan bullfights."

It would be interesting to look up the canonical laws which at one time forbade priests to attend *corridas*; one of the principal reasons for this prohibition was doubtless the strong element of paganism in the bullfight ritual, which Hemingway saw from the very first.

The bullfight involves a sort of liturgical emotion; it is a moving sacrifice that is almost religious in character. This is evident from the fact that the *torero* who dies does not die alone, and also from the fact that the death of the *torero* in the bullring is quite unlike that of a champion racing driver or an airplane pilot in competition. For the *fiesta brava* is not just another spectacle, but a very special sort of one that *necessarily* ends in death—that of the bull, and sometimes that of the matador. And that is also why it so fascinated Ernesto. Therefore, along with the dramatic "orgy" of *The Sun Also Rises*, one would also have to quote, as in a very special sort of theological treatise, the entire text of *Death in the Afternoon*, that work which a French critic has described as "more a treatise on the Spanish character than a treatise on bullfighting."

And the *corrida* is defined and distinguished from all other spectacles, fiestas, and sports, in *The Sun Also Rises*:

> "Nobody ever lives their life all the way up except bullfighters."

Yes, yes, Don Gregorio Corrochano: Ordóñez (like any good matador on a quiet, courageous afternoon) *imparted* death twice, because as he fought his two bulls—and as the other *toreros* fought theirs—he was living a sacrament, a sacrifice, his own possible destruction and therefore the possible destruction of those for whom he was officiating, of those who were taking communion with him in this blood, in a manner of speaking. And the name Ordóñez stands here for that of every other valiant, honest bullfighter.

I said, feeling rather out of my element:

"I'm *imparting* an invitation to you gentlemen to have a glass of wine with me."

"How about gin?" the man with the glasses said.

"Or whisky?" the fat man said.

"I invite you to impart, compart, repart, share, and take communion with me in this wine, which is what the bulls would invite you to do if they could."

"This guy's quite a learned scholar," the fat man said.

"Don't a string of words like that remind you a little bit of a mass?" the man with the round glasses said, looking at me as though I were butting in on a private conversation.

"I'm standing anybody to a drink who wants one," I said to the waiter. And they all took me up on my offer after the fat man had explained, in a quiet, very polite voice:

"This man is a learned professor, and he's asking us to have a drink with him."

"He can buy us drinks all night long if he wants to," the man with the glasses said in a cordial tone of voice.

But as the waiter started serving everybody, a whole bunch of people from the Bullfighters' Association, or the Good Samaritan Club, or the Union of Brave Bulls, or whatever, flocked to the bar. I was keeping track of the tab in my head, and since I have never mistaken myself for a philanthropic matador, I paid up the first chance I got, elbowed my way through the mob around the bar, turned around at the door, *imparted* my blessings on Cerro Corrochano, and fled to the street.

The nasty little man with glasses was the only one who came to the door, shouting after me, to everybody's amusement: "Hey there, you great genius, don't go yet. . . . We haven't had the elevation of the Host yet. . . ."

Meanwhile the fat man was beating his chest with his fist as though it were a drum in the *plaza* and whooping with laughter: "Some people are crazy, really crazy! The world is full of madmen!" he shouted.

4   I went down the little back streets leading directly to the Paseo del Prado. Hidden in one doorway was a night watchman with his gray duster over his shoulder, *imparting* love with a plump young *chacha*.

"Have fun!" I called out once I was well past them.

I went into La Espuela. There wasn't a single first-rate matador in the place. You hardly ever run into one in Madrid any more; almost all of them are out touring the provinces trying to get themselves gored. But the regular customers were discussing a subject that everybody had been talking about lately: bulls as God makes them and *toros afeitados* —ones whose horns have been shaved before a fight. "Haven't you ever seen a bull 'barbered'?" someone was saying. "The bullfighter asks the bull: 'How would you like your hair cut? Shall I leave your sideburns a little longer? That's quite fashionable nowadays.' And the bull replies, very gravely: 'I'd like you not to cut off this little curl between my horns.' And the *torero* answers in a jovial voice: 'Don't worry— you'll like the haircut I'm going to give you!'"

So the night was turning out the way it was bound to: talking bullfighting. And a night that begins with bullfight talk always ends up either in the police station or in bed with a woman. Naturally, the second possibility is preferable.

Insolent, sly girls as hard to handle as cows on the loose had already begun to appear on the streets—ladies of the evening, and the night was all theirs now.

There was a flower seller with lovely blossoms for sale in the doorway of the Teatro Español, an unusual sight in summer—but maybe she'd been hired to stand there by the people in the Tourist Office. And floating along the sidewalk like shipwreck victims or waving their arms on the corners or circulating among the taxis were the same prostitutes as always, because today's old ones were yesterday's young ones. Certain subtleties were beginning to be involved, thank God, in the business of fornication—such nice discriminations as that made by the pedant in *El Lazarillo de Manzanares*, who maintained that "it never gets dark in Madrid" and therefore it's the "Norway of moonlit nights." What a dull clod!

What I shouldn't do was mix drinks, because Pernod and red wine don't sit well together, as I could see already, and if I drank beer on top of them, which was what the clear Madrid night seemed to call for, I might be even worse off.

I was in the Flamenco quarter now, and I went into one of the bars plastered with bullfight posters like the ones Ernesto had at his place in Havana (one of them was from San Sebastián, as I remember) and also in Ketchum.

I had come to the right place; the pot was boiling, so furiously it was about to spill over, in fact. Ernesto's name and Manolete's had been entered in the lists, as they couldn't help but be.

Somebody mentioned Clarito, the bullfight critic. "Clarito's clearly a clarion," I said to myself, enjoying my little alliterative slogan. But Clarito's clarion cries had become a strident bugle call summoning the troops to battle, and this crowd in the bar obviously couldn't tell shadow from substance, or appreciate the difference between a spectacle and a sacrifice—even though Ernesto had said from the very beginning, and insisted in his last book, that bullfights never interested him as spectacle. One of the waiters was searching among the bottles and the receipts and even the little box for tips, and finally he came up with what he'd been looking for: a clipping of Clarito's article about Ernesto. He leaned over the water faucet and the big bottles of red and white wine, and began to read Clarito's article aloud, in the voice of a sacristan in a convent:

> It was never a question of his hearing bells ring in his head [this very witty remark has been repeated hundreds of times by all sorts of semi-illiterates, those who have gotten their facts, both in wartime and in peacetime, from police informers or from lists of names]; he simply couldn't tell which bell it was that was ringing. During the war he confused the bells ringing for the Caudillo and those ringing for La Pasionaria; and he was unable to distinguish those that were ringing for Manolete and those that were ringing for his successors. . . .

"Clarito's clearly a clarion," I said softly, but to my surprise the men with and without mustaches, the women with and without blemishes, on their reputation or otherwise, standing along the bar, spoke up like a Greek chorus:

"That's putting it clearly enough!"

"Good for Clarito!"

"Clarito's crystal-clear!"

And Clarito wasn't one of the worst critics, either. But he'd had to put up with Ernesto's outrageous behavior (the *fiesta brava* and the honor of pen-pushers faithful to the star matadors had been dragged in the mud), and had dared to say, from the most distinguished and most noble tribunal of bullfighting, that *The Sun Also Rises* was a colorless, tasteless, insipid novel.

"Remember what Hemingway said about Manolete . . . that angel?"

"People kept whispering things in his ear."

"Can you imagine, that Judas denied that Manolete was a great *torero!*"

"But he never saw him in the bullring!"

Had Ernesto been any less respectful toward Manolete than toward Ordóñez's father, Niño de la Palma, whom he had called a yellow-bellied coward? Had he been any kinder to Sánchez Mejías among the older generation of bullfighters, and to Dominguín among today's generation?

I am one of those who believe that Ernesto's fervent enthusiasm for Antonio Ordóñez in his last years was childish and turned what had been solid rock into meringue; but this was just one more evidence of blindness on the part of a man and artist who in the twilight of his life had endeavored to renew a familiar dialogue with what is only a myth and a re-created fantasy. At certain times, Ernesto's adoration and his solicitude had made me blush for him. But all that was very understandable. After his downfall, Cayetano Ordóñez was a name not to be mentioned. And Antoñito had been what Ernesto had never dared write about him, an artistic genius and a fine person whom you couldn't describe as "invincible" or "unbeatable" because it might bring him bad luck and be the death of him. Ernesto had always looked on Antonio with awe, and a sort of tenderness that is not easy to describe, though there is no doubt that it was a very healthy thing, so healthy that at times it was the one thing about Ernesto that made him seem a real man, an ordinary human being in the presence of his great idol. To use a bullfighting analogy, because Antonio was not only Ernesto's favorite but also a master of his art, when he was fighting in the ring it was as if he were the only bullfighter alive. To Ernesto, Antonio was the one and only.

Was it true that Ernesto had never seen Manolete in the bullring, not even in Latin America? I'm not at all sure of that, and have had my doubts for some time, because Ernesto was usually very reluctant to talk about anything he hadn't seen or experienced firsthand. I could remember Mary describing Manolete perfectly; she is one of those women who can paint an absolutely lifelike portrait or sketch a cruel caricature of someone in just a few strokes. She had never forgotten meeting him, and loved to tell about it.

They could talk about Manolete all they wanted. Probably none of these parasites who hung around with third-rate bullfighters had ever been as close to Manolete as I had in the last days of his life, because I had had two quite intimate conversations with him, one just a few days before he was fatally gored by the Miura bull in Linares. Nonetheless, I hadn't written one line about my meeting with him, not even the day the news of his death had reached me at the Universidad Internacional de Santander. I had shut myself up in my room and refused to come out even to eat. The last conversation we had had together had been so frank and intimate that publishing an account of it would have seemed a sort of blasphemy to me. But *toreros* have always made me feel more tongue-tied than inspired.

One day Manolete's name had come up in a very private conversation I was having with Ernesto. And I had a few solemn words to say about the very sober *torero* from Córdoba, where stoicism is an endemic disease, even in the best of families.

"He was cold and distant," Ernesto said.

"That's not true," I replied.

"He was a melancholy sort of man."

"That's true," I answered.

"He had complexes," Ernesto insisted.

"You're wrong," I said. "It's true, though, that people who didn't know him usually thought he had."

"He didn't have the least little spark of imagination."

"He was a very serene man."

"He was a jinx."

"He was introspective, but a kind man, kinder to other people than he was to himself."

Ernesto didn't like hearing Manolete being described in those terms, especially by me. So I said no more. Ernesto liked it that I knew when to keep my mouth shut. Moreover, when he thought I was likely to disagree with him or argue with him about his own very personal views of bullfighting, he very often was quite reluctant to spar with me, and I knew I didn't have the strength to face this giant. He had made his mind up, once and for all, about Manolete, as he had about Dominguín. He had written:

> . . . Chicuelo did everything backwards that he could, looking at the crowd as the bull moved under his extended arm to remind them of Manolete who with his manager had brought bullfighting to its second lowest ebb and richest epoch and then been

1. Hemingway was basically an anarchist, but the concerns of his art gave him a deep-seated respect for justice. In spite of his fascination with wars, his was the soul of a pacifist. (EDICIONES DESTINO)

2. Photographer Robert Capa photographed a young Ernesto in Spain, sharing the adventures of Spanish cronies. (ROBERT CAPA)

3. Ernesto's great passion for the Sanfermines and for Spain always put him in a euphoric mood, which ended in his singing the "riau-riau," a popular Navarrese song during these holidays. (MASPONS, BARCELONA)

4. It wasn't all excitement and frenzy at the Sanfermines. Sometimes an international reporter or a professor would come along and Ernesto would have a polite chat with him. (MASPONS, BARCELONA)

5. Wine, women, song, and guitars. . . . Ernesto, in Pamplona, invitin
one and all to come have a glass of wine with him. People thronge
about him continuously, until finally he could stand it no longer an
would make his escape like a man pursued. (MASPONS, BARCELONA)

6. Hemingway mingling with the townspeople at the San Fermín fiesta i
Pamplona, after dancing in the Plaza. He always claimed that "Spain is
country to live in, not to die in." (MASPONS, BARCELONA)

7. In this historic picture, Ernesto has just met Antonio Ordóñez. (CANO Y GUERRA, FOTÓGRAFO TAURINO)

8. From his very first meeting with the *torero* Antonio Ordóñez (the son of the bullfighter Niño de la Palma, who was the model for the young matador and hero of *The Sun Also Rises*), Ernesto was fascinated by Antonio, whom he regarded as even more handsome and courageous than his father. From the moment Ernesto returned to Spain in 1953, he followed his new idol from one bullring to another all over the country, mesmerized by the fact that Ordóñez might very well meet his death in any one of the *corridas* he fought. This obsession of his is dramatically reflected in his articles for *Life* magazine, which he entitled *The Dangerous Summer*. (MASPONS, BARCELONA)

9. Hemingway and his wife Mary waiting for the running of the bulls to begin in the streets of Pamplona. (MAGNUM)

killed and dying had become a demigod and so escaped criticism however.

Ernesto couldn't forgive Dominguín for the splendid and rather frivolous life he led, and he couldn't forgive Manolete for having allowed himself to be fatally gored in the bullring. Whenever Manolete's name was mentioned, Ernesto would wince in disgust and refuse to take part in the conversation. But there was always somebody who spoke up for Manolete. What Ernesto wrote in *The Dangerous Summer* was his final word on the subject:

> . . . but the public loves these tricks since they were taught that Manolete was a great bullfighter and so this must be great bullfighting. It will be years before they know that Manolete was a great bullfighter with cheap tricks and that he used the cheap tricks because the public wanted them. He was fighting before an ignorant public that enjoyed being defrauded.

People kept streaming in and out of the bar. They were doubtless the very same sort of individuals to whom "The Unbeatable" or "The Invincible" shouts from the middle of the bullring: "You swine, you bastards." Of course: Clarito was clearly a clarion. And they went on shooting their mouths off. I knew their kind: people who hang around the bullring, vultures too, in a certain sense, who even take a peck or two at the matador every so often. One of the things I never could understand about Ernesto was how he could be so patient with people like that. I could understand very well how he could be so enthusiastic about the spectacle of the bullring, and even about the "Spanish beauties," the *majas* in the stands; how he could be a paternal, passionate, fanatic admirer of his favorite bullfighters; but what I couldn't understand was how Ernesto, who was so short-tempered and impatient with other people, could be so credulous and so indulgent toward all the tramps and scoundrels who hang around the bullring.

Because they are shy and unsure of themselves, or perhaps because they secretly like being fawned upon and toadied to, great men often surround themselves with mediocre people and even riff-raff, people with no intellectual interests, buffoons who laugh and joke to conceal their inner chaos, troublemakers who find it to their advantage to stir up the most absurd sort of quarrels. Yet these same great, sensitive-souled celebrities will go out of their way to avoid people who are sincerely interested in them or be barely polite or snappish or sarcastic in their dealings with them.

This was yet another point of resemblance between Ernesto and Don Pío Baroja, whose intimates, for the most part, were also an irritating bunch of mediocre, coarse, vulgar sycophants.

Copying the example of the *toreros*, Ernesto surrounded himself with a sort of entourage of riff-raff. He had many very respectable friends, but was also surrounded by many hangers-on, a whole raft of toadies whom he couldn't do without but nonetheless secretly despised. They were the last remaining traces of a certain ambition of Ernesto's, to be at once a prince and a rogue, and in a certain sense they made him feel invulnerable.

The last time Ernesto and I were together, Aaron Hotchner had been there, and I had found him rather a wet blanket. He was something of an enigma, a sophisticated, freckle-faced man who might perhaps best be described as that typical character in American literature, the person who could easily become either a Bible-thumper or a bum.

"He's a smart cookie," Ernesto whispered to me.

"I can see that."

"He has lots of connections in television and the movies and knows his way around."

"I gather you've known each other a long time."

"Yes, we're more or less old friends."

"He's obviously very fond of you."

"He's as faithful as a bird dog. But I don't trust anybody—you know that. I did once, and the guy tried to hop in bed with me!"

The thing I disliked most about Hotchner was his two-faced behavior toward people who were Ernesto's real friends, people such as Juanito Quintana and even Ordóñez. Though he was very clever at hiding his true feelings, you could tell that Hotchner was really a hypocrite. But he put up a very good front as Ernesto's mild-mannered, obedient servant.

It was Ordóñez, as I remember, who first called him "Freckles," and the nickname stuck. He pretended not to mind and was good-natured about everything, but he was such a toady at times that it was sickening.

Ernesto rather liked Hotchner's funny stories and put up with his drivel, but at times his obsequiousness got on Ernesto's nerves and bored him to tears. Hotchner did his best all summer long to make the imaginary duel between Ordóñez and Dominguín a real one; in moments when Ernesto was tense or had no one around for company, he was half convinced he was witnessing a genuine "civil war" in the bullfight world, though I for my part thought the whole affair was a big laugh, and almost everyone else did too.

As an expert at grinding out publicity in the United States, Hotchner knew what a big splash Ernesto's articles were going to make, and was already bragging about what a coup they would be.

I felt very bad about those *Life* articles, called *The Dangerous Summer*, to tell the truth, because it seemed to me that the whole farce was beneath Ernesto and that he should have refused to have anything to do with it.

"Freckles" was never open and aboveboard. His mild manner and his air of shy diffidence seemed to me quite a clever cover-up for his exploitation of Ernesto.

The blood of all these vulgar parasites in the bar was still boiling because of what Ernesto had written in *The Dangerous Summer*. They were saying:

"When the hour of truth came . . ."

"The moment when you have to go in close to the horns . . ."

"That's right. When the hour of truth came and he saw that he was taking a worse beating than the padded horses in the bullring, he split wide open."

"Like a melon."

Ernesto had laughed at almost everything, even himself at times, but he had never laughed at Spain. He uttered the very word Spain the way a patriarch pronounces the name of his wife in the company of other women. On the road, in taverns, in the bullrings, whenever Ernesto mentioned anything Spanish, I swear there was always a special note of tenderness in his voice. And all that riff-raff there in the bar—butchers, gypsies, black marketeers, traveling salesmen, bootblacks, queers, spongers, pimps, penny-a-liners, bums—were raving on and on about Ernesto. I had been in this very bar with him one other time, and that night there hadn't been any talk about shaved or unshaved horns, about cheap tricks or costly ones. I remembered that one of the men in the bar had called out to Ernesto: "You stand head and shoulders above everybody else!"

It was a funny remark you could take both literally and figuratively, and all the people in the bar had applauded. After we had left the place, Ernesto had commented on the savory popular speech of the people of Madrid, one of the few places left in the world where there was real personal imagination and wit. If he were here tonight, his ears would burn. Maybe that was another reason why he had killed himself, because he would have found it hard to have to defend himself on every street corner in Spain.

Someone said: "It was all because of Antoñito."

And another man piped up: "Antoñito kept whispering in his ear."

If Ordóñez had walked in at that moment, they would all have shut up immediately, of course.

Everything Ernesto wrote about bullfighting in *The Sun Also Rises*, *Death in the Afternoon*, and *The Dangerous Summer*, he wrote in places like this bar, or at any rate he had learned a great deal hanging around in them, especially the jargon of the bullfight world.

Despite all the gossip in Spain, Ernesto's friendship with Ordóñez had not been as intimate or as important as people believe, despite the fact that the two of them called each other "associate" and all the rest of it. Spaniards—who are evil-tongued as well as master coiners of wise aphorisms—were out for blood the minute they read such paragraphs as:

> Antonio lay naked on the bed except for a hand towel as big as a leaf. I noticed the eyes first; the darkest, brightest, merriest eyes anybody ever looked into and the mischief urchin grin and could not help seeing the scar welts on the right thigh.

The photograph that showed Ernesto sitting on the edge of Ordóñez's bed practically on top of the wounded *torero* had caused the most vulgar and vicious sort of talk, all over Spain and elsewhere. Most people were quite willing to believe that in Hemingway's very exclusive circle of intimates the most shameless vices were tolerated. Could that have been the reason why such odd sorts as Edgar Neville had tried to get Ernesto to come to his parties and when Ernesto refused had spread the most outlandish rumors about him?

Suddenly there was a prolonged *shhhh* and everybody at the bar shut up. The waiter with the collection of grease-stained clippings had brought out another one.

"I bet you can't guess who wrote this one!" he shouted. And without waiting for an answer, he added, very confidentially, "It's by Curro Castañares."

The waiter read a hopelessly confused sermon by this famous bull-fight critic, stumbling over many of the words, but when he got to the phrases "queer *aficionado*" and "sectarian follower of the art of bull-fighting," he read them very slowly and repeated them several times. His awestruck audience kept up a running comment:

"He drew blood there."

"The sword struck home that time."

They were all behaving like the *monosabios*, the red-shirted bullring attendants who rush over to get the picador out of trouble. I couldn't take them all on, but I was so angry I would have to choose the one that repelled me most and have it out with him. I looked them over one by one, but it was no easy task to pick out a victim, much less a worthy adversary. I had been very upset when I came in, and when they started clowning and joking about Ernesto, I simply had to resort to fisticuffs to work off my indignation. The minute I realized that I was going to fight them, I looked around for a bottle. Hitting somebody over the head with one may not be as noble as a duel with pistols or a bout in the boxing ring, but sometimes it settles lots of things.

At that moment an angel from heaven came to my aid, in the guise of a whore, a prostitute as age-old as a shark, as untidy as a blackbird's nest, as smelly as a guinea pig, as sweet as raspberry jam. This angel, miraculously sent to me from heaven above, took me by the hand and whispered to me, in a voice tinged with mystery: "Come with me, there's somebody here who wants to help you."

I followed her, a little bit afraid that this sinuous snake was casting a spell over me. She seemed to be anxious to save my honor, but on the other hand she might be making me risk losing it altogether, not to mention the danger of breaking my neck or my jaw or a rib. But that's the way it goes in Flamenco places.

"You're welcome here, you're most welcome," a short, very gaunt-looking man said to me.

"Who are you?" I asked.

"I'm the proprietor. You're most welcome here," he replied in a soft voice.

"Thank you, thank you very much," I replied mechanically.

"If the shoe fits put it on," somebody said. "And if not . . ."

"Don't pay any attention," the proprietor said.

"They're all stewed to the gills," the prostitute chimed in.

The proprietor went over to the bar and said something to the waiter who had read the clipping, and he put all his articles from the newspapers away under the cash register. The snickers had turned to laughter now; they were laughing in my face, in fact. How long could I stand this?

"They're a little potted, you know what I mean?" the prostitute said.

"Potted? They're bastards, that's what they are," I answered.

"Don't pay any attention to them," the proprietor said again, raising his hands in priestly benediction to quiet everybody down.

Alcohol seldom made Ernesto actually pick a fight with anybody, but he sometimes became argumentative and almost cruel when he was drinking. But that wasn't all. He was usually talkative, though not eloquent, and ordinarily his speech was slow and deliberate, with every word carefully weighed. Alcohol more or less stirred up the coals of his memory, and then the sparks of reminiscence, of pure nostalgia would fly. His conversation at times like that was terse but intense, full of long silences but also pulsing with life.

No, the alcohol I had drunk wouldn't get me into trouble tonight, because I would fight it, as though it were the stupidest ass of all in this bunch of stupid brutes. I was in my element now, and glorying in it, and it was Ernesto's element too; if he were still alive he would have liked being here, no matter how painful the experience might have been for him. I would concentrate on the most important thing now, make a real effort to imagine what had happened in Ketchum. Faced with his sudden, frightening death, how had Mary, that gentle person, gone about wrapping Ernesto in his shroud? Had she shuddered and sent him off to nothingness with this token from one person and that from another in his coffin? Had she sent him to his grave as a passionate anarchist with no flag in his lapel? In the robes of a mystical monk with no credo and no fixed rule? As a universal bystander, part militant and part sportsman, dressed in the garments of a rich but homeless vagabond? There was no way of knowing. Perhaps it had all been done in great haste, as when the bull in the ring gores the horse and both intestines and sawdust spill out and an attendant rushes over and covers them with a merciful piece of canvas.

Somebody pounded violently on one of the tables, spilling the glasses of wine. As I remember, it was a man in a pinstripe suit and a white tie. A little short guy with a flat nose got very angry and yelled at him in a high-pitched voice. The man in the pinstripe suit and the white tie, who looked like a gypsy, stammered:

"Everybody keeps calling him Old Wh-wh-whiskers." And having managed to get that much out, he went on: "What size do you wear?" addressing the man who had made the remark about the shoe fitting.

"Listen to the guy! He sounds like a crow," the short man said.

"That g-guy you call Old Whiskers had a first n-n-name and a last n-n-name." Having contrived to get that much out, the man with the stutter seemed more sure of himself and pounded on the table again, but this time the glasses didn't spill.

The waiter decided to put his two cents' worth in. He lowered his voice and said confidentially that it was because Old Whiskers was such a close friend of Ordóñez's that he called him affectionate nicknames like Toñete or Toñín. Everybody hooted, and when they had quieted down, the man stammered:

"Stop calling him Old Wh-wh-whiskers!"

"O.k. then, the writer," the little guy with the flat nose said.

"Yeah, the writer," the waiter said.

"He was a writer from the t-t-top of his head to the t-t-tip of his t-t-toes," the man stammered, barely getting the words out this time.

"Old Whiskers was a great man," somebody who hadn't spoken up before said.

"Don't call him Old Whiskers! He had a name. And he was as decent a man as any one of us here." And on seeing that he'd gotten all that out without any trouble, the stutterer drained his glass.

"It certainly didn't show," the man with the flat nose said.

I couldn't bear it another minute and got up to leave. But the prostitute said to me, in a quiet, very gentle voice, "Don't go away mad. Don't pay any attention to these jungle savages."

The proprietor put a glass of what he referred to as his "special reserve" in my hand, and offered me a cigar. It wouldn't be polite to leave now, so I sat down again. Then I began talking in a very quiet voice, as though I were talking to myself, to shut out the noise from the bar. I can't remember exactly what I said, but it was a relief to talk about Ernesto, much as a person who is mentally ill gets rid of his depression by raving deliriously.

"Do these men know that Ernesto proved that there is a parallel between Golgotha and the Bullring, between Christ Crucified and the Matador? And Ernesto wasn't at all irreverent or blasphemous," I said softly. "I know for a fact that he was sometimes shocked at how readily Spaniards shit on God and the Holy Virgin, if you'll pardon my language."

"I know what you mean," the prostitute said.

"Christ's hours on the cross were like the hour of truth for the *toreros*. Do you see what I mean? Bullfighting to Ernesto wasn't selling blood for money, which is what it is to the Herods and Caiaphases and Pilates and Judases in the world of the *fiesta brava*."

The owner practically had tears in his eyes. I think he was rather impressed. I went on:

"When Ernesto said that 'a crucifixion of six carefully selected Christs will take place in the Monumental Golgotha of Madrid,' he wasn't being blasphemous, or at least that wasn't his intention, because in his own way he believed in Christ. Do you know what that means?"

The prostitute wiped the sweat off my forehead with a paper napkin.

"And when Ernesto, who was quite certain that what he wrote wasn't going to be censored by the authorities (a fact we mustn't overlook), goes on to say that

'the following well-known, accredited and notable crucifiers will officiate, each accompanied by his cuadrilla of nailers, hammerers, cross-raisers and spade-men . . . ,'

he is not poking fun at the Man who *wanted* to die. Do you see what I mean? The Man who *wanted* to die is Christ.

"But did Ernesto, as you call him, believe in God?" the proprietor asked in a furtive whisper. (I noted that he didn't ask whether he believed in Christ.)

"He had more faith in God than all the rest of us put together, and the word Christ gave him gooseflesh. I know—I saw the goose-pimples with my very own eyes."

The prostitute put her hand on my shoulder. And the proprietor poured some more of his "special reserve" into my heavy, fluted glass.

"You apparently knew him well," the proprietor said.

"He must have been a very lonely man to have killed himself," the whore said.

"That wasn't why at all, dear," I said. "Ernesto had completed his orbit; he'd gone through the entire cycle."

"What do you mean by that?" she asked.

"What I mean is that he had reached his goal, or at least believed that there was no further goal to strive for. It's also quite likely that Ernesto wasn't happy about having become that sort of person, for he had always tried to climb higher and higher. But when he attained what for many people would be the *summum bonum*, he realized it really wasn't much of anything, felt cheated, and did away with himself . . ."

"He was a bad man, then."

"Not so bad."

"Don't tell me that somebody who's got everything and kills himself nonetheless, isn't possessed of the devil."

"He didn't have everything. He didn't have complete confidence in himself, for one thing, and he tried to prove to himself that the fear of dying, and the fear of killing himself in particular, was something childish and unimportant, something he could overcome through an act of supreme indifference."

"So the fool went ahead and killed himself."

"As he put it: 'Death is a sovereign remedy for all misfortunes.'"

"Some remedy!"

"The smell of death made him dizzy; it intoxicated him more than whisky or vodka. Death has a special odor, which very sensitive souls can detect, and he got a whiff of it, when he was in the Clinic perhaps, or when he came back home. . . . He probably suspected that he would die a lingering death, and couldn't bear the thought."

"He was a coward, then."

"He was a real he-man, but as defenseless as a little kid who's scared."

Our host put two lobsters on the table in front of us, and a sauce with little bits of onion and peppers floating in it. The prostitute didn't want any.

"All right, I'll eat both of them," I said.

"Go ahead—I hope you enjoy them."

The men at the bar weren't talking about Ernesto any more. They were jabbering away about *estatuarias* and *faroles*, about *toreros* as rigid and still as marble angels on tombstones, and *toreros* as jerky and laughable as Las Fallas puppets.

"Do you know what Ernesto used to call this?" I said to the proprietor, pointing to my glass of wine.

"Everybody knows what it's called: bull's blood."

"No—he used to call it Christ's blood."

"Don't say that!" the prostitute exclaimed, and then added in a reverent tone of voice: "God might punish you."

"Ernesto wasn't being irreverent or blasphemous when he called it Christ's blood. Christ to him was the total divinization of that dark, blind, fatal force we call the realm of Nature, which is what the bull represents. But Christ was also intelligence, will, courage, the drive to excel, supreme art, everything the *torero* represents, that is to say, power over death. The bull and the bullfighter are symbols of a transcendental combat, and Christ is at the very center of it, reigning not only over the life of the senses but also the life of the spirit. . . ."

"You'll make yourself sick if you keep brooding about it," she said. "We should get him some broth or something . . ."

The proprietor got up from his chair. But I went on with what I was saying.

"Bullfighting was a miraculous solution for him, a discovery that guided both his life and his art. From the very first *corridas* he ever attended, he began to see that life is the great *corrida*, because it is so unpredictable. The *corrida* may be a few trancelike moments of great valor, an instant of serenity when the bull brushes past the cape, the beautiful sensation of pure courage on a quiet afternoon. . . . But it may also be helplessness, a ridiculous lack of guts, craven cowardice in the face of the brave bull, a sword flung in the air, an ignominious retreat, a grotesque leap, livid shame at the edge of the ring where the bull has been clumsily butchered."

The proprietor came back with a steaming cupful of thick, dirty-white broth with a couple of stale eggs in it. But it burned my tongue, and I set it aside to cool.

"Ernesto knew what he liked to drink and where to get it. He adored hanging out in the taverns of Madrid and told me more than once that he'd made his best friends out drinking. The sort of people he liked best were the ones who seem to have a fear of going to bed and stay up talking (or sitting not saying a word) till the wee hours of the morning. Do you know what he said about Valdepeñas? He said: 'On a hot day it is cool from the shade and the wind.' And he was quite right. Just think, he'll never drink any again. . . ." And I reverently drained my glass.

Somebody called the prostitute to the phone. I took a closer look at the horde of oddball creatures at the bar and decided they were actors on summer vacation, with perhaps a few dancers and a sword-handler or two among them. But most of them were actors. Why hadn't I realized this before?

"How about another drink?" the proprietor asked.

"Yes, please—put it in the broth, will you?"

"Would you like sherry in it?"

"No, no—some Valdepeñas, the wine he called 'the poor man's Tavel' and always recommended highly, providing nobody had been stupid enough to chill it."

"He knew what he was talking about."

"He knew a lot about wines. In recent years he drank the very best rosés, since he had plenty of money, but he never scorned Valdepeñas.

He would drink four or five bottles of it at a meal; that's why he'd gotten such a paunch. He used to say that Spanish wine 'cools you and then lights the fire that you need' if only to prove that your glass is still in front of you and hasn't disappeared. But he could hold his liquor, better than almost anybody, so he goes on to say that 'the next glass cools you and only lights the fire if the engine needs it.' And as for the third glass . . ."

"In other words, the engine always needs it."

"And if it needs it in the beginning, it starts needing it more and more."

The prostitute had come back. She had no idea what we were talking about, and looked as though she was upset about something.

I got to my feet. I might never get out of there if I didn't leave now. The proprietor didn't want me to go and wouldn't take a cent from me. But this whole scene, a sort of offbeat funeral service for Ernesto, was beginning to seem sadder and sadder, and the actors and the gypsies at the bar were bound to bring up the Manolete business again any minute now.

The prostitute had obviously had bad news of some sort. She'd come back from the phone looking dismayed and dejected, like a little bird when somebody puts a hat over it. Maybe she had a little girl who was sick, or a younger brother with polio she was taking care of, or a husband waiting for her on the corner to pocket her day's earnings. And here she was, consoling a poor man grieving for a friend who had killed himself because he wasn't allowed to drink any more and because alcohol neither refreshed him nor lubricated his motor any more. . . .

I thanked both of them politely, said good night, and left.

I stood there on the corner of the Carrera de San Jerónimo, not knowing what to do next.

Ernesto and I had once gone to the bar of the Hotel Palace around this same time of night, though it had been in the fall, and as we were walking toward the Puerta del Sol he had stopped right where I was standing now and said, "When I came to Madrid the first time, things were pretty bad. They were terrible, in fact, and I had a rough time of it. I lived up the street there, and had almost no money. When I look back on those days now, it scares me."

"And were you happy?"

"Yes, sort of, but a person without money has very little freedom, and a person without freedom . . ."

I could see him in my mind's eye now, standing there as though rooted to the spot, peering anxiously in all directions.

"Later on I saw this street entirely torn up by Fascist shells. There was nothing left of it," he went on.

"What do you remember most about our war?"

"Shit on your war."

He ran his hand through his beard, a gesture that somehow seemed both placid and obsessive. After a moment's silence, he went on, as though swallowing saliva: "The whole thing was absurd, nonsensical, incomprehensible . . ."

I didn't say anything. When he fell into this strange sort of mood, it was better to let him do the talking. Since he spoke very slowly, I would often have time to see the connection between what he was saying and things he'd written or recalled at other times.

"Didn't you know I was in the front lines in a tank at Brunete? There are lots of things people don't know. The place where the fat was really in the fire was Teruel. It was a real mess. The troops were one place, the plans someplace else, and the armaments God only knows where. If it weren't for the fact that so many men, and such good ones, died there, I could laugh my head off just remembering that whole farce. The fighting was going on around the cemetery, the seminary, and the insane asylum. The Fascists counterattacked furiously, with a whole bunch of tanks and planes. They had gotten themselves in a bad spot and wanted out. It was a bad situation for us, too, because we'd goofed, too, and taken up a very poor position. Then somebody or other decided he was a great tactician with a marvelous idea—straight out of Goya. Since we were defending those few decisive meters to save the skins of the loonies in the asylum, why not let them defend themselves? We're all more or less nuts anyway. No sooner said than done. We equipped the patients from head to foot, the whole outfit: rifles, wine-skins, bottles of cognac. And those loonies proved to be very reliable. They defended the terrain like wild beasts, and it was quite a sight to see them moving about with such *esprit de corps* and such determination, shouting 'No pasarán, no pasarán' at the top of their lungs. The troops barricaded themselves behind their parapets like madmen, and the real madmen fired from the rooftops and chimneys, crouching behind mattresses or whatever else they could scrounge up, shouting 'Viva, viva la guerra!' It was a fierce battle, but the loonies leaped into the breaches opened in our lines by the Fascists and proved to be just as highly disciplined as the men in the International Brigades. Maybe even more so. It was amazing. They didn't even fall back when their comrades got killed, and were so fired up they would have willingly sacrificed their lives. 'Why are these madmen so willing to die for the Republic?' I asked myself. There wasn't one of them that turned out to be a traitor or a coward or refused to obey orders. What an afternoon, what a night, what a morning! Those hours seemed endless at the time, but they were unforgettable. It was a fantastic thing, because even when they saw their comrades fall, not one man gave up. It was a death worthy of madmen; the *locos* of Teruel must be the greatest madmen in all of Spain."

"I wouldn't go that far—those where I come from would be a match for them any day."

"I've never been to Murcia."

"Well, you'll have to go there."

"We'll go together some time."

"What happened to the *locos?*"

"Thanks to them, we were able to evacuate the regular troops in a more orderly way. That night was the closest I ever came to getting my ass shot off, but as you see I saved my skin."

"Yes, I can see that. So that was the closest call you ever had during the war?"

"I had a couple of very close shaves flying over Rebel territory, too."

He never talked about the current situation in Spain. It was as though he'd sworn not to. I didn't want to make him angry or press him. I remembered a bit of dialogue he had written:

"Are you a Communist?"

"No, I'm an anti-Fascist."

Nonetheless I wanted to take advantage of this intimate moment to get something straight, and I asked him, rather hesitantly, "Did you ever carry a rifle? Or rather, did you ever fire it?"

"Everybody shoots in wars, but my job wasn't really killing people— it was trying to keep myself from getting killed."

"So you were often in real danger."

"About as much danger as the enemy facing me."

Ernesto had not been in Madrid during the entire siege. He had been active during the battle for the city, however. He came and went, encouraging people, criticizing. His role in Madrid was principally that of a technical adviser and morale officer indoctrinating the troops, and he was more interested in being a guide than in being a captain. And as he visited the battlefronts to urge his comrades on, they in turn communicated something of their fervor to him, causing him to feel that he was both an inspired and inspiring front-line witness.

Though he attempted to veil the tragedy by the use of a heightened, often lyrical language, it is nonetheless quite evident that life behind the lines bored him and sickened him, because the front lines were where the bloodiest and most ignominious acts took place.

". . . we are not yet in the time of fairs and festivals."

"But this will be a fair and festival today," another said. "The

Fair of Liberty and from this day, when these are extinguished the town and the land are ours."

"We thresh fascists today," said one, "and out of the chaff comes the freedom of this pueblo."

"We must administer it well to deserve it," said another.

This was the other side of the coin of the great dream, and the heart-rending price to be paid for cruelty. That was why he added:

> . . . It was like after a storm or a flood or a battle and everyone was tired and no one spoke much. I myself felt hollow and not well and I was full of shame and a sense of wrongdoing and I had a great feeling of oppression and of bad to come. . . .

I could still see him in my mind's eye, standing there on the corner of the Carrera de San Jerónimo, rubbing his hand across his eyes, those eyes that were not blue, as a number of Spaniards who have tried to draw his portrait have described them, but like a deep lake in the north country where he was born, with little green and dark-gray specks at the edge. And beneath these bright eyes were freckled cheeks, and those blotches like stigmata carefully concealed beneath his splendid beard.

He was lost in his own thoughts, and I don't know whether he heard me when I said, "You must have seen many terrible things."

But he came back from the far country of memory then and said, rather gravely, "You can take my word for it: there's no other country like Spain. I like it better than any other country in the world."

These were almost exactly the same words that Robert Jordan utters a number of times in *For Whom the Bell Tolls*:

"There are no other countries like Spain."

Ordinarily, Ernesto had a slow, careful way of speaking, gravely weighing every word. But whenever he spoke of Spain it was as though a faucet had been turned on, and the words came pouring out like a joyous hymn. At such times, you didn't dare mention the things that weren't going as well as they appeared to be, or the things that were clearly going very badly in Spain. Or even those good things that were the cause or the consequence of all the other things.

"This is a good country to live in—and live for," he would say ecstatically.

You wished you could have as pure and generous a love for it as Ernesto, but that was not always possible.

He wanted to separate the good from the bad, to be not merely a writer who described people and places and events, but a moralist, an ideological guiding light. Was any page he ever wrote more powerful and more truthful than his description of the Rebel forces attacking El Sordo's position in *For Whom the Bell Tolls?*

Ernesto always regarded the Spanish Falangist movement as nothing more than a servile copy of Nazism, or more accurately, a Celto-Iberian brand of Fascism, and he was unwilling to concede that the Falangist program for the country might bring about genuine reforms. In his view, nationalist movements that become organized political parties produce nothing but a lot of fruitless, high-flown talk. I had heard him say more than once that the Falangists wanted to do the right thing but weren't able to, that Falangism was perhaps a genuine expression of the will of the people—as a number of Spaniards had testified—but that the cry for justice had been stifled, through outright violence at first and later through a sophisticated campaign of lies and half-truths. Even though he admitted that some of the Falangists were whole men physically, he was convinced that they were spiritually castrated and had no workable program. It was a shame, but they had been caught from the beginning between the devil and the deep blue sea, between militarism on the one hand and a tradition-minded society that resisted any sort of change on the other. It was not only hollow rhetoric and empty speculation that had led them astray, but also their espousing of an outworn ideal that no longer fitted the situation in Europe. The Falangists might be acceptable and even good men personally, but as a plan and a political system Falangism was inappropriate and even anachronistic. Because he had a violent antipathy for all parties that destroyed human personality, that had no charity or mercy, that preached redemption through despotism, he could not bear Falangism. For the same reasons, he was also a thoroughgoing anti-Communist.

"But you know that almost every feature of Spanish life is a unique phenomenon," I reminded him. "We're different from everybody else."

"But the label is more important than the contents in this country now. It's a mask that doesn't impress me."

"The Falangists may not be able to preserve the traditional moral values, but at least they're trying to preserve a certain aesthetic," I insisted.

"It's an aesthetic of pretentious dandies," he answered.

Ernesto's arguments had impressed me. I might have replied that not all Falangists were pretentious *señoritos*. I might have added that he would have more in common with the Falangists than with the Carlists; he might enjoy going out drinking with the latter or running bulls with them or hunting with them, but it would be quite a trick to get them to talk about the future, or the imperfect or the perfect either, for that matter. And it seemed to me that Miguel Primo de Rivera, for one, had been fairly decent to him in 1953, when Ernesto was allowed back in Spain, but he guessed what I was thinking and said, "I don't deny that there may be a gentleman or two among the Spanish Fascists. What I meant was that the movement as such, with its flags and its legions and its Roman squares, seems to me to be an anachronism."

Sometimes he would end conversations like this with the words, "I haven't said a thing, mind you."

And at other times he might wind up his harsh criticism of the Spanish leaders by saying, "I don't deny there may be one or two decent ones, like Rafael for instance."

And one time he had said something even more revealing, referring to the Falangist emblem and Franco: "Listen, arrows are o.k., taken separately, but I don't like them in bunches. I don't go along with oxen, or rather ox yokes, either. That's also more or less the reason why I told those guys who are pulling the wool over the eyes of the Russian people to go to hell. . . ."

His scorn for the Carlists doubtless stemmed from the fact that their ideals left over from an earlier age made them almost legendary figures. They had been convinced that they were waging a crusade, or something close to it, and therefore drank and fucked and killed with a sort of sacred fury. But at least they hadn't gone in for bureaucracy, endless lists of proscribed names, factionalism, and imperialist rhetoric, nor had they used religion as a cover-up for their eagerness to run the country (with them it was the other way around, in fact), nor had they been inclined to pass off acts of vengeance and plunder as a program of liberation during the struggle.

"For some strange reason, I hardly ever saw Falangists fighting in the front lines."

"Well, they died too—lots of them," I answered.

"That may well be—but not as many of them as they killed, behind the lines especially."

Ernesto had his own picture of the Spanish Civil War, and there wasn't anything or anybody who could make him change it. In order not to be obliged to retouch it, he usually refused to even talk about it. His loyalties were as deeply entrenched as the Republicans defending Madrid. He was not only proud to have been in Asturias, in Estremadura, in the Battle of the Ebro, and in Brunete; he also maintained that he felt privileged to have been in Madrid during the siege. Those days were an important part of his life and a rock-solid pillar of faith in his very brief personal credo. The Spanish Civil War to Ernesto was first and foremost a romantic crusade, and he fervently embraced everything that made him feel like a crusader.

"I was much more kindly disposed toward the Carlists."

"That's because you saw them in the front lines for the most part."

It was no use pressing the point. Ernesto had lived his novel in real life, and his novel in turn was simply a passionate reflection of his own personal experiences. María asks Robert Jordan if in the fighting the next day they are going to kill the Falangists who have cut off all her hair and shamelessly raped her, and Robert answers:

> "They do not fight. They kill at the rear. It is not them we fight in battle."

In Ernesto's eyes, the Spanish War had been full of acts of violence on the one hand and absurd bickering on the other, a tragedy and a farce, a mystique of terror and a violation of the dignity of the human person. In the last analysis, this was what the war had added up to. As if he had guessed what I was thinking, he said, "The ones who paid in the end were the Spanish people."

This was the same line of reasoning Robert Jordan had pursued when he wondered, in a moment of despair, whether there had ever been a people whose cruelest enemies were so obviously its own leaders.

But many years were to go by before Ernesto felt he could even hint at his real opinions, and at no time did he ever discuss the subject openly. When he was told that *For Whom the Bell Tolls* was being sold under the counter in Spain, like contraband drugs, he laughed, but he never joked about the Spanish situation in public.

I was sorry I couldn't discuss the war freely with him, but I always kept my ears open for whatever hints he might drop. And I was even sorrier now, that our dialogue had suddenly been broken off, forever.

There were a great many things that I had long been pondering and would have liked to discuss with him. Given the chance, Ernesto might have been willing to answer my questions someday during an intimate conversation. There had been countless things about his novel on the Spanish War that had attracted my attention, but I couldn't remember them now, or remembered them only vaguely. It had occurred to me, for instance, that Ernesto had tried to construct his novels as though they were plays, as though he were thinking more or less in terms of their effect on a stage. There were certain phrases in his fiction, for instance, that were reminiscent of bravura passages in plays that an audience will inevitably applaud. I don't think this was a deliberate trick on his part, but rather a sort of naïve searching for dramatic effect. If he had had any real talent as a playwright, he could never have written *The Fifth Column*.

The most notable theatrical, or perhaps cinematic, element of *For Whom the Bell Tolls* is his tendency to make his characters either all black or all white, as happens in even the very best of American novels, perhaps because of the influence of Westerns.

Ernesto's hero is always more or less an anti-hero. He cannot be defeated, of course, but he will nonetheless be demolished, crushed, undone. In this novel the hero is apparently saved, however, and what saves him—both at the beginning and at the end of his heroic endeavor—is love, a sudden, passionate, Hollywood sort of love, quite poetic but just a touch conventional; it is a passion that is decidedly carnal in the beginning, and deliberately so, but as it fuses with the ideological passion of the book, it passes from the romantic to the spiritual to the sublime. Ernesto's tremendous love for Spain made him forget all his theories about fictional protagonists, and the lack of heroism in this novel is compensated for by the ideological passions of the war and above all by the intense fervor of the characters, a fervor that wounds and personal derelictions cannot diminish. Robert Jordan decides to be reasonable and no longer play the hero, but he dies fighting. His only heroism lies in the fact that he is killed by the enemies of his ideal rather than going through with his decision to die by his own hand, an anguished, cowardly death. The moment when Jordan thinks back on his father's cowardly suicide makes him more human perhaps, but more importantly, it makes him a Hemingway character through and through.

The Spanish passion, with all its fury and all its skepticism, all its warmth and all its fatalism, is the insistent ground bass of the book, on which there are superimposed the sort of adventures common in American fiction. Author and protagonist alike are convinced that the only things of interest in life and in literature are the pleasures of the moment and personal sacrifice. How else could it have been in a country where revolution was waged in exactly the same spirit in which the bull and the matador fight to the death?

It is difficult to understand why there are a number of completely unauthentic details in a novel written with such a love of reality and in such a realistic style: the fact, for instance, that the peasant guerrillas do not take their clothes off at night, fearing that someone will steal them while they are asleep. In Castile, between Segovia and Ávila, among shepherds?

It is most unlikely that they would behave in this way, even in the middle of a civil war.

Another thing that bothered me was all the praying the characters in the novel do. In a guerrilla band of the sort that Hemingway depicts, it is highly improbable that there would have been a man like Joaquín, who begins with an Ave Maria and winds up with a *Señor Mío Jesucristo* every time he sees Fascist planes overhead. Anselmo also prays when he sees that El Sordo's group has been wiped out. Could Ernesto have included these prayers as a kind of counterpoint to the prayer of the Carlist lieutenant, Berrendo, later on in the book? Joaquín might conceivably mutter a prayer under his breath out of fear, but that Anselmo should pray for divine guidance in carrying out the orders of the foreign demolition expert strains belief. There is too much addressing Heaven, even though many prayers were said during the Spanish

Civil War. Those in the front lines prayed, those in the rear prayed, those in the jails on both sides prayed (some more than others), those who were about to be killed prayed, and sometimes even those who were about to kill prayed, or made their victims pray. But the most common sort of prayer on both sides during the Spanish Civil War was a blasphemous curse.

One day Ernesto said to me, as though to relieve his conscience, "I know you're a Catholic, and unlike me, you even go to mass. But I assure you I've given up all hope of finding any trace of the spirit of the gospel or of Christian charity in Spanish Catholicism."

"I know—it's not easy to find."

"Not easy! It'd almost be a miracle. Believing in the resurrection of the dead wouldn't be nearly as hard!"

I didn't say a word. I would have forgiven Ernesto anything. At heart he was a good, noble, sincere person, though admittedly vainglorious, shy, mixed up, and a bit of a liar sometimes, a man with almost unconquerable inner fears and anxieties. Even though deep down he had respected the Lord's will, he had gone to a coward's grave in the end. But in the back of his mind, hadn't he always harbored the vague idea that suicide was a courageous act? Even though, in the days when he was still sound of mind and body, he had not hesitated to call his own father a coward for killing himself?

I had sat down at a table in a sidewalk café. The waiter passed by several times without asking me what I wanted. I wondered how he knew I preferred to be left alone there under the stars, praying for my dear friend in my own way. Looking up at the sky made me feel as if I were witnessing God's judgment of His servant Ernesto, and I would have liked to think that He was not counting his suicide as an ineffaceable black mark against him. Surely it ought to count for something that Ernesto had always seemed a wonderfully decent, just, and even pious person.

There were still a few kids in the square chasing each other about and bursting into song from time to time. They should all have been home in bed at this hour. It was dinnertime, and I would have to find some place to get some solid food into my stomach.

I got up and suddenly crossed myself, as though the thoughts running through my mind had been a kind of prayer. I hurried down the street then, wondering what people who had seen me cross myself would think. They'd doubtless shake their heads and remark that there were all sorts of nuts in this world. And they'd be right on that score.

I would eat somewhere on my way home.

I don't know why, but suddenly I remembered Ernesto's many cats, and one of them in particular, Colón, a big tom as dignified as a university professor, who used to sit on Ernesto's shoulder at table. Had Ernesto taken Colón with him to Ketchum? One of his most horrifying stories is "The Natural History of the Dead," in which he first describes dead mules and then compares the death of soldiers on the battlefield to the way cats die:

> Others would die like cats; a skull broken in and iron in the brain, they lie alive two days like cats that crawl into the coal bin with a bullet in the brain and will not die until you cut their heads off. Maybe cats do not die then, they say they have nine lives. . . .

Nine lives? I remembered writing something about Ernesto having seven lives like a cat, at the time of the false bulletin announcing his death. And he had said: "Thanks, my friend; I've often thought about a cat's seven lives."

He had specifically mentioned *seven* lives—I remembered that very distinctly. In fact, I had said to myself at the time: "This man even knows the Spanish proverb about a cat's seven lives," and I decided I'd have to look up this passage later and see if he'd really said "nine." I would also have to think about all the rest of "The Natural History of the Dead," full of macabre words such as *decomposition, worms, death in bed*. And I mustn't forget the lines:

"I do not know, but most men die like animals, not men."

Like animals? Like mules, like cats?

"Like animals. Not men."

"Suffering is a bestial thing," he had said as we were waiting together while Ordóñez was being operated on.

A bestial thing? Also something more than that. Ernesto had written Juanito Quintana:

"Antonio has suffered a great deal—I've experienced quite a lot of pain myself, and I appreciate what he's going through—but he endures pain like a Cheyenne from the North country."

What had Ernesto's reaction been when Antonio Ordóñez had displayed his religious faith so openly after his brush with death?

Almost the only thing Ernesto had talked about in his last few letters was his health, as when he wrote:

"Everything has turned out very well for me too. I'm down to 200 lbs. now. And I must say I'm not in a rut. . . ."

"My eyes are very tired, though there may be something more serious the matter with them. I must have them checked and as soon as I finish this job I'll have to look after my health. . . ."

"I'm fine, better than when we last saw each other. But there are still a few things wrong internally, so I'm not in absolutely perfect health. But both of us are getting better all the time. . . ."

"I weigh 204 lbs., and my appetite is good. . . ."

"I'm as strong as a bull. . . ."

When he bared his torso or his biceps and displayed his scars; when he beat his chest or shadowboxed in his hotel room; when he crowned himself with grape leaves and got half tight and sang; when he walked in the hills, with his rifle at the ready, stepping carefully and holding his breath; when he plunged into a river and joyously splashed about like a mating shark; when the waiters and the country folk stood about in a noisy Castilian tavern or inn on some holiday, watching in openmouthed amazement as he downed gigantic meals; when he applauded his hero Antonio or a bull because he had been brave, or a mere *banderillero* for having come so close he almost grazed the bull's horns; when . . .

When he sent us that telegram saying that he would not be coming for the San Fermín fiesta, what was going through his mind? Some vague danger always seemed to threaten him; but he had a very special gift for keeping his friends from feeling depressed, and things were always lively when he was around. But hadn't he already made up his mind, or half made up his mind, to do what he did, when he sent that telegram? I could scarcely believe that he had pulled the trigger just when the San Fermín festival was beginning, at the very hour when the rockets opening the fiesta were being set off and the bulls were being let out of the stockade to run in the streets, that cloudless hour as clear as anisette, that darkly tragic hour as beautiful as wine sparkling in glasses and the ringing cry of young blood in the streets.

A short, pudgy man and a hollow-eyed, frightened-looking girl were necking furiously opposite the lions in front of the Congresso de Diputados, in the dark shadow of the little Cervantes Garden, a tiny plot of ground that serves as the symbolic tomb of the most famous but least-read writer in Spain.

Without offering my soul either to God or to the Devil, I entered the tumble-down building I had come to visit and headed up the stairs. A snarling cat fled to an inner courtyard.

It is horrible to see cats suffer (a subject that Ernesto had both written about and discussed at great length with me one night when he felt like staying up till all hours). Almost as horrible as seeing a man suffer after several long months of medical treatment. When you get out of the hospital, you're not the same man. You're like a cat in a dry well with smooth cement sides. . . .

How easy it was! The easiest thing in the world. At a moment when your mind is temporarily clouded, you grab the lion-hunting rifle, you assume a dignified position, and you pull the trigger. What happened next? Or, for that matter, had anything happened after that? There was a very loud noise, as if a door had fallen flat on the pavement. And the person who might have been able to tell you what had happened next couldn't say a word now, couldn't tell you if he had realized what had happened between the instant he squeezed the trigger and the blinding instant that immediately followed, like a great red flash of light. Perhaps committing suicide is easier than we think. Have you ever seen the way a dove dies when you hold its head under water? Or a rabbit when you cut its innocent little head off? Or a horse when the bull gores it and it takes a deep, deep breath? Or a bull, when the enormous pupils of its eyes reflect the white handkerchiefs waving and the women's rouge as it slowly sinks to its knees in the sand of the bullring? And a *torero*, who unerringly puts his hand right over the mortal wound, and on seeing the great red stain can still say, "It's only a little blood!" Why spend so much time thinking about what it is like to die, of the cold and the sweat that cling to the soul, of the absurd emptiness that steals over you like the sun setting on a planet made of snow? The whole trick is to squeeze the trigger, that fang of death, very, very gently (there is no need to squeeze it hard), more or less as you would jokingly embrace an old whore, that hideous old trollop whom you feel an urge to fuck despite her ugliness, because you realize the moment you see her that she's fucked you before, perhaps in some other, previous life now long forgotten . . .

According to the nameplates downstairs, there were two *pensiones*, or rather one private apartment and a *pensión*. The stairs creaked mournfully and so did the banister when I grabbed hold of it. The whole building was ancient, filthy dirty, stinking. I lit a cigarette and was startled by my own shadow projected on the wall.

But I had made up my mind. I would have to go through with this sometime. It was as if the dead man had left me specific tasks to do. And I would be forced to carry them out—as though they were military orders.

On one of the landings, I met two nuns whispering to each other as they hurried down the stairs. I was about to murmur a polite "Good evening," but they did what nuns always do: they rushed past me, crossing themselves.

This was strange, because if they were nursing sisters coming to spend the night at the bedside of someone who was ill, they would be entering the building, not leaving it. Or maybe they were the day shift. In any case, it was no hour for nuns to be out on the streets. In the dim light on the stairway I could see that one of them, the older one, had a mole on her cheek with hairs growing out of it and a complexion that was the same sallow, waxen color as a church taper. The other one, a squat, plump creature, had the face and the bearing of a sprightly peasant girl. If she stumbled on the stairs, I was certain, she would roll to the bottom like an apple.

On one of the landings there was a little, triangular bench against the wall, and I sat down to plan the visit I was about to make. I'll ring the bell and somebody will come to the door, I said to myself. And I'll say, very calmly: "I'd just like to have a look around." And before they answer, I'll add: "With your permission, of course." They may be taken aback by that. So the best thing to do then would be to show them the newspaper with the photograph and say something like: "Don't you recognize me?" And modestly add: "You may have seen my picture in the papers before." And if they're still suspicious, I can say: "Yes, I've been photographed a number of times with this great friend of Spain. When he or I came from America. When they gave me that prize I've already eaten up." . . . I just wanted to find out a few things, to see if I could turn up anybody who had known him when he was still a nobody, or almost a nobody. Little by little I would reconstruct his past. I would interview everyone, from the small fry who hung around the bullrings to the doctors who had treated him and any of his comrades from the days of the siege of Madrid. His closest friend from those days might be Heaven only knew where now, an employee in an insurance agency or a scientific publishing company or a barman in a big hotel or even the owner of a chain of cafeterias. I already knew who some of these people were, and it would be an interesting project to gather unpublished firsthand data. So that some day we Spaniards might be able to erect a monument to him that would be worthy of him, not a monument in bronze or marble, not a monument of hollow, false words, but something beautiful, something worthy of him because it is spare and simple.

"Well, let's get on with the *corrida*—this looks like quite a bull," I said to myself, getting to my feet.

I knocked at one of the doors. Nobody answered. I knocked twice more and a blond woman with very white skin, as though it were powdered with flour, finally came to the door. She had a newspaper in her hand, open to the page with a photo of Ernesto in a sweatshirt. As I peeked through the door, I saw a number of girls scamper down the hall like frisky young goats.

I was a little flustered, but said in the most dignified tone of voice that I could muster: "Could you tell me if this has always been a *pensión*?"

"I beg your pardon? Are you Nieves's father, by any chance?"

"Isn't this a *pensión*?"

"Have you ever received a card from us?"

102

"I thought this was a boardinghouse."

The woman, whose face looked like rice pudding with red pepper in it, scowled and slammed the door in my face.

"Listen, Señora."

Overcome with curiosity, she opened the door a crack and said through pouting lips, "Try upstairs."

Before I could even thank her, she slammed the door in my face again. But as I walked down the hall to the stairs, the door opened once more and I heard her mutter, in a voice like a witch casting a spell, "Why don't you ask the night watchman?"

The night watchman? Was it that late already? I went up several more flights of rickety, dimly lit stairs. The banister kept swaying—and not because I was tight. I had trouble finding the doorbells in the gloom, and rang every one I found.

One door opened finally and immediately slammed shut again, like a sudden earthquake. I stood there stammering, "Listen, listen . . ."

Someone inside laughed uproariously. I looked through a crack in the door and was dumfounded: A woman wearing a tunic with yellow butterflies on it was waltzing around and around at the end of the corridor, where I could see a dreadful sketch of Sancho Panza with an earthen jar in his hand.

Was this the place Ernesto had told me about? If I had seen a couple of priests in the hallway—Galician priests, of course—I would have been sure I was in the right place.

Ernesto had first visited Spain in 1922, and then for a longer time in 1923. He had lived here in the Carrera de San Jerónimo in a *pensión*. I was certain of that. It was hardly likely, of course, that the very bed he had slept in was still in one of the bedrooms, or his own chair still in the dining room after so many years and a civil war—but stranger things have happened, and I stood there not knowing what to think. I could still hear people laughing inside.

But there was one more floor above, so I climbed the last flight of stairs. It was pitch black on the top floor, and I groped my way toward the door inch by inch; I could hear music, but I didn't know if it was a radio or someone playing an instrument, perhaps a clarinet. I knocked, and the music stopped. After a while, I heard footsteps, and finally a man came to the door with a surprised look on his face and an odd-looking trumpet in his hand.

"I'm sorry," he said, inviting me in with a wave of his hand. "I've been waiting for you for quite a while, and since you hadn't shown up, I began practicing. If you don't mind, we'll talk here," he said, turning the light on in a little room whose walls were plastered with diplomas and photographs of people who obviously were long dead and buried.

"I beg your pardon," I managed to whisper.

"I'm the one who should apologize," he said, pointing to a thread-bare, red armchair.

But I just stood there at a loss for words, and then, finally, I said, "I think you might be able to help me. I'd be very much obliged if you'd tell me how many years you've lived here."

"What a strange question! Why do you want to know?"

"I'm a newspaper reporter."

"A newspaper reporter? Well, I'll be damned!" he exclaimed, tapping his foot impatiently.

"I'm a journalist and writer and I'm trying to find out if you or any-one else in the building can give me some information about the *pensión* that used to be here some forty years ago . . ."

"You mean you're not the man who phoned me about bombardon lessons?"

"No, sir."

"Well, sir, in that case you're wasting my time, and time is taking me to my grave," he said, tapping his foot again.

But he looked like a kind man.

"Let me explain. I want to see if I can find out more about Ernesto Hemingway, who committed suicide on Sunday, as you may have heard. He lived here in this building. . . . And I just wanted to know if . . ."

This gaunt man with protruding Adam's apple and prominent cheek-bones above side whiskers, turned paler and paler, then suddenly col-lapsed on the floor and lay there doubled over. I pulled at his arm, say-ing over and over: "Señor, please! What's wrong? I'm right here. Please, Señor, what's the matter?" But he just lay there with his bombardon be-side him, looking as though he were about to breathe his last.

I confess that at that point I proved to be both a coward and a heart-less wretch, because I ran out of the room and down the stairs as fast as my legs would carry me. I made such a racket I was surprised that none of the tenants so much as looked out their doors to see what was hap-pening, but the very fact that they didn't, made me scramble down the stairs all the faster.

As I rushed out the door, I bumped into a man with a musical instru-ment under his arm. I hoped he'd go straight upstairs. I crossed over to the sidewalk opposite, hoping no one was following me, and kept cau-tiously glancing back at the balconies as I made my way down the street.

I reached Zorilla just as the Jesuit priests were closing the church on the corner. I went in one door and out another.

Then I reluctantly made my way back to the building, more or less prepared to climb all those stairs again, but also feeling a strong urge to take to my heels and make myself scarce. I crossed the street and stood in the doorway of the building again. I had just remembered that Ernesto had once confessed that he was not very devout but thought the Jesuits were a good bunch.

"Why in the world do you say that?" I had asked him.

"There are moments in life when you feel like becoming a Trappist monk, just as sometimes you feel like pulling up stakes altogether because you're in people's way or because you belong somewhere else. . . . I don't know if . . . you . . . have any idea what I'm talking about." And then he added: "It's all quite clear in my own mind, though. One lifetime is all we have to get ourselves a pretty good reputation, if not a brilliant one, and you have to fight the bulls you get when the lots are drawn."

Then he said, "The Jesuits are dangerous and have lots of power, you know."

"I know. I have close relatives who are Jesuits, but they don't seem to have much pull—or maybe they're such good souls they've never tried to have any."

"They tell me there's another type of Jesuit that's much more corrupt, though." And when he saw the surprised look on my face, he added, "What's all this business about the Opus Dei, anyway?"

"To tell you the truth, I have no idea," I answered.

"Are they really all that secretive?"

"So much so that probably most of the members of the movement don't know what it's all about."

"I've always thought Spanish religious life was more like a *corrida* than a circus. I admire their fervor. I even have a certain liking for those tough-minded Spanish Inquisitors who spoke and wrote in tongues of fire. That's also why I admire Loyola and his followers. I have much less respect for people who are mealymouthed."

He fell silent for a moment and sat there eying me, and then he went on: "I don't know anything about all that, and I don't want to know anything, but I don't mind telling you that Loyola is okay in my book. And I can tell you that I needed the Jesuits once—really needed them, though I won't tell you why. It was a life-and-death matter to me, though. And they were right there when I needed them. Yes, they were right there on the spot, and they haven't ever mentioned the debt I owe them, or the one they owe me. They were very decent to me"—and Ernesto put his finger to his lips to indicate that he wasn't going to say one more word. He'd gotten what he wanted to tell me off his chest. It would be a long time before I heard any more about this incident, and perhaps I never would. I was amazed. Who would ever have suspected that Ernesto had some idea of what troublemakers the members of our very Spanish secret society were? What sort of human mystery was at the bottom of his relations with the Company of Jesus or the intervention of some Jesuit on his behalf? Did he dislike the Opus Dei because of specific things he had been told about it, or was his hatred of what it stood for instinctive?

One day someone had come to Ernesto and told him a pack of lies about me, the worst one being that I was both a member of Opus Dei and a devoted follower of Ruiz-Jiménez, the anti-Franco liberal leader— as if those two horses of a very different color could ever be yoked together. Many Spaniards had such a false picture of Hemingway that they thought they could break up our friendship by telling him things like that—the sort of people who were convinced he was a rabid atheist, a destroyer of churches, a fanatic unbeliever. How little they knew him! He was not only an uncommonly religious man, although not a church-goer, but also had the greatest respect for other people's sincere religious beliefs.

"I think you're very brave to be a Catholic. I'm one too, but a pretty lukewarm one—I don't take it very seriously," he said to me one day.

And seeing the surprised look on my face, he added: "I'm not kidding. I really am a Catholic, though I never say so publicly and don't like to talk about it. . . . And I don't want you to tell anybody either."

"Don't worry—I won't say a word."

I did tell my wife, however, and swore her to secrecy. Ernesto and I had had that conversation in 1956, and I found out during our visit to Pamplona in 1959 that he'd been telling the truth. (More about this later.)

The watchman appeared, and the two musicians were out on the balcony now, one of them running about like a madman and the other looking down with the bombardon in his hand.

I stole away inconspicuously, and went into the Casa Manolo, opposite the Teatro de la Zarzuela. There was hardly anyone in the place. The waiter came over and, without my even asking, set a bottle of miraculous Valdepeñas wine in front of me. Then he said to me, almost reproachfully, "Well, what's it going to be?"

"A bull."

"Dead or alive?"

"Alive, very much alive."

"Horns and all?"

"Without horns, if possible."

"We have some very nice filets tonight."

"Some nice filets, you say? What I really would like is a trout, perhaps one of those nice fat ones that the friars of El Paular pull out of their sleeves. Could I have a nice Navarrese trout instead of one of your very nice filets? Eating a trout from Navarre is a sort of promise I've made myself—in honor of a friend of mine who can't be here to eat one with me."

"Is your friend a long way from here?"

"Quite far away."

"Doubtless there aren't any trout streams where he is."

"I'm not really sure, but my guess is that there isn't a single trout stream where my friend is right now."

"He must be quite far away, then."

"Oh, yes indeed. About as far away as you can get from here."

"How do you know there aren't any trout streams there?"

"There may be some. Maybe that's why my friend went so far away— he might have been trying to find one. He was always hunting for new ones."

"Was he that fond of trout?"

"He liked them as much as he did bulls, and that's saying a lot."

The waiter went off shaking his head.

Weren't there any trout in France? Of course there were. But what he liked best was Navarrese trout—the only ones as good as bulls. While Hadley spent her time playing stringed instruments and singing like a nightingale from heaven, Ernesto went trout fishing and saw his first bullfight. And bulls became his lord and master and trout fishing a pastime that allowed him to think.

And always there was Spain: always the same fascination, the same terrible temptation.

Ernesto's first visits to Spain marked him forever. He never forgot arriving in Spain and going about the streets without the least idea of what was going on, nosing about cautiously, not so much because of his limited budget but because he was afraid, keeping an eye peeled for guys like the bombardon player who might have a razor on them, being wary of girls who had carnations in their hair and syphilis too, perhaps. Ernesto went all over Spain, very much on his guard at first, then with much more self-confidence, and finally, once he had become a disciple of the art of bullfighting, with more or less an outright devil-may-care swagger. In the beginning, he may have thought of Spain as simply a quiet place for a vacation, but later it got into his blood and he was eager to spend more and more time there.

"I felt I was a fool for going back, but I stood in line with my passport," Jake Barnes confesses.

What a rough time Ernesto had had in those days when he was timid and wary but determined to come back! Spain was like an offering on the altar of a barbarous and magic God. Naturally he never went to fashionable cocktail parties and didn't hang around with bigwigs; his haunts were little inns and winding back streets. He arrived in Spain at a critical time, but he never mixed with intellectuals and never got caught up in political or aesthetic quarrels. When he went to the Congress or the old headquarters of the Socialist Party or the Ciudad Universitaria, it was only as a sort of sedative after the tense hours in the *plaza de toros*. But the place where he felt most at home and most stimulated was always the Prado Museum.

The word Madrid made him tingle with excitement.

"We'll be seeing each other soon there. As soon as I give this thing I'm writing the *coup de grâce*."

"I'm sure you'll finish it off in great style."

"I may have lost a little of my touch, but not all of it. This is just the beginning."

He probably couldn't have killed himself in Spain, or in Havana either. There were too many memories there for a sentimentalist like Ernesto. The one place he could do the deed was in Ketchum, a cold, neutral zone where he had no guardian angel, a spot to which he had no strong emotional attachment. The doctors had warned him: "You mustn't do anything strenuous; you mustn't read or write or let yourself get upset. . . ." Hot soup, but no garlic in it. Trout, but no ham with it. Lemonade and orangeade and Coca-Cola, but no alcohol. The doctors had insisted that he mustn't drink, or eat big meals, or fuck, but it was madness to forbid a man like Ernesto, whose whole life and work were built around such things, to indulge in them.

I looked through the evening papers. How pale, how pointless, how ridiculous all the pieces about Ernesto were, including my own, which disconcerted me and made me blush when I read it. The reporters had fulfilled their assignment by reeling off a whole lot of nonsense: they called him a citizen of the world, a Madrileño by adoption; they made a big thing of his having offered his Nobel Prize to Don Pío Baroja; they made ideological propaganda out of his visits to Spain, passing him off as a sinner who had repented of his misdeeds, or a convert; they repeated *ad nauseam* that success had come very easily to him and life had continually smiled on him.

Ernesto needed Spain more and more, and that was why he kept coming back. I'm almost certain that if he had come back in 1961—as he had wanted to, though he never made it—he would have found it very hard to leave, and I think he would have stayed. And I repeat: he wouldn't have killed himself here. All his jokes about Ordóñez being his partner in business ("We started being partners or *socios* in 1956. The real basis of this business relationship was that I would look after the book end of the business and he would handle the bull end") and other jokes about going into the real estate business on the Costa del Sol and selling property to tourists betrayed a more or less subconscious desire to settle down in Spain, to make it his *querencia*, as when the bull chooses the spot in the ring where he wants to die even though he is still prepared to lunge left and right with his horns and share his death with others. . . . Ernesto felt full of vitality and was still very self-confident when he was in Spain in 1959, as he had not been for a long time in Havana and certainly not in his own country. Spain was no longer a trench to hole up in for self-protection, but a reserved seat for the work of creation.

"How's Paris, Ernesto?" I had asked him.

"I'm beginning to be fed up with it."

"I can't believe it."

"Neither can I, but it's true."

"You carry Paris around with you in your mind."

"Yes, but I have Spain in my blood."

"What about London?"

"The one unforgettable memory I have of London is Mary. And a war where I got to know a few bloody strategists all too well, and met up with the worst pedants I've ever had to deal with in my entire life."

"You don't say! You must have run into quite a few of them in Spain."

"I sure did! But everything comes in giant sizes in Spain: the biggest criminal, the biggest coward, the biggest traitor, the biggest fanatic, the biggest idealist, the biggest saint, the biggest madman—they're all the real article, whatever they are. That's why you can measure how much of a tyrant or a liberal, how gutless or how brave you really are when you come to Spain."

Everything was quite simple to Ernesto. A glass of wine was only a glass of wine, but it could be drunk both to cheer yourself up when you were depressed or to sober yourself up when you were dizzy with happiness.

One day I asked him, as one writer to another, "What do you mean when you say in *The Sun Also Rises* that 'the Norte station in Madrid is the end of the line'?"

"Did I say that?"

And he had to go look the passage up, because he was very proud of being as accurate as the clock in the bullring. When he wrote those words, Ernesto had seen only the North of Spain. He had never been to the South, to Andalusia, and I'm fairly sure he had had a certain prejudice against it. (And on his visits to the South in recent years his stays in that part of Spain were no longer spent at a humble inn along the wayside but on an elegant country estate.) Fortunately he began to be acquainted with "torrid Spain" when he went to Valencia, that city bubbling over with life, early in the twenties, one summer when he was following the *toreros* around the bullfight circuit. He tagged along with them as though he were just another lowly matador's *peón*, but instead of carting around sword cases and a chest full of bullfighting capes, he carried a schoolchild's composition book around with him wherever he went, for in it he was doggedly scribbling the rough draft of his first novel, having begun it both with certain misgivings as to his gifts as a novelist and with great expectations.

Valencia had brought angry tears to his eyes when he came back there in 1936, during the Civil War. It was the city in *For Whom the Bell Tolls* where Pilar and the bullfighter Finito had made passionate love twenty-four hours a day in a little room with a balcony overlooking the beach, with a cold pitcher of beer close at hand, because diligent fornicating makes you both thirsty and hungry; they spent several days there that were like a dream because they hardly ever left the room except to go down to the sandy beach to watch the oxen drag the boats up out of the water. It was Ernesto's own experiences he was describing, of course. And Valencia was also the place where Ernesto, like Pilar, discovered many new pleasures, such as stuffing himself with prawns fresh from the sea, sprinkled with lime juice, the place where he first ate strips of huge red peppers, the biggest ones he had ever seen, the place where for the first time he had his fill of garlic and onions and fucking and all the rest. . . . He told me once:

"If you wanted to get the clap the easy way, all you had to do was visit Valencia; it was one of the roughest cities in the world."

Those were the golden years in Ernesto's life. He remembered the smell of burned powder from the *feria* firecrackers, and the eels dripping with oil:

> . . . as tiny as bean sprouts and curled in all directions and so
> tender they disappeared in the mouth without chewing.

And paella in its saffron splendor, full of bits of seafood, was a messenger from the Valencian sun that turned the swamplands into a torrid, shimmering haze, and the crayfish made you want desperately to fondle the breasts of young girls.

Valencia was more or less where Ernesto became a man. The youngster who had been awakened to his virility by the bulls in Pamplona and awakened to sex in this Mediterranean city now experienced his maleness to the fullest, for his previous experiences had been those of the adolescent, tumbling girls in the grass under the sheltering trees and on the lakeshores, little storybook peccadillos, not grave, biblical sins. Even though war had sunk its huge talons not only into his back but into his very guts, it had never made him experience the sort of boundless frenzy that can consume a man when he makes passionate love.

"Do you know what's really great after you've burned yourself out in bed with a woman?" he said to me once.

"A glass of wine," I answered.

"That's not bad, but two big slices of melon and half a dozen or maybe even a dozen tangerines are even better."

(". . . We made love in the room with the strip wood blinds hanging over the balcony and a breeze through the opening of the top of the door which turned on hinges. We made love there, the room dark in the day time from the hanging blinds, and from the streets there was the scent of the flower market and the smell of burned powder from the firecrackers . . . ," he had Pilar say in *For Whom the Bell Tolls*.)

"I could *really* eat and drink in those days!" Ernesto exclaimed.

I burst out laughing, and as often happened, Ernesto answered with a laugh that began as a deep rumbling chuckle and ended in a wild, uproarious guffaw. His laughter was sometimes as disconcerting as a madman's.

The trout still hadn't arrived. Maybe they'd really gone to El Paular for it. I got up from the table and headed for the door. What, if anything, was playing at the Teatro de la Zarzuela?

But at that moment the waiter came with the trout, as hot as a passionate marquise whose husband stays up till all hours poring over his books on heraldry, archaeology, numismatics, or such other damsels as he has not yet deflowered. My sexy trout would soon get cold, though, so I lifted up its beautiful bright sides and immediately found the ham hidden inside. How nice and warm the trout was, how delicious it smelled—and it tasted just as good. It slid down my throat like butter.

"I'd like a salad, please," I said to the waiter.

Ernesto detested metaphysical arguments and high-flown philosophical discussions that force you to carry on the conversation with an absolutely blank look in your eye and bleat like a young ram dreaming of mounting a ewe. He had little time for class or caste distinctions either. So he would sleep with a little black girl if he happened to feel like it, though he had a few scruples about it afterward, and would refuse to have anything to do with big tycoons, diplomats, and aristocrats if they didn't measure up to his standards.

I was now out on the pavement again, remembering how Ernesto used to stride down the streets of the city, like a dignified caretaker solemnly treading the tiled floor of a mausoleum for gods with their heads blown off. The pavement in Madrid is as shiny as a mirror, and once you've seen blood shed on it you never forget it. And you never forget the blood shed every afternoon in the bullring, or the blood shed in the trenches during a civil war. . . .

Dear Ernesto:

I don't know if you know that my body still can't draw breath, much less my soul.

You were always such a painstaking man—even when you seemed to be doing things in the most haphazard way, on the spur of the moment—and you have rounded off the last paragraph like the most finical prose stylist. You have deliberately, conscientiously, responsibly contrived to hammer home the nail that had been partially driven into you and stood quivering between your chest and your shoulder.

Very well. What else could you have done? Retire and live on your income? You may claim that the balance sheet had already been drawn up or that your cup of bitterness was full to overflowing, or that the *corrida* was over. But, dear Ernesto, you left one thing still only half done. There's one question you haven't answered at all: Is killing yourself a good thing to do? Is it a sovereign, free act? Or is it a disgraceful, fumbling miscalculation by a person who holds himself straight and tall in the presence of others until one day he suddenly allows them to glimpse his hopeless demoralization?

At the cost of great effort and endless patience you won a triumphant victory over stale, artificial writing and renewed the art of storytelling, but you paid for it with your life, and this aesthetic victory, this heroic victory bore no relation to your ethical values or even to your most heartfelt human values. What I mean by that is that even though you carefully concealed the fact, you were basically a man in terrible despair—and always had been. Wasn't it despair—not metaphysical despair but despair at life itself—that lay at the very core of your existence, that trapped you in a narrow well shaft with no handholds? The fact is, my dear Ernesto, that just as you contrived to transform your reckless, chaotic, strife-ridden life into a work of art, thereby concealing the fact that it was a shameful, headlong escape, so too your death has a grandeur about it that makes us fail to see it for what it really is. . . . The counterpart of the Nebuchadnezzar with feet of clay is the giant with a burlap heart.

I said all this aloud as I walked along, and more than one passerby stared at me. But I was more astonished than any of them, because in the space of just a few hours my thoughts had spun around and around like a carpenter's drill, and the untouchable majesty that this very same figure had had in my mind early that morning was now beginning to seem seriously flawed.

I went back down the street behind the Palacio de las Cortes, and when I reached the *pensión* building again, I saw that the two men had disappeared from the balcony. I suddenly remembered Ernesto crossing the tiny little square nearby in four long strides. You almost had to run to keep up with him.

"Ernesto, how did you manage to make ends meet when you lived here?" I had asked him.

"I barely managed to stay alive. I wrote articles, just as you're doing today, and most of the ones on bullfighting got published, though not all of them."

"Would you have liked being a *torero*? And is it true that you saved John Dos Passos from getting gored in Pamplona around 1924?"

"When you know as much as the bull—or more—it isn't easy. I lived up there in that *pensión* for several months. They called me *"el inglé"*— the Englishman. I had a really rough go of it sometimes, but the *pensión* was cheap and there were always people from the "bullfighting world" staying there. The place was a real melting pot, because among the boarders there were not only *picadores* and *banderilleros* and students and chorus girls, but also priests and fairies. I'd come in with the newspaper under my arm, and everybody in the dining room would immediately start whispering, 'Here comes *el inglé!*' 'The *inglé* has just arrived!' 'What a sourpuss that *inglé* is!' I think it was mostly the students who were responsible for all the fuss—they were always trying to stir up some sort of trouble. They gave me a hard time, but I kept my mouth shut. I didn't say a word for days on end, because I needed to pick up a vocabulary in Spanish, dirty words especially. They're the most expressive—Spanish is such a colorful language."

"Did you write that article for *Esquire* about dirty words in Spanish while you were staying in that *pensión?*"

"Yes, though I have to admit I pulled a few punches when I translated them into English."

"I can't tell you how upset people get about dirty words here in Spain."

"They do in my country too. Well, anyway, I lived up there with the whole lot of them, boning up on dirty words. They all talked a mile a minute, laughing and joking and making fun of everything. Some of them were pretty annoying. But the whole experience was invaluable to me. They talked about everything under the sun. What shocked me most was that they said really terrible things about priests, even though they were Catholics. None of them had the least respect for the most sacred things. I've never been like that myself—do you know why?

Because I've always avoided getting mixed up with this whole God business. . . ."

After a moment's pause, he went on: "They talked about bullfighting from dawn till dark and said lots of things that were really stupid. One night when somebody made a dirty crack about a *torero*, I couldn't stand it any longer and started pounding on the table and shouting: "I'll shit on the mother of anybody who dares repeat that, and if he doesn't take it back, I'll tell him to his face that he's a whoring son of a bitch."

"Those were your very words?"

"Yep. Nobody let out so much as a peep. There wasn't a sound in the room—like when the matador goes in for the kill. I was standing there in front of all the tables, so mad I could hardly see straight. I'd been drinking, but so had they. Then I kicked a chair over and shouted: "Nobody with any balls would tell a joke like that . . . you're all a bunch of yellow-bellied cowards. . . ." Nobody said a word. Then I yelled in an even louder voice, "That *torero* you're talking about is a friend of mine!"

He told me then that the bullfighter they'd been running down was Niño de la Palma. (It was okay for Ernesto to call him a coward, but nobody else had the right to.)

"Have you ever told Antonio that story?"

"No. Why should I? But I can assure you that when those wretches saw me standing there shouting at the top of my lungs, they thought I'd lost my mind. One of them, the loudmouth who'd gotten me mad in the first place, kept saying: "Listen, didn't you say he was an *inglé?* He's an *inglé* and he sounds just like my uncle in Granada!"

"It was a smart move."

"It certainly was! From that day on, they were very polite to me. In fact, some of them were almost too polite, which might have made me get mad all over again, except that I realized they were just trying to stay on their best behavior. You can't imagine how well-mannered they were all of a sudden: "Good morning, Señor," "Good evening, Señor," "I hope you enjoy your dinner," "May you sleep well." As I remember, that was where I first began to discover that Spain has both its good side and its bad side."

"That's not news to *me*, my friend."

"The whole secret is knowing when to talk and when to keep your mouth shut, keeping your eyes peeled, fucking or getting fucked at just the right moment."

"You've described two Galician priests in that *pensión*, haven't you? Hiding in a corner gorging themselves . . . and handing out advice."

"I've never hung around with priests. I think it's bad luck."

But I remembered a passage in one of his works that had made a great impression on me, since I'd been brought up on *The Lives of the Martyrs*. In *For Whom the Bell Tolls* someone says to Pablo after the priest has been brutally murdered in the village massacre:

> "You didn't like it about the priest?" because I knew he hated priests even worse than he hated fascists.
> "He was a disillusionment to me," Pablo said sadly.
>
> "I thought you hated priests."
> "Yes," said Pablo and cut some more bread. "But a *Spanish* priest. A *Spanish* priest should die very well."
> "I think he died well enough," I said. "Being deprived of all formality."
> "No," Pablo said. "To me he was a great disillusionment. All day I had waited for the death of the priest. . . . I expected something of a culmination. I had never seen a priest die."

Apparently the death of the Spanish *padre* had not been as exemplary as his executioner thought it should have been.

What was most admirable about Ernesto was that he never considered himself an oracle. He spoke in the name of no person and no cause, and when he looked upon himself as a great destroyer you could only feel sorry for him.

As I remember, that day we went to the bar of the Hotel Palace after that, for some reason. The place was full of foreigners who knew him and came over to say hello. He exchanged a few words with all of them, but then he suddenly became very distant and stood there at the bar counter talking for a moment with the waiters, lost in a world of his own, his shoulders slightly hunched over and a lock of gray hair falling over his forehead. I remember all that quite well, and I also remember that later he had stood there joking with a Cuban friend about a tube of pills that the latter had just given him and trading dirty jokes with him, without even introducing me. But when the man left, Ernesto had turned to me and said, "That stupid idiot's going to land in jail."

I decided to drop in at the bar at the Palace. But it was very dark and gloomy in there, or at least it seemed so to me. I didn't even bother to exchange a few words with the waiters.

I said to myself: "Why not go talk to the night watchman?" I had been nosing about the building like a criminal who can't resist returning to the scene of the crime. The classic writers tell us that even in summer the breezes in Madrid are soft and delicately perfumed, but there was nothing classical about this night. The air was dead and stifling.

Bunches of young girls kept entering the foyer of the building. How odd! They looked like respectable enough young ladies. Moreover, I had seen two nuns leaving the place earlier in the evening. The night watchman hadn't appeared to let these girls in yet, and they were standing there cackling like hens. The watchman finally came lumbering along, pounding his pike on the pavement, and unlocked the door for them. It was obvious that the bullfight crowd of Ernesto's day and their successors had moved on to the Hotel Victoria, and that this one-time hangout of people from the bullring had been converted into a residence hall for decent young ladies, half-decent ones, and perhaps a few who weren't decent at all, because there is room for all kinds in the vineyards of the Lord.

A whole bunch of stupid-looking, obviously well-heeled tourists were coming up the street from the Hotel Palace, laughing very loudly. They had every right to, of course. Though it's quite true that Americans never lack for anything, it's also true that they pay a higher price for everything than anybody else, including getting fucked. So they had a perfect right to laugh louder than anybody else. One of them came over to me and asked me what the building with the lions was. I told him that it was the Pantheon of Illustrious Men. He was very impressed, and thanked me effusively for the information. A few minutes later the street was almost deserted again. After thinking the matter over carefully, and screwing up my courage—because night watchmen can be as humble as field flowers or as prickly as thistles, depending on which way the wind is blowing—I asked this one, "Do you know if this building has always been a *pensión?*"

"The people who live here are decent sorts, I'll tell you that right now."

"Oh, I'm sure they are. I just wanted to ask you whether you knew if it used to be a boardinghouse that took in *toreros* and all sorts of people, even priests."

The watchman looked me up and down, and finally said, "I think you may have the wrong building."

"That's quite possible."

"I can't answer your question, because I've only been here since last Saturday. My friend the regular night watchman got a bad case of typhoid swimming in the Manzanares and I'm *supplementing* him here."

I gave him a tip, mostly because of that fancy last word of his: *suplimentándole*. It wasn't going to be easy to get information about Ernesto's first stay in Madrid in those years when what he wanted most in the world was to come to Spain. He'd decided that, after a conversation with Gertrude Stein ("Lard-Ass," as he used to call her behind her back) in the course of which she had shown him a photograph of herself sitting in the front row at the bullring in Valencia with Joselito and El Gallo standing down below. Her urging him to go to Spain was the best advice anyone ever gave him in his life. And his amazement when he first set eyes on the capital of Spain ("and the world") was rather like the shock a greenhorn gets the first time he walks down a street lined with bordellos.

I remembered a passage in *The Sun Also Rises:*

"Did I want to stay myself in person in the Hotel Montana?"
Of that as yet I was undecided, but it would give me pleasure
if my bags were brought up from the ground floor in order that
they might not be stolen.

All tourists, American ones especially, have always tempted Spaniards to take up thievery as a full-time occupation, and when Ernesto first arrived in Madrid, he kept feeling his breast pocket to make sure his wallet was still there. He was in the Court of Miracles at last, and all around him were the marvelous sights described by the classic authors: "The Oratory of Heaven," "The Prosperous Metropolis of the Scepter and the Plough."

On the next corner was another night watchman, who looked as though he might be better informed. This one was making the pavement and the sidewalk shake as he strode down the street with his pike.

"Does the name 'Hotel Montana' mean anything to you?" I asked him.

"Montana, Montana . . . No, I don't remember any place by that name."

"There was a 'Hotel Montana' somewhere around here. I think it was that building over there," I said, pointing. "It was a *pensión* where all sorts of people lived—*toreros*, students, priests, soldiers . . ."

"Montana, Montana. The only name like that I remember is the Montaña Barracks."

I gave him another *duro*, though what I really felt like giving him was a kick in the pants. I definitely recalled Ernesto writing, "Nothing was ever stolen in the Hotel Montana. In other fondas, yes. Not there. No."

Maybe Ernesto had forgotten the *tilde* and meant the Hotel Montaña. But he always pronounced that ñ sound right in the words *coño* and *puñeta*.

But what interested me most was Ernesto's personal reminiscences about the place. They were not simply the fleeting memories of a reporter passing through town. I remembered very well what he had told me:

"That's where I was baptized a Madrileño."

"In other words, a Christian," I had said jokingly.

"No, I was a Christian before I came here, and I've been one ever since. But not an 'old Christian,' as you Spaniards once called people who were born in the faith. I'm one of those Christians who are direct descendants of that great crab-eater, John the Baptist—the one whose head got offered on a platter to that old fairy Herod, like a delicious deep-sea crab."

It wasn't easy following Ernesto's trail, but his stay in the Hotel Montana was really an unimportant little detail. I wondered what sort of information I would turn up if instead of going to the Africa bush to see what the lions and the rhinoceroses had to say about him, I could explore Marlene Dietrich's memories and feelings, or Ava Gardner's. To do a good job of it, I would also have to track down an anti-Fascist guerrilla somewhere, if there was one still alive, and hear what he had to say, and I would have to go to Havana and talk with the fishermen and the mysterious habitués of the Floridita. I'd also have to go to the Casa Botín, which Ernesto had described as "one of the best restaurants in the world." But to go there, I'd have to have a wallet with a little more folding money in it. You really can't order a calf's head or roast lamb or suckling pig without ordering a good wine to go with it.

". . . We ate roast young suckling pig and drank *rioja alta* . . . I ate a very big meal and drank three bottles of *rioja alta*," Ernesto had written in *The Sun Also Rises*.

"A meal there now is a disaster," he had said to me the last time he was in Madrid.

"Has Spanish cuisine slid that far downhill?"

"No, that's not it at all. The place has gotten terribly crowded. There's always a whole raft of tourists there, like a plague of locusts, and they immediately pull out a folder of traveler's checks."

I would have to go to Casa Botín someday when my pockets were well lined and see if I couldn't make up for the pile of paper money I'd leave behind, by filling up sheets of paper that would bring Ernesto the discoverer of Madrid back to life.

I would have to make careful plans. You can't write enduring literature without a plan. I would go ahead one step at a time, after having thought the whole thing through beforehand, so that it would be something more than a sentimental journey. I would travel on an empty stomach and not drink a drop of wine. If soldiers don't eat before a battle they fight much more bravely, and if *toreros* enter the bullring with an empty belly they have double their usual skill. We writers are like hunters: when we come face to face with a tiger, a night watchman, a prostitute, a wild boar, a university professor, a mountain lion, or a notary, we need a cool head and a steady hand. That was Ernesto's philosophy, and it turned out to be a very practical one, because if a hunter doesn't have his guts under control, he's lost. Like the bellows of an old church organ, they wheeze and fart grotesquely. Keep a careful grip on your shotgun and your guts, you hunters. That's excellent advice straight from Don Ernesto.

5 The city was the same as always, of course, though on this lazy summer night it seemed like a sort of refreshing oasis, despite the suffocating heat, for at many of the windows people were watering their plants with pitchers or sprinkling cans.

I said good-by to the lions from across the street and went to the Iberia terminal to wait for a taxi. How I wished I could buy a ticket then and there and board a plane for Ketchum! It would arrive at dawn, just as the sun was coming up, since I would gain several hours during the flight because of the time change. But a taxi home was all I could afford right now, and tomorrow would be another day. That is to say, I could have a decent hot meal then with the money I'd gotten for my piece on Ernesto, plus an advance, and the whole cycle would begin all over again. I'd keep writing a piece a day to stay alive. That was the ridiculous fate in store for me, and Ernesto had said to me again and again, "Leave journalism, once and for all. Even though you may not even have enough money the next day to buy yourself a glass of wine."

How wonderful it would be to have money! I'd fly to Ketchum and put my arms around Mary and question her as to what had really happened, or simply keep my eyes and ears open. But by now she would at least have received that telegram that had left me with a nearly empty wallet.

I was alone in my shabby apartment again. A couple of enormous cockroaches were running down the hall, like two bulls that had strayed from the San Fermín fiesta. I went over to the bookcase, looked at the row of books by and about Ernesto, and took down Gustav Regler's *The*

Great Crusade. With patience and perseverance and the aid of a dictionary, I might get a clearer picture of Ernesto's life from this book. For tonight, though, I'd have my work cut out for me just getting through Ernesto's preface, written in Camagüey, Cuba, in 1940; I was still in the groves of academe that year, struggling with the *Enchiridion Symbolorum*. It was in the preface to *The Great Crusade* that Ernesto described how the Eleventh Brigade had been totally wiped out in the terrible battle of Teruel. Was the head of this brigade that Hungarian who detested journalists and was shipped off to Moscow, where he was given the very formal military "review" his disastrous defeat had earned him? In this preface Ernesto mentions a report he wrote, which eventually reached the famous General Lucasz, whose unit Ernesto the combatant-correspondent had always praised highly. He also briefly mentions the Fifteenth Brigade, one that started out as the Fifth Brigade and later was called the Eleventh, the First, the Twelfth, and the Second—merely a juggling of numbers to make the enemy think that the Loyalists had more troops than they actually did. This brigade was the one that had stayed on in Jarama, and I had fought these men on the road to Madrid when I was still scarcely more than a child: my rifle, at any rate had weighed more than I had.

It was plain to see that what Ernesto had told me in conversation was all there in his books. The defense of Madrid and the battles of Guadalajara and Arganda had been a dream, a happy dream, to him.

"To think that we might have won the war!"

"Was there ever such a possibility?"

"We could have won it if it hadn't been for the disgraceful behavior of certain people and the nit-picking of certain others."

My receipt for the telegram I'd sent Mary was lying on the table.

As I rinsed my mouth out in the bathroom, I looked at myself in the mirror and said to myself, "Well, I'll just have to face up to it: he died the way he lived."

There was one thing I objected to, or rather, was anxious to set straight: Ernesto hadn't died "with his boots on," as one of the Barcelona newspapers had put it. He'd finally gotten to the fiesta of Saint End-of-the-Road, but he'd carefully planned his itinerary a long time before. All I had to do was use my ears to hear, rather than my eyes to see, and listen to what he had said in all those books sitting there on the shelves and lying open in front of me. "I wouldn't want to be that old." "An old man is a nasty thing." They'd gotten there too late to help this time, much too late. But what about the other times he'd almost died? Had he really been trying to kill himself?

"*Any one has a right to do it, he thought.*" So anybody has a right, then, to kill himself on a July morning when the red poppies are like warm kisses amid the ripe ears of grain? "*But it isn't a good thing to do.*"

Of course not. *"I understand it but I do not approve of it."* Of course: if to understand is to forgive, I could understand this act but I could not forgive even my beloved Ernesto for having gone through with it. What happens is that a man pokes and prods the idea of death, and of suicide in particular, so long, and doubtless so masochistically, that finally he knows all about it, and at the same time he has no idea what it's all about. It's like putting your hand up the panties of that "beloved" who both fascinated and disgusted Ernesto so much. I would have to get my thoughts in order and remember what I had read.

"You have to be awfully occupied with yourself to do a thing like that." Occupied with yourself? You also have to be sick, totally demoralized, crazy. But was Ernesto crazy? *"He wasn't any son of a bitch though. He was just a coward and that was the worst luck any man could have."* Precisely. *"Maybe I'll just do it now. I guess I'm not awfully good at pain. Listen, if I do that now you wouldn't understand, would you?"* Was the pain of this death that was his and his alone, and at the same time the exact copy of his father's death, so deep then?

Thinking of his grandfather and his father, Jordan-Ernesto says to himself: *"But suppose the fear he had to go through and dominate and just get rid of finally in four years of that and then in the Indian fighting, although in that, mostly there couldn't have been so much fear, made a* cobarde *out of the other one the way second generation bullfighters almost always are?"* (Ernesto often used the Spanish word for coward in italics.) But this was before the marvelous, sublime summer with Antonio Ordóñez, whose father Ernesto "wouldn't give shit for" (Ernesto's own words, repeated in a furtive whisper to his intimate friends), while Antonio was pure class and his style the very essence of the art of bullfighting. When he talked about his own father, Ernesto always said that he had fallen into a trap, and though he himself had cleverly tried to avoid that same trap, he too had fallen into it, not at the very end of his life but long before, when he was still hardly more than a child. *"Who do you suppose has it easier? Ones with religion or just taking it straight? It comforts them very much but we know there is no thing to fear."* If there was nothing to fear, why did Ernesto spend his whole life fearing death and seeking it? And then the trap snaps shut. *"It is only missing it that's bad. Dying is only bad when it takes a long time and hurts so much that it humiliates you."* Aye, there's the rub: for me, for you, for everyone. That's why you don't find many people who are masters of the philosophy of dying. Everyone dies his own death. And the way *you* chose of course, Ernesto, was blowing your brains out. It's as plain as day now that, of all your works, *For Whom the Bell Tolls*—a war novel—was the one in which you turned the sack full of your delirious fears and anxieties upside down and emptied them all out. I am fascinated by the fact that

María, who wants to do everything for her hero and lover, wants most of all to clean and oil Robert Jordan's pistol. When he promises to show her how to do it, she says, almost joyously: "If you will teach me to shoot it either one of us could shoot the other and himself, or herself, if one were wounded and it were necessary to avoid capture." Whereupon the valiant Jordan (who has chosen to carry the very pistol that his father shot himself with—though it was a shotgun that Ernesto's father killed himself with) answers, like someone who sees a clear path ahead: "Very interesting."

It was time to go to bed, but I could now see the whole thing very clearly: Ernesto was obsessed with the idea that he would kill himself just as his father had, and had tried at one and the same time to escape that destiny and pursue it, and perhaps both his everyday life and all his writings were an attempt to overcome this terror and postpone this fatal step. All his dramatic encounters with death—both as a youngster and as a grown man—were duels in which the opponent to be bested was the fear and cowardice that haunted him like bloodstained ghosts.

I sat down at my typewriter.

But just a few moments later I heard loud voices in the courtyard. I could hear empty bottles and jars raining down on the roof and the cement floor of the ice-cream store downstairs.

I poked my head out the window to see what was going on. There was often a lot of shouting and complaining about the noise from the store, but this time the outcry didn't sound the same. And the moment the neighbors spied me at the window, a great chorus of angry voices yelled, "Cut out that racket!"

It wasn't the freezer in the ice-cream store they were complaining about this time, because the motor wasn't running. It was my typewriter they meant. A hysterical voice shouted, "Can't you do your writing some other time?"

I turned out all but one small light, feeling as though I'd committed a crime, and sat on the balcony in the dark for a while. But there were still lights on in lots of the windows, and people were still shouting that I had no right to type at that hour, that I'd disturbed the whole neighborhood, that this wasn't a civilized country any more, that it was the American influence in Spain that was responsible for such outrages. And at that moment a real American—one from Kansas or Illinois or maybe Idaho—piped up, shouting something in English that nobody understood. And a great chorus of voices shouted back:

"Go back where you came from, Yank!"

"Shut up, you bastard!"

"Isn't that disgusting? The only thing those Americans come here for is to fuck, and then they have the nerve to complain!"

I laughed despite myself, because I felt as cross as a bear, and went back inside in much the same mood that Ernesto would have been in if he'd suddenly come back to life and were crawling back into his den. I tumbled into bed with all my clothes on, and must have fallen asleep the minute my head hit the pillow.

The one light was still on when I woke up, at dawn, and I had to climb out of bed and turn it off. I was dripping with sweat, and went to get a drink of water. I had a splitting headache, too, and searched all over the apartment for some aspirin without finding any. And to top it all off, I couldn't help remembering how ridiculous my behavior the day before had been: my utterly pointless wandering all over the city, all the things I'd said that made no sense even to me, all the things I'd done that seemed very peculiar now that I thought about them.

It was still very early, a few minutes before four, but I couldn't drop off to sleep again. I couldn't get the disturbing thought out of my mind that there was something I ought to remember about Ernesto, but I had no idea what it was I'd forgotten. I picked up Regler's book again, and reached for paper and pen. But I couldn't bring myself to write down a single note. I lit a cigarette and blew smoke rings at the lamp for a while, and then lay down again and eventually fell asleep.

It was almost nine when I woke up again. I went straight to the telephone, even though I realized that this was no time to call a *torero*. Even if Ordóñez was in town, he was no doubt still asleep. I picked up the phone two or three times to call him, but finally decided I wouldn't disturb him for a while. After all, the poor man deserved some rest—he'd killed two bulls on the afternoon that his friend's corpse lay shattered to bits halfway around the world, and he had traveled several hundred kilometers after the *corrida*, if he returned to Madrid.

At that moment the phone rang. It was a magazine editor calling, begging me to write a piece about Ernesto, a very special one: I wasn't to say a word about bullfighting or bulls, and not a word, of course, about the whole civil war business. It struck me as an impossible assignment: was there any book of Ernesto's dealing with Spain that wasn't centered on bullfighting? You can't read three consecutive pages anywhere in *For Whom the Bell Tolls*, for instance, without Ernesto or Robert Jordan or the guerrillas mentioning something having to do with the bullring. There is really only one setting in Ernesto's books about Spain, the *plaza de toros*, and two central characters: the bull and the bullfighter. Even the Spanish Civil War was only an extended metaphor to Ernesto: one long, tragic bullfight. I told the editor I couldn't write a piece like that, and was glad when I had turned down the job.

How could anyone fail to see that the battle between the two factions depicted in the novel was only an echo of the inner battle Ernesto

124

had long fought in his effort to understand the basic problem confronting the Spanish people? *For Whom the Bell Tolls* was not a novelistic treatment of events he had witnessed during the Spanish Civil War, but an attempt to enter into almost mystical communion with the reality of Spain. All the characters—whether "Reds" or Fascists—are desperately searching for their own definition of Spain. And the author's own painful vision of this country so close to his heart comes into sharper and sharper focus with every page.

It was not his hero, Robert Jordan, but Ernesto himself, who came to Spain to participate in the war, to witness at first hand not the final decisive battle, which never took place, but the haunting tragedy of a people fighting for its very existence. To tell what it was like, he had to invent a hero cut from the same cloth as himself, a hero with ideals as lofty as his own, a hero as capable of sacrifices, a man both as generous and as frustrated as himself. He had to invent a hero who was a typical adventurer, yet at the same time possessed of the sentimentality of a mixed-up adolescent and a profound sense of justice. His hero had to be a witness capable, in short, of understanding the stark, solemn drama of this great *corrida*.

One day in the Floridita, in Havana, Ernesto introduced me to a man who appeared to be a rather close friend of his with the words, "Here's a buddy of mine who used to be a doctor at a bullring in Spain."

"That must be a very special branch of surgery," I said ingenuously. "They tell me horn wounds are very dangerous."

"Machine-gun wounds are more dangerous," Ernesto replied, as though letting me in on a great secret.

I suddenly realized he was speaking from personal experience.

And, another day, he said to me in the bar of the Hotel Palace:

"Ask this buddy of mine what happened the day I leaped into the ring and fought as an amateur against a bull as big as a tank. . . ."

"No, it was the other way around," his friend said. "It was a tank as big as a bull. . . ."

Ernesto's most treasured and proudest memories were of war and bullfighting. He often associated the two. One day I told him what the war had been like for me: it had begun in a seminary and ended in a prison for counterespionage agents, and in between I had been in the front lines a good part of the time. Ernesto had commented, "It's plain to see that you were a good *banderillero*."

I had seen the film *For Whom the Bell Tolls* in Mexico in 1958. When Ernesto said something about the war one day in Havana and I mentioned that I had seen the film, he said to me, "You were in the *corrida* yourself, so forget what you saw."

I had *For Whom the Bell Tolls* in front of me now. I leafed through this novel that had moved me so deeply, but found that I simply could not settle down and study any one passage. I would start reading a page and immediately find myself so amazed and so annoyed I couldn't go on. How could Ernesto have put such high-flown concepts and such fancy words in the mouths of a band of humble, unschooled guerrilla fighters?

This had not been either the first or the last time that Ernesto's way of dealing with the most daring and embarrassing subjects had been a strange blend of the exotic and the naïve. Could this puerility, this sort of ingenuousness as a storyteller be the key to his style? For the hundredth time, I was fascinated by this book. It seemed to me that it contained too much philosophizing and too many background facts about the Civil War, though I must say that the effect of passages that were too rhetorical or inaccurate was counterbalanced by the book's lofty and generous idealism. What I was reading was real, vividly real in some places, but in other places, unfortunately, the book seemed very stilted and cliché-ridden. But it was a fascinating novel nonetheless. Ernesto had been terribly anxious to get to the bottom of the tragic truth about Spain, but what he had really explored was his own truth about Spain, and what he had primarily borne witness to was his own personal tragedy.

From time to time I consulted the English edition to see how the insults and blasphemies had been rendered in the original. I could see that the hand of a master had blended all the many contrasting colors in the book. The worst obscenities were followed by the most tender, most noble words, and as always I found the book as a whole deeply moving. Certain scenes still puzzled me, however, and once again I found them very hard to swallow. I simply couldn't believe that María, who is a decent young girl from a middle-class family as well as a Republican, would willingly give herself to a man simply because he was about to blow up a bridge. The rather conventional passion in the love scenes struck me as a somewhat awkward symbolic counterpart of the charge of dynamite that Robert Jordan is going to place under the bridge. I was not at all shocked by Ernesto's euphemistic word *muck*. I do find it hard to believe, however, that Robert and Agustín—a Spanish youngster who is impressed by the moral purity of this band of guerrillas—would use such vulgar language in their conversations together. María is not a very convincing mixture of innocence and sexual ardor, and it strains belief that she would be so forward in the presence of the other members of the guerrilla band. María is Spanish, after all, and I don't believe any Spanish girl behaved that unconventionally in the year 1936, even in the most liberal circles.

But the book was impressive nonetheless, because what is most vivid and most striking about it is not this or that erotic scene in the sleeping bag or this or that political conversation in the cave, but another sort of emotion that Ernesto conveys beautifully despite all his novelistic tricks and facile devices to keep the reader's interest from flagging. Many episodes are so powerful and the narrative pace so intense that the defects of the book seem merely incidental.

Why was it that this novel had not had the success it deserved in Spain? To begin with, very few people had read it. The edition published in Argentina had been smuggled into the country and sold under the counter, and therefore it had commanded a very high price. If it had been readily available, Spanish readers would have discovered that the book, despite the many things about it that were gratuitous and facile, was a marvelously realistic one that went far beyond mere cleverness or pedestrian reportage. All the expert little technical and psychological touches, the many subtle shadings of courage and cowardice, each carefully embodied in the behavior of a specific character, the many monologues and dialogues that at times are marvelous stories in and of themselves, in the end make the reader forget the lack of verisimilitude of this or that situation or the artificiality of this or that conversation.

I sat there, drenched with sweat because I was so upset, wiping my forehead not only to get rid of the beads of perspiration, but to rid myself of the nightmare that was haunting me. I kept lighting cigarettes, and then forgetting them until they started to burn the table and I would suddenly smell them.

I reread several times the barbarous scene in which the town Fascists are slaughtered in the square, and had to get up and get a drink of water. It was a nightmarish scene that made your throat as parched as when you harvest grain or pick grapes.

There are very few descriptions of a collective massacre as powerful as this episode in Ernesto's novel. In this brutal scene he used everything he had learned at the bullring to depict the horror of war, in *Death in the Afternoon*.

> [Spaniards] know death is the inescapable reality, the one thing any man may be sure of; the only security . . . . they think a great deal about death and when they have a religion they have one which believes that life is much shorter than death. Having this feeling they take an intelligent interest in death and when they can see it being given, avoided, refused, and accepted in the afternoon for a nominal price of admission they pay their money and go to the bullring.

The scene in the public square in *For Whom the Bell Tolls* is a masterful study of a vulgar, brutal, vile mass killing, in the style of Goya, a bloody, drunken orgy.

And once more one wonders: What sort of hatred hidden in the hearts of Spaniards made an entire town—grown men and women, oldsters, children—look on the massacre of their neighbors as a great fiesta, the fiesta to end all fiestas, the "bullfight of the century," the most exciting *corrida* ever?

There was no doubt that horrible things had happened in Spain, and I had seen some of them at close hand, so close that at times I had been spattered with blood—and more than once it had been the blood of innocent victims.

The trouble was that even though I was deeply moved by the book I also had certain reservations about it, for it was quite obvious that many of the horrors Ernesto depicts could not have happened in the geographical sector in which he situates the action.

First of all, there were no such cases of mass slaughter in towns in Segovia. Nor were there any around Avila. People in that part of Spain were not as passionately involved in the revolutionary movement or as eager for vengeance as in other regions, such as La Mancha or Estremadura.

Since of all things Spanish Ernesto was most familiar with the world of bullfighting, he doubtless was very pleased when he stumbled upon the device of the bullfight as the basic metaphor for his depiction of the bloody spirit of revenge that the beginning of the revolution had aroused.

As I knew all too well, barbarous things, really horrible things, had happened in many places. But there was no basis in fact for setting this scene of collective sadism in a little town in the mountains outside of Madrid. Ernesto must have heard a whole litany of atrocities that had occurred in other places, and in his simplistic way decided to lump them all together in one symbolic scene.

The killing of Spaniards by Spaniards often was sheer butchery, but such executions as these, which were always meant to serve as collective punishment or as an example, very seldom, if ever, took on the air of a great fiesta. I myself had witnessed certain happenings that were almost as brutal. Nonetheless this scene of a human *corrida* in the middle of Castile strains belief. But did this lack of historical authenticity really invalidate the point Ernesto was trying to make or mar the artistic effect of the book? The episode was impressive nonetheless. Even though it was not historically accurate, it was still a striking use of metaphor. In Ernesto's hands the bullfight theme takes on epic proportions, becoming the overarching symbol of a noble struggle for freedom. But doesn't he also use this basic metaphor ironically? In this scene we see not brave matadors but butchers, not noble bulls but vulgar beasts, an entire town becomes an enraged mob, a ritual drama turned into a brutal slaughter, a *plaza de toros* that has become an ignominious cattle pen.

The Spanish war had been something more than a grotesque *corrida*, something more than drunken bullies clumsily butchering their neighbors in a savage mass slaughter. If only Ernesto had had a greater religious awareness, founded on something more than his innermost fears and a childish sense of apprehension! In the *corrida* with the bull and against him, the matador not only confronts the dark power that is the very source of a man's virility; he also reverently worships that other immortal, extrahuman power, God, that mystery that remains nameless no matter what we label it. The Spanish War, for Ernesto, was an embodiment of every aspect of the myth of the bullfight, from the worship of virility to blood communion to a sort of hymn of the bridegroom at a nuptial feast. The Spanish War came to represent Ernesto's blood wedding with age-old, eternal Spain, at once life-loving and mystical, hideously cruel and wonderfully human.

But even though he dealt with it in terms of the most moving symbol of Spain—bullfighting, a sacrificial rite, and the Iberian bull, the bestower of eternal life—the Spanish War was too vast a theme even for Ernesto. I need hardly say that it was also too vast a theme for all those who have approached the subject by way of rhetoric, solemn superpatriotic speechifying, mountains of newspaper articles, floods of righteous indignation, dire prophecy, empty lyricism, ideological demagoguery, cheap trickery, spurious mysticism, self-serving sociology, and a mortal fear of the truth, exploiting the Spanish people's feelings to make money from the epic *corrida* that cost the lives of hundreds of thousands—the great bullfight in which not only noble purebred bulls but vicious mavericks met their death, those three bloody years in which seasoned matadors and clumsy amateurs, brave volunteers and cowardly shirkers, executioners and victims, heroes and traitors on both sides gave the world a tremendous lesson in the art of killing and the art of dying. The Spanish Civil War had been, and still was, a formidable bull.

But Ernesto's book had at least forced people to think, and would continue to do so. It would be one of the greatest contributions to a balanced view of the war, for it was very far removed from the usual run of hypocritical apologias and far superior to the venomous tracts that both sides had put out.

It was quite clear that Ernesto had failed to appreciate certain rather important nuances, but he had at least grasped the larger meaning of the great *corrida*. The events of the book take place in Castile, however, and therefore the excessive violence of many scenes strains belief. Admittedly there were many atrocities committed in that bloody period, but it is quite unbelievable that young boys in a little town in Castile would corner the terrified, defenseless daughter of the mayor, who has just seen her mother and father shot to death and had her hair publicly shorn off, drag her to the town hall, and collectively rape her in her father's office. Perhaps Ernesto had heard similar horror stories during the siege of Madrid and had written this revealing rape scene to dramatize the violence of people's passions and hatreds.

The acts of terror and barbarism that the war brought in its wake would provide more than enough material for many horrifying books; but a day will come when someone will also tell us of the many quiet acts of humanity that also took place, both in the rear and in the front lines.

But this was the least of it. What was even more important was that Ernesto had gone to the very limits of the monstrous, precisely because this was the only way that he could achieve the inner catharsis he needed so desperately. Very few readers have noted that in the midst of all the many deeds of violence committed by both sides in the novel, Ernesto's characters are constantly gnawed by doubt and remorse. The book thus depicts not only the armed struggle, but also, the inner conflict that was the novel's real subject, despite the fact that Ernesto carefully concealed his theme. The bitter taste of guilt is the secret wellspring of the entire book, for Ernesto was anxious not only to save the social body of Spain through drastic surgery but also to communicate the spirit that underlay the heroic struggle. Hence when the characters speak of the crimes of which they were the authors or the victims, they do so almost as if they were in the confessional, as though they feel that their souls can begin to be healed only by recounting these crimes. One might even go so far as to say that at the heart of this intensely personal novel—which seems on the surface to be merely sensational reportage—there is a sober condemnation of a country that claims to be Christian but at times falls prey to the most pagan temptation, because it is one thing to preach sermons and quite another to love one's brother even if he is a Republican or a Monarchist. What Ernesto tried to prove in the novel is that with men such as this, men of such savage purity, revolution is impossible, because for such men revolution will inevitably be accompanied by bloodshed.

But how can a war be won and a revolutionary change take place unless every last person on the other side is killed, in the trenches or somewhere else, unless every last one of your neighbors who does not share your views is liquidated?

It was too early to be telephoning Ordóñez, who by dint of much hard work is able to live the life of a petty monarch. *Toreros* sleep late in the morning, though sometimes they stay up so late they don't even bother going to bed. But they keep such hours when they're young matadors. Later on, when they have ranches and herds of bulls, they find it a great pleasure to get up very early in the morning out in the countryside.

No one answered at Ordóñez's house however, and I hung up. Could Antonio have gone to Ketchum?

I sat down at my typewriter. What was I going to write? An article? For the time being I would simply copy down the passage about the death of the bull, word for word. Then I might perhaps make a comparative analysis of the death of the bull and the death of one of the local "Falangist" leaders. (Ernesto had been much too free in his use of the words "Falangist" and "Fascist" in his descriptions of the town.) Then, after that, I might try to point out the similarities between the slaughter in the public square of the little village and the rape of María, the girl whose mother and father had been shot to death outside the slaughterhouse. Would there have been such a pat parallel between these two events in real life? I had certain reservations on that score. A whore who has slept with all the boys for miles around might have gotten what was coming to her in a gruesome *fiesta* like that in a small town in Castile, but a decent young girl simply would not have been raped by young lads who had known her all her life, especially not collectively in a semipublic place. . . . Hadn't Ernesto strayed a long way from the truth in this episode?

I had to tell Ernesto he'd been wrong. But how could I? I'd never have a chance now even to hint as much. There were many women raped, of course, during our Civil War—as happens in every war, civil or otherwise—but a very large percentage of them had been raped by Moors or foreigners, who knew nothing about our customs and our ordinary patterns of life. These rapes were committed by groups of soldiers passing through who had momentarily been carried away after winning a victory or were taking their revenge after a defeat on the battlefield by mistreating civilians. But it beggared belief that a young girl in a small village would be collectively raped by her fellow townsmen. It has often been pointed out that the Spanish male is fiercely individualistic and extremely circumspect about his fornicating even in the midst of an orgy, and therefore Ernesto's story is simply unbelievable, despite the fact that he has Jordan remark that there are as many different kinds of Spaniards as there are Americans. No, there are a few kinds we don't have in Spain.

I quite agree that we Spaniards are prepared, quite prepared, "to kill with excessive ease," as old Anselmo puts it, precisely because we are unwilling to give up our privileged role as the "people of the auto-da-fe," in Jordan's words. But let us also not forget that "it is a sin to kill a man"—a fact that is the moral salvation of Robert Jordan and other characters in the novel, and of the author too, of course.

Yes, there were deaths during the Civil War, thousands of them, but furtive secret, shameful ones, not murders organized as a great fiesta and carried out with wholesale violence and sadism. There were gross travesties of justice and even a fair number of executions, both of individual prisoners and of entire groups, that were entirely uncalled for, but I defy anyone to produce eyewitness evidence that the entire population of a town ever gathered to applaud each act of murder, or stepped in to finish the victims off themselves when the "experts" proved clumsy. This image is a violation not so much of the historical facts as of the psychological truth of the Spanish character.

But as I sat there at the typewriter, I found myself unable to write a single lucid, straightforward, convincing line. I went to the phone and ordered a strong cup of tea from the pizzeria downstairs.

I went on with my study of the novel then. The bull with the horns curving sharply downward that Finito was fighting was staring at the red cloth. The crowd had fallen silent:

> She saw him now clearly as he furled the heavy flannel cloth around the stick; the flannel hanging blood-heavy from the passes where it had swept over the bull's head and shoulders and the wet streaming shine of his withers and on down and over his back as the bull raised into the air and the banderillas clattered.

There was a knock at the door. I took the tray with one hand and handed the delivery boy a tip with the other.

> She saw Finito stand five paces from the bull's head profiled, the bull standing still and heavy, and draw the sword slowly up until it was level with his shoulder and then sight along the dipping blade at a point he could not yet see because the bull's head was higher than his eyes. He would bring that head down with the sweep his left arm would make with the wet, heavy cloth; but now he rocked back a little on his heels and sighted along the blade, profiled in front of the splintered horn; the bull's chest heaving and his eyes watching the cloth.

This was not a mere routine description. It was a poster of the *torero* Finito in action, a short, dark-haired, sober-faced matador with sad eyes and sunken cheeks and deep wrinkles in his very dark, sweat-soaked forehead, standing in profile sighting for the kill.

Was Finito—a tramp, a drunk, and a coward, a fear-wracked *torero* and a failure—merely a literary device? It would be very much worth my while to examine the text patiently, because if Ernesto waved the bullfighter's cape and the bloodstained muleta at us Spaniards from the very beginning of this Civil War novel, it was for a serious reason. Significantly, the bull's horns had entered Finito's body through his buttock and exited through his liver. There is another figure from the world of professional bullfighting in the novel, Pablo, who also becomes drenched with blood, but this time it is human blood, for his adversary is a different kind of bull and he fights a different kind of *corrida*, one that begins as a sort of passionate amateur bullfight early one morning and eventually becomes a tactical and strategic war fought with the powers of intellect.

Finito was the only professional matador in the book. And Ernesto respected bullfighting too much to make Pablo, a vulgar bullring horse supplier, a valiant *torero*. Since a *corrida* was something noble to Ernesto, an almost ritual offering, it is Andrés who symbolizes the real spirit of the bullfight in this overarching metaphor that starts with the ugly bullbaiting in the square and ends in martyrdom.

The janitor knocked at my door. Did I want milk delivered? He also handed me the receipt for the gas bill and said, "Since they know you're only going to be away for the summer, I don't think they'll shut it off."

"Thanks, don't worry about it," I said, and closed the door.

I picked up the book again.

> Pablo organized it all as he did the attack on the barracks. First he had the entrances to the streets blocked off with carts as though to organize the plaza for a *capea*. An amateur bull fight.

I was eager to reread the entire episode, but at the same time the thought of doing so repelled me. Once I started, I would have to read it through to the end, for this *corrida* in the village square was much more of a formal ritual than the execution scene. It was also much more depressing. Why was it that Ernesto had dealt with this entire episode as though he were a punctilious bullfight critic, from the very moment that the first human "bull" appears, staring fixedly at the audience, till the moment when the last victim is dragged to the cliff above the river? I was sorry that Ernesto had mixed together the macabre and the festive, the atmosphere of a gay fiesta and bloody, criminal acts. But perhaps I was repelled by this image because it was engraved on my heart, because Ernesto's description of it was so close to the truth, even though such an event had never occurred anywhere in Spain.

"I'm still convinced you don't like bullfighting, José Luis," he had said to me one day.

"That's not true—I like it very much, but I wouldn't want to see a *corrida* every day," I replied.

From his very first days in Spain as a young man, when the art of bullfighting came to him as a sudden revelation, the *corrida* had always seemed something superhuman to Ernesto. The *torero* seemed a god to him at the moment of the kill, and the audience also seemed to him to be fulfilling a sacred function as it witnessed the moment of truth. But when would the tourists who flocked to Spain by the thousands after reading *The Sun Also Rises* and *Death in the Afternoon* ever understand this? Killing while at the same time risking being killed was a revelation to Ernesto, almost a parable of divine justice. Nevertheless the prisoners killed in the square in the novel were disarmed, mere beasts being helplessly slaughtered, unfortunate creatures as well as guilty ones, who would have been utter failures even in a *tienta* testing their courage before being shipped off to the bullring. Perhaps it was precisely because Ernesto knew how rare perfection is in the bullring that the cruel *corrida* in the novel has all the coarseness, the jeering disrespect, the injustice, the insensibility, the sarcasm displayed by the audience at a bad bullfight.

But I would have to emphasize one point again and again: episodes such as that simply did not take place in Castile. In other parts of Spain there had been even more inhuman instances of Celto-Iberian cruelty: I have never heard of Spaniards condemned to death being given a chance to have a priest hear their confessions before being executed, for instance, as happens in Ernesto's novel.

I could not have explained why it pained me so much that Ernesto had not captured the real image of Spain's martyrdom—the martyrdom suffered by both sides, for each was both the victim and the executioner of the other. The war had been a grim reaper in the month of July 1936—the harvest month, when sacks of grain are brought to the granaries. There had been much less of a feeling of mercy for the enemy than that depicted in Ernesto's book, and another kind of cruelty, a much blinder, less sensational, and less overt sort than that described in the novel.

In any event, each of these bulls—the brave ones and the cowardly ones alike—is fated to die its own death. Because there is a little of everything in every *corrida*. And Pablo is everywhere, the organizer of this bullfight in *For Whom the Bell Tolls*.

The *corrida* is about to begin. The men have formed two compact lines stretching down to the river. They have had their coffee and a drink, and now the rude jostling, the shouts, the spitting, the obscenities begin.

"I have never killed a man," he said.

"Then you will learn," the peasant next to him said.

The men have flails and sickles and shepherds' crooks and scythes and reaping hooks in their hands. They will serve as pikes, and the men will be *picadores* or *banderilleros* as the bull passes their way. Will these bulls take their punishment as they should? Some of the men tremble at the thought that they will have to fight the village priest too—one more bull. "There are always *toreros* who don't like killing, who are afraid to kill." Would the priest be a really fierce, dangerous bull? No, that was too much to expect. But the others might prove worthy opponents, though doubtless a little dazed, for after having been shut up in the city hall they would come out into the bright sunlight as though emerging from the dark pen at the bullring. Which of these bulls would prove the bravest: the mayor, the shopkeeper, the landowner? A hushed silence. It is a matter of minutes now, of seconds. Pablo will sound the trumpet beginning the *corrida* any moment. His men, the matadors (or the crucifiers, as Ernesto suggests more than once in this passage), are still in the bull's territory. There is also sex in the air, and feminine voices shouting for the *corrida* to begin, as at the bullring, for the women of the town are also present, glistening with sweat as at the *plaza de toros*, drinking the intoxicating wine of the *corrida*, muttering the words of the bordello, stinking of the vomit of death. Meanwhile the prisoners—the bulls—are praying, for like the *torero* the bull, too, feels immortal at a certain point in a *corrida*. The priest gives them his blessing to impart this feeling of immortality.

"That it should start then. That it should start."

But the crowd must wait a moment longer while a man with a water-hose wets down the sand. The men and women separate, still anxiously waiting for the *corrida* to begin.

> There was no noise now in the plaza as all were waiting to see who it was that would come out. Then a drunkard shouted in a great voice: "*Que salga el toro!* Let the bull out!"

The mayor comes out first, but his spirit is broken, and he doesn't put up a very good fight.

"*Que salga el toroooo!*"

The owner of the mill and feed store is next. He walks down the double line, staring at the matadors, and is clubbed in the head. If all of the *toros* are this cowardly, the *corrida* is going to be a fiasco—they may have to give the townspeople their money back. Where in this bullfight are the three classical stages of a *corrida: levantado, parado,* and *aplomado?* The matadors can't show off their skills with bad bulls like these.

The landowner appears next, a bull that is not on the defensive. He has come out of the enclosure quite willingly, and says:

"To die is nothing. The only bad thing is to die at the hands of this *canalla.*"

The old landowner is very brave and shouts:

"*Arriba España!*"

135

This brave bull excites the audience, and they are now in no mood to pardon any of the victims. And as in every *corrida*, a gentle bull now appears, Don Faustino, who has always wanted to be an amateur bullfighter. This is the bull the crowd has been waiting for. He has his *querencia* all picked out: he would like nothing better than to return to the town hall. The crowd jeers at him and mocks him, and finally he is dragged to the edge of the cliff.

The crowd starts handing around bottles of *anís* and *coñac*. Bloodshed calls for more bloodshed. And also:

"To kill gives much thirst."

The shopkeeper Don Guillermo Martín comes out now, the man who has sold the crowd their flails, their herdsmen's clubs, and their wooden pitchforks. Ernesto adds that Don Guillermo is a Fascist, and to prove it he mentions that he is a subscriber to *El Debate*—a rather glaring inaccuracy. Don Guillermo, a nearsighted man, halts and looks up at the balcony of the "apartment house" where he lives, another little detail that doesn't quite fit. It's almost as if Ernesto were as drunk now as the crowd in the square, because at this point he has Don Guillermo engage in a long dialogue with his wife on the balcony, a pious hypocrite who is responsible for her husband's being a Fascist, another incident that does not ring true. Then the bullfight goes on; a drunken bystander leaps on Don Guillermo's shoulders and bashes his head in with a bottle. The hideous spectacle approaches its climax, the moment when the last deathblow is dealt, though at times this *corrida* has been more like a circus than a bullfight. For the most part, the bulls have not charged as they should, and there are still a fair number of them left, including the village priest. The gate leading from the bull enclosure opens again. Will we now see the art of bullfighting in all its splendor, some really elegant passes at the very edge of the ring, something that might be compared to the death of gods?

No, no such thing happens. A big, fat man, a moneylender and insurance agent, appears, to be greeted by nothing more than a derisive shout from the crowd, who then kill him by knocking his head against the sidewalk of the arcade. Is a human being any better than a dumb beast if there are bulls a hundred times nobler than a man?

Ernesto did not present a proud image of a noble sport. Ernesto knew his subject well, for he never wrote about anything he did not have intimate, firsthand knowledge of. If he dealt with war in terms of a *corrida*, it was because he himself had confronted the enemy as in a bullring . . . and because he had seen with his own eyes both the sheer courage and the sheer cruelty of the Spanish people.

Even when he spoke of love, Ernesto often could not help dealing with it in terms of the matador and the bull, the red cloth and horns. And there would always be an Augustín, hoping for justice and order through revolution, the greatest running of the bulls of all. Or an Andrés:

> He looked forward all the year to that moment when the bull would come out into the square on that day when you watched his eyes while he made his choice of whom in the square he would attack in that sudden head-lowering, horn-reaching, quick cat-gallop that stopped your heart dead when it started. He had looked forward to that moment all the year when he was a boy. . . .

This time there was no postponing the great *corrida*, the battle of the Spanish people. But will he be granted the great good fortune of playing a personal role in it? Andrés wonders. Amateur bullfights are only a boisterous diversion, and what loomed on the horizon was all-out war. The hour had come when he would be put to the test as a fighter for the cause of the people. The time for noisy merrymaking in the streets was over—or almost over—and something more personal, more dramatic, more sobering was now in store. Would the man who had faced the bull's horns with such cool courage be found wanting in war?

At the critical moment when the bridge that symbolizes the triumph of the revolutionary cause must be blown up, Anselmo's courage does not fail him, for he, too, has already bravely faced the bull's horns in spirit. And for Andrés as for Anselmo, the responsibility of fighting for a revolutionary cause was a grave risk, but at the same time, his efforts, and those of all the guerrilla band, might bear splendid fruit. He would not allow himself to fail—not for his own sake, but for the sake of the others.

The Spanish translation has the word *cola* for tail, rather than *rabo*. In Spanish you can talk about the *cola* of a shark or a swordfish, but when Spaniards speak of a bull's tail they always use the word *rabo*. Translating Ernesto's books, especially the ones about Spain, into Spanish is no easy task if one is not familiar with the vocabulary of bullfighting, as obviously Señora Olga Sanz, his Argentinian translator, was not.

I leafed through the book again and again. At times I wasn't quite sure whether I was reading about Finito in the *plaza de toros* in Valencia or about Pablo in the village square finishing off a lot of very cowardly bulls. . . . The prisoners were still gathered around the priest in the reception room of the city hall, among the tables and benches, hoping and praying. Pablo is again the key figure, literally this time, for he has in his hand the key to the door, one a good foot long.

The *corrida* ends abruptly. When the door opens, no bulls rush out;

137

instead the mob rushes in. But it is the priest, the imparter of absolution, who is the center of attention, who is attacked most viciously. And we cannot shut our eyes to Pilar's laconic summing up of the massacre:

> "It would have been better for the town if they had thrown over twenty or thirty of the drunkards, especially those of the red-and-black scarves. . . ."

We are thus witness to the feeling of revulsion of an author whom André Maurois describes as "the post-Christian novelist," a man who nonetheless believed in the teachings of the Bible all his life. Even though the "Reds" at whose side he fought might have been discomfited thereby, he forthrightly condemned evil and injustice. Let us not forget that Ernesto was a man of principle.

This sort of examination of conscience was to place Ernesto far above both contending factions, even though his loyalties lay with those who he thought had right on their side and would be Spain's salvation.

Who can deny that Ernesto always endeavored to bare every sort of evil, not only condemning the iniquity buried deep in the human heart but also exposing the passing temptations to slyly get the better of one's fellows in everyday life? A writer must be prepared not only to understand evil but to pass harsh judgment on evildoers. Who can say that when Ernesto turned up in Spain in 1931, leading his son by the hand, as though to teach the boy a great lesson even though he himself thoroughly disliked pedagogues, he came to our country merely to see bullfights and keep close track of the rise or fall of his idols? There were undoubtedly other reasons as well. He came to Spain the moment he heard that it had been declared a republic, because he hoped that this might be the beginning of an exciting revolution, a bloodless one that would transform this country so close to his heart.

"How did the situation in Spain strike you in 1931?" I once asked him.

"It was terribly dull."

"What do you mean?"

"The whole thing was just a bunch of fancy words."

"What had you expected to find here?"

"I hadn't come looking for metaphysical miracles or marvelous socioeconomic plans. I came in search of a people, and found it surrounded on every hand by clowns and rascals."

"What leader impressed you most?"

"I wouldn't have given two pesetas for any of them. All I heard was rhetoric—cheap rhetoric. It was a shame—a great shame."

Ernesto was grateful to Spain precisely because our country and our people had awakened a sense of vocation in him that went far beyond merely being charmed as a writer by our picturesque customs. He not only discovered an extraordinarily powerful myth in bullfighting, something far surpassing the struggle for existence; his life was changed when he came face to face with the dramatic violence of our country, the blinding clarity of our cloudless skies, and more importantly, the imperturbable serenity of our people, a product both of our fatalism and of our deep religious faith. In Spain Ernesto the pagan turns Christian, the man who lives by his instincts becomes a mystic yearning for the Absolute, and the man pursued by the loathsome whore, Death, sometimes feels that he must preach the glad tidings that man will indeed enjoy the immortality he dreams of. The man who had been a disillusioned puritan from a very early age, the hero who felt himself a failure after his dramatic encounter with life, the perplexed and untried artist whose work was turning stale and sour within him was to discover passion and anxiety, gnawing worry and conflict, drama and style in our country. In Spain he was to discover not only a certain lofty idealism but also patterns of everyday behavior that forge character. In *The Sun Also Rises*, Brett Ashley forswears making a lapdog of the bullfighter, and when the innocent young girl, María, creeps into the foreigner's sleeping bag in *For Whom the Bell Tolls*, their love-making has an ineffable beauty.

I went to my filing cabinet and started looking through some folders. Where was that photograph of Ernesto extinguishing, with one shot, a lighted cigarette in Ordóñez's mouth, like an act in a sideshow? I'd seen him do it several times in a row, the cigarette getting shorter and shorter with every shot, and he never missed, but I wouldn't have dreamed of offering myself as a target, even if I'd been drinking and was as high as a kite. I had had a chance to observe Ernesto closely during his last stay in Madrid and had realized what was behind his nervous mannerisms, his indecision, his fits of temper, his sour moods. . . . The photo had been a revealing one, the perfect image of a championship bout between a matador and a hunter, between an elusive prey and an expert rifleman.

I looked at my watch and was disturbed to see that it was almost noon. I still hadn't reached Ordóñez, but when I called this time, I had better luck. He agreed to meet me late that afternoon, an appropriate time of day to be seeing a *torero*. But the minute I hung up, I realized that Antonio's voice had sounded not only grief-stricken but also a bit confused, almost remorseful. I could still remember, as if it had been only yesterday, the joking conversations between him and Ernesto:

"How's the Company doing since the last board of directors' meeting?" Ernesto had asked him one day.

"The company treasurer says business is booming," Antonio answered.

"Well, if the treasurer says so, I'm sure it's true," Ernesto said.

"I think we'll have to raise more capital and buy real estate on the Costa del Sol," Ordóñez answered with a straight face.

"Well, if you say so, it's as good as done already," Ernesto replied, shaking hands with Antonio as though they were two business partners who had just concluded an important deal.

I could see them now, patting each other on the back and putting on a good show, because they always pretended, especially in public, that they were in business together, which wasn't true at all. But at the same time they also unconsciously pretended that they were intimate friends, which wasn't true either. They got along very well with each other, but that was really as far as it went. Joking back and forth was absolutely essential to their relationship, since they had very little in common except their interest in bullfighting.

Had Ordóñez ever gotten to know the real Ernesto? He respected him and was a fervent admirer of his, but I don't think he really appreciated him either as a person or as a writer, for he had read very few of his works. Now that Ernesto was dead, perhaps Ordóñez would cease to be merely his grateful admirer (for there was no question that Ernesto had helped smooth Antonio's path to fame and fortune), and begin to study his works and understand him better. It had been an extraordinary stroke of good luck for Ordóñez to meet up with Ernesto, a bright meteor who had made Ordóñez's name a household word from one end of the globe to the other: Ernesto was a talented writer, of course, but even more important, he could greatly further Antonio's career. As Ordóñez got to know this famous celebrity better, he realized his weaknesses, but at the same time he began to be more than a casual friend of Ernesto's and came to admire him for more profound reasons. But it was very hard to cement a deep and lasting friendship with Ernesto the artist, because, for one thing, Ernesto was always so much in the public eye that there was seldom a time or a place where a person could get to know him better. To Ordóñez, Ernesto was a top celebrity who was a past master at keeping the eyes of the entire world trained on him. Since Antonio knew Ernesto's weak points as a bullfight critic, he was inclined to underestimate the value of his other works. But Antonio was doubtless greatly shaken by Ernesto's death. He knew very well how fond of him this Nobel Prize winner had been; in fact, there had been times when Ernesto's affection for him almost grated on his nerves. Ernesto was not only a good friend; he was also a devoted older brother, almost a father, or a father-figure, who doted on him because of his talent in the bullring and indulgently forgave his protégé all his little human faults in the world outside.

Ernesto, on the other hand, had been obliged to tag along after Ordóñez like a humble attendant in his retinue, and had shared Antonio's destiny with all his heart and soul ever since they had first met, worshiping his art and his person to such an extent that it was almost like a love affair. Even though Ernesto may have been tempted at times to put an end to this passionate involvement with Antonio, he was neither free enough nor strong enough to do so. When Ordóñez was in the bullring, Ernesto trembled for him and rejoiced with him to such a point that his identification with him was both ineffable and frightening; outside the bullring, he had found the idol that every artist needs.

I had often noticed how tense Ernesto was when Ordóñez was fighting, how nervous he was before one of his *corridas*, how intoxicated he was afterward if Antonio had fought well, and also how upset and depressed he was when Ordóñez had had a bad afternoon in the ring—though he would never admit it.

"Could there possibly be anybody better than him, José Luis?" Ernesto used to ask me.

"Antonio's really great," I answered.

"He's the one and only—there's nobody like him."

"There are others."

"Yes, that's right: there are others. But they're not Antonio."

And then there was his remark about *corridas* without Antonio on the bullfight card:

"It's not worth the trouble."

"What's not worth the trouble?"

"Seeing a *corrida* when Antonio's not fighting. He's the only real man fighting and killing in the bullring today."

But at times he had surprising misgivings about Ordóñez:

"If anything happens to him, I hope I'm not there to see it."

"What could happen to him? Nothing's going to happen to him."

"I hope God's listening."

"Of course He is. And the bulls are listening too. You don't seem to have much confidence in the master from Ronda."

"It's not that I lack confidence in him; sometimes I trust him too much. Everything Antonio does is too good to be true."

"Well, there's nothing to be afraid of, then."

"I'd sooner have something bad happen to me than to him."

"Nothing bad can happen to Antonio."

"You're right. He's beyond any sort of fear or doubt. He's far luckier than any ordinary mortal. Antonio's almost a god," Ernesto said, getting up from his chair and reverently knocking on wood.

I got up from the table and stood staring at the many windows overlooking the immense courtyard. Some bricklayers working on a scaffolding were singing something that sounded a little bit like a funeral hymn, at least to my ears. I went out on the balcony to stretch my legs a bit and the bricklayers on the scaffolding called out:

"The lucky bastard! He's just getting up!"

"Some people really have a soft life."

Like a fool, I felt guilty and went back inside.

I went downstairs to the pizzeria to have something to eat, but the minute the waiter set my plate in front of me I realized I wasn't hungry. I sat there reading *Burning Brand*, the series of diaries of Cesare Pavese, a great admirer of Ernesto's. His books reek of suicide too, and as you read his writings you come to realize that he is going to kill himself sooner or later. This frustrated Hemingway hero says:

> The frenzy for self-destruction has to be felt. I am not talking of a suicide. People like ourselves—in love with life, enjoying the unexpected and the pleasures of human intercourse—cannot get as far as suicide except through some imprudence.

Some imprudence? Absent-mindedly toying with a rifle, for instance, or clutching it the way a Buddhist monk clutches the torch he will use to set himself on fire?

As Pavese writes in *Burning Brand*:

> And then suicide seems like one of those mythical acts of heroism, those affirmations, in fables, of the dignity of Man in the face of Destiny, that make interesting statues but have nothing to do with us.

Pavese is wrong about suicide leaving us indifferent. Even a man who kills himself is not indifferent to his death.

> The self-destroyer is a different type, more despairing, but more practical. He has a compulsion to discover every fault, every baseness in his own nature; then he views these tendencies so leniently that they become mere nothings. He looks for more, enjoys them, finds them intoxicating.

This is Ernesto's own personal story, and the secret story of his characters as well.

> He is more sure of himself than any conqueror of the past, and he knows that the thread connecting him with tomorrow, with the potentialities of life, with a prodigious future, is a stronger cable—when it comes to the ultimate strain—than any faith or integrity.
>
> The self-destroyer is, above all, a comedian and his own

patron. He never misses an opportunity to listen to himself. He is an optimist, hoping for everything in life.

Could there possibly be a more lifelike portrait of Ernesto? And Pavese goes on:

He cannot endure solitude.

What had gone through Ernesto's mind and soul in those months in the hospital as he lay alone in bed listening to the hideous cackling of madness?

But he lives in constant peril that one day, all unawares, he will be seized with a craze for creating something or setting everything in proper order. Then he suffers unceasingly and may even kill himself.

That's the great trap, as Ernesto would say.

Consider this point carefully: nowadays, suicide is just a way of disappearing. It is carried out timidly, quietly, and falls flat. It is no longer an action, only a submission.

What other explanations could there be for Ernesto's suicide besides those that he had provided in his works and in his life? The score of his life had to end with a great tragic roll on the bass drum, echoing and re-echoing through space like the tolling of the bell for a dead man.

Reading Pavese had knocked all the wind out of my sails. I couldn't even choke down my salad. The people in the pizzeria were the same ones who usually ate there: the fat lady with glasses of the sort nuns wear, who is more or less the neighborhood bawd; the red-cheeked gypsy who sells neckties; the very-dark-skinned little man with long curly hair (quite the fashion in that neighborhood), who seems to find it as easy to get out of jail as to get in; office girls and typists, and a few men who looked like good middle-class citizens and were doubtless grass widowers on the loose during the summer.

As I left the pizzeria, I met the parish priest in this new section of town, a man of the cloth who is quite an attractive combination of the old and the new, the modern and the old-fashioned. He gave me a quick rundown of the latest developments in the parish: it seemed that the city government had gone back on its promise to give the Church an empty lot for new parish buildings. I wasn't at all surprised to hear this, because lots in this new neighborhood were going up many millions of pesetas in value every year. The Archbishop's Office was applying pressure, however, and probably would eventually get the space, though the plans now were to use most of it for an office building for Acción Católica and other church agencies. The priest didn't like the prospect at all but doubtless would have to resign himself to it. He had grabbed my arm and I was obliged to walk all the way to the parish house with him. We said good-by in front of the church, and I promised to attend a meeting he was going to call when his parishioners got back from their summer vacations.

As I stood there alone outside the church, I realized that I hadn't yet said an "Our Father" for Ernesto, as he certainly would have done for me had I drowned in the Mediterranean or been run over by a truck or died of poisoning from eating canned mushrooms. Once inside the little church, a strange sense of joy and gratitude overcame me. Despite everything, despite having taken his own life, Ernesto was going to have a Catholic funeral and be buried in sacred ground. The priest in Ketchum—the one from the chapel of the Virgin of the Snows, if I remembered rightly—had not hesitated to grant this desperate wanderer eternal rest in the arms of God.

I sat there thinking of all Ernesto's restless spiritual meanderings. They were not just touching; they were heartbreaking. But even so, he was not a stranger to the mystery of Grace. No one could ever call him an unreligious man or an agnostic. For all any of us knew, the many joys and perverted pleasures of life that he had sought so feverishly and found so unsatisfying had made him increasingly aware of the great conflict between his present life in this world and his future life in eternity, even though he had studiously avoided any sort of religious examination of conscience.

Had he gone to meet his Maker with self-doubts that would bring him eternal salvation, or had he been incapable all his life of expressing such thoughts even to himself? He had fought a spiritual battle within his soul his whole life long, and from time to time he had managed to glimpse the light through tiny chinks in the thick wall of his everyday life. But this inner struggle threatened to inflict on his soul more unbearably painful wounds than any his body had ever suffered in his passionate, exhausting battles for the lofty human causes he believed in.

Faith, a comfortable, simple, innocent faith, was rather easy to come by, and I am fairly certain that this sort of faith never failed Ernesto; but faith in an afterlife would have required too much of him. It was not that Ernesto lacked the will to believe in eternal life; rather, the mystery of death filled him with such fear and trembling that he was unable to face the thought. There was a paralyzing gap between Ernesto's faith and Ernesto's works. He had the greatest respect for everything having to do with religion, and in a way this respectful attitude toward everything sacred was the only thing that made his ignorance of the true spirit of religion tolerable. Instead of seeking God and praying, he went his own way in silence, apparently unconcerned about his soul but in reality terrified as to its ultimate fate. Weren't the apathy and pessimism that had overcome him part of the drama being played out in his soul, a drama that was really a kind of wordless prayer for love and hope to descend upon him from beyond the borders of our earthly world?

More than once, to my great amazement, I had seen him prostrate himself before the Mystery of God among men, and had had convincing proof of his attachment to the Catholic Church as a protective presence on this earth—for both sentimental and historical reasons—as well as his attachment to something even more positive and spiritually strengthening, the powerful, living spirit of Catholicism. I am certain that he told very few people he was a Catholic, either because he was too proud to bow entirely to the Church or was afraid he would be labeled an opportunist no matter what he said on the subject.

He had admitted a number of times, however, that he was a Catholic, though not a practicing one. He kept all of his inner life a carefully hidden secret; his spiritual life was as vague and timid as his outward enjoyment of life was frank and open. We can know little about his religious life beyond what he revealed in his writings, though he was always a strange romantic, who stubbornly kept all his innermost anxieties to himself. Nonetheless, how can we fail to see that scattered throughout his works are many profoundly Christian thoughts, many evidences of a true spirit of charity, a passion for justice, a yearning for an eternal peace in a blessed afterworld far more precious than all the promises of this world?

He did not have sufficient formal training as a philosopher and serious student of theology to trust himself to make definite pronouncements with regard to official Church dogma, nor was he at all interested in being a model, practicing Catholic. There was one important factor that had to be taken into account, however: his upbringing in the critical years of his life, during childhood and adolescence. He had come from a strict, rigid, puritan background and immediately upon leaving home had plunged into an anarchical and unbridled pursuit of the violent pleasures of life. There was bound to be a violent conflict between his instinctive lust for life and the austere traditional religious beliefs he had been brought up in. As a result, all of his powers of concentration came to be focused on the work of art. His writing was to fill the vacuum left by his disenchantment with religion, and all the other empty places as well, including that left by love.

But did he feel no ties at all to anything above and beyond his work as a writer and the sort of exciting life that inspires works of art? We know that he had respectfully accepted the teachings of the Bible in his early years, and came to respect them even more during his long years of dedicated labor in the vineyards of literature, and we also know that every so often he would drop in at his parish church or a chapel somewhere. At times such as this, his attitude was not so much one of fervent devotion as of quiet reflection. Usually he did not kneel, though I had seen him do so on two or three occasions, and had also seen him cross himself as any good Catholic would and solemnly recite an "Our Father" without stumbling over a single syllable.

Though he had little respect for church dogma or conventional forms of worship, I noticed more than once that he was greatly displeased by almost everything that smacked of atheism and thoroughly disapproved of any sort of mockery of sacred things. Blasphemous remarks about Christ or the Virgin didn't sit well with him at all, and he disdainfully turned a deaf ear to any sort of vicious joke about church ritual, priests, or religious processions. His own irreverent remarks never went beyond the casual sort of mild jest that any good Catholic might indulge in with close friends. He might occasionally criticize the Church for this or that minor fault, but I only wish that the many practicing Catholics who have dragged Ernesto's name in the mud for his lack of religious faith had his sense of respect for sacred things. He might tell the crudest joke in the world about other things, but he avoided any sort of ir-reverence, blasphemy, apostasy, or taking the name of the Lord in vain as he would the Devil himself. He disapproved of anything of that sort, and never indulged in that kind of talk himself. I can safely say that I never heard him pronounce the word "God" except in awe, with an almost biblical fear, or as the name for a terribly serious problem that faith might shed a glimmer of light on, though no mortal could ever hope to understand it or solve it.

I had just remembered what he said to me one day as we were leaving a church in Madrid: "I may not be a good Catholic, but I'm glad my friends are. People like Antonio, for instance."

Out of a deep sense of modesty, undoubtedly, he gave you only the smallest hint of his real feelings when such serious subjects came up in conversation. I knew that he would never reveal his most intimate be-liefs, but the rare moments when he would give you a brief glimpse of his innermost concerns were always very moving. We had gone on talking about religion that day, and he had said to me, "I'm as deeply attached to the Catholic Church as you are." Since usually he was dis-concertingly sarcastic about almost everything, I found this solemn pro-nouncement of his at the door of the Church of San José, with his hand over his heart, extremely revealing.

I would have to go to some trouble to get to the bottom of all this, but, for the moment, as Ernesto lay dead but not yet buried, those few words of his were enough. Perhaps the key to the mystery lay in Pauline, his second wife, a practicing Catholic. Their marriage may well have given Ernesto something more than the satisfaction of becom-ing a father.

If Ernesto ordinarily refused to discuss his religious beliefs, because he considered them nobody's business but his own, he was even less inclined to reveal any of the intimate details of his personal life. And usually when he did condescend to talk about them, what he said was either an outrageous lie or a sarcastic mock confession that no one could possibly believe, including himself.

Perhaps it was this romantic side of his personality that made Ernesto feel so much at home in Spain. In any event, he was always much more warmly sentimental and less prickly here than elsewhere. Whereas in London or Paris he was always very much on his guard, the moment he arrived in Madrid he was very relaxed and outgoing—as much so, at any rate, as a person as defensive, secretive, and mistrustful as Ernesto could ever be.

His religious fervor—and his Catholicism in particular—was doubtless most intense during his marriage to his second wife. His tortured soul searching stemmed from something more than intellectual doubt. I am convinced that the source of his inner turmoil was not so much the sort of melodramatic intellectual conflict that Unamuno fell prey to as it was an emotional problem, and that at a particularly trying time in his life Ernesto clung to Catholicism as a rather simplistic and naïve way of attaining a certain necessary peace of mind. As he searched his innermost heart, he one day found that the word *hope* was intimately related to Pauline's God.

There was one curious fact, a minor detail, that stuck in my memory like a mysterious key to the truth. It seemed like a very trivial thing, but I couldn't help remembering it: when Ernesto sat down at the table for a meal, he was never abstemious and couldn't understand why anybody else should be, but once when we were about to enjoy one of our phenomenal banquets on a very solemn religious holiday, before I could say a single word about how inappropriate our feasting was, he said, "We really mustn't gorge ourselves today."

"As a matter of fact, we should be fasting," I replied.

"Well, as long as that doesn't include alcohol, I'm all for it," he had answered.

And the meal he ordered that day was a very modest one.

And another time, after his disenchantment with Fidel Castro, I had asked him, "Is your Nobel medal still pinned to the mantle of the Virgen del Cobre?"

"I don't think anybody's dared lay a finger on it yet, and I don't suppose they ever will. Would they remove it here in Spain if I'd pinned it to the Virgen del Pilar, even though I fought on the side of the 'Reds'?"

"I see what you mean: it would offend the Cubans' sense of national pride."

"What's more, it would offend me. It wasn't a gift to the patron saint of Cuba to get in good with the Cubans, as certain reporters claimed. It was because it made me very happy to give my medal to her, even happier than if I'd given it to Mary, who also deserved it. I imagine you're happy about it too, since you're not one of those people who go around saying things like 'Hemingway, the prophet of the faithless,' 'a shameless pagan,' 'a fatalist without a soul,' and all that garbage. . . ."

Moreover, when we went to the cemetery together to see Baroja laid to rest, Ernesto was upset to see that Don Pío was being buried in a non-Catholic cemetery. Many Spaniards regarded this as Don Pío's last defiant act of rebellion against the social order, but it saddened Ernesto and he kept saying, "That poor old man, that poor old man."

He had said an *Our Father* and crossed himself in the funeral home, and he did so again at the cemetery, thereby shocking a number of simple-minded idiots.

"Come on, let's get out of here," he had said. And then he had added: "That poor old man, such a decent person—he deserved better."

"That's how it goes in Spain; someday they'll dig his body up and bury it in a more illustrious gravesite—not here, in this obscure spot, among foreigners, victims of the firing squad, and suicides. . . ."

Ernesto winced, and I realized immediately why he had, for I suddenly remembered how his father had died. To relieve the tension, I said, "Don Pío and I often talked together, you know, and in one of our last conversations about the supernatural he said to me: 'What penicillin doesn't cure, holy water won't cure either.' "

Ernesto pretended he hadn't heard and said again, "That old man deserved better."

"I know what you mean," I said. "He ought to have had a different kind of life."

"And a different kind of death," Ernesto added.

What other kind of peaceful, comfortable death had he been referring to? I had no idea what card he was betting his money on, because once he had said to me, out of a clear blue sky, "Do you think there's such a thing as a life after death?"

"Who knows!" I had replied, being very well aware of what the credo of the Church is but not wanting to indulge in propaganda.

"Well, I've never visited the beyond," he said slyly.

"Oh, we've all been there once or twice," I replied.

"Well, maybe we'll all meet in the sweet by-and-by. Who knows?" he said.

"I certainly hope so," I answered.

Ernesto had always enjoyed playing the role of the man of mystery, not as a game but out of necessity. To him it was a means of self-defense, a refuge.

Speaking of Baroja's funeral, he had also said, "I've never seen anybody as rabid as a Spanish Catholic who thinks he's acting in God's own name."

I had thought he simply meant they were disgusting. But then he'd added, "They're like mad dogs."

"Usually it's because they don't know any better," I'd said.

And as though agreeing that there might be a certain truth in that, he had said, "I'm sure you heard what they said this morning and saw all those cowards in the cemetery. They're ashamed to pray, themselves, but, at the same time, they're quite capable of killing other people because they refuse to pray."

I couldn't help but remember, despite myself, the cruel passage in *For Whom the Bell Tolls* where Robert Jordan confesses his innermost feelings about our country, a passage that had earned Ernesto a heap of abuse from Spanish critics, who accused him of being everything from a slanderer of our national character to a capricious, inconsistent back-biter. In it he had written:

> Those are the flowers of Spanish chivalry. What a people they have been. What sons of bitches from Cortez, Pizarro, Menendez de Avila all down through Enrique Lister to Pablo. And what wonderful people. There is no finer and no worse people in the world. No kinder people and no crueler. And who understands them? Not me, because if I did I would forgive it all. To understand is to forgive. That's not true. Forgiveness has been exaggerated. Forgiveness is a Christian idea and Spain has never been a Christian country.

These lines were an outspoken condemnation, but they were only the beginning.

I understood why Ernesto had been so irritated, and I found it hard to forgive the critics who had taken up arms against him or failed to see his point. Just as I found it hard to forgive the man—a snotty bastard, and mediocre writer to boot, who had snidely asked Ernesto, "Why is it you're not writing anything like *For Whom the Bell Tolls* now?"

I knew how hard it had been for Ernesto to control his temper, and had remarked, "Don't pay any attention—the man's a miserable wretch."

"He's not just a miserable wretch—he's a son of a bitch," Ernesto had replied.

I had gotten absolutely nowhere—I was a mere nobody—when as Don Pío lay dying I had tried to break through the wall of indifference and stupid bigotry that had so isolated him. I had asked a high church official to accompany me and a highly regarded university professor when we went to visit Don Pío on his deathbed, and this illustrious dignitary had replied in a cutting tone of voice, "Don Pío? May he die as he has lived."

It was enough to break your heart, as were Ernesto's bitter words:

> [Spain] has always had its own special idol worship within the Church. *Otra Virgen más.* I suppose that was why they had to destroy the virgins of their enemies. Surely it was deeper with them, with the Spanish religious fanatics, than it was with the people. The people had grown away from the Church because the Church was in the government and the government had always been rotten. This was the only country that the Reformation never reached. They were paying for the Inquisition now, all right.

Wasn't this passage written with a very Spanish passion, and haven't Spanish writers, among them the most blatant propagandists, penned much more uncharitable phrases?

I am absolutely certain that throughout his life Ernesto had believed to the end that he could win a victory over the flesh and the senses and that his faith would fill the gaps in his own credo. There was obviously something that he could not destroy with an automatic rifle, and it would mean a great deal to me if I could discover any sort of proof that his secret battle and his despair were signs not only of his fascination for death but of a yearning for eternal life.

Nothingness, and the nothingness of nothingness, were little more than words, Ernesto's siren song to death. Above and beyond his fascination with nothingness, at its very heart there was an acute anxiety and a keen awareness of an everlasting peace that transcended all the ephemeral adventures of this world. For Ernesto, the unknown was something more than another dimension; it also had to do with a tortured, wounded, hopeless feeling of abandonment. It was a question that would be resolved only at that point where the sincerity of Ernesto the mortal man—who had suffered pain counter to his very nature—and the sufficient grace of God would be conjoined.

I had always felt that Ernesto was a crippled man who had looked upon himself as a pathetic, abandoned orphan all his life. But I had also been dimly aware that he was a prey to an invincible fear of death, that all the victories he had won over the "Bald Lady" were empty, melodramatic triumphs. But at the same time, I could see that Ernesto, in his very heart of hearts, still cherished a sort of hope that might have been his salvation. Even though he turned a deaf ear to religious dogma and had no very clear conception of the meaning of the liturgy and the traditional rites of the Church, that did not mean that he had no more than vague stirrings of faith and vague desires of one day meeting his God, a God, that is to say, whom he desperately searched for in an endless "dark night of the soul" and hoped to find patiently waiting for him someday at the gates of paradise, where the story of Ernest Hemingway's life on this earth would be recorded like the transcription of a haunting nightmare. . . . What record would there be of his nebulous, pain-wracked spiritual wanderings? Few men standing at the bar of eternal judgment would have been forced to plead so desperately for their salvation by invoking the beauty and the undeserved felicity of their works. An artist who has lived such an active life, and at the same time been such an eloquent witness of the misery of the human condition, will not automatically attain the eternal rest that he deserves. But because Ernesto had both loved and suffered so much, he should rightfully be pardoned. His life might appear to be a violation of the established order of things, but in reality it had merely been proof of his impatience with the ways of the world, and his deep mistrust of them.

I found it particularly consoling that the parish priest in Ketchum had respected the family's wishes and despite such a scandalous suicide had allowed Ernesto the notorious vagabond to be buried in sacred ground in accordance with the holy rites of the Catholic Church.

At this point, I clung to certain passages in Ernesto's books that were like searing nails, such as this one, for instance, in *The Sun Also Rises*:

> "Listen, Jake," he said, "are you really a Catholic?"
> "Technically."
> "What does that mean?"
> "I don't know."

Or another conversation in this same novel:

> "You might pray," I laughed.
> "Never does me any good. I've never gotten anything I prayed for. Have you?"
> "Oh, yes."
> "Oh, rot," said Brett. "Maybe it works for some people though. You don't look very religious, Jake."
> "I'm pretty religious."

Or the passage in *The Old Man and the Sea*, at the climactic moment of the old fisherman's life:

> "I am not religious," he said. "But I will say ten Our Fathers and ten Hail Marys that I should catch this fish, and I promise to make a pilgrimage to the Virgin of Cobre if I catch him. That is a promise."
> He commenced to say his prayers mechanically. Sometimes he would be so tired that he could not remember the prayer and

then he would say them fast so that they would come automatically. Hail Marys are easier to say than Our Fathers, he thought.

"Hail Mary full of Grace the Lord is with thee. Blessed art thou among women and blessed is the fruit of thy womb, Jesus. Holy Mary, Mother of God, pray for us sinners now and at the hour of our death. Amen." Then he added: "Blessed Virgin, pray for the death of this fish. Wonderful though he is."

"I could not fail myself and die on a fish like this," he said. "Now that I have him coming so beautifully, God help me endure. I'll say a hundred Our Fathers and a hundred Hail Marys. But I cannot say them now. Consider them said," he thought. "I'll say them later."

In the short story "Now I Lay Me" (what a beautiful title!) the protagonist prays, mostly "for them," for other people, but, with his usual frankness, Ernesto notes that he cannot get past the words "On earth as it is in Heaven."

But perhaps this path led nowhere. Did all this prove anything? Of course not. The only proof I had of anything was that I had heard Ernesto recite the Our Father, not once but several times. And I also kept remembering his words:

"Didn't you know that I was a Catholic?"

"Does that mean that you aren't one now?"

"I confess I'm a bad one."

But this was also proof of something more. More than once, Ernesto had been on the point of confessing the whole truth about his marriage to Pauline, but had stopped at the very threshold. My personal impression was that this had been an important period in his life, for it had brought him consolation and happiness, but, at the same time, it had been a time of much greater inner struggle than any of his other marriages.

"I can't be a good Catholic, because I'm a sinner," he had said.

"But I believe that all of us who call ourselves Christians are sinners."

"But I'm not a good Christian; I've never managed to be one."

One fine day, like a person telling an exciting story and identifying wholeheartedly with the rebellious gesture that he was recounting, Ernesto told me how his son Patrick had come to him, rifle in hand, and uttered an almost biblical phrase: "Father, I've come to you for my rightful inheritance." He had been proud of his son's self-assertiveness, and had laughingly said, "He's a great kid."

Whenever he spoke of profound spiritual things, Ernesto pretended to be very downcast, as melancholy as a widower who had lost all his enthusiasm for long-cherished beliefs. I had once heard him murmur, after

10. Even after he became famous, Hemingway remained on intimate terms with the friends he had met when he first visited Spain. Here he is chatting with old Marceliano, the innkeeper who befriended him when he was an unknown. He loved going off to a corner table with him to talk about old times. (MASPONS, BARCELONA)

11. In this photo taken at the 1959 San Fermín fiesta, Ernesto is standing next to the author of this book. In the foreground are Aaron Hotchner, the author of *Papa Hemingway* (eating an ice-cream cone), and the Irish girl, "Miss Valerie," whom Ernesto brought to the United States. She married Ernesto's son, Dr. Gregory Hemingway. (MASPONS, BARCELONA)

12. Standing next to Ordóñez the matador, Ernesto, with a red carnation in his buttonhole, talked with us about what could happen during a bull-fight. Almost anything is possible in the course of a corrida, even death, but in a way it is a glorious death. (MASPONS, BARCELONA)

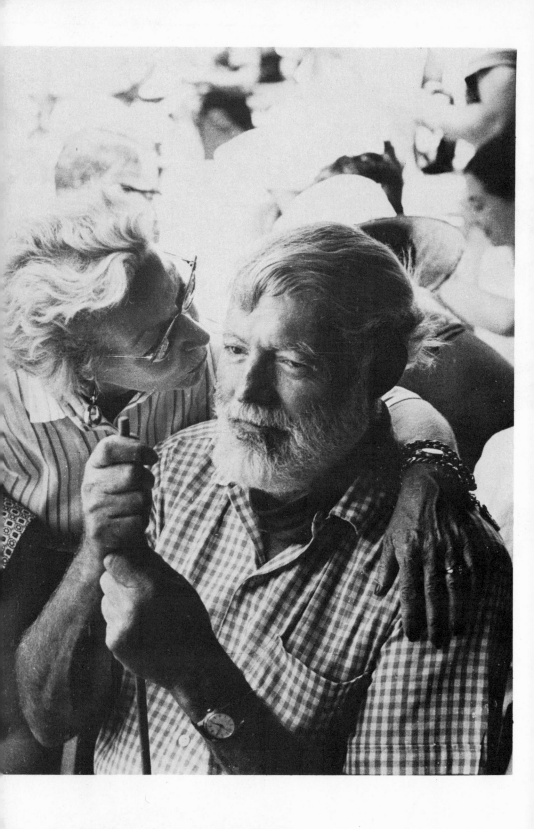

13 and 14. Mary Hemingway never left Ernesto's side during his last fiesta in Pamplona. (MASPONS, BARCELONA)

15. Ernesto. (JOHN BRYSON)

16. Hemingway and his wife Mary with Juanito Quintana, the close friend who introduced him to the world of bullfighting and to many of the top bullfighters—among them Maera and Niño de la Palma. (EDICIONES DESTINO)

17. Ernesto among the spectators at the bullfight. (MAGNUM)

18. Ernest Hemingway, American winner of the Nobel Prize for Literature, poses with the matador Antonio Ordóñez after the *torero's* return to the bullring at Linares. Ordóñez had recently been gored at Palma, Majorca, and again near Dax, France. (WIDE WORLD PHOTOS)

19. Ernesto watches a bullfight at Pamplona, with Antonio Ordóñez. (UNITED PRESS INTERNATIONAL)

having long pondered his "personal civil war," as though trying to conceal his passionate idealism, "If only a healthy anarchism could be combined with a living spirit of Christianity!"

But he regretted having said that, and immediately began criticizing revolutionary leaders in Spain in the same terms as in *The Dangerous Summer,* where he had written that during the Civil War he had seen such terrible things that he had stopped praying for himself and prayed only for others.

Praying for others may be a commonplace thing, but praying for the salvation of other people's souls without regard for one's own is very close to the spirit of the gospel.

But all this merely brought me back to the disturbing question: Why does a man kill himself? And once more I found myself at the very edge of the abyss, in that ambiguous world in which pagan powers were not only the source of evil but also the source of the impulse to control the unhealthy desires that had ruined half Ernesto's life, if not all of it.

> Once you accept the rule of death thou shalt not kill is an easily and a naturally obeyed commandment.

Ernesto had not minced words when he wrote that in *Death in the Afternoon.* But he had immediately added what might appear to be no more than a form of disciplining the will, though in reality it had led him to the very edge of self-destruction:

> But when a man is still in rebellion against death he has pleasure in taking to himself one of the Godlike attributes; that of giving it.

Why not deal oneself the deathblow then? Wasn't that a way of overcoming one's miserable human condition as a mere mortal? If a man is also suffering from a debilitating mental illness that clouds his mind and makes him so delirious that he feels absolutely empty and seems to be simply drifting from one disaster to another, his instinctive defenses and his respect for himself as the repository of a treasure that does not belong to him will soon vanish.

Just a year before, he had told his biographer, Singer, "It's the same with my life. From a distance it looks very beautiful and exciting, but the closer you can come the more scars you see; look at my body. Look at my face. Look at what is under the beard."

Hadn't he said almost the same thing to me, and even worse things? "There's no point in praying for courage when you've become a ridiculous burden on others. The thing to pray for is one moment of lucidity that will make you forget all the rest. . . ."

He had said that to me a number of times. Sometimes I took it as an ironic remark meant to show me how much he really valued his life and his soul. But the last time he told me that, it seemed to me that he was hinting that something terrible was about to happen to him, and I was suddenly afraid for him. Because after uttering those words, he appeared to be lost in thought and started wandering aimlessly about the room with a faraway look in his eyes, fingering his glass of whisky but not drinking it, as though it were poison.

He felt that there was little he could do any more. And even more revealing: there was very little he could write.

Summer in Madrid is not just hot; it is stifling. Getting from my neighborhood to Ferraz 42 at four o'clock in the afternoon was as heroic a feat as fighting two Miura bulls in a row.

It was time for the *corrida* to begin. On the way to Ordóñez's, I tried to recall everything Ernesto had said about him. He had talked about him constantly, in the most flattering terms: "He's a great kid, isn't he?" "He's stupendous." "He's very handsome and a very decent guy." "There's nobody like him." "I'd die if anything ever happened to him; but he's so good he doesn't deserve to have anything bad happen to him." "I'm so fond of him—he means more to me than a son." I got quite used to this string of compliments that Ernesto constantly came out with, almost without realizing it, though he meant them all wholeheartedly; they were not just empty phrases.

When Ordóñez was gored in Aranjuez, I saw Ernesto in a state of mind I had never seen him in before; one minute he'd swear a blue streak and the next minute he'd start praying. It was "Damn this whole fucking thing" one minute and "I've said a prayer to the Virgen del Cobre and she'll save him" the next. He kept pacing nervously back and forth, kicking his feet and mumbling to himself, and then curled up in a ball in a chair like a man possessed. "Didn't I swear to myself that I'd never be friends with any *torero*? Why did I ever get involved with one— one like this especially?" he muttered.

But what splendid moments he had had watching Antonio in the ring! The critics called Ordóñez "the prodigy of the bullring," "the Plato of bullfighting," "the Michelangelo of the *corrida*," "the Napoleon of *verónicas*," "the Picasso of the cape," and so on, and Ernesto would sit reading such things in open-mouthed amazement, and would always add that no other *torero* had the personality, the courage, the depth of emotion that Antonio displayed in the ring. When some bullfight critic or other outdid himself and spoke of Antonio's "world as secret as the Catacombs" or his "universe as aesthetic as the Divine Comedy" or his "passes as full of grace as the Hail Mary" or his "moments as stellar as the emergence of Aphrodite from the foamy waves" or "his passion as an artist, a style at once bold and delicate, like Goya's painting," Ernesto was prepared to be somewhat cordial to the man and pay for his fancy metaphors in American dollars. One day in a tavern the leader of a troupe of Flamenco performers spotted the two of them and sang, almost in a whisper:

> Long live Pedro Romero,
> Who invented bullfighting;
> And Antonio Ordóñez,
> Its most glorious prophet.

And Ernesto had casually handed him a greenback, as though he quite expected to pay people for praising Ordóñez.

"Look what it says here in the paper about you," Ernesto would say to Antonio, and hand him the piece with all the most complimentary phrases underlined: "the peak of perfection," "a purity as immaculate as an Annunciation by the Beato di Fiesole," "the master favored us with his magic taurine Word," "the artist allowed us to see and admire his art in all its wondrous beauty, as one might unveil a newly discovered painting by El Greco. . . ." And then Ernesto would say: "Does that please you? How about that! You can count the *toreros* who've had things like that said about them on the fingers of one hand." Then he would go on reading the clippings: "The word that this genius passes on to us by way of the muleta has the stamp of eternity." Sometimes they went on and on, and he didn't read them all the way through or even show them to Antonio: "Of everything that has gone to make up life and history, that is imperishable because it is of the essence and has deep roots, because it does not age with the passing of time or become outmoded as fashions change. . . ." Reading things like that always put Ernesto in a good mood.

Sometimes Antonio, who has always been a modest man with a fine sense of humor, would interrupt him: "I wonder when we'll fight another *corrida* as impressive as *The Old Man and the Sea*."

"Yes, that was a great afternoon."

And if Antonio was in a teasing mood, he might say, "They tell me it was mostly ghostwritten . . ."

But to see Ernesto's enthusiasm for Ordóñez at fever pitch, you had to be on hand when Antonio went around the ring with two ears in his hand and halted in front of him, as though paying him homage. I used to watch Ernesto when Antonio was fighting. He followed his every move so intently he didn't even blink. It was something more than the ecstasy of watching a consummate artist perform. There was passion in his eyes: at once a kind of ritual suffering and a keen sensual pleasure. He liked it that Ordóñez's passes were so controlled, his cape work so logical, his gestures so elegant, but above all he liked it that Ordóñez had the perfect stature for a bullfighter. And Ordóñez was touched by this old superaficionado's devotion, just as his father,

Niño de la Palma, had had a certain fondness for Ernesto as a young man, though their friendship had not kept Ernesto from one day calling him a coward and a fake.

What had Antoñito's feelings been when he heard the news? Ernesto would have been more grief-stricken had it been Antonio who had died, because Antonio was something essential to him, whereas Ernesto was not that indispensable to Ordóñez. Ernesto's devotion to him had become a jealous, total, exhausting kind of worship in the end. Would Ernesto have turned on him eventually, the way he had on almost all the friends who were really devoted to him? During Ernesto's last visit to Spain, I had noticed—or thought I had noticed—certain signs that he wanted to be left alone, to hole up in his hotel room and search for striking, unusual adjectives to describe this living embodiment of the dreams of his youth. He had finally met a *real* bullfighter, and what was more, a young, likable, courageous, affectionate one. But it drove him crazy when Antonio would put his arm over his shoulder and say, "What a great life you writers lead—all you have to do is keep pushing the pen around."

All the way to Ordóñez's I kept wondering why he hadn't flown to Ketchum. And he hadn't said a word about going to the funeral when I had talked to him on the phone. One newspaper reporter with a lively imagination had written a long piece describing the matador's reactions on viewing his friend's dead body, and had also mentioned that Ordóñez had been appointed Ernesto's executor.

Toward the last, Ernesto hadn't seemed quite as fond of Antonio as he had once been. He kept stealing cautious glances at him, as though it pained him to look at him, and yet at the same time he had seemed to be delighted when Antonio fought well and downcast on those rare occasions when he fought badly. It was as though he felt a little ashamed of having been that carried away by a bullfighter. But I also had to remember that Ordóñez was not only a good matador but the sort of bullfighter Ernesto had dreamed of for years, the ideal model for a writer. At the door of the operating room that day in Aranjuez I had heard Ernesto say repeatedly:

"Can't you see he's just a kid?"

The roots of all of this lay far back in the past. In *The Sun Also Rises* Ernesto had written of the bullfighter Romero, who had been modeled on Antonio's father, Niño de la Palma:

"That Romero lad is just a child."
"He's a damned good-looking boy," I said. "When we were up in his room, I never saw a better-looking kid."
"How old do you suppose he is?"

"Nineteen or twenty."

"Just imagine it."

And in another passage:

Romero's face was very brown. He had very nice manners.

And also:

I noticed his skin. It was clear and smooth and very brown.

And:

"My God, he's a lovely boy," Brett said.

And finally:

Romero listened very seriously. Then he turned to me. He was the best-looking boy I have ever seen.

But this was very little compared to what Ernesto was to write and do on Antonio's behalf, for he looked upon him as the resurrection of a *torero* god, the living image of all the mythical matadors who had ever lived. If he was dissatisfied with *The Dangerous Summer*, it was not because he regretted what he had said about Manolete or was worried about having assigned Dominguín an inferior role, but because Antonio deserved even better. He could not do him justice in a piece of reporting, and would have liked to immortalize his idol by making him the hero of a novel. That was what he regretted not having done.

The newspapers had made a big thing of the whole Hemingway-Ordóñez affair, and had even reported that they were in business together, doubtless because the two of them had often jokingly spoken of being "fifty-fifty partners." And at least one bullfight critic, Curro Castañares, had even gone so far as to make certain nasty insinuations about "Ernesto's senile devotion to Cayetano's son."

But Ordóñez had merely been a beloved, affectionate friend, a resurrected idol, the ideal bullfighter in the flesh. And also a charming, likable youngster who always called Ernesto "Papa."

"Listen, Papa." "Come on, Papa." "See you later, Papa."

The possibility that something might happen to Ordóñez during a *corrida* made Ernesto even more deeply attached to him. And Ordóñez for his part couldn't help feeling flattered that one of the greatest authors in the world, or at any rate one of the most famous ones, had chosen to write about him. Ernesto was bound to be impressed by Antonio, just as Antonio was bound to have his head turned by Ernesto's interest.

Nonetheless, they were never as close friends as has generally been supposed. Ernesto was a writer and Ordóñez was a subject. That was what they had in common, though they came to admire each other more and more as Antonio gradually began to appreciate what a great writer Ernesto was and Ernesto discovered what a kind, decent, good man Antonio was, a side of himself that this famous *torero* was sometimes obliged to conceal because it did not fit the public's image of a bullfighter. Ordóñez had begun to read some of Ernesto's books, and everyone in the world knew who Ernesto's favorite bullfighter was. But the two of them pretended not to take literature, the press, or even bulls seriously, though they both knew that this was only a kind of private joke between them.

After his fulsome praise of Ordóñez, about the only thing that Ernesto could do with the other *toreros* was to discreetly dismiss them. How much grief and remorse and wasted time and energy the whole *Dangerous Summer* project was to cost him! But it was too late now to regret having taken it on—or to regret anything else, for that matter. This job of reporting had been nothing more nor less than a crushing burden that had left him exhausted when he reached the end of the road.

I was thinking about all this and many other things on my way to Ordóñez's, and suddenly I could see Ernesto clearly in my mind's eye, a majestic figure tirelessly following Ordóñez from one bullring to another and one hotel to the next. I also had a vivid picture in my mind of the two of them brimming over with good spirits after a *corrida* when Antonio had fought especially well.

There was something almost religious about Ernesto's devotion to his idol. He not only prayed for him; he made promises and vows whenever he thought Antonio was in particular danger. Before a *corrida* he would tiptoe into his room very quietly, as though overcome with awe. If he allowed himself to crack a joke, he made sure that it was a really funny one that would cheer Antonio up, and never one that would remind him that he was about to enter the ring for yet another fearful and dangerous *corrida*. When Antonio left for the bullring, Ernesto would clap him on the back or give his arm a friendly squeeze. If Antonio felt like talking, he'd sit down on the bed next to him and do his best to make amusing conversation without ever resorting to dirty jokes or frivolous gossip. During the *corrida* his eyes followed Antonio's every move in rapt fascination. He might make some comment about the bull or the *caudrilla*, but would never say a word about Antonio. After the *corrida*, particularly if Ordóñez had fought brilliantly, he would be more effusive and give his friend a hearty embrace and perhaps even a kiss and stand there next to him drinking a toast to him along with all the others. Then he would leave him to enjoy his triumph by himself and walk off, his shoulders sagging a bit, and looking a little depressed. But he knew perfectly well that a *torero* has an obligation to his faithful. He must have vastly admired Ordóñez's art and been very much attached to him as a person, it seems to me, to be able to put up with that strange crowd, half tatterdemalion bums and half elegant men about town, that inevitably tags along after matadors. This king of the bullring was bound to be surrounded by such courtiers, and Ernesto somehow managed to tolerate them. The most important thing in this world, the *corrida* itself, demanded such sacrifices, including playing the role of number one courtier.

I personally believe that, from the very beginning, Ernesto had so totally identified himself with the bullfighter that he had an intuitive understanding of the central mystery and the ritual meaning of the *corrida*. He had as profound an understanding of the very essence of bullfighting as any non-professional can ever achieve. But he also began studying our *fiesta brava* objectively, doggedly gathering all the information he could and attending hundreds of bullfights. He was not content to remain a simple *aficionado*, or even a passionate *aficionado*, which is what the Spanish bullfight bigots have tried to make him out to be. If Ernesto managed to earn a reputation as the most important writer on bullfighting outside of Spain and, despite what many people say, one of the most important ones within Spain, it was not because of all his pointless and occasionally very regrettable commentaries on the superficial aspects of bullfighting, or because of his descriptions of the art of this or that famous *torero*, but because of his total dedication to the *corrida*, which often sheds important light on his own personal tauromachy. There are pages of his on our fiesta that are destined to sweep away all the soggy rhetoric and all the false lyricism that clutters the brains of the majority of our so-called bullfight critics. There are pages of Ernesto's about bullfighting that will be indispensable to anyone who wishes to study seriously the deeper meaning of our national fiesta. And for that reason alone, I believe that Ernesto deserves greater respect from those whose lives are centered on bulls, bullfighters, and the Fiesta Brava.

Perhaps I should keep my mouth shut about the Ordóñez affair, too. The less said about the intimate details the better. It would probably be best not to write about any of these things that had crossed my mind. The whole bullfighting world is a nest of vipers. And the last thing in the world I was prepared to do was to cross swords with the high priests of bullfighting, who are perhaps better at sinking their fangs into innocent calves and heifers than anything else.

The bus was almost empty. All sorts of memories kept popping up unexpectedly all during this trip across Madrid on the upper deck of a bus.

One of these memories was quite painful, and I wished I had never remembered the whole incident. The last time I'd seen Ordóñez, we'd gone to a restaurant, the Valentín, with Julio Aparicio. I remembered that we had walked up Mesonero Romanos together as far as Torres Bermejas, and just as we were about to go into a coffeehouse, the two of them had gotten into a fistfight with a journalist, Antonio Olano. It had all happened so fast I was dumfounded. It was like a scene in a movie that a director had set up beforehand.

Another memory, this one a joyous one, was the last San Fermín fiesta with Ernesto. We had danced like *simbas*, the Pamplona word for carnival dancers, all the way from the hotel to the square. Domecq's son had been with us. Since then, he has begun what promises to be a brilliant career as a *rejoneador*, a bullfighter on horseback. Domecq and I had had seats high up on the sunny side of the ring, and between bulls we drank whole bottles, wineskins, and canteens of this and that. We were doubtless pretty high and every once in a while we'd wave our handkerchiefs and scream "Paaaapaaa," "Paaaa-aaaa-paaaa," "Paaa-aaaaaaapaaaaaaaa" at the top of our lungs. Ernesto was sitting on the far side of the ring in the shade, and finally he spotted us and began shouting and jumping up and down too. That was Ernesto's last San Fermín fiesta. It was a wonderful afternoon—or rather lots of afternoons, all of them marvelous.

When we got back to the hotel after the *corrida*, Ernesto bawled Ordóñez out. Antonio had been gored in the leg during the running of the bulls in the streets and he shouldn't have jumped around and danced that way. It might be dangerous!

"What was that you said?" the conductor on the bus asked me.

"I just remarked that you've made these wooden seats feel nice and cool sprinkling them down that way."

"We do the best we can," he replied, pointing to an earthenware jar in the corner.

"Well, that's the best anybody can do."

"That's what I always say."

He headed toward the stairs, looking very dignified and shaking his coin box like a rattle.

The San Fermín fiesta in 1959 had been Ernesto's last spree. It was the key to everything. All the "local color," the Irish girl, "Freckles" Hotchner, the girl students, the very likable doctor George Saviers and his wife Pat, Bill Davis and company, the whole crowd of flippant, affected, conceited bit players in this drama who had flocked around the fabulous Ernesto had made it all seem more like the grand finale of a stupendous *opera buffa,* where amid all the cheap swaggering and the vulgar sentimentalism there are a few marvelous moments and wonderfully touching, genuine emotion. The priests and priestesses in the chorus were frauds, but they had nonetheless made this twilight of a Goliath who was soon to blow his brains out a glorious epic spectacle.

Ernesto kept turning to me and making confidential remarks about Davis: "He's really a very faithful friend. He'd lay down his life for me," he whispered.

And then, a few moments later: "He drives like the devil himself, though. He scares me sometimes."

Then he dropped the subject of Davis and started in on Hotchner: "He's a little precious, but he's a very smart cookie."

"I can see that he's very fond of you," I replied.

Then, a little while later, he'd whispered, "I don't really trust him, though."

Remembering what Ernesto had said about Hotchner naturally reminded me of the Irish girl who had come to play a more and more important role in that cast of kooks at the San Fermín fiesta. "Freckles" had kept whispering in Ernesto's ear, and Ernesto had tried to convince himself that this rather ordinary-looking girl with a mysterious, charming personality could fill the great empty spot in his heart. It was really a rather cruel irony. At one point he took me aside and said, "You keep eying her."

"Who, me?"

"You seem quite taken with her."

"Oh, Ernesto! Come on!"

"Listen, she's all yours."

But all this was merely the opening scene in the *opera buffa.* Next came the enthusiastic chorus of girl students who kept pretending they were innocent young things. Ernesto said to me: "Where do you suppose their maidenheads went?"

The whole thing became more and more unreal in my memory, as it had perhaps been back then, too, for in the midst of that uproarious circus Ernesto had been threading his way across the last great abyss of his life.

And at this point I remembered the figure who to my way of thinking had kept her dignity throughout the whole business. Mary Hemingway knew very well what was gold and what was mere tinsel in the bullfight world, what was theatrical show and what was truly courageous and noble. Mary and Ordóñez knew the difference between picturesque rascals and crass opportunists. At one point Antonio said to Ernesto, "I can see that 'Freckles' is a great help to you."

And Ernesto replied, " 'Freckles' is tops, in my estimation."

"And your 'nigger' is a hard worker."

"He's my bodyguard."

"But what would you be without Mary?" Antonio said slyly. And then he added, "You must pay her very well."

"I don't think she has any reason to complain," Ernesto replied.

"She does more for you than anybody," Antonio went on. "What would you be without her?"

"It would be absolute disaster," Ernesto replied. And added, "What would you be without Carmen?"

"A total wreck," Ordóñez said.

"We'd both be total wrecks," Ernesto said.

"That's right—we'd be total wrecks," Ordóñez agreed.

I found all these memories amusing, just as it was very amusing to remember Quintana, a great gentleman and one of Ernesto's oldest friends, laughing indulgently; or Matías sitting quietly watching, for all this commotion that Ernesto was the center of struck him as a sort of absurd carnival. Matías knew publicity hounds and spongers when he saw them. At this very moment, Matías, decent, even-tempered, philosophical Matías, was no doubt thinking of poor Ernesto and perhaps remembering how the crowd in Pamplona would whisper: "Look, there's Old Whiskers, the lucky dog." But the thoughts running through my mind were doubtless not as noble as Matías'. I was thinking of all the parasites in the bullfight world, the "chiselers," as Ernesto called them, the exploiters of bullfighters, the bull-butchers, the fawning fans of the Nobel Prize winner, the rascals and clowns of the carnival that had now ended forever, and wondering what they were doing right this minute. Some of them would be silently wheeling around the corpse in great circles, like vultures looking for a choice morsel, and others might be just a little touched and search for some memory in the bottom of their hearts that might persuade them that what they felt was genuine grief.

I got off the bus at the Plaza de España and walked down the street in the shade of the trees. There were crowds of kids waiting in line to get on buses that would take them to a swimming pool. I went over to a refreshment stand and ordered a beer. It wouldn't do to arrive at Ordóñez's ahead of time.

There was one thing in particular that was troubling me. Should I come right out and speak of suicide, since I was quite certain that Ernesto had killed himself, or should I resort to that expression so common in the world of bullfighting, "bad luck"? I must not forget that Ordóñez had recently been going through a religious crisis, or rather had embraced the Catholic faith with even more fervor than before. I remembered what Ernesto had said about him:

"He's a good man, a really good man."

"What's more, he's a true Christian who faithfully follows the teachings of the Church," I said.

"Yes, I've noticed a number of traits of character in Antonio that are quite uncommon in bullfighters."

"He's a practicing Catholic. A really good Catholic. He wants to live his life as honorably as he fights bulls," I said.

"I'm sure that he's been deeply moved by the death of someone he loved very much. His very best trait is that he's absolutely fearless. There's not an ounce of fear in him," Ernesto said.

"He's learning to control his fear perfectly. But I'm quite sure he's scared stiff now and again," I replied.

"Have you seen Ordóñez in the bullring, drinking from a water jug? When a *torero's* shitting in his pants with fear, he's not able to rinse his mouth and inconspicuously spit the water out in a corner somewhere so as not to offend people's sensibilities. He's not scared at all."

The joking and the leg-pulling and the clowning between Ernesto and Antonio, their enigmatic relationship to each other, had come to an end now. The "kidnaper" of young girls, the fatalist on the most familiar terms with the Great Whore—Death—the winner of every sort of honor, the spendthrift who had gone through thousands and thousands of dollars, the novelist whose own life was so much like a novel, had now written the final paragraph of the story of his life. Art for art's sake and life for life's sake had ended in death for death's sake. Like one of the gods of the bullring, Ernesto had died while fighting his adversary. But it would be best not to say a word about all that.

Every step I took was bringing me closer to the Calle Ferraz. I have never been one to invade the privacy of bullfighters, to try to establish any sort of relationship with them other than the most respectful friendship, and for some reason I worship great bullfighters almost as much as I worship the priesthood. This may be because of the ceremony that continuously surrounds them, not only in their moments of splendor but in their everyday life. In the *callejones*, in the bullring, in banquet halls, in restaurants, along the streets, in infirmaries and hospitals, they are always heroes and enjoy being surrounded by a retinue of worshipful fans, who reverently admire their wrists and their calves, their slender waists and their beautiful asses. When you are with them, you must behave one minute as though you were a guest at a wedding, and as though you were a mourner at a wake the next. This constant shifting back and forth between the atmosphere of a fiesta and that of a funeral has always struck me as both very unnerving and very exhausting: not so much in and of itself, but because it requires such toadying, such single-minded fawning. The *torero* himself is altogether worthy of admiration if he fights courageously and serenely, nobly and gracefully; but the fact remains that bullfighters—even the greatest of them—oblige even the craftiest rapscallions and the most cynical hangers-on to be patient and long-suffering and cater to their every whim. There are few arts surrounded by so much corruption and so much emotional blackmail as the so-called "divine art of tauromachy."

Down by the Calle Ferraz, in the ruins of the Montaña Barracks, where disaster had first struck my family during the Civil War, some boys were playing *pelota*, with oldsters standing on the sidelines watching. All I could see were several figures in shirtsleeves and the only thing I could hear was the smack of the ball against the wall, and now and again the usual shouts of approval, or groans of dismay when one of the players missed a shot.

I could remember clearly now how Ernesto had behaved while Antonio was on the operating table. He was absolutely crushed, and kept wandering in and out of the operating room and pacing up and down, unable to sit still. It wasn't simply nervousness; it was more like a very peculiar sort of hysteria. As we waited there for news of how the operation was going, I saw an Ernesto I had never seen before: a hesitant, terrified, almost desperate man. From time to time, he seemed to withdraw into a world of his own, muttering incoherent words and phrases over and over, and then falling into a very revealing, gloomy silence. I don't really know how Dr. Tamames, who has the reputation of being a rather sharp-tempered genius in the operating room, was able to be so patient with him. It was as though Ernesto was determined not only to see Antonio's wound but to touch it with his very own fingers, and every once in a while he would mention the names of other specialists he knew personally and other hospitals he was familiar with. As Dr. Tamames wielded his clamps and scissors and scalpels, Ernesto kept asking, over and over:

"What about his femoral artery? Is his femoral artery okay?"

Ernesto was so paternal he seemed childish. He would exaggerate the danger to Antonio's life one minute and play it down the next, he would buttonhole curious bystanders and question them, voice his mistrust in all doctors and pray out loud, try to cheer us up one minute and communicate his fear to us the next, and then go off in a corner by himself, and when he couldn't stand waiting it out there another minute, he would retreat to a nearby bar and drink. I couldn't help remembering a paragraph from *Death in the Afternoon*:

Cayetano Ordonez looked like a bullfighter, he acted like a bullfighter and for one season he was a bullfighter. . . . At the end of the season he was gored severely and painfully in the thigh, very near the femoral artery.

That was the end of him.

That is doubtless why he kept asking over and over again as Antonio was being operated on:

"How about his femoral artery? Is his femoral artery okay?"

What had happened to the father might well happen to the son. But there was something that held even greater terror for Ernesto, and his tortured mind kept wavering between the real and the imagined, between literature and life. I was suddenly reminded of another paragraph in *Death in the Afternoon*, which has become one of the most famous passages he ever wrote:

If you see Niño de la Palma the chances are you will see cowardice in its least attractive form; its fat rumped, prematurely bald from using hair fixatives, prematurely senile form. He, of all the young bullfighters who came up in the ten years after Belmonte's first retirement, raised the most false hopes and proved the greatest disappointment.

Knowing Ernesto, it was obvious to me that he could only have written those words because Cayetano Ordóñez had both disappointed and irritated him, because he both admired him and felt scorn for him. (How could Antonio have forgiven Ernesto for writing such harsh words about his father? He may never have read them. Or perhaps he simply preferred to ignore them.) But such a thing would never happen to Niño de la Palma's son. The son was far braver; he was far superior to his father in every way.

When Antonio saw "Papa" poke his head in the door of his room at the sanitorium, his face lit up, he grinned from ear to ear, and whooped for joy.

"Hey there, genius, come on in!" he shouted to Ernesto.

Ernesto was so concerned about the wound in Antonio's leg that you would have thought he was waiting outside a delivery room for news that he was the father of a bouncing baby boy. Antonio started to get out of bed then, and Ernesto immediately rushed to his side the minute his feet hit the floor:

"Careful, Matador, you might fall."

"Nonsense! It's the Nobel Prize Winner who's shaky on his pins."

"Hang on tight—I don't want you to fall."

"You're the one who's a total wreck. What would become of you without me?"

"Stretch your leg out very carefully."

"Never mind my leg."

"Put your foot on the floor very gently."

"Okay, I'll put it down as gently as if it were a double-barreled shotgun."

"That's it precisely—or rather, as if it were a double-balled shotgun—a pair of *cojones*, as the classical writers put it."

"I hope they stand the test of time."

"The classical authors, you mean?"

"No, my balls!"

"Don't forget that they were in pretty serious danger."

"I'll do my best to keep that in mind."

As Antonio gradually recovered from his wound, Ernesto stopped being so gloomy and depressed and began bubbling over with such high spirits that he seemed almost childlike. Any other *torero* would have been an invalid for the rest of his life after having been gored so severely. But Ordóñez was not only an extremely brave man; he was also a very lucky one, and Ernesto found this so reassuring that he suddenly seemed years younger.

"Antonio will be back in the bullring soon and there won't be another *torero* who can touch him," I said, knowing how happy it made Ernesto to hear things like that.

"I hope God's listening," he replied.

"Antonio thrives on danger. Horn wounds purify his soul the way torture implements cleanse the souls of martyrs."

"But he shouldn't push his luck too far," Ernesto answered.

I was in front of Ordóñez's house now. I saw by my watch that it was exactly the hour Ordóñez had set for my visit. A drop of sweat was trickling down my back like a worm crawling along my spine. But once it reached my belt it went no farther.

I was afraid to ring the bell. And I stood there at the front door of his house wondering what sort of scene awaited me inside. Would Antonio's wife, Carmen, be there? Would their children come running to the door? I hoped they weren't home.

It may sound silly, but I had the feeling that there, inside Ordóñez's house, in the middle of one of those elegant reception rooms that *toreros* have in their homes, I would find Ernesto's huge body dangling from the ceiling like a slaughtered bull, that I would see before me his great broad face, his thick neck, his reddish hair, his piercing eyes, his pursed mouth, and his flared nostrils of a wild beast in heat.

He would not even have in his eyes that faraway, inscrutable, but utterly frank look that the pupils of dead men's eyes have, nor that skeptical but mesmerizing air about him that all dead people have, that terribly disconcerting peacefulness, that imposing horizontal solemnity of the dead.

In my mind's eye I saw him with his shoulders all hunched over, his massive chest thrust out, and his round belly bulging. Perhaps they had left his legs and ankles uncovered there in Ketchum; people might see that he had the haunches of a sportsman gone to seed, with blobs of flabby fat all over them.

"Listen, José Luis, is it true that lots of people in your home town hang themselves?" he had asked me.

"The number varies from year to year—there are some years that give you better reasons to hang yourself than others."

"We'll have to visit your home town together sometime."

"You'll be glad we did, I'm certain of that."

In my town, people ordinarily commit suicide by hanging themselves from the branch of a tree—usually an olive tree or a fig tree. But occasionally one *aficionado* or another has chosen a fragile fruit tree and the branch has given way and saved his life, although in most cases he has a funny, wry neck for the rest of his life, thereby serving as a macabre example of plans that have gone awry because they have been carried out halfheartedly.

I tried to imagine what Ernesto looked like after the fatal shotgun burst, but I simply couldn't. Ernesto's majesty, his grandeur remained untouched, in my mind's eye at least, by the horror of his terrible self-slaughter. But undoubtedly his head had been shattered to bits. Had they covered his face so that no one could see? What sort of a day was it there in Ketchum? Was the sun shining on the freshly mown grass, were there low-lying clouds weaving in and out of the branches of the trees, or was a dreary rain beating against the windowpanes and the timbers of the house?

I finally rang the bell and was immediately ushered into a huge salon with an oil painting of the matador dominating the dimly lit room. A heavy silence had fallen over the whole house. As I stood there looking at the painting of Ordóñez and eying the solid, middle-class furnishings, the trappings of a *nouveau riche* who has amassed a considerable fortune, I thought I saw someone peek in the door—I wasn't sure whether it was a woman or a little girl—and then suddenly dart back down the hall. Antonio finally appeared, looking utterly crushed, even more grief-stricken that I had expected to find him—more downcast, I am almost inclined to say, than the day I saw him bury his own father.

I can't describe the feelings that both of us shared at that moment, because we could scarcely get a single word out and simply threw ourselves in each other's arms, our faces streaming with tears.

Both of us had lost all self-control, and neither of us thought it ridiculous that the other had completely given way to his emotions. We were each of us unable to say one word, and when we finally managed to blurt out a few disjointed phrases, it was no more than an absurd litany of rhetorical questions and grief-stricken laments:

"Why in the world do you suppose he did a thing like that?" I said over and over.

"I just can't believe it; it can't possibly be true," Antonio kept saying.

"He must have been utterly mad."

"It just can't be true. . . . I still can't believe it."

After a moment, we both fell silent, and simply stood there sobbing. I kept saying, again and again: "Why in the world do you suppose he did a thing like that?" not as an accusation but as a kind of lament.

And with a faraway look in his eye, never once uttering the word suicide, Antonio kept crying:

"He's destroyed our lives, too."

"Yes, it's true, he's destroyed our lives, too."

"I'm a dead man now. The news of his death has been a mortal blow."

"But why, why? Why did he do a thing like that?"

We realized then what a gaping hole Ernesto had left in our lives: we would never again take refuge behind his broad shoulders, as friends zealously guarding his reputation. It was as though by ending his life Ernesto had left us defenseless, trapped in a corner, with people pointing accusing fingers at us.

Antonio kept saying with a note of great concern in his voice but in the vaguest way:

"We simply must do something on his behalf."

And I kept saying:

"Yes, we can't just sit here and do nothing."

We sat facing each other there in that dark room, like two flickering shadows fighting the inescapable truth.

It was not only that a beloved friend has passed on. It was the way he had died, an act of utter blindness that could not be said to have been a momentary affliction, a weakness that could not be imputed to a temporary lack of will power. There was something about Ernesto, there had always been something about him, that made it quite likely that he would die by his own hand. The very fact that we were careful not to mention the word suicide—or I for my part at any rate deliberately forebore to mention it—was the fateful confirmation of all our forebodings.

As a kind of temporary relief and distraction, I told Ordóñez about my trip from Benicasim, and confessed that from the very first I had had a presentiment of what had in fact happened. And Ordóñez told me about the *corrida* he had fought after receiving the news, the saddest one in his entire life, with a minute of silent tribute to Ernesto, and a black mourning band on his suit of lights.

As we searched for some explanation of what had happened, I was about to mention the blotch on Ernesto's face, that angry red blotch that had so marred his noble face. Very few people had realized how much that bright red patch, extending from the bridge of his nose almost down to his mouth and up to his eye, that kept peeling off in scaly white flakes, worried Ernesto. One of the many times that I had seen him peer obsessively into his mirror to examine his face, he had upset me terribly by remarking, as though muttering to himself:

"I'm really worried about my eye."

"What's wrong with it?"

"It's nothing, really—I just need a new pair of glasses."

"That's no problem," I said to him. "I'll take you to a good oculist —a man who's also a great admirer of yours."

"If I have any more trouble with my eyes, I'll let you know. For the moment, I can still shoot a rifle pretty damned well . . . and I don't think I miss very often," he answered, crouching down as though taking aim at an imaginary target.

But Antonio Ordóñez was in no state to confront this sort of revelation. What he was most concerned about at the moment was whether or not he ought to attend the funeral, though it was quite obvious from the first that he had not made any plans as yet to fly to Ketchum. He still hadn't really accepted the fact that Ernesto was dead, and kept talking about the telegram he was expecting confirming their meeting in Pamplona. Antonio had had news recently from Ketchum that had rather confused him. Both Ernesto's doctor friend and Mary had assured him that Ernesto's stay in the Mayo Clinic had been very beneficial and that he was all set to work again, and even kick up his heels a bit, but had lost a lot of weight.

"He was so fond of you," Ordóñez said.

"He was so fond of you, too," I answered.

"Both of us owe him a great deal," Ordóñez replied.

"We both died a little when we learned that he'd died," I said, and on hearing my voice break as I uttered those words, I said no more.

The entire Niño de la Palma affair seemed to have happened long, long before, almost like a story long since forgotten, for Ernesto had worshiped Antonio to such a point that he came to regard him as the very exemplar of all the virtues of the *torero*. To Ernesto, he was not so much a real person as the living incarnation of the ideal matador.

"I loved Ernesto like a father," Antonio said. "And the whole thing is still like a dream; I can't believe what's happened."

"Both of us owe him so much," I replied.

The words we exchanged were terribly painful, but the cause of our pain was remote, inaccessible. We might have pictured him in our minds, with his brains blown to bits, his heart forever stopped, his hand an inert weight, but we simply could not imagine him dead, for to us Ernesto represented the very opposite of death, despite the fact that we often pictured him to ourselves as a hesitant, timorous Hamlet.

I finally ventured to say, "If you decide to go to the funeral, I'd like you to tell Mary . . ."

"No, I'm not going. I simply can't face seeing 'Papa' dead. Poor old 'Papa'!" Antonio said pityingly.

Ordóñez hadn't decided not to go to Ernesto's funeral because he stood to lose money if he did since he had many *corridas* scheduled in Pamplona in the next few days. I understood perfectly why he had decided not to go, and knew that "Papa" would have thought he was doing the right thing. Ordóñez would go to Pamplona, the birthplace of Hemingway's very first novel, and fight a bull there, as Ernesto would have wanted him to do; he would stand there in the bullring wearing a black armband on his matador's suit and ask the audience to observe a moment of silence for his dead friend.

Then Ordóñez said, "We must pray for him. I can assure you I've spent the entire day praying."

"I'm certain you have. I've been praying, too," I said.

"I've arranged to have masses said for him," he sobbed.

"That was exactly the right thing to do; Ernesto would have liked that."

"There are very few people who knew Ernesto as well as you and I did!"

"His death was so absurd, so unexpected."

"Like a bolt from the blue."

How long did the two of us stay there in that dark room, remembering the past, but exchanging only a very few words? Antonio sat there all hunched over in his armchair, like a bird with its head tucked under its wing; I kept moving about in my chair and changing position, because I was a little frightened by my feeling of utter lethargy. The matador's portrait was hanging there on the wall between us in that dark room. But Ernesto would never again see Antonio in his suit of lights, in his country clothes, in his elegant silk pajamas, in bathing trunks, or merrily whirling about the dance floor at a party, nor would he ever again relive that nightmare moment when the bullring attendants picked Antonio up off the sand and carried him to the infirmary, where the first thing Ordóñez was conscious of when he came to was Ernesto's hairy, freckled hands wiping the sweat from his forehead like a

Sister of Charity. I was on the point of reminding Ordóñez of one of Ernesto's most recent long letters to his old friend and confidant, Juanito Quintana, a letter that all of us who were close friends of Ernesto's had discussed endlessly after Antonio's most recent goring. In it he had written: "Antonio has suffered a great deal—I've experienced quite a lot of pain myself, and I appreciate what he's going through—but he endures pain like a Cheyenne from the North country. That youngster has as much balls as he has talent, and as you know, he's the greatest artist in the bullring the world has ever seen. The whole thing has turned out just as we had a feeling it would, and Carmen has behaved throughout like a saint and a heroine from the good old days when there were really great ones. . . ."

Or perhaps I might tell Ordóñez about the time that Ernesto had remarked to me: "Listen, José Luis, I've seen just about every kind of bull, including really fierce ones, bulls with horns as hard as rock, bulls with fire coming out of their nostrils, bulls that ran on gasoline or butane, *toros* from every bull ranch in Spain, but I assure you I've never seen anyone as graceful and as brave as Antonio in my whole life."

I decided, however, that it was better to say nothing and stop pondering, once and for all, the question preying on both our minds:

"Why in the world do you suppose he did a thing like that?"

Bullfighting had been a far from negligible factor in Ernesto's recent depression. As a writer, he had chosen an invincible idol as the hero of his romantic and very well-paid bullfight epic, *The Dangerous Summer*. But how had Ernesto's impassioned tribute to his idol been received? He had been left lying belly up in the horse enclosure, ripped apart by the sharp-honed knives of professional butchers. Vengeful, vulgar butchers had pounced upon his warm, poetic, affectionate piece of reporting and reduced it to a pile of bloody entrails. What had been the response, in Spain and other Spanish-speaking countries, when Ernesto had naïvely challenged bullfight *aficionados?* Sly, insulting letters, articles by writers with an ax to grind, slanderous gossip about him in the newspapers, anonymous poison-pen letters. Ernesto had had to face up to this whole series of shameless attacks on him at the very moment when his health was most seriously endangered and his morale was at its very lowest point, in those months just before he entered the Mayo Clinic, where he was treated not only for liver trouble and heart disease but for mental disturbances as well. The doctors not only forbade him to travel, to consume his usual Gargantuan meals, to drink as much as he would like to have, to hunt, to fish, to go to bullfights; they also ordered him to avoid any sort of emotional stress or violent argument. The last few glowing coals of romantic love, the childish affairs of a man already past the prime of life, were no pleasure at all to him; they were torture, a blow to his ego and an obsession. All these things had left him with a haggard, drawn face and dirty hands, like a gambler caught using marked cards. The shadows were descending, and a horde of miserable good-for-nothings, nit-pickers, soreheads, vicious enemies, and vulgar parasites descended upon him. Hamstrung by his doctor's strict orders to avoid any sort of emotional stress, and thus forced to hold his tongue, Ernesto was utterly defenseless, the mere shadow of his former self, a shackled bull fallen into the hands of sadists and cheap exploiters of his enviable gifts as a man and artist.

I should like to believe that at that moment Ordóñez was also remembering with heartfelt grief the glory that had come to surround him because his name and Ernesto's had been so closely linked. When certain people die, they take a part of us with them, leaving us immeasurably poorer, whereas others, with boundless generosity, leave the very best of themselves behind for us when they pass on, an imperishable monument of triumph upon triumph. There are certain people who leave a kind of chorus of blessings hovering round about our heads when they die, despite the pain we feel as they bid us farewell forever, as they unexpectedly take their leave of us. Whether such people are blessed or cursed by fortune in the end is not what matters; what is most important is that they were glorious human beings. In this respect, too, there had never been anyone quite the equal of Ernesto.

"He was such a decent person," Antonio said.

"He was such a good man, and so few people had any idea what he was really like," I replied.

"I still can't believe it," Ordóñez said yet again.

"Ernesto the giant was such a great man."

"Why did it all have to end the way it did?"

The two of us sat there tirelessly lamenting Ernesto's tragic death. But from time to time, as if the echo of the fateful shotgun blast were ringing in our ears, we would suddenly fall silent. During these silences, the same thoughts were doubtless running through both Ordóñez's mind and mine, though Antonio was much more circumspect than I was, for he had not once mentioned the word suicide, whereas I had already accepted it as certain fact that Ernesto had taken his own life. Will they perform an autopsy on him? I wondered. Will they allow him to be buried according to the sacred rites of the Church? Perhaps the word "accident" would prove useful. How few people had any idea of Ernesto's heartfelt desire to be a good Christian, or knew that he was a convert to Catholicism, at least outwardly, for he had lacked the will to submit completely to the Church.

I thought above all of Mary, because Ordóñez had several times said, "Poor Mary, poor Mary," and I had sent that telegram to assure her that I shared her grief in these lonely hours. Ordóñez had been right, absolutely right, to refuse to accept the obvious truth, because Ernesto's death was something that had no place in the world of real facts, despite its being a gruesome, bloody reality.

Could it be that words cause things to happen, could it be that when certain words are repeated too often, words such as *death*, they hasten the fateful hour rather than conjure it away? The word *death* hung suspended just above our heads there in that dark room; Ordóñez had many *corridas* coming up, both in Spain and in Latin America, and I, too, had an almost inevitable rendezvous with death, perhaps in some corner of the globe where I least expected it.

Ernesto had gone to *his* rendezvous with death with a bold swagger; he had faced the bull's horns squarely, and killed in the most dangerous way possible, *recibiendo*.

Ordóñez had gotten to his feet and was standing there sadly shaking his head. It was terribly hard for him to accept the incontrovertible fact that Ernesto had set a trap for himself that was as cunning as it was cruel. Nonetheless, there was nothing either of us could do except face the truth and accept it. And since there was no longer any point in beating around the bush, both of us went on with our sad litany in mourning for Ernesto:

"God has surely forgiven him."

"He was a great man."

"He'd suffered terribly."

"He'd loved many things passionately."

"What's happened is so unfair."

"We must do something for him."

"He deserves anything we can possibly do for him."

I was still in a state of shock, and began voicing some very confused conclusions I had come to about Ernesto as a person. I remember that I particularly emphasized his stoicism, above and beyond all his frantic pleasure-seeking, and most important of all, his authentically religious searching for ultimate truths, for I regarded Ernesto as a much more religious man than many others who die beating their chests and saying their *mea culpa* without feeling any sort of real contrition. Both Antonio and I must have been absolutely blind not to have realized that even though Ernesto gave the outward appearance of being an absolutely solid monolith, he was inwardly a human being in utter agony, as soft and as perishable as clay. In very vague turns of phrase, even more vague than the words I had written in a number of articles when Ernesto was still alive, which he had pointed to with an ad-monishing forefinger, I said to Ordóñez:

"I'm convinced that Ernesto might have been the greatest mystic of our time. But he was such a simple person, raised by his family and educated in such a haphazard way; he had come face to face with the misery of this world in such a painful way, so early in his life. . . ."

Ordóñez gave no indication that he had any idea what I was talking about, and just stood there gazing at me with a faraway, stunned, vacant look in his eyes. I wanted so much to unburden myself and be completely frank with him, and would have given anything to describe what ravages a demoniacal pride can wreck when it rears its ugly head in a person as sentimental as Ernesto.

It was enough to make almost anyone burst into tears. With his handsome beard, his snow-white hair, and his radiant smile, Ernesto was far more than simply a prematurely senile old man when he killed himself. I remembered how much it pleased him to be called *viejo*, "old one." And hadn't he given almost his very last book the title *The Old Man and the Sea* and made a *viejo* the hero of it, a man far advanced in years, possessed of the wisdom of a lifetime, a wisdom as old as time itself because he had garnered it from the sea, the oldest and wisest thing on our entire planet?

Antonio and I just stood there, not quite knowing how to say good-by to each other.

"We must see each other more often now," Antonio said to me.

"Yes, we really must," I replied.

"Are you going to go to Pamplona?" he asked me.

"I don't think I'll go this year. I can't picture Pamplona without Ernesto."

"What awful luck," Ordóñez said in a dejected tone of voice.

"But we really must do something on his behalf," I replied.

Ordóñez simply stood there like a great, silent cypress tree, his shoulders sagging a bit and a blank look in his eye. The whole room was a shadowy blur now.

We walked toward the door together, muttering the same stupid phrases to each other yet again:

"I simply can't believe it," Antonio said.

"I can't either," I replied.

"Why oh why didn't he come to the San Fermín fiesta, when he was apparently looking forward to it so much?"

"I'm not at all sure you'll believe me, but I've been afraid something like this would happen for a long time now. Haven't you had that feeling too?" I answered.

"I haven't the faintest idea why things turned out this way."

"I've been expecting the worst for a long time now, as I just told you," I replied.

"It's the hand of fate," Antonio said finally, collapsing in a chair again.

The painting by Echeverría, the mirrors, the porcelain figures, the fur rugs, the satin-upholstered furniture there in the room behind us were like a splendid twilight slowly fading. We were almost at the door now. Antonio seemed terribly downcast and hesitant, trying his best not to burst into tears. I, too, found nothing to say, not because I was deliberately holding my tongue but because I was absolutely grief-stricken. And Antonio said once more:

"We have to do something, there must be something we can do."

"Yes, we have to do something," I agreed.

We embraced each other, I went out the door, and Antonio closed it very softly, almost timidly, behind me. I kept saying to myself, over and over again: "We must do something, anything we possibly can. . . ." And with these words echoing in my mind, I suddenly found myself at a newsstand on the Paseo de Rosales.

What a terrible disaster! I saw from the headlines that a dam had burst—heaven only knew why, though doubtless it was because the builders had made profits on the side by using shoddy materials, or because the engineers had botched the whole job, or because the figures run through the calculators were wrong, or because someone connected with the project had seen a chance to pocket a tidy sum for himself; there was no way of knowing, and doubtless no one would ever get to the bottom of the whole affair. But whatever was behind it all, the sad truth was that an entire town had been wiped out, and the majority of its inhabitants had been drowned as they slept in their beds. The town that had been inundated had a very poetic name: Rivadelago, Lakeside Village. A really nice name, but that was all that was left of it now.

Out of a hypocritical sense of charity, the papers, or at least one or two of them, had featured stories about what they called Ernesto's *paganism*. But does a pagan take his own life in such a violent way? If Ernesto the man had been a real pagan, living his whole life singing hymns of praise to the pleasures of this world, it would have been only to be expected that his life would end amid the greatest possible euphoria. And would a "pagan" writer have written such desperate, such intense, such moral, such spiritually uplifting works for readers able to understand him?

I sat down on a wrought-iron chair, surveying the jagged mountain peaks that surround Madrid, a view with the subtlest of colors and the most delicate shadows. At nearby tables, groups of young boys and girls were searching for words as they played some sort of game I couldn't make head or tail of. There were also a number of young boys and girls stealthily trying to feel each other up, plus several married couples whose one diversion seemed to be fighting with each other and scolding their children.

Antonio's words were still echoing in my mind: "We must do something for Ernesto, anything we can." But at that point I had no idea what I could do for Ernesto. The festival of San Fermín was about to begin, but a San Fermín fiesta with his body lying in state thousands of miles away, in Idaho, would be more or less like Holy Week without the comforting assurance that there would be a joyous Resurrection Sunday.

It was getting dark now. A rose-colored twilight was descending. It was as if a great flood of red ink were flowing down the slopes of the Sierra. Then, little by little, the color of the sky and the earth faded to the pale gold, the gray, the somber black of the portrait of Antonio. Twilight descended as slowly as when a bull brought to its knees gazes all about the bullring very quietly, not yet expecting the final *coup de grâce*. The mountains stood out all around, as naked as the skull of the "Great Bald One," the great whore, Death. Flickering lights suddenly appeared here and there.

I heard a train whistle then, which made me imagine myself boarding the train for Pamplona, where I would relive the San Fermín festival of other years in the past, those endless nights, those wee hours of the morning when Ernesto had sung his farewell to life, surrounded by beautiful women and his many friends.

Night slowly fell, and at Ordóñez's there would still be just enough light to catch a glimpse of the portrait of the *torero* in his pale-gold bullfight costume. But Ernesto would be there in that room too, feeling even more lonely than Antonio, more lonely than he had ever been before. The San Fermín fiesta would go on as though nothing had happened, and Antonio would soon be packing his suitcase for the trip to Pamplona, where I had gone to meet the dead man in 1953 and come back for the fiesta with him again, year after year, with the 1959 San Fermines the most unforgettable fiesta of all. . . .

6 I shall go back to the year 1959, then, the year that Ernesto
joined in the *riau-riau* most joyously and most frenetically, the last time
he ran in the streets before the bulls of life, with Death already treading
on his heels.

We had agreed to meet in the Plaza del Castillo, and I had no
trouble finding him. He was there in his checked shirt, wearing the red
bandana of Pamplona merrymakers around his neck, his baseball cap
covering his gray hair cut in a bang over his forehead like a teen-ager,
leaning on an ashwood cane. There he was, with his one and only vade
mecum for the fiesta, a big glass of wine, in front of him.

"Bring another bottle—nice and cool," were his first words to the
waiter after greeting me.

The waiter's reply was the same as always: "What a boozehound this
guy is! But he sure can hold his liquor!"

It was still early in the morning, and Ernesto hadn't yet put any food
into that great belly of his. But in twenty-four hours in Pamplona, not
to mention the seven long days of the fiesta, you do a lot more living
than you ever figured you would. Before joining in the strenuous
dancing in the streets, Ernesto would have to have a delicious lunch,
washed down with great quantities of red wine—though occasionally,
for a change, he also was in the habit of drinking French chablis, and if
it was a really elegant repast, an excellent rosé.

The fiesta at Pamplona, as in *The Sun Also Rises*, would be one
long drinking bout, around the clock for seven days and seven nights.
You had to join in the festivities heart and soul, so the merrymakers,
following an age-old tradition, went to confession and communion the

first day of the fiesta. Then, after that, it was anything goes, and the San Fermín *feria* became a superspectacular sporting event, which you were obliged to take part in till the last dog died, without faking it or ever once dropping out.

For Ernesto, the fiesta at Pamplona was far from being a relaxing vacation, because he was both living the present intensely and reliving all the years of the past, and during these days spent in Navarre he felt in the pink of condition physically, as full of great dreams as when he had first arrived in Spain as a wounded war veteran just out of the service and a newlywed.

It was one of these periods of apparent idle roistering that inspired *The Sun Also Rises*, that novel of a lost generation that is still being devoured by countless readers today, the majority of whom fail to appreciate what a miracle of art this work is. The week-long fiesta of San Fermín had such a profound and decisive effect on Ernesto that it was a sort of phenomenal revelation to him, and his memories of it eventually spurred him to write his "bible of Spanish bullfighting"—a work that was both a celebration of life by a man who lived it to the hilt and the contemplation of a mystic—a book he titled *Death in the Afternoon*, a treatise on our typically Spanish *fiesta brava* that very few Spaniards have ever read.

Just seeing Ernesto in person in the Plaza del Castillo—or the "Plaza Mayor," as he often called it in his writings—was a thrilling sight, a joyous, lively spectacle in and of itself. He had not come to Pamplona as a magician promising to perform miracles or a plaster saint promising to heal souls or a philosopher making an on-the-spot study of the depravity of a town that has come up with a combination of paganism and Christianity that adds up to a week-long orgy. No, Ernesto was there for the same reasons as always: because he was an impassioned *aficionado* who had found that he could forget himself and feel the pulse of life itself amid all the riotous merrymaking and the excitement of the running of the bulls in the streets.

He was constantly surrounded by a great crowd of people, and would sit cheerily chatting both with dull Americans who were pestering him and any of the townspeople brash enough or daring enough to say a few words to him. Many of them, the foreigners in particular, had a copy of *The Sun Also Rises* in their hands and wanted him to inscribe a personal dedication to them in it, and he would patiently write whatever they wanted him to, signing his name as cheerfully for priests as for prostitutes. Every once in a while, reporters, both Spanish newsmen and journalists from other countries, would approach him and beg him to say a few words. His eyes never leaving the great crowd of people in the plaza, Ernesto would reply very shyly, "I've already said all I have to say in my books."

And a number of times he was approached by such dreadful boors and such awful pests, often several sheets to the wind, that he was forced to drive them away by brandishing his cane or shaking his fists.

Like the characters in *The Sun Also Rises*, Ernesto appeared on the surface to be frivolous and rowdy and a great eater and drinker, but underneath he was terribly depressed and bored. His outward boisterousness and exuberance served to conceal an inner loneliness that was absolutely total, an inner drama that was like a dose of hemlock downed against his will. Women would often come up and give him a big kiss, even though his wife was sitting right there beside him. But all these trappings of fame and glory merely served to hide his inner torment.

But that day there on the terrace of the café was only a preparation for the next day, when all the church bells of Pamplona would begin to peal and rockets would be shot off as the signal to send the bulls racing down the streets, chasing a great throng of youngsters with nerves of steel. In a matter of approximately three minutes the bulls would run the two kilometers between the Puerta Rochapea and the *plaza de toros*, the streets would ring with shouts of terror, but once the youngsters had given voice to their fear they would master it completely, and there would be tumultuous, exuberant shouts of sheer joy. This intense, dramatic way of braving death in the flower of youth was what filled Ernesto's heart with such nostalgia and such fervor. The bulls would thunder down the streets like locomotives racing along without rails, their horns brushing the chests of youngsters, who adored this traditional rite. And all of this tumult would be sharply counterpointed by the sound of a very primitive sort of music, the whole fiesta a curious blend of religion and a hunting party.

It was the night before the opening of the fiesta. Ernesto had received invitations to watch the running of the bulls from any number of balconies, beginning with the ones at the city hall. But as usual he would not accept any of them. His favorite spot for watching the running of the bulls was one of the steep, narrow streets of the town, the Calle Estafeta for instance. And he planned someday to go to the bullring to watch the crowd of youngsters running before the bulls pour into the *plaza de toros*, stark drama turning into a joyous hymn to life pouring from the throats of exuberant youngsters wearing white shirts, red neckerchiefs, and rope sandals. It would all be over in just a few minutes, a scene straight out of one of Goya's etchings or drawings, in which life and death suddenly touch and become one.

There was no need to hurry. We had all the rest of the morning ahead of us. Quite a few people were content to start the day with coffee and doughnuts or rolls, claiming it was too early to begin drinking. It was going to be a long fiesta, and the thing to do was to pace yourself and drink slowly, for the Sanfermines shouldn't be a drunken orgy but a time of perfect happiness shared with intimate friends. Ernesto was never a compulsive boozer, downing one glass after another; he would sit for hours slowly sipping whatever it was he was drinking.

Every so often, a youngster would come over and offer him a drink out of his wineskin, and Ernesto would always take a sip, almost as if it were some sort of solemn religious rite. And occasionally some foreigner who didn't understand what the whole ceremony was all about would hold out a bottle of Coca-Cola to Ernesto, and he would say:

"Sure I'll have a drink of it if you'll let me add a few other things to it." And he'd grab the waiter's tray and go from table to table picking up various drinks and pouring them all together, to everyone's vast amusement, to make a famous concoction he claimed was called *potingue*, a drink novice bullfighters were weaned on, according to him.

The whole plaza was one mad whirl, reflected in Ernesto's sea-green eyes, and at times, when warm tears at the memory of other years at Pamplona threatened to brim over, he would hide behind his dark glasses. I saw a huge crowd collect around him, shouting, "Viva Ernesto Hemingway," and applauding—because he'd become a sort of patriarch of the whole San Fermín *feria*, and to a certain extent he really was the father of it, for it was Ernesto who first had made it a world-famous fiesta. As I watched him there in one of his favorite haunts, his *querencia*, absorbed in memories that went back many years, I thought to myself: "He's a Job, he's become as long-suffering as Job." And I was quite right to think so.

We went for a stroll around the town then. Ernesto strode along just ahead of me, looking very serious and dignified, like a priest in a church procession; he had a gait like no one else in the world, moving his shoulders at every step. I noticed that his broad back still narrowed to a V at the waist, but from the front he had almost no waistline, for directly below his great chest he had a huge paunch, a simply enormous belly. But he walked along at a brisk pace, because he was still very agile, and his legs, although very slender, incredibly slender for such a big man, were very strong, the legs of a man born to wade through icy torrents and climb to the tops of mountains, waiting for a trout or a bear to come along: it hardly mattered which, since he was equally fond of fishing and hunting.

The whole crowd was walking in the direction of the city hall, the boys with their shirts open almost down to the navel because it was so hot, and the girls all wearing as few wispy garments as decency permitted, but nonethless looking perfectly chaste, as though the purity of the sacred music being sung had somehow extinguished the flames of passion in their hearts. In a few minutes the sexton would ring the bell that was the signal to let the bulls loose, and a little puff of white smoke would linger in the sky after the skyrockets were set off, breaking the dignified silence that reigns all the rest of the year in the Plaza del Castillo. In a few seconds now, the dam would burst, and people's hearts would begin to dance like bulls rushing out of their pens ready to make the sacrifice of their lives a festive occasion.

Ernesto turned around and said to me, "The fiesta's always exactly the same, but every time I come to Pamplona it's as though I'd never seen it before."

"So it's true it makes you feel like a youngster again?"

"I've always been young in heart, and I still am."

There was no need for him to swear that that was true. When you were with him there at Pamplona, you felt young too, so young that you solemnly promised that the next day you'd run in the streets in front of the bulls like just one more stout lad from Navarre.

"I'd certainly like to run with the bulls—but you have to start taking care of yourself so you'll be in good shape if you want to participate in the *encierro*," Ernesto said.

He had become ravenously hungry all of a sudden. And when Ernesto was famished, it was like waving a red rag at a bull. We went on down the street, arm in arm, to the Casa Marceliano, owned by Matías, a man who had been his friend ever since Ernesto had first turned up in Pamplona as a mere youngster, a man who had taken Ernesto under his wing when he was still an unknown reporter who was perhaps going to write a book about the San Fermín fiesta. Matías had given him bed and board and never pestered "Mister Ernesto" to pay his bill when he arrived with a wallet that was hardly bulging and he was not yet famous, even in his own household, for anything but a few foolish escapades. Before going into this beloved haunt of Ernesto's, I disappeared for a time. The market was nearby, and I wanted to buy a few little appetizers that Ernesto was especially fond of: radishes, celery, capers, scallions, pickled peppers, green cloves of garlic, cod, fresh tuna, Spanish olives, and whatever else I could find, because Ernesto, the victor of so many battles, who still had enough energy to refuse to grow old, deserved every favorite tidbit of his that I could possibly offer him.

Ernesto knew how to seek out the sort of company he most enjoyed. He was sometimes a bit tightfisted with his money, but this time it was as though he wanted to celebrate something important, to give a farewell banquet or something of the sort. Those of us who were there in Pamplona with him were tried and true friends, who could stroll arm in arm with him in the garden and the cloisters of mutual friendship, talk to him in his solitary cell of loneliness as to a brother. Nothing made Ernesto prouder than the close friends he had made, because, as he often used to say, he had carefully chosen each of them himself after weeding out a whole bunch of candidates.

A college professor with or without a list of publications to his credit, a famous photographer or a rank amateur with nothing but a Brownie, a film or television writer who might be a big name in the business or a complete unknown, an author with either a well-established reputation or not a single work yet published, a celebrated journalist with a syndicated column or a mere cub reporter might approach him, and Ernesto would exchange at least a few words with any of them. Pamplona was the only place in the world where anybody and everybody could talk to Ernesto. Everywhere else, he was always very selective about the company he kept. And people who hung about him simply because they were nosy, because they were trying to wangle confidences out of him, didn't hang around very long. Ernesto had his own special technique for giving them the cold shoulder or the brush-off without ever being downright discourteous to them.

Even when nuisances with colossal nerve forced themselves on him, he seldom lost his temper. But, once he did, there would be a terrible scene, because Ernesto had an impressive vocabulary of insults and swear words at his command. Quite often he had every reason to defend himself not only by demolishing his adversaries with a burst of booming laughter but by practically biting their heads off; he was on-stage every minute, so people not only shouted, "Viva Ernesto," but also sometimes made insulting remarks or jeered at him. There came a time, however, when his closest friends began to act as bodyguards to prevent anyone from invading his privacy. But when he was alone with old friends, Ernesto was free to play the clown if he liked or to be his real self, frank and open and completely unpretentious.

I found myself sitting next to an American with a vulgar, careworn face, who every once in a while would drop his pose of a man of mystery and say something mildly funny. It was Hotchner, dressed more or less in the traditional costume of a participant in the fiesta of San Fermín, except for his plaid shirt. On second thought, I decided he looked exactly like a farm hand on a ranch in the Far West. When Ernesto had introduced us to each other, he had said: "Hotchner's a colleague of mine. He's done some good work in television and done a fine job of looking after my interests."

Hotchner was delighted by all the excitement in Pamplona, even though the festivities had scarcely begun. He had entirely the wrong idea about one thing, though: he was quite certain that the fiesta of San Fermín would end in a great, collective orgy. At one point, Ernesto turned to me and whispered in my ear: "Hotchner's a good friend of mine, but he's a sharp customer."

I thought Ernesto meant that as a compliment, and I said, "Yes, it's quite obvious he's an awfully clever fellow."

"Yes, he's terribly intelligent, but he's also out for number one."

Sitting opposite me were a married couple with faces wreathed in smiles, two very friendly, outgoing, charming people. The husband was wearing a white shirt with the sleeves rolled up and the wife seemed just a little bit more self-assured than her husband, as though she was quite accustomed to moving in select social circles. As we had strolled around the town, Ernesto had said to me, "They're a delightful couple. The husband is a physician, a local doctor we keep in very close touch with in case something goes wrong with my motor."

I found Doctor George and his wife most congenial, and I was glad that Mary was able to have the pleasure of their company, since it must have been very hard on her to spend hour after hour there in the midst of all that uproar. Moreover, the presence of the Irish girl and the two other young girls whom Ernesto jokingly called "my kidnap victims" had put Mary in a rather awkward position, since Ernesto had started making advances to them more or less as a joke, but was quite willing to go further. Mary knew very well that it would ruin everything if she crossed Ernesto and sent him into a tantrum, that she ought to do her best to make him happy during the Pamplona fiesta. So she tried hard to conceal her real feelings, to ignore his apparent willingness to stray down the primrose path; his lack of attention to her, words or acts of his that were the predictable consequence of the whole festive atmosphere.

Seeing Mary sitting there looking so calm and dignified, paying no attention to the way Ernesto and the others were carrying on, I realized what a wonderful person she was. If Ernesto were someday to lose his mind, he might possibly come to hate her, but for the moment she was the person he loved best in all the world. He couldn't live without her. But when he lost his temper over some silly thing or threw a childish tantrum, as when Mary had broken her foot, Ernesto could be surly and demanding and a sort of petty despot, and I thought to myself that his first three wives must have often had a pretty rough time of it. Ernesto liked excitement; he was moody and selfish and always on the go, a feverishly intense person and at the same time a man who was often very depressed. I was certain it hadn't been a bed of roses for any of them. I have no idea who got fed up with whom first in his previous marriages, nor was I able to arrive at any sort of general conclusion, since his three wives before Mary had all been so different, but it was quite obvious that Ernesto was a destroyer of women, and I was inclined to believe that he destroyed them not by what he did to them but by what he failed to do. That was why I admired Mary's patience and dignity and energy from the very first day I met her, even though at the time she was just recovering from a whole series of marital crises. And doubtless there would be more of them. I was quite certain that Ernesto, the giant destroyer of his own illusions, was a very difficult man to live with.

Mary had liked my book *América de cabo a rabo—America from Head to Tail*—and was especially pleased that I had dedicated it to her. When we were with friends, she would often say, "José Luis has written a fine book about America, you know."

"Yes, I know, and he's also written another one: *Death Under My Arm*," someone from the bullfight world might chime in.

"No, it's called *With Death on My Back*," Ernesto would pipe up.

And everybody would laugh. Mary knew a great deal about literature, and was, I suspected, the person responsible for getting Ernesto back to writing again, so she was the one I always turned to when I could no longer bear all the empty chitchat of the others.

The Irish girl looked as though she'd been starving to death when she arrived, and had just discovered that such a thing as wine existed. She blushed, she dozed, she kept stroking herself, and constantly acted more or less like a little bitch in heat. She was a very pretty little creature, who was to lose a great many things at the fiesta, but also gain a lot of others.

The other two girls in Ernesto's intimate circle there at Pamplona were nice girls, university students in a gay mood, very smart, very sophisticated young women, who felt as though they were playing a role in some sort of drama, though they weren't exactly certain what the script called for. If the Irish girl was as warm and sentimental as a little nesting sparrow, these two were great migratory birds with powerful wings that could easily span oceans. They were very good-looking but they struck me as cold, calculating creatures, at least at this stage of the fiesta.

Up to this point, it had been a very patriarchal fiesta, for if Ernesto had not been there presiding over the festivities, we would have been merely a motley crew of merrymakers. And then there was Mary, whose presence reminded us from time to time that this fiesta was also something of a matriarchy. Most interestingly, we all loved Ernesto the man even more than we admired Ernesto the writer. When you came to know and love Ernesto, it was quite easy and in fact quite the proper thing to do to forget that he was a great writer. It would never have occurred to anyone in our inner circle to quote from his books or recite some famous passage, though occasionally some boob would pop up at our table and do just that.

How far was the Irish girl willing to go with Ernesto? What did the two "kidnaped" American girls have to lose, since it was fairly obvious that they'd already lost their maidenheads? The excitement of having the three of them around had brought Ernesto close to a state of absolute delirium, though he would recover his sanity after a while, like a madman wandering about the streets who suddenly recognizes his own house, like a crazy gambler who stares and stares at his cards when he's upped the ante too high, as though trying to deny the fact that he's bet on a very bad hand.

The fiesta was getting better and better. Ordóñez would be arriving any moment now, and our marvelous host was going around taking our orders, and would soon be bringing us appetizers to nibble on while we waited for lunch. Matías always seemed to me to be the very soul of hospitality, an innkeeper straight out of the Middle Ages.

Juanito Quintana turned up just then, and I noticed that Hotchner took an instant dislike to him. I also noticed that the moment Juanito appeared, Ernesto paid no attention to any of the rest of us, including the women, and the two of them immediately began talking bullfighting. Juanito had just seen the bulls for the first *corrida* of the fiesta, and he was as enthused as a general inspecting the tanks that will clear the way for the infantry when the offensive begins. He drew up a chair, sat down next to Ernesto, and told him that there were a number of balconies, including the one upstairs at the city hall, that were at his disposal if he wanted to watch the running of the bulls in the streets from one of them. But Ernesto said he'd rather watch from one of the streets, on the first day at any rate, and Juanito agreed that that was a fine idea.

We sat there drinking and nibbling at this and that, though we hadn't yet settled down to the serious business of eating what promised to be a huge lunch. There were fewer bit players popping up at our table now, but all the ones who did drop by congratulated Ernesto for being a *pamplónica* by adoption. As a matter of fact, if the mayors and the other city officials of Pamplona hadn't been so afraid of certain people's reaction, they would have named Ernesto "Pamplona's favorite son" during his lifetime, or given him the gold medal of Navarre, and Ernesto would immediately have pinned it on the mantle of San Fermín, a French martyr who, were it not for his bishops' vestments and miter, would look exactly like a plump tavern keeper who had given up French cuisine and its cheese and taken to cooking Navarre style, with lots of garlic, after crossing the border.

Quintana sat there talking, his face beaming, playing to the hilt his role as the ever-young, genial Juanito, a marvelously human man whom Ernesto greatly admired. Hotchner's nose was obviously out of joint on seeing what intimate friends the great maestro and this Celto-Iberian whom Hotchner considered a mere matador's peón were, though Quintana, being a Basque, was always very dignified, even when he was bubbling over with enthusiasm. Both when Juanito had been the skipper at Pamplona and Ernesto just an able seaman, and now that it was the other way around, Juanito had always been the perfect gentleman with Ernesto, and he was doing his best not to appear to be overprotective of his old friend, because it would have offended him.

I know that Juanito was the first real Spanish friend that Ernesto had ever had, and I am very much inclined to believe that he was his closest Spanish friend, though I know that Ernesto always spoke most affectionately of Dr. Medinaveitia and a number of Spaniards in exile whom he was truly fond of and admired enormously. But Juanito was the "mother hen," you might say, to Hemingway the young reporter who was bedazzled by the whole world of bullfighting, the purgatory and the heaven of the matador and the bull, though I shall forbear to call it a hell as well, for we are taught that hell is the inability to love, and men such as Ernesto are passionate men, imbued with the noblest passion. Yes, Quintana for Ernesto was the informal but learned teacher, sufficiently learned to cause that globe-trotting reporter to formally enroll for a course in "The Art of Bullfighting" under Juanito's tutelage, a course that the student will certainly never pass if he is incapable of understanding life and death as a spectacle that embraces both the bestial and the divine. All Ernesto's impressions and experiences in and around the bullring had been something like an intensive extension course, but until he met Quintana he had never had any really intimate contact with the sacred rites of bullfighting. Juanito took him into the *toreros'* dressing rooms as they rested before donning their suit of lights; he took him to the ceremonies where bullfighters are officially recognized as full matadors; he took him over to bullfighters to talk with them just before they entered the bullring, as they were resting between bulls, and after the last bull of the afternoon had been killed. This dignified little innkeeper was the person who had taught Ernesto what bullfighting was really all about. Thanks to Juanito, Ernesto saw *toreros* surrounded by their worshipful fans, among whom there were always women, both virgins and prostitutes, ready and willing to offer their bodies on the altar of sex as personified by the bull and the bullfighter, to give themselves to the master of that obscure force that is at once bestial and godlike.

What Ernesto discovered through Juanito Quintana, around the year 1922, was an entirely new world, something he'd never even dreamed existed, and Ernesto, who sought heroes to worship his whole life long, immediately realized that the matador answers our heed for mystery on this earth. In Ernesto's very first articles, he was already taking his first steps inside that sacred circle where the bull and the bullfighter, the victim and the priest, the celebrant of the rite and the faithful become one in a ceremony in which each gesture is artistically linked to the next to form a perfect whole. From a less lofty point of view, it might also be maintained that Quintana poisoned Ernesto's mind, that he was the *agent provocateur* who "hooked" Ernesto on the only metaphysic he would ever truly believe in, though admittedly this spectacle of Prometheus freeing himself of his bonds led Ernesto at certain moments in his life to ponder loftier and deeper mysteries.

The wine was flowing abundantly at our table, the very best wine, Matías' special reserve, which he produced only on the most solemn occasions. More and more people kept dropping by, but Quintana saw to it that Ernesto's adoring fans merely waved to him from the doorway, or if he allowed some of them to come in, he made sure that they stayed only a few moments and stole quietly out of the master's temple.

After munching the appetizers that Matías had produced, we were to have our private lunch in one of the large upstairs rooms, rooms with bare, whitewashed walls and nothing in them but immaculate wooden tables and plain, straight-backed chairs.

Matías kept running upstairs and down—in his work clothes (we were all quite sure that he never took off his apron and probably even slept in it)—bringing us drinks and plopping down in a chair next to Ernesto every so often, slowly sipping a drink, his cheeks gradually growing redder and redder, whispering bits of gossip to Ernesto, to the latter's great delight, little secrets that were hardly earth-shaking, of course, but brought back many memories the two of them had shared down through the many years they had been friends.

It was not a great festive celebration, but there was a certain ritual that had to be observed. Ordóñez would be turning up any moment now, along with some of his promoters, his *cuadrilla,* other matadors, bullfight photographers and critics, the endless parade of people in the bullfight world that was always the same and always different. It was the one sort of celebration that always makes people's thoughts turn to the beyond, or at any rate the thoughts of people such as Ernesto. The presence of the *torero,* or his absence, always reminds us, like it or not, that all of us are mortal.

We were there at the very spot where Ernesto's baptism as a bullfight *aficionado* had taken place, sitting in the very inn that he had turned up at more than thirty years before, now, with nothing but a fisherman's knapsack, a bunch of pencils, a note pad, and a couple of books. Ernesto squinted his eyes and looked down the blindingly bright sunlit street outside. In Pamplona he had discovered something more than an exciting spectacle, because as he became more and more fascinated by the art of bullfighting, he also discovered a whole new lexicon, a subject, and a vocation. What sort of career as a journalist would Ernesto have had after the year 1921 had he not recognized in the two horns of the bull the symbol of the dilemma of his own life? What is there left of the rest of his articles, his verses, and some of the short stories he wrote in these early years before he wrote his first novel? He already was able to capture the atmosphere surrounding a place or an event, he already knew how to bring a character to life on the printed page, his writing was intuitively pithy and vividly realistic, but was it worth all that effort to set such fleeting events of the moment down on paper?

His very first article on bullfighting, an account of the first *corrida* he had ever seen, had been something more than a bit of picturesque local color as viewed through the eyes of a foreigner, and the image of the bull and the bullfighter was to become a central one both in his life and his work.

"Is it true, Ernesto, that you wanted to become a bullfighter after seeing your first few *corridas*?" I once asked him.

"Yes, that's quite true. I thought it would be as easy as pie," he replied.

"And what happened then?"

"I became a laughingstock: everybody thought I was terribly funny when I made a few stabs at it; even my friends thought it was a laugh riot."

"So you gave up bullfighting in the nick of time."

"I didn't give it up, because I'd never really started. I'm quite content now to be just a spectator. . . ."

But Ernesto was never just a coldly analytical spectator; he was a passionate witness of the mystery of the *corrida*. That was why he couldn't stand the bullfight critics, those same critics who now spoke of him rather scornfully. But how could a critic such as Corrochano, for one, forget the prophetic words Ernesto had written about Corrochano's son Alfredo, an utter failure as a bullfighter, just as Ernesto, a red-headed Yankee and great boozer, had predicted?

"After having many brushes with life and death, bullfighting is the only serious thing it has been my privilege not only to witness, but to *participate* in," Ernesto once laconically told me.

Spaniards have always been miles away from understanding Ernesto, but even European and American critics have not sufficiently emphasized the fact that it is not mere happenstance that Ernesto's first major work from the artistic point of view is *The Sun Also Rises*, that collection of bits and pieces of shattered lives centering around the *corrida* and its imagery. Isn't it quite obvious that Ernesto, having reached the very peak of his fame, wanted to go back to the very beginning, and was desperately eager to write what he had left unsaid both in *The Sun Also Rises* and in *Death in the Afternoon*? *Life* magazine was going to pay him more than $1.50 a word for the next installment of

The Dangerous Summer, more than thirty thousand dollars in all. That was why Ernesto was so withdrawn, so edgy: he was desperately attempting to relive his whole past life.

During the fifteen years following the Spanish Civil War, when Ernesto was unable to visit Spain, as he would have liked so much to do, Juanito Quintana had sent him, year after year, the programs of the most talked-about *corridas* and all the bullfight magazines reporting the ups and downs of the careers of *matadores* and *novilleros.* Wherever Ernesto happened to be—in Havana, in Ketchum, in Africa—he followed events in the bullfight world very closely, for it was a universe that interested him much more than politics and life in literary circles.

Along with her bulls, Spain is one of the keys of Ernest Hemingway's metaphysics. His entire body of work, the subjects he chose, his characters, were all marked with the imprint of the *corrida,* and every one of his ideas and reflections, even the most lofty of them, on man's fate and his hope for eternity, were always expressed through images drawn from bullfighting, and thus ample proof that he considered the bullring and the *corrida* the very symbols of the human condition and man's tragic fate on this earth.

"I want to drop by and see the saint," he said.

"I'll go with you if you like," I said.

I didn't dare to discuss the subject any further. Anything that Ernesto had ever told me about his religious beliefs had always poured out spontaneously, and I knew he would clam up if I questioned him. One day, shortly after we became friends, I had asked him: "Tell me, what does God represent to you?" I had framed my question that way because it seemed stupid to come right out and ask him: Tell me, do you believe in God?

And Ernesto had replied in that half-joking, half-serious way of his, "Well, God to me is something like the greatest killer of bulls ever."

"Somebody in the class of Maera, Belmonte, Joselito, Ordóñez, Dominguín . . . ," I said.

"All those guys were great matadors, some of them greater than others, but even so they were just great *aficionados.* They killed only because it was a power conferred on them."

"I don't follow you at all," I said.

"What I mean is that it was quite possible that they themselves might die, whereas God . . ."

I must have had a very odd look on my face, because he added, "I don't mean to be blasphemous. A Catholic shouldn't ever be blasphemous."

He stared at me intently then, and said:

"Don't tell me you didn't know I was a Catholic."

I was totally at a loss for words, because at that time I was not yet on intimate terms with him.

"I'm not a very good one, but I'm a Catholic nonetheless. I've never renounced my faith," he said.

I was sitting there digging into my food and downing my wine, enjoying both immensely, and Ernesto evidently decided it was a good time to give me a bit of advice:

"José Luis, take the bull by the horns and leave journalism before it's too late."

"But what would my family and I live on if I did?" I replied.

"I know what you mean. But you just have to climb out of bed some morning, with your mind all made up that that's what you're going to do, and then do it. It's impossible for a *torero* to be anything but a *torero*. He can't even be a good husband."

He went on talking then about what it was like to be a writer. Writing a good novel wasn't a matter of fighting just one great *corrida* on a quiet afternoon with good bulls, but fighting lots of good *corridas*, on lots of afternoons, even if there was a nasty breeze blowing and the bulls weren't charging right. You had to make your passes at your chosen theme the way the *torero* makes his passes at the bull, fighting as close in as possible, with grace and style, but also with dignity and total command of the situation. Just as he preferred to see bullfighting by a *torero* with a very personal style rather than seeing clever tricks by a bullring star who is merely showing off, so in literature he preferred a bare, spare style rather than tricky technical gimmicks and fancy figures of speech. A first-rate *torero* and a first-rate writer were both masters of their art, and writing a novel was very much like fighting a *corrida*, for the novelist, like the matador, is alone in the ring at the moment of the kill, at the hour of truth. He insisted he wasn't telling me all this simply to hear himself talk, but because he had seen more than two thousand *corridas* in his life, and thus bullfighting was in his very blood. And then, finally, he said:

"Nerves of steel, calm judgment, great courage and great art, perfection, and greater and greater fearlessness. That's the great lesson bullfighters teach us."

"You haven't told me anything I didn't know already," I murmured.

"I don't mean merely in the bullring facing the bull, but in life as well, and in front of a blank sheet of paper too, I hardly need add."

Matías came upstairs again, with a waiter carrying a trayful of dishes and jugs. Juanito was talking to Mary about how many foreigners there were in Pamplona this year and politely answering the questions the doctor and his wife were asking him as to whether many people were likely to be injured during the running of the bulls in the streets, while the two Yankee girl students were expressing their surprise on being told that there would be no fistfights or any sort of violence among the huge crowd of youngsters at the fiesta.

Two *toreros* from South America entered the room then, not great stars, but bullfighters who greatly respected Ernesto and, what was more, belonged to Antonio's "clan."

"We'll be seeing some good bulls," they announced.

"What do they look like?"

"Will they put up a good fight?"

The lot of bulls for the first *corrida* looked quite promising, it appeared.

I noticed, however, that the moment the word *toro* was mentioned and the *toreros* appeared, Ernesto lost interest in everything else, except perhaps eating and drinking. Life, death, the world, women, religion, art could all be explained in bullfighting terms. Statements Ernesto had made that I had read in the papers or seen quoted in profiles of him suddenly came to mind, one for instance in the weekly magazine *Arts*, in which he had said that he had already k.o.ed Turgenev and Maupassant and was hoping to knock Stendhal out of the ring, thanks to what he had learned from watching bullfights.

That was a battle that was really on the up and up, a much more crucial match than the "civil war" that Ernesto was convinced was taking shape between Ordóñez and Dominguín.

"But Ernesto, what about those of us who don't fight a *corrida* somewhere every Sunday and Thursday afternoon?" I asked.

"Life is one big bullring for them too, and there isn't any way out of the ring for anybody," he answered.

"So the only thing you can do is fight the bulls as best you can?"

"Yep, that's it exactly. The only thing you can do is fight your bulls, and there are only two possible outcomes: either you kill the bull or the bull kills you," he answered.

The proximity of the three young girls excited Ernesto the way a red cape excites a bull. He couldn't keep himself from casting covert glances at the affectionate little Irish girl with the unkempt hair, or touching her. He seemed to be very fond of her, and the expression in his eyes as he looked at her was most unusual for him. As a general rule, Ernesto, who was really a very shy man at heart, fled from strikingly beautiful women. If he occasionally eyed a very pretty female, it was always with a certain skepticism, the disillusionment of a man who has found very little pleasure even in lovemaking. Ernesto had long before made the painful discovery that beneath the soft skin, the white teeth, the fresh lips of women, the warm wet down of their crotches, there was nothing but disillusionment, failure, bitterness. How could there have been so much talk for so many years of Ernesto the lusty enjoyer of all life's pleasures, when at heart he had always been a sad, disillusioned, cynical person?

People from Tafalla and Estella invaded the room shouting: "Hurrah for the fermented juice of the grape!" and "Long live our bearded friend!"

People were playing Galician bagpipes and drums and an accordion and a couple of guitars in the doorway. We could also hear skyrockets going off and church bells ringing. The fiesta had really gotten under way now. The momentary intruders didn't bother us, and the uproar in the streets was just innocent merrymaking.

"I'm so happy you came," Ernesto said to me.

"You knew I would," I answered.

"We're going to have a really great time. There's one thing, though: we're going to have to pray that nothing happens to Antonio."

"What could happen to him? He'll be fine—and have a great time too."

"I'm having a fine time myself."

It was true: He later wrote the same thing in *The Dangerous Summer*.

Ernesto was still something of a carouser, but not nearly the one he'd been in the twenties. And his cronies now were certainly much more sedate than the ones back in those days, and the drinking bouts wouldn't be as scandalous as they had once been, and much more fun, really. In Ernesto's crowd this year there was no one I knew of who was impotent, and no female anything like that very decent whore, that heavy-drinking English aristocrat with the hot pants, the famous Lady Brett Ashley. Ernesto had told us about the funeral of the woman she had been modeled after: her pallbearers were her inseparable drinking buddies, all of them stewed to the gills, who kept making lewd and insulting remarks about her and finally dropped the coffin, exposing the dead body of the beautiful redhead who had killed herself drinking and fucking.

Seeing Ernesto in such a glowing mood, we all understood precisely why he had written in utter seriousness:

My return to Spain is a pilgrimage of loving devotion.

And what was more, he had come with Mary, thus violating his own firm tenet that you should never come to the fiesta in Pamplona with your own lawfully wedded wife.

Fortunately Mary was being very sensible and good-natured about the whole thing. And we were all very pleased that she, too, seemed to be having a fine time.

Out on the street, someone was singing a sort of fandango, in a voice that was terribly off key, in honor of Antonio:

> Antonio Ordóñez, what great style you have
> And what fame as a *torero*
> And what an absolute master you are
> On the sand of the bullring

Everybody down there on the street applauded, and Ernesto got up from his chair and shouted down for all of them to come on up and have a drink.

And at that very moment, Ordóñez appeared, with several of the members of his *cuadrilla* and a bunch of his cronies. As I remember, that was when Cano, the photographer, asked us all to come downstairs to have our pictures taken, or a number of us anyway, and took a photo of Ernesto and his friends, both those of the days of yore and those he had made more recently. Ernesto embraced Antonio and said, "Everything's going just great. I'm terribly happy."

He would later write, like a last will and testament and a sort of vaccination against being carried away by any other sudden bursts of enthusiasm, that this had been the happiest two weeks of his life.

It was plain to see that that was true, that he was deeply touched; he was embracing everyone and allowing them to embrace him. And the *toreros* who were friends of Antonio's may have been feeling twinges of envy, but they nonetheless thoroughly approved of the improvised songs people were singing in Antonio's honor:

> We savor the lingering taste of wine on our palates
> Just as we savor the *corrida*
> If it's Antonio Ordóñez who's fighting in the bullring.

A San Fermín celebrant who had tied his neckerchief to a long stick as if it were a *muleta* made imaginary passes at a bull until another *pamplónica* charged him with a three-legged stool and he suddenly withdrew from the *corrida*.

The air of a great fiesta was even more noticeable now, because the presence of the great matador from Ronda, the son of Niño de la Palma, as long-time *aficionados* kept repeating to Ernesto's nostalgic delight, had enlivened the festivities considerably. The women were all making sheep's eyes at him, and he was openly flirting with all of them. He was wearing the most informal sort of dress, tight pants and a silk ascot. His voice had that rasp in it that at times made him sound like a simple peasant and at other times like a cabaret entertainer.

They all came back then, after watching the bulls being unloaded, and told us what their horns and all the rest looked like. Ernesto was positively drooling as he sat there watching the gestures and posturings of that youngster who seemed to be merely a dashing, handsome social lion, though when the trumpet sounded for the beginning of the *corrida*, he would suddenly become a real hero.

If Ernesto's first love among all the countries in the world was Spain, it was because Spain was the magic link in the chain of his art, the one place on this earth where the human tragedy was played out before one's very eyes. Regardless of whether he is a humble man who is practically starving to death or a rich landowner with a whole herd of fighting bulls, the matador, a lone man in the middle of the arena, is one of the most human figures of our time, because he willingly confronts the possibility that he may die in the ring, though his death will never be a humiliation or a defeat if he fights the bull honorably. The *torero*, who is just another human being, like all the rest of us, is invincible when he confronts his adversary with courage and acquits himself honorably. A bullfighter may be fatally gored and his lifeless body removed from the *plaza de toros*, as happens frequently, but his death is always a glorious one. A *torero* is never a man defeated, so long as he has proven himself both a courageous fighter and an artist whose intelligence has proved superior to his instincts.

Ernesto guarded Antonio as though he were a rare museum piece, constantly keeping tabs on him, asking him all sorts of personal questions, advising him, scolding him. Ernesto kept a sharp eye on everything Antonio ate or drank, made sure he rested and relaxed, and so on; as a matter of fact, he took much better care of Antonio than he did of himself.

"Are you going to run with the bulls?" Antonio asked me.

"I'll give it a try."

"He won't chicken out," Ernesto chimed in, and stuck his hand out as though we'd just made a deal.

Even though the San Fermín celebrants who run with the bulls in the streets are merely summer revelers or amateur sportsmen running a sort of thrilling foot race, they nonetheless deserve a certain respect. But according to Ernesto, the *corrida*, and what precedes and follows it, has nothing to do with either revelry or sport. It is the greatest human tragedy of all. Hence, going to a bullfight, watching it, following it requires that the true *aficionado* fight a moral battle against any sort of licence that is simply self-indulgence or hedonism. Precisely because it is such a beautiful form of dying, and because the *corrida* gives the *torero* the possibility of overcoming death and being immortal for an instant, it demands great sacrifice, a spirit that must be forged, if not by ascetic self-denial, by a firm, deeply rooted, stoic force of will.

"You're not going to run, though," Ernesto said to Antonio.

"No, you're the one who's not going to run, because you're such an old man," the matador replied affectionately.

"You really shouldn't run," Ernesto insisted.

"We'll see."

"You're a sly old dog, you know, and you're surrounded by women here. . . . Let's have a few passes *por lo bajo* and *por lo alto* out of you; how about it?" Ernesto whispered to Antonio with a twinkle in his eye. "We'll see if you leave any broads for the rest of us," he added, winking at me.

Ordóñez seldom over ate, although once in a great while he might drink a fair amount, and though he might occasionally be quite taken with a woman, it was always only a mild infatuation, never a passionate love affair. Quite aside from the fact that his wife, Carmen, kept a sharp eye on him, his conscience and his respect for his profession kept him from straying very far down the primrose path, though from time to time he did play around a little, perhaps to show himself and others that he was capable of being carried away.

A couple of resounding bangs on the marble table brought me out of my daydream. The Paseo de Rosales is just the right sort of spot to take a trip outside of time and space. How long had I sat there at that table after leaving Ordóñez's house?

"You were having a little cat nap, eh, friend?" the waiter said to me.

"No, I wasn't asleep."

"That's what they all say," he replied. "This place doesn't seem like a bad spot at all to take a little siesta. I sure wish I could cork off a while. But I'm through here for the day now," he said, handing me the check for my drink. "And then it's behind the wheel for me . . . a couple of hours driving a taxi," he went on in a confidential, mock-theatrical tone of voice.

As night fell, it seemed to be getting lighter and lighter for some odd reason. Perhaps it was just that my eyes were getting accustomed to the dark and therefore the sky looked brighter and brighter. And every so often a star streaked down from the Milky Way, as poorly placed banderillas sometimes fall from the back of a bull. And I thought to myself: "Where could I possibly go now that would be better than right here?" Though no answer to that question came readily to mind, I nonetheless got to my feet, paid the check, and walked on down the street.

It was a mortal sin to leave the Paseo de Rosales, but I did, strolling along the edge of the tree-lined parapet, and when I got to another combination outdoor café-bar and newsstand on the corner, I sat down again. But I was hungry now, so this time I ordered some fried potatoes and olives.

The view of the Sierra was even more beautiful from here, and the couples petting at the tables even more passionate. I continued my stroll down memory lane:

"She's all yours. . . ." Ernesto said.

"No, she's yours. . . . Go to it," I answered.

"No, she's yours," he insisted.

"Heaven only knows who she belongs to. Maybe she's her own woman."

This was all just a pleasant way of whiling away the time. The Irish girl with the wild mop of hair, the burning eyes, the pink cheeks sprinkled with freckles, was flushed with excitement. She seemed a quite innocent girl, however, and her apparent eagerness to bed with Ernesto was probably mostly a matter of wishful thinking on her part. Ernesto was a superdeity in her eyes as she sat there watching people from all over the world line up to get his autograph.

In that whole excited mob of men and women in Ernesto's inner circle, the person who seemed most dignified and level-headed was his family doctor from Ketchum, who was wordlessly watching his patient consume great quantities of cheese and cutlets and fried peppers and sausages and crayfish and above all glass after glass of wine. The doctor's wife was perfectly charming, fighting off fatigue like a child, and asking every sort of question imaginable.

The most standoffish and wary of the group was "Freckles" Hotchner, lolling in his chair looking like a crafty gypsy and watching all of us with that strange expression of his, half lustful and half on the defensive. He was laughing and applauding and singing and taking it all in, but despite his apparent air of easy camaraderie, it was quite noticeable that he was subtly playing the role of ringmaster. He was very careful to be properly attentive to Mary and extremely polite to her and the other guests, but he kept his eye on Ernesto every minute, watching his every move and listening to his every word, especially when he was approached by journalists or photographers. "Freckles" was in complete control of the situation, and I wasn't at all surprised that he had earned lots of money for Ernesto by signing him up with the television networks and mass-circulation American magazines, though I was quite certain Hotchner had been motivated by something other than worshipful admiration for a great writer.

As for Bill Davis, he looked like just another Navarrese peasant. Most of the time he acted like a farmer who was a bit hard of hearing, and every so often he would get terribly bored and doze off, but all in all he was as well-behaved and as polite as an English sailor when he's not three sheets to the wind.

Ernesto was very anxious for all of us to get to be good buddies and stick together like grains of rice in a good paella. So when he heard the *chistu* players coming down the street, he began to sing the *riau-riau* in the great booming voice of a whale fisherman, and those of us around the table swayed back and forth in time to the music like shipmates carrying out the orders of the skipper of our pirate ship.

The fiesta had really gotten off the ground now. The city was one great swarm of people, from the valleys and the seashore, from the mountains and the truck farms round about, for there are still a few around Pamplona, though not many. The strolling musicians and the dancers had begun wandering about the streets; the whole city was singing and dancing; and as twilight fell, the revelry was becoming more and more delirious.

Then Ernesto got up from his chair and said, "Let's go outside."

There was much more applause for Ernesto now, and we all laughed and danced along beside him as he joined the great throng advancing toward us like a river, with upraised arms and pounding hearts. We all mingled with the joyous crowd, each of us aglow with the same bright flame.

"It's love of a city," I said to the Irish girl.

"It's love of a man," she said in her charming, hesitant Spanish.

We entered a vast, damp, rustic tavern that looked more like a cellar. The *kilikis* and the *zaldiokomadikos*—the giant carnival figures carried through the streets during the Sanfermines—were bobbing and weaving just outside the door, and the crowd was having a great time watching them nodding and bowing.

"They're just the same," he said.

"Who's just the same?" I said, not knowing what he meant.

"Those things," he replied, pointing to the huge traditional figures, the *"gigantes y cabezudos,"* being paraded through the street.

"Oh, they've probably been touched up a bit," I commented.

Passions were cooling a little, there was less jealousy in the air, and we were all feeling like lifelong friends now. Ernesto had a great talent for soothing ruffled feathers and smoothing over the rough spots.

We went outside again, and immediately found ourselves surrounded by deafening whistles, bagpipes, and cymbals. It was not only dried skins and bright metal that made it seem as though we had been caught up in a whirlwind; we were also swept along by a great wave of warm, sweating bodies, but it was young flesh, boys and girls whose innocence was like a rainbow between one thundershower and another. And the sidewalks were lined with great mobs of people waiting for the saint to be carried by in the procession.

All of us felt terribly young, but the doctor was worried about how excited Ernesto was, and kept taking his pulse, like someone who keeps consulting his wristwatch as he waits for a train, and, each time, Ernesto would roar, "I'm as strong as a bull!"

"But not just any bull, not even a Miura," I chimed in.

The doctor nodded in agreement. And "Freckles" said, in his halting Spanish, "He's the best matador in the whole country."

Ernesto was giving out autographs to Spaniards and foreigners with the patience of a saint, cheerfully signing their bits of paper "to my friend so-and-so" when they told him their names, then giving each of them a hearty handshake.

A peasant walking just behind us madly tootling a trumpet, his face as red as a beet, said to us as we arrived at the door of the sanctuary, "Are you going in to see the 'saint with the dark skin' too?"

"Sure," Ernesto replied.

"There aren't many saints like him," the peasant said.

"You're right, there!" Ernesto replied. "But the funny thing is, even after so many years of running the bulls at Pamplona, we still don't know if San Fermín likes or dislikes them."

"What makes you think he dislikes bulls? I bet he likes *toros* as much as I like turnips, cod, and the cunts of . . . old ladies," the peasant said with a laugh.

There was hardly room for one more person in the tiny little church, for it was packed with sweaty bodies. Once inside, Ernesto looked all around, as though trying to catch a glimpse of something he was very familiar with and very fond of. And to my great surprise, he knelt at one of the prie-dieus. He didn't look anything like a peasant, but his attitude was as reverent as any simple farmer's. I watched him and noted that his lips were moving. What was he praying for, what was he promising, what was he repenting of, what was he confessing? Where had I come across this image before?

> I knelt and started to pray and prayed for everybody I thought of . . . and all the time I was kneeling with my forehead on the wood in front of me, and was thinking of myself as praying, I was a little ashamed. . . .

These words from *The Sun Also Rises*, written so many years before, seemed as fresh and new as when a grimy fresco is washed down with a damp sponge. Ernesto may even have been praying for me. This little church was a much more moving and intimate place than the cold, empty church described in the book. At any event, Ernesto was on his knees praying. I felt a need to pray for *him* then, for him to be cured of that terrible blotch on his face, of the tremor in his hands I had recently begun to notice, for him to be able to write much more, for him to be able to drink without endangering his health, for him to have the courage to run before the bulls even though he was really too old for such feats of bravado. And once again I remembered how the p. had ended:

> . . . I was a little ashamed, and regretted that I was such a rotten Catholic, but realized there was nothing I could do about it, at least for a while, and maybe never, but that anyway it was a grand religion, and I only wished I felt religious and maybe I would the next time.

We soon met up with the rest of the group, with Davis leading the women—Davis the silent kidnaper, the superfaithful organizer, the keeper of the keys, the mailman, the administrator, the huckster, the laconic drinking buddy, the bodyguard ready to put up his dukes and protect Ernesto at the slightest sign of trouble. He might pull almost anything out of one of his pockets: a check, a doctor's prescription, tickets for bullfights, a mysterious telegram, a Colt .45. Perhaps he liked fooling people by pretending to be just a hayseed with lots of *pesetas* socked away.

"Antonio's waiting for you at Yoldi's," I said to Ernesto.

Mary was tired and I took her back to the little chalet in the new part of the city that she and Ernesto were staying in.

"He seems as strong as an ox," I said to Mary.

"That's always been my biggest problem: trying to decide how much he can take. But I've always been wrong, because he's always been able to take far more than I possibly imagined he could."

"That can get pretty exhausting."

"*You* know how he can wear you out," she answered.

You either had to keep up with Ernesto or stay away from him. If you were anywhere around him and yielded to the temptation to keep him company—a temptation that was very hard to resist—you very soon felt like a boat caught in a giant hurricane.

I went back to Yoldi's, where I found Ernesto and Antonio standing just outside the door. Before San Fermín week began, Ernesto would start scaring up bunches of tickets for good seats at the bullring. He naturally had the choicest seats firmly booked for himself, but he also wanted all his friends to share the excitement of the *corrida*. Everything was all arranged and we all had passes, so there would be no difficulty getting in. If Ernesto was short of tickets for his friends and found that he could wangle them no other way, there was always his money clip, and green bills would appear like slices of bait for a fishhook.

Antonio was standing there with his retinue of second-rate matador cronies and members of their *cuadrillas*, laughing and joking with Ernesto. The two of them had first gotten to know each other right there in Pamplona, or rather the author and the youngster, the bearded patriarch and the young gypsy had first met there, in the year 1953.

Everything that Ernesto was later to labor so hard to describe in *The Dangerous Summer* was already there in the matador's eyes, and one might even go so far as to say that, in certain sense, it was all already written.

I noticed the eyes first; the darkest, brightest, merriest eyes anybody ever looked into. . . .

And Ernesto the author would no longer have to pull out of the secret recesses of his mind all the things he had never been able to set down on paper about Antonio's father. He had met his idol in the flesh now, an idol he felt obliged to worship, but also a beloved friend he felt obliged to watch over and care for. The more fervently Ernesto worshiped Antonio, the more this youngster took on the stature of a mythical figure. And the happier that made Ernesto.

But Antonio had not come to Pamplona to run before the bulls in the streets. He had come to the fiesta to do something much more difficult: to make people forget the minor faults that had marred his performances in previous years and lay the groundwork for an enduring reputation that no one would ever again question. This promised to be his moment of greatest glory, and Ernesto hovered about him constantly, absolutely fascinated, utterly captivated by him. The very first time he had seen Antonio fight, Ernesto had written, in *The Dangerous Summer*:

Watching Antonio with the bull I saw that he had everything his father had in the great days.

Ernesto was standing there frowning, watching Antonio joking with his friends there in the middle of the sidewalk. There was a distraught look on Ernesto's face, almost as though it distressed him or hurt him to see that Antonio did not seem to be living up to the role of a god incarnate that he, the world-famous bullfight *aficionado*, had conferred upon him. Antonio was too natural, too outgoing, too happy and exuberant. Ernesto had mentioned in *The Dangerous Summer* Antonio's "mischief urchin grin." But to Ernesto, Ordóñez was nonetheless much more than the mere youngster he still seemed to be, standing there in his informal sports clothes, with his usual slightly condescending, mocking smile on his face. Everything that Ernesto had ever dreamed of in the way of life and color, movement and grace, art and sensitivity, was there just two steps away: Antonio, making a fool of himself, kidding around, playing the clown. Nonetheless Antonio could have no possible rival in Ernesto's eyes. He was the very incarnation of the bullfighter, the incomparable master in the bullring, and what was more, he was a very nice youngster, warmhearted and affectionate and handsome. How very few times there has been such a miraculous fusion of the artist and his handiwork, of statuesque beauty and grace! Ernesto was enamored, more than enamored of Antonio's ideal physical beauty, as his idol constantly confronted death, the great enemy of every sort of beauty in the ring. And that is also why it sometimes pained him simply to look at this youngster, whose presence was not enough to blot out the thought of the terrible dangers Ordóñez so often confronted.

Ernesto came over to me and said, "He's his father all over again, but better."

"Better because he's more talented, and more courageous?"

"He's better in every way, a better bullfighter, a better person."

"Did you have something against Cayetano?"

"Do you have something against Antonio?"

"I saw Cayetano lying in his coffin, and he seemed to me to look like all dead people do—wasted away to nothing."

"It's sad when a *torero* dies in bed, but there are certain sorts of death in the bullring that I'm not certain I'd have the courage to witness."

"Were you ever on as intimate terms with Cayetano as with Antonio?"

"It was different. We spent a fair amount of time together, but Cayetano wasn't like Antonio. Antonio's one in a million. In the beginning, his father had lots of style and lots of balls and he led a very decent life as a *torero*. Before taking up bullfighting he'd been a shoemaker, a baker, and a cook's helper. For a while he was absolutely tops in the ring, but later on he slid downhill like all the rest of them . . ."

"What did you like most about him?"

"He could control the bull better than anybody . . ."

"Anything else?"

"His passes were sweeping and slow and harmonious, very majestic and beautifully linked."

"How was he at killing?"

"When he began to allow his fear to get the better of him, he turned into a coward and a clown."

Antonio was talking about bullfighting with some impresarios and agents and other people who make their living from bullfights. Ernesto went over to them, pretended to pass an angry onrushing bull with a cape, and at the end of the pass, they all shouted in chorus:

"Oleeeeeeeee!"

When he came back, the two of us went on with our chat there in the dark.

"I've heard that it was very sad watching Cayetano slide downhill."

"Niño de la Palma was a *torero* through and through, but every once in a while he'd have a terrible afternoon, when he would suddenly lose all his spontaneity and all his majestic dignity. He didn't seem like the same man at all on afternoons like that. I think there were times when he was absolutely overcome with apathy and indifference. It wasn't so much a fear of the bulls as it was fear of himself, not fatigue but a sort of very odd lethargy that was so contagious everyone felt it. A terribly sad look would come over his face, as if there weren't the slightest spark of life left in him . . ."

"What do you think his best season was?"

"Well, the one I'd pick as his very best was 1925, the year I started *The Sun Also Rises*."

"I think Antonio is much more sure of himself and much more mature than his father ever was."

"I often think of Niño de la Palma, but Antonio is incomparably better."

The first draft of *The Sun Also Rises* was written from July to October 1925, in Spain. Ernesto began it in Valencia, continued working on it in Madrid and San Sebastián, and when he left Spain the rough draft of it was finished but not the final draft. It was during the following winter that he began revising it and polishing it up, in Austria, in the snow.

It was Hemingway's pal Scott Fitzgerald who had acted as an intermediary for him, recommending Ernesto's manuscript to Maxwell Perkins, editor of Scribner's in New York.

Ernesto sent a number of confidential letters to Fitzgerald, all couched, however, in carefully chiseled phrases with an eye to their literary effect. As when he wrote to Fitzgerald on first discovering bullfighting that paradise to him would be a *plaza de toros* with two good seats permanently reserved for him. But something else was needed to complete the picture of ideal happiness, and paradise also meant a trout stream near Pamplona set aside for his exclusive use.

It didn't matter that the days when Hemingway and Fitzgerald had been cronies and Ernesto had discovered bullfighting lay far in the past. When he returned to Spain, Ernesto was able to fuse his love of the boxing ring and his love of the bullring.

But the boxing ring did not occupy nearly as high a place in his scale of values as the bullring. The boxing ring enclosed with ropes is nothing at all like the bull arena, where the mad flurry of betting is preceded and followed by a deathly silence, and even the part of the bullfight that is sheer spectacle is charged with a drama that is incomprehensible for anyone who has not identified with it completely.

But we kept rolling down the streets of Pamplona like a great ball. How patiently Ernesto went through the entire routine: waiting around, making phone calls, following the bullfight circuit, rushing back and forth, controlling his temper, applauding like everybody else, making harsh remarks, apologizing, going into ecstasies, vomiting. . . . Ernesto put up with all of it in order to remain close to the world of bullfighting, that mixture of shameless toadying, publicity, pedantry, and commercialism. He must have been extremely fond of Antonio to have so devotedly dogged his idol's every footstep. During this time, he took me aside one day and said, as though sharing a great revelation with me:

"Tell me something, José Luis. Since you're obviously so fond of Antonio, how come you've never written one line about him?"

"I will someday."

"I'm quite sure that would please him a lot."

"It would please me too."

"You really ought to."

"Maybe someday I can do a decent job of it."

Ernesto wasn't trying to get publicity for Antonio or anything of the sort, since Antonio has always had fervent and well-paid critics who have praised him lavishly. What Ernesto apparently wanted was to make Ordóñez a legendary figure by having me write a novel with Antonio as the hero. But I couldn't work up much enthusiasm for the idea. And the two or three times that Ernesto tried to explain to me why the duel between Dominguín and Ordóñez was so important, the whole thing left me rather cold. I didn't really understand what all the fuss was about. They had managed to kindle some sort of fire that "dangerous summer," but I never felt warmed by it. But "Freckles" was delighted at the thought of how much money they were going to make, what with all the talk of a great rivalry between the two matadors.

There were certain days, and particularly certain hours, when Ernesto became practically delirious thinking about Ordóñez: the hours before or after a *corrida*. When Antonio wasn't fighting, Ernesto felt he had to fire his enthusiasm for him some other way. Antonio was not only his beloved friend, he was his passion and his dream, his own personal creation, and a proof of his gifts of prophecy. Antonio was not only a human being but an art object. How many times I heard Ernesto exclaim: "Look at him, will you? Just look at him! Have you ever seen anybody anywhere near his equal?"

Antonio was Ernesto's living myth. He bitterly regretted that he had wasted everything he had learned about bullfighting in earlier books, including that first novel whose hero had been modeled on Antonio's own father. His book about Antonio's fights should be fresh and sparkling and new. It would be his masterwork, the crowning work of his career. He had carelessly squandered his greatest treasure in his earlier books. Ordóñez, his own creation, was the perfect protagonist, a hero whose name deserved to become a household word in the farthest corners of the world, where people had never even heard of bull-fighting.

I remembered some of the almost childishly naïve confidences he had shared with me. One day, for instance, he said to me:

"I trust you. I believe you've got real powers of intuition. Is it true, José Luis, that Antonio's not going to die?"

"I suppose you mean die in the bullring?"

"Yes."

"I think Antonio knows lots and lots about bulls and that if the bulls come to know as much about him, they'll all have the greatest respect for him."

"Antonio doesn't deserve to have anything bad happen to him."

"Nothing's going to happen to him."

"He's not going to have any ordinary sort of mishap, at least."

"Why did you ask me that question, though?"

"Because sometimes I have a feeling in my bones that something bad is going to happen, and I have bad dreams, really demoniacal ones."

"I think Antonio's fate is already written in the stars. I don't know whether he'll die a tragic death or not, there's no way of knowing, but I don't really think he will. I think he's got a lucky star . . ."

"I hope to God you're right . . ."

And he felt immensely relieved. What had my words freed him of—those "demoniacal nightmares"? At any event, I felt that it was the great temptation, the exhausting struggle between his needs as an artist and his feelings about his beloved friend that in the end finally un-balanced Ernesto's mind. He dreamed of writing a great epic about his idol, but would he be capable of writing it? Such a work almost demanded that Antonio die in the ring, and Ernesto had a premonition and a very great fear that that was how Antonio would die (what part did Ernesto's unconscious, unavowable wishes play in this fear that came close to being abject terror?); Antonio's death in the bullring was almost a necessity in order to crown not only Ernesto's work of art, but the legend, the myth of Antonio. Perhaps that was why Ernesto had called them "demoniacal dreams." The temptation had been too great . . .

I do not believe it would be straying too far from the truth to main-tain that this strange psychic ambivalence was the cause of the guilt complex that so clouded his mind in the last months of his life. I am sure that Ernesto had already unconsciously imagined Antonio's death in the ring a thousand times in his tortured mind, and could almost have set it down on paper. And that was why he was obliged to take such scrupulous care of his friend, to pray so often for him, to indulge his every whim, for Antonio was at one and the same time the creature of his imagination, the hero of the epic he would write, and a beloved personal friend, there at his side, in the flesh. It was enough to unbalance anyone's mind.

As the day drew to a close and another just like it began, we were all dead on our feet, about to collapse, yet Antonio and Ernesto kept standing there joking with each other. Antonio, who was always as much of a tease as a schoolboy, said to him: "We're tied for the highest honors, and will keep splitting fifty-fifty. I'm the best *torero* in the world and you're the best writer. The best Nobel of them all."

"You're very generous," Ernesto answered.

"But you writers really live a soft life. Everything's so easy for you. Look, everybody else is doing all the work and you're reaping all the glory."

Antonio is rather a simple man, and in the back of his mind, this wasn't simply a joking matter. Antonio could never understand the inner fits of rage that sometimes overcame Ernesto, or his inner torture.

When Ernesto would sometimes leave Antonio and his rowdy cronies and come over and take me aside, I often thought he had something important to tell me. But all he would say was something like, "Do you think this is Antonio's finest moment, his moment of greatest glory?"

"I think Antonio is going to go much further," I would answer. "Antonio is going to be the greatest *matador* ever, the one and only."

"I believe you're absolutely right. But you think he may die in the bullring, you're convinced he's taking great risks, aren't you?"

And immediately, as though he had put his finger on a painful wound or as though he wanted or needed to drive the evil thought out of his mind, Ernesto would cross himself or say, "Get thee behind me, Satan."

At such times, it was quite apparent that his mind was becoming a little unhinged, and I knew he was suffering terribly. Later on, I realized or at least thought I had caught a glimpse of the real cause of his attacks of acute anxiety. After not having visited Spain for fifteen years, he doubtless believed that bullfighting was more or less the same as in his youth, when a *torero* was much more likely to die if he was gored in the ring. Hence, in my opinion and in the opinion of many others, Ernesto's fears for Antonio's life were somewhat unrealistic and exaggerated, and it was for precisely this reason that certain journalists and cheap tabloids hinted that the relations between the two of them were suspect. But this was not true at all. Ernesto and Ordóñez were never as close friends as most people thought; what most attracted

Ernesto to Antonio was the thought of making his idol the protagonist of a great work of art. With Antonio as his hero, he could write his great bullfight epic, something even better than *The Old Man and the Sea*. But what if Antonio were to die in the bullring, what if "something were to happen to Antonio," as Ernesto always put it? If that came to pass, the death of Robert Jordan as he blows up the bridge would be nothing compared to Antonio's glorious death, the most sublime death imaginable. But how could he possibly even entertain such a thought? "Get thee behind me, Satan."

We told Antonio we'd meet him, at dinnertime, at Las Pocholas, and the two of us walked back toward the Plaza del Castillo. Ernesto strode along the sidewalk with the dignity and the pleased look of some-one who has just regained something that has rightfully belonged to him for a long time. His literary life had really begun with *The Sun Also Rises*. When Hadley Richardson, Ernesto's first wife, divorced him, he very generously gave her the manuscript of this very first novel of his, which Hadley later sold to the actress Ann Harding for ten thousand dollars, a rather tidy sum; but that was not the end of it, for, a while later, the actress sold it to someone else for twenty thousand dollars. The price of the manuscript had doubled in just a few years, but several years later it had risen even higher, for the film producer Darryl F. Zanuck was forced to shell out the unbelievable sum of two hundred thousand dollars to purchase this much-sought-after original manu-script.

But all this was simply an indication of Ernesto's growing financial success; his stock as an excellent writer also continued to rise steadily, and people began to cease speaking of "a piece of reporting" with a tinge of scorn, as if it were a very minor genre. And that was a real achievement.

After taking a look all around the Plaza, Ernesto headed straight for the terrace of the Choko.

"In the old days I used to hang out at the Iruña, over there across the way, but in recent years it's gotten to be a terribly dull place. What's more, I've heard that the Iruña was where the Fascist generals used to hang out," he said to me.

But the Choko wasn't the only place Ernesto frequented. There were several other bars around, such as the Kutz and El Torino, and since it was going to be a long day, there would be plenty of time to drop in at those hangouts too.

Everyone in Pamplona was still applauding and acclaiming Ernesto. Not only the local townspeople but Spaniards from all over the country lined up with foreigners to pay their respects to Ernesto. Our sweat-soaked shirts were sticking to our backs, and every once in a while Davis or Hotchner or one of the girls or I would get up and try to keep the mob from pestering Ernesto and let him rest for a few minutes at least. He was sitting there answering questions, talking with people, signing autographs like an automaton. And every once in a while a faraway, bewildered, almost disappointed look would come over his face. Perhaps he was already thinking the thoughts that he was later to set down on paper, the sad realization that almost all of his comrades of the Civil War days had disappeared now.

Suddenly I was eager to ask him a few questions about people he'd met and events he had witnessed in his past.

"What was Belmonte like in the days you knew him?" I asked him at one point when he was taking a breather.

"He was a rather quiet sort, never very outgoing," Ernesto answered.

"Was he perhaps shy?" I asked.

"He was kind of an odd sort. He was more or less of a bore until he loosened up a little. But once he let go and started kidding around, he was fun to be with, but that didn't happen very often. Usually he was pretty much of a wet blanket, more or less a naturally unhappy person, a real sad sack."

"Is that so?"

"Yes, he always got on my nerves a little."

Ernesto had a great talent for drawing little profiles of people. And as he went on with his little thumbnail sketch of Belmonte, that taciturn *torero* who could suddenly surprise you by coming out with some really droll remark, I was thinking about the sad night we had gone to Julio Camba's wake with Sebastián Miranda and the rather dotty lady whose oddball behavior had made the whole tragic but mordantly funny scene something straight out of Goya. Belmonte's bone-deep sadness, his dry wit, his jokes that betrayed childish fears and a terribly pessimistic outlook on life, had always made a deep impression on me. But Sebastián Miranda had managed to allay my fears about Belmonte's suicidal tendencies.

Ernesto was lost in thought again, and you felt that he was concentrating on everything he had written thus far and everything he was about to write, his remark for instance about the *corrida* at Aranjuez:

> In this section of the country the people who knew about real bulls and real bullfighting had been exterminated on both sides in the Civil War.

Wasn't this something of an exaggeration? But Ernesto really believed that, and had said as much time and time again. Perhaps he didn't really appreciate the fact that in Spain people knew a lot about bullfighting, even though they didn't go to *corridas* regularly. I am quite willing to concede that you may find *aficionados* in the stands at the *plaza de toros*, but it's in the streets, in the very air, that you will discover the secret of the Spanish people's love of bullfighting. Our talk about life, death, God, history, politics, love, war is always full of bullfighting images. Was it true that the Spanish Civil War had really severed the very roots of our profound love of bullfighting? There was no doubt, in any event, that the war had been such a crucial turning point in Ernesto's life that everything had seemed totally different to him afterward.

But his ideas and his feelings with regard to everything Spanish deserved the greatest respect. They were entirely his own. In *The Dangerous Summer*, he had written that "animals have been fought in capeas that have previously killed more than ten men." And he had also written that nowadays it was only tourists who attended professional bullfights.

As a matter of fact, amateur bullfights such as those Ernesto mentions are still held in many parts of Spain, occasionally bringing some village lad's life to a sudden end in a way that is as senseless as it is terrifying. And it was also quite true that tourists, mostly Americans with a copy of *The Sun Also Rises* in their hands, were mobbing Hemingway's sanctuary. That was why he was sitting there staring scornfully at them, as though he were offended and infuriated and scandalized. And every so often he would get up out of his chair and bellow at them to drive them all away.

The Plaza del Castillo was like a breakwater in a busy port. People of all descriptions kept arriving in great waves, and it seemed as though the little tables in the bars would be swept away at any moment by this veritable human tide of dancing, singing merrymakers.

But the *fiesta brava* had not really begun yet. Though the wooden barricades had already been erected along the streets where the bulls were to be run, from the military hospital to the telephone building, with a number of tiny plazas and winding alleyways, the stairs of the city hall, and two very narrow little streets, Mercaderes and Estafeta, along the route, the stars of the fiesta, the bulls, still had not appeared: the bulls, with their superhuman offering, with death perched on the tips of their two horns, the possible death of any one of those young lads walking down the street at this moment arm in arm with his sweetheart; the bulls, whose headlong stampede through the streets would make a man of each one of these lads.

"Will you run with the bulls tomorrow, José Luis?"

"I'll have a try at it."

Meanwhile the "kidnap victims" were talking about Antonio, calling him in their hesitant, faulty Spanish a *majo* (a gay blade), a *macho* (a real he-man), and even a *chulo* (a cutie-pie), though I don't think they really knew what the words meant. "Antonio's a real looker, a neat guy," they kept saying.

"I bet *you* and *you* and *you* would be only to happy to sleep with him, right?" Ernesto chimed in, pointing at each of them in turn.

Nothing could spoil the San Fermín fiesta for Ernesto; he was entering into it with all his heart and soul, a part of the very myth that he himself created.

"Waiter!" he shouted. "Bring us a couple more bottles, but make sure they're nice and cold."

"I beg your pardon?"

"I want them to be ice coooold!"

By now there were quite a few noisy drunks around, and every once in a while some boorish roisterer would elbow his way into our intimate little circle. Ernesto tried his best to keep his temper, but from time to time he'd leap up from his chair, hopping mad, and bellow, "Can't you let us do our celebrating in peace?"

"No offense meant," the intruder would say.

We would step in then and try to shoo them away politely, but finally Ernesto would wave his arms and shout angrily:

"Clear out of here, the whole drrrrunken lot of you!" growling his r's in his throat like a fearful clap of thunder.

The rest of us had to intervene then and beg the louts to leave:

"Come on, clear out, won't you? You're being ridiculous."

"Stop pestering this great man who's been much nicer to you than you deserve."

In the middle of the day, the Plaza del Castillo was as quiet as a beach after a fleet of pirate ships has sailed away. It was time to go eat dinner. There were lots of places, both inside and outside of town, where Ernesto might find a quiet little corner to have dinner with his friends. Usually Ernesto chose the restaurant and the menu himself beforehand. But everything about Ernesto, even the meals he ate with his most intimate friends, inevitably became a sort of spectacle, and we practically had to fight the journalists and photographers off with our bare fists.

"Can't you see that the man's exhausted, that suppertime will be the only rest he'll have?" we pleaded.

Sometimes they would go away and sometimes they wouldn't. Often the photographers and reporters were trying to do their jobs conscientiously and were simply nosing about in search of a story.

As it happened, just as we were going into the quiet little restaurant where we were going to have dinner, we ran across a bullfight critic who couldn't stand the sight of Ernesto. (I must admit that there was nothing very unusual about that; most of the other bullfight critics also thoroughly disliked him.)

"Isn't there some other place where ordinary mortals like us can eat in peace?" Ernesto remarked when he saw him.

We went somewhere else for dinner; nobody seemed to have noticed what had happened except me, for Ernesto had taken my arm a few moments before and I had been standing right next to him. This was scarcely the first time that such a thing had happened. Ernesto's presence in Spain—whether at the San Fermín fiesta, in the streets of Madrid, at a hunting preserve, in the Prado Museum, or in a gas station— did not always cause people to burst into applause the moment they recognized him. He was often greeted by insulting remarks and gibes. Many people took Ernesto for a great publicity hound and reacted as if all the hubbub that constantly surrounded him was his way of promoting himself, of keeping himself in the limelight. But they were wrong. You could both admire and criticize Ernesto for very well-founded reasons, but he could never rightfully be accused of being a publicity hound or cleverly blowing his own horn. He was famous *despite* the fact that he did almost nothing to promote his own image in the public eye.

To get back to the subject of bullfighting, Ernesto had been the writer largely responsible for making reporting on bullfighting a serious literary genre, and that is precisely what the pen-pushers, the hack bullfight critics, had never forgiven him for, since their own reporting was loaded with adjectives and adverbs and verbs used as substantives, a style as heavy as the bullfighters' trunks stuffed with equipment that their attendants cart around from one bullring to the next.

As we ate dinner, what we talked about around the table was how much the bull must suffer when they shave his horns in the bullpen, and how the poor *torero*, even if Sofia Loren were to suddenly hop into bed with him, would simply have to close his eyes like a saint and dream of the Miura bulls awaiting him the next day. We also mentioned the fact that practically every baby born in Navarre is conceived during the San Fermín fiesta, though if your name is Fermín it's not an absolutely certain sign that you were fathered on that saint's day or even the day before or the day after. The *feria* of San Fermín today was naturally nothing like it had been years ago, and it was doubtless the great throngs of foreign girls who had poured into Pamplona for the fiesta that were responsible for the fact that used condoms had appeared by the hundreds at the foot of the walls of the city, in the parks, and on the riverbanks.

"It makes people horny to see all those bulls," Ernesto commented. "Even the bullfighter sometimes get horny," he added.

"And maybe the bulls do too!" somebody piped up.

"Yes, that might very well be," Ernesto replied. "That's why you don't often get horn wounds in the chest and very seldom in the heart. When you get a *cornada*, it's usually in the groin, the inside of the thighs, the belly, the balls . . ."

It was the first night of the fiesta, merely a sample of all the others to follow during the rest of the week-long celebration. We strolled slowly, almost solemnly, down the streets where the following morning the bulls would be treading on the very heels of the delirious, excited youngsters fleeing before them.

We agreed to meet on a certain street corner the next morning if we missed each other at Ernesto and Mary's chalet.

I took a couple of turns around the plaza by myself then, watching the square gradually empty. I collapsed in a chair on the terrace outside one of the bars and began staring at the sky. Most probably, there were no bullfights on the moon, despite the fact that it looked like a bullring adrift in space, but were there perhaps courage and passion, war and love, on Mars or Venus?

Suddenly people began shaking me by the arm.

"The bulls are coming!" they shouted.

"Here come the *toroooooos!*"

I woke from my half doze and leaped to my feet in a panic, and they all whooped with laughter. Then I cursed the whore of a mother who'd borne them, and they thought it was very funny. We all stood there exchanging great bear hugs, and then made the rounds of the town together, drinking and singing.

7

"Look, your jacket's lying there on the ground—somebody might make off with it," the waiter said to me.

Sad and fatigued, I had hung it on the back of one of those comfortable chairs there in the café-bar on the Paseo de Rosales, and I couldn't understand how it could have fallen to the ground. Because there was no one else around except the waiter and me, I didn't want to embarrass him by searching through the pockets to see if anything was missing.

I paid the check, left the waiter a tip, and walked on down the street. The balconies of some of the buildings were deserted, and whole families were sitting outside on others. It was that hour of night in Madrid in summertime when families open all their windows and french doors, and endless conversations were going on from one balcony to another. The radios were turned up full blast, and you could hear every word of the soap operas, full of the usual trite domestic crises, as you walked down the street.

I went past Ordóñez's house again on the way home. I couldn't see a single light on anywhere inside; the house was as quiet and deserted as a tomb. And I thought to myself: "Antonio can't possibly go to Pamplona. He must have said he was going just to hear himself talk. I'm sure he'll be on his way to Idaho early tomorrow morning . . ." It was the least he could do.

But perhaps Ordóñez would merely kneel in prayer, thus paying back in kind the words Ernesto had written in *The Dangerous Summer*:

> I prayed for all those I had in hock to Fortune, for all friends with cancer, for all girls, living and dead, and that Antonio would have good bulls that afternoon.

They were very simple words, but also very revealing ones. It was something more than just an empty phrase.

I walked slowly on toward the Plaza de España.

On stormy nights in Madrid—both in summer and in winter—one always lands up in the Gran Vía somehow, a fine shelter from the gusts of wind and rain. Fortunately there aren't very many storms in Madrid, either in summer or in winter.

Ernesto had written in *Death in the Afternoon:*

To go to bed at night in Madrid marks you as a little queer.

Like a bull making its way to the watering trough, I decided I would drop in at the Chicote, one of Hemingway's frequent stopping-off places when he was out roaming the streets of the city during his first stay in Madrid.

I felt a need to say good-by for him to all his favorite haunts in Madrid that he would never see again. Madrid, "the capital of the world," as he had called it, would never see Ernesto again either, but at least he had left us his descriptions of it, a violent, bloody, fascinating fresco. For one thing is certain: however much critics in other parts of the world might wrack their brains trying to explain Ernesto's works, they would be forced to admit in the end that without Madrid, without the sidewalks of Madrid, without that strange mixture that is the style of Madrid at its very purest, part Velázquez and part Goya, and the impression that they made on Ernesto's Yankee sensibilities and his Yankee mind, the meaning of his best books would be impossible to unravel. Madrid had been the crucible in which Ernesto had fused the Celto-Iberian and the cosmopolitan, enthusiasm and desperation, passion and candor, the brutally realistic and the delicately sensitive—that amalgam all his very own that is the key to his stylistic canon.

Even though Ernesto had discovered the colorful world of bullfighting in Pamplona, even though he had been impressed with Spaniards' sense of freedom and honor as he wandered all over Spain watching the people of the country and listening to them, even though his naturally lethargic spirit had been quickened in Spain, both in wartime and in peacetime, all this would have been a mere patina, not real substance, if Ernesto had not eventually come to identify completely with the soul of the Spanish people as reflected in the mirror of Madrid. In Spain, and particularly in Madrid, this bored, insecure, complex man had discovered a passion for life, a heroic ethic, and artistic simplicity. There is no question that this is so, for it is no secret to anyone that it is in his works set in Spain or those portraying Spanish characters locked in combat that we see his violent philosophy of life, his weakness, his cowardice, his pagan pleasure-seeking take on both more subtle tones and a more sweeping, more imperious majesty. It was Spain that had awakened his pride in his craft and in his manhood, as he came to know Spaniards who often lived on the very edge of poverty but whose code of conduct made them behave at all times like perfect gentlemen. If *toreros* risked their lives every Sunday afternoon in the bullring, many other people—whom one might be inclined to dismiss as tatterdemalion scamps on seeing how they were dressed or hearing their rough speech—had from the first taught Ernesto a very important lesson. "All you Spaniards really *think* about life," he had often said to me.

It was the time of day when the Gran Vía is not only a shelter from the storm but a veritable beehive of activity, that hour of the day when Ernesto, the devourer of the instant, frivolousness incarnate, had discovered metaphysical truths in anything and everything: in the cries of blind men hawking their lottery tickets; in the chatter of the barman handing out drinks and advice over the counter; in the obscene invitations whispered by a streetwalker in the ear of a wealthy visiting merchant from Barcelona or Bilbao; in the quiet footfalls of patients on the way to their doctor's office or parents on their way to the seminary to visit their son studying for the priesthood; in an Andalusian dandy's boastful tales of his sexual prowesses, and his innocent listeners' wide-eyed amazement; in the way a priest crosses the street and stealthily slips down some alleyway in search of who knows what consolations; in the marvelous dignity with which some besotted customer in a lowly tavern comments on the death of a comrade; in the absolute composure of the man doomed to die . . .

Ernesto knew very well that among Madrileños there were—and still are—any number of sly rascals and not only among bullfight *aficionados*, that there are many who would not hesitate for a moment to gore their own fathers, that Madrileños have hides as scarred and pitted as the centuries-old, weathered stone statues of Guisando bulls. Nonetheless he wanted to, he needed to, he learned how to distill transcendent truths from even the most fleeting sights. A stork on a tower in Castile was a call to the world beyond; the pink juice of a watermelon streaming down the beard of a peasant was a summons to enjoy life; the red and yellow earth of La Mancha was a thirst for the ideal; and a *plaza de toros* a cathedral where God is present in person, not as the official presiding over the *corrida* but as a spectator watching each pass intently, even though He knows beforehand how each of them will be linked together.

I had ridden with Ernesto down this very street in the Lancia that his chauffeur, Adamo, drove with the arrogance of an Italian Renaissance prince, and remembered that Ernesto had asked him twice:

"Adamo, do you believe in Madrid?"

"Do I like Madrid, you mean?"

"No, I'm asking you if you believe in Madrid."

"Is there any reason I should?"

"If you ask so many questions, it's because you don't believe in Madrid. But I hope with all my heart and soul that someday you will."

It was a sort of joke, just as it would have been a sort of joke if at that moment I were to raise my eyes and say that the moon shining down on the roofs and the towers of the city was mine, all mine. Nonetheless, Ernesto had not been content merely to visit Madrid; he had also smelt it, touched it, felt it, tasted it, endured it, loved it . . .

We had gone into a bar then, that day, and as Adamo sat there delicately peeling his shrimps, Ernesto whispered in my ear: "We'll take him to Guadalajara someday, and even farther north, to Brihuega. This guy was one of the ones who were going to take Madrid," he said, winking at me. "Didn't you know that?"

"How could I have known?"

"That's why I wanted him to 'fess up' about it."

The marvelous thing about Ernesto was that when he decided to open up, it always happened in the most surprising places. When you least expected, as some clerk was wrapping up a book or some sausages or some rifle cartridges that Ernesto had bought, he might dumfound you by suddenly revealing some secret about himself. And that day with Adamo, following the same train of thought, he went on: "It's not easy to understand how such a rebellious people patiently accept whatever mysterious calamity either God or the Devil visits upon them."

"Don't you believe it. Here in Spain, too . . ."

"Yes, yes, I know: here in Spain, too, there are people who spit in God's eye, and even kill themselves sometimes. But a people that sees the bull's dead body dragged out of the ring and applauds if it's been a brave one, a people that jeers and boos at anybody who trembles when he sees the bull's horns coming at him, is prepared for the *corrida* of life. Because life here in this world is a *corrida*, nothing more nor less than a *corrida*. . . . Will you be awarded ears and a tail and maybe even a hoof? White handkerchiefs waving, applause, the crowd shouting *ole* and *viva*, or coward, cheater, scoundrel . . . a real *corrida!*"

There was something of the reek of a great slab of meat in a slaughterhouse about Ernesto, certainly. Thus both when he entered a *plaza de toros* and when he walked about in the streets, the buzzards and the butchers gathered around, just waiting, with their sharp beaks and keen knives.

I hesitated for a moment at the entrance to the Chicote. It was not the right sort of place for a long, sentimental chat with long-time friends, though I was hardly likely to run into old girl friends now married to *toreros* or *toreros* I'd once known who had married lady writers, two professions that don't seem to mix very well, but I went in anyway. As always, it was a bar that seemed to inspire sober thoughts about man's fate, and the women inside looked more like mourners at a funeral than vestal virgins.

One day as we stopped at the door of the Chicote, Ernesto had said to me, "I don't really want to go in there."

"How come?" I asked him.

"It brings back lots of bad memories. And when I hear talk of its being a favorite hangout of 'intellectuals,' it makes me laugh. I don't think it very likely that Unamuno would ever have written *The Tragic Sense of Life* at one of the tables in there."

"I'm sure he wouldn't have. Nor *The Agony of Christianity* either. Everybody knows the Chicote is scarcely an Athenian academy."

"On the other hand, in the old days it was also something more than a place to pick up a whore. You might say I cut my wisdom teeth nibbling on olives in the Chicote."

And as we walked on down the street, Ernesto explained what it had been like in the months when Madrid was besieged by the Nationalist troops. Those were the days when you could get yourself not only a girl to sleep with you for the night but even a fiancée or a wife in exchange for a can of black beans or corned beef or sausages, a kilo of sugar, or a few slices of codfish. The city seemed doomed, and life there very precarious. And yet there was a tremendous vitality about it, even though an exploding shell might reduce the dreams of a lifetime to a heap of dust and bleeding flesh at any moment. And Ernesto had gone on describing all the things he had seen from the windows and heard in the elegant bars along the Gran Vía.

I found an empty stool at the bar, sat down, and ordered a gin and soda.

The Chicote had changed a great deal, yet it was quite easy to imagine Ernesto sitting in a corner drinking and writing his articles about the Spanish Civil War. I could almost see the encouraging news bulletins pouring in, like rapidly advancing tanks, or news of the disastrous failure of operations he had such high hopes for limping in like crippled mules.

Those bars, during the war, must have been like seething caldrons, in which the story of the war was brewed. Public figures, both great leaders and two-bit politicians, commissars and generals, spies and agit-prop agents made such places a stage for their boasting and bragging, for the recounting of their bloody deeds, for their demagoguery and their plotting. It was in bars like this that Ernesto had sat amid alcoholic fumes

216

and clouds of cigar and cigarette smoke, working on his bloody panto-mime of the Spanish Civil War, his frantic ballet of the Spanish people up in arms, the great *corrida* fought in the name of justice.

In those days there weren't any matadors or beautiful señoritas or bull breeders or even *toros* available for the fiesta. But there were ani-sette and cognac, beer and vermouth and whisky, if only for a chosen few. Things were very different now, though; there was something for everybody, for the pretty little "turtledove," for the playful "little rab-bit"; for the diplomat whom the war had put out of a job and for the colonel living on a pension; for the businessman not yet retired and raking in the profits; for the powerful industrialist and for the manu-facturer who'd gone bankrupt; for the cuckold, the honest man, the pa-tient man, the stoic; for the tormented, fawning fairy kept by a lover; for the professor with a university chair and the professor emeritus; for journalists with and without jobs; for prostitutes with and without an official police card. For every male and every female there were a thousand different kinds of cocktails available; since all of Spain was "different" now, naturally an internationally famous bar would also be "different" . . .

When I had once asked Ernesto: "What memories of our Civil War have remained the most vivid in your mind?" he had replied:

"The times when I sat drinking at the same table with outright crimi-nals. The same people who kept insisting, both before and after down-ing their drinks, that 'killing was an ugly business, a very ugly business' but that 'there was nothing else to be done.'"

"They doubtless killed other people to save their own lives," I said.

"No, that wasn't the reason. They always insisted they were killing other people 'merely to save the Republic and win the war.'"

"Oh, I see."

"It's as if I could still feel some of them breathing down my neck this very minute. It's as though I can still hear them bragging about their heroic exploits and see them playing the fake martyr to this day."

"I know what you mean."

"I remember having bellowed, 'That's no way to win a war,' at them more than once. But they'd all been thoroughly brainwashed, and would all answer, like a bunch of parrots: 'How long do *you* think we should put off fighting a revolution?' They not only killed people for the pleasure of killing, but because they were scared shitless. And what's more, they hated their enemies. But those on the other side had dirty hands too. Killing's an ugly business, a very ugly business, I can assure you."

I had only to remember *For Whom the Bell Tolls*, the book that is a mass confession of the blood shed among Spaniards. There was Pilar,

217

for instance, that character who is part witch, part gypsy, part Saint Teresa, part bawd, part tragic mother, whose only words after the death of Don Guillermo are:

". . . I felt a feeling of shame and distaste. . . ."

She says this as the peasants are filing out of the village square as if they were wending their way home from the bullring after a great *corrida*. They are suffering both from a guilty conscience and terrible cramps in the belly.

There is one little touch in *For Whom the Bell Tolls* that appears to be a mere minor detail, but is in fact very subtle and revealing. One of the drunken townsmen who has taken part in the collective slaughter tries repeatedly to set fire to the corpse of the town moneylender, Anastasio Rivas. But he attempts to do so not by pouring gasoline or wood alcohol over the man's dead body, but anisette, the common drink at fiestas and amateur bullfights. Was this a mere happenstance, or a symbol that Ernesto had carefully chosen?

There were many such apparently accidental symbols in this novel that is one long lament for Spain. What, for instance, is the object that reveals that the solemn hour for the mass slaughter of those shut up in the city hall has come? It is the key in Pablo's hand.

The bull cannot come out of its pen till the door is opened, the prisoner condemned to death cannot leave his cell until they open the door, the bridegroom goes into the nuptial chamber key in hand, the *torero's* only key is his sword, as the priest's only key is the cross of Our Lord. But with keys such as these one unlocks the gates of death and enters eternity.

The Chicote wasn't a very lively spot that night. A few people dropped in every once in a while to have a look around, but most of them stayed only a few minutes.

Women kept getting up from corner tables and leaving the place. They didn't look like very fresh blossoms, despite the fact that they were wearing bright-colored flower-print dresses. Some of them were quite tanned, making you wonder when and where they sunbathed, and others looked pale and had great circles under their eyes, making you wonder where they spent these moonlit nights. But, then, most people spend the summer in Madrid at swimming pools and sitting out on the balconies till all hours. Their faces were heavily made up, and you could see from their eyes that no matter how many men they slept with there was no pleasure in it for them. There were some whose skin was peeling off in great flakes, and others whose skin had great cracks in it, like a dry river bed. There weren't many tourists around, or visitors from the provinces with bulging wallets. Over by the door there were a few foreign couples gaily downing the barman's latest concoctions that he was passing off as traditional drinks from before the Spanish Civil War—or who knows what war.

Ernesto hadn't wanted to go into the Chicote that day I'd been with him, but here I was tonight, sitting at the bar with a buxom, middle-aged tart on each side of me, thinking about the story Ernesto had been inspired to write sitting at one of the corner tables in this very bar, for it was here that Ernesto would jot down his notes and then later, in the Hotel Florida, he would go over them and little by little sort them out and put them all together.

"You look as droopy as a weeping willow tree," the woman sitting on my right remarked, a strawberry blonde with a doll's face, all decked out in flashy gold earrings and lots of gold rings and bracelets.

"He looks like he needs a little cheering up," the slightly cross-eyed blonde on my left said.

But I was thinking about Castro, the next bull about to be killed in the great human slaughter in *For Whom the Bell Tolls*, sitting there in the city hall watching Pablo's every move, as the others about to be killed begin praying more fervently than ever. Pablo's one act at that moment is fraught with meaning: he merely points to the key to the door of the city hall. His gesture is the secret signal for the extermination of all this herd of bulls there in the room. It is at this point that Pablo barricades the door with tables and chairs and sits down at the head of the table, as if he were the mayor of the town now, with his shotgun in front of him. Yes, what had earlier been a fairly bloody amateur bullfight organized on the spur of the moment is now to become a cruel and deliberate slaughter, a grim parody of a bullfight. There are passages in this novel that are almost unforgettable, a mixture of the sinister bareness and spareness of Solana's paintings and the sardonic humor of Baroja.

"What a dead night!" the strawberry blonde with all the gold bangles and lots of gold caps on her teeth to match remarked.

"Yeah, business is really lousy!" the other blonde, whose cross-eyed wink was a weapon in her professional arsenal, chimed in.

The hustler on my right slid off her stool and said she was going to make a phone call, a discreet way of admitting defeat; she'd doubtless decided she wasn't going to get anywhere with me.

The whore on my left slid over to the stool on my right, perhaps thinking that the cross-eyed squint in her right eye wouldn't be so noticeable from there.

"Some nights you couldn't peddle so much as an umbrella even if it was pouring," she said.

The waiter, an old friend of mine, set a dish of olives and potatoes down in front of me.

I dashed for the lavatory, feeling sick to my stomach. But I felt better after I'd taken a great, long, endless piss. It wasn't just getting rid of all that alcohol in my system that made me feel relieved. Expelling something inside us that disgusts us and is ripping our guts apart is more than just a temporary remedy.

Sad-faced voluptuaries, lonely lushes, little bands of aimless drifters kept coming into the bar. Many of them stayed only a few moments, and then went on to some other bar like robots, looking for something they were hardly likely ever to find. Others sat there at the bartender's elbow, grimly downing one drink after another as if it were some sort of duty. A brunette perched on one of the bar stools was allowing both the man on her right and the man on her left to feel her up, with a look of utter indifference on her face. The women who had stationed themselves strategically around the room were standing there like cows in a manger, trying to see what sort of effect their thighs or their bosoms in their low-cut dresses were having on the men in the room by watching the looks in their eyes. Others kept getting up and going to the powder room or the telephone, chatting away among themselves like girls in a boarding school. In one corner, a group of men who seemed to have no interest whatsoever in the buying and selling of female flesh that was going on all around were jotting a bunch of figures down on a corner of a newspaper.

Madrid today was a gay, bustling city, dreaming of prosperity, not anything like the Madrid of the old days. But during the war, when Ernesto had used to round up all his cronies for a party where fanatics espousing opposing ideologies, spies and counterspies, army officers from different countries who supposedly were all on the same side but countermanded each other's orders on the battlefield, and fearless, jealous newspaper correspondents who hated each other's guts all rubbed elbows, these bars that were now sex bazaars had been the red-hot grill that had reduced their ideals to cinders, the slaughterhouse that had killed their great dreams, the back room where contracts for murder had been negotiated that later were executed in cold blood.

"It must have been a den of thieves well worth seeing back then," I had said to Ernesto.

"Don't kid yourself—it wasn't nearly as fascinating as you might think. They were all a bunch of dull, hairsplitting intellectuals. So much so that when you got a chance to talk to an ordinary man in the street it was a real privilege."

This more or less explains why Ernesto was so easily taken in by the tales of horror that were recounted or made up out of whole cloth as a sort of excuse for their own bloodthirsty crimes by the fanatics that Ernesto was constantly surrounded by.

"I've always thought there must have been certain moments of fantastic collective fervor," I said.

"Yes, that's quite true; the common people were fanatically loyal to the Republican cause and had lots of guts, but most of the rest of them were just a bunch of sophisticated intellectuals dabbling in revolution, the sort of people who were cruel because they knew they didn't have the courage to be heroes. Even though the ordinary Spaniard was as unruly as a bull on the loose, he was still what I liked best about the whole bloody business."

Just as today the talk in the Chicote is about *corridas* and soccer matches, about the top matadors and the way they've performed, or what's happened in international competitions, so during the war the talk was all about military operations, battles at the Cuesta de las Perdices, Pingarrón, or Brunete, or about how best to carry out the revolution, seizure of private property, labor unions, popular tribunals, co-operatives, public welfare funds, and so on, or when time dragged, about which commissars or commanders were the most bloodthirsty butchers, or about the colonel who died trying to pass over to the Republican side after having been caught writing subversive pamphlets, or the crazy Falangist who had cut his tongue off with a piece of glass in some prison barracks to make certain he wouldn't "sing," or a priest whom the Loyalists had forced to utter a blasphemy and then promptly executed for having done so, according to the men on the firing squad who had shot him . . .

Just another Spanish priest, like the one in *For Whom the Bell Tolls* who so disappointed Pablo.

One of the whores—the plumpest one—had finally picked up a john, a man as skinny as a beanpole, the son of a Bilbao shipowner, with more vices than pesetas.

Everybody was laughing at one man, who had fallen asleep on one of the bar stools and was teetering back and forth in perfect balance. There were also a number of drowsy tipplers sitting there staring glassy-eyed at the row upon row of multicolored bottles. They could see their reflection in the mirror behind the bar and appeared to be anxious to reassure themselves that their faces looked perfectly normal. Every once in a while one of them would start mumbling to himself.

The bootblack came by selling lottery tickets, and then a woman selling flowers, but I waved them both away. Men tempted by the sins of the flesh kept coming in, and for each man there were three priestesses ready to take him into the confessional. The market was supersaturated. And all of them were flitting about like drunken butterflies, like dotty widows.

It was the same crowd as usual there in the Chicote, flotsam and jetsam floating from bar to bar. But many of the men sitting there in the bar and many of those dropping in on the prowl for tail looked as downcast and indifferent and grim-faced as I did.

"What do you think would have happened to you if you'd ever been taken prisoner, Ernesto?" I once asked him.

"I think it would have been curtains for me," he answered.

"I'm quite sure they would have exchanged you for some bigwig Nationalist prisoner."

"I don't think so. That civil war of yours produced the coldest fish imaginable, on both sides. I don't think the good offices of neutral parties—is that the right expression?—would have saved me."

"You would have had a pretty rough time of it, I admit, if you'd fallen into the hands of the Moorish troops at Carabanchel."

"They captured a friend of mind. He was a poet, a good poet who had every chance of becoming a first-rate one. He was one of the world's true innocents, who had dreamed for years of coming to Spain and was going about the countryside playing his violin. They caught him one freezing December night and forced him to perch in a tree like a nightingale, playing folksongs from his country on his fiddle. Early the next morning they set fire to the tree with their bird still in it . . . fiddling like mad to try to get them to spare his life."

Why hadn't Ernesto ever used that story in any of his books, or so many others that would come suddenly pouring out when he'd downed a great many whiskies or martinis in a row? He had an inexhaustible supply of material stored up in his memory. Too much, I suddenly realized, thinking about the episode of Pablo and the priest in *For Whom the Bell Tolls:*

"You didn't like it about the priest?" because I knew he hated priests even worse than he hated fascists.

"He was a disillusionment to me," Pablo said sadly.

So many people were singing that we had to almost shout to hear one another.

"Why?"

"He died very badly," Pablo said. "He had very little dignity."

"How did you want him to have dignity when he was being chased by the mob?" I said. "I thought he had much dignity all the time before. All the dignity that one could have."

"Yes," Pablo said. "But in the last minute he was frightened."

"Who wouldn't be?" I said. "Did you see what they were chasing him with?"

"Why would I not see?" Pablo said. "But I find he died badly."

"In such circumstances any one dies badly," I told him. "What do you want for your money? Everything that happened in the *Ayuntamiento* was scabrous."

"Yes," said Pablo. "There was little organization. But a priest. He has an example to set."

"I thought you hated priests."

"Yes," said Pablo and cut some more bread. "But a *Spanish* priest. A *Spanish* priest should die very well."

How could I help but hear passages from Ernesto's writings echoing and re-echoing in my mind, especially passages from those books that he had begun to write or research in Spain? "He was a Spanish priest." What did Ernesto expect of a Spanish priest? Hadn't he expected every Spaniard to display the extraordinary courage of the hero and the extraordinary faith of the martyr, not to mention the extraordinary cruelty of the savage?

The two men who had just come in the door weren't on the prowl for tail. They were cops who had a photograph of somebody they were looking for, but their man wasn't in the bar.

The Chicote was getting me down. The place was dead that night, and the dreary *corrida* going on was depressing me and making me feel uncomfortable. I headed for the door, and all the heifers and cows on the loose there in the Chicote looked disappointed, doubtless thinking they'd let another possible customer get away.

I stood in the doorway of that noisy place, not knowing where to go next, and finally strode across the street and into El Abra, another high-class joint that was a first cousin to the Chicote.

The women in there were darting around like fish in an aquarium when you dip a sieve in it. The front of the bar looked like a vivarium full of rare species of plants and animals: full-blown dahlias and solitary whales, pale pink magnolias and slender glowworms. Some of them were tarts who'd taken up their profession only a short time before, and others were old pros who'd been streetwalkers for twenty years, since just after the war. El Abra was like a drained swimming pool full of stranded water bugs.

The johns standing elbow to elbow at the front bar were mostly American GIs, tourists, and well-heeled conventioners. Farther back in the room there was a long bar off to one side, with regular or semiregular customers, pub crawlers and popular bullfighters' assistants sitting around in comfortable armchairs. The atmosphere there in El Abra was very informal: the girls kept going in and out, circulating around the room there was a long bar off to one side, with regular or semiregu-
to each other, picking fights with each other one minute and laughing fit to kill the next, joking and kidding around with the customers in the

223

front of the room, who stood there looking very uneasy and unsure of themselves and peering about hoping to spy an empty bar stool.

At the very back of the room there was a pianist whose fingers never left the keyboard except to reach for the drink that once in a great while somebody would send over to him. He usually played sentimental little ditties all evening long, but on nights when the place was very crowded —after an important soccer match or a fine *corrida*—he might offer a rendition of Falla's Ritual Fire Dance or "La Paloma." And on more serious occasions, such as religious holidays, he might even give out with Pergolesi's "Stabat Mater" or "In a Monastery Garden." He had about as much spark to him as an oyster, and sat there at the keyboard night after night looking bored to tears, quite obviously out of his element.

I elbowed my way to the back of the room, and as I was about to go down the narrow flight of stairs leading to the telephone, the washroom, and the little bar downstairs that only real habitués knew about, I heard someone murmur my name. I looked around and spotted two old cronies I'd used to pal around with before I was married, and an oddball journalist, a real night owl, who had once interviewed me. I didn't feel much like spending the rest of this evening that had gotten off to such a dreary start with them, and was surprised to find them in Madrid on this summer night; I would have expected them to be off on summer vacation, lazing on a beach somewhere.

I went over and said hello to them, and told them I'd be back in a minute.

People who hang about on the fringes of the literary world are an envious lot. No one has deprived them of any rightful sort of inheritance in the world of letters, but having failed as writers themselves, they are such jealous backbiters that you would think that literature was a treasure that established men of letters had stolen from them.

"So you're one of those guys who makes his dates with whores downstairs so nobody will see, are you?" Ramón said to me as I started down the stairs, just to needle me a little, as usual.

When I came back upstairs and sat down with them, the first one to open his mouth was Luis:

"Well, the *corrida's* over now for your great master. It was quite a performance: from *delirium vitae* to *delirium mortis* in one fell swoop. He took Death's pulse so many times he finally killed himself. You do agree, don't you, that he killed himself—that it wasn't an 'accident,' as all the newspapers reported?" he said.

"Yes, I think he killed himself," I replied.

"Well, we've seen the last of Old Whiskers' wenching and carousing and globe-trotting and hanging around the bullring," he went on, sipping mechanically at his drink.

224

20. The author of this book arranged for Hemingway to meet the great Basque novelist Pío Baroja, in 1956. Here we are at the door of Baroja's house. Ernesto had worn a business suit and tie for the occasion—something he rarely did. (BASABE, MADRID)

21. During his visit to the dying Spanish novelist, Ernesto sat for a moment in Baroja's armchair. It has been claimed that Ernesto served as a pallbearer at Baroja's funeral, but in fact he refused to do so, saying that the honor of carrying Baroja's coffin belonged to Spanish writers. (EDICIONES DESTINO AND BASABE, MADRID)

22. Sitting beside the bed of the dying novelist Pío Baroja. The dedication of his first novel, *The Sun Also Rises*, reads: "To Baroja, with admiration from his disciple." (BASABE, MADRID)

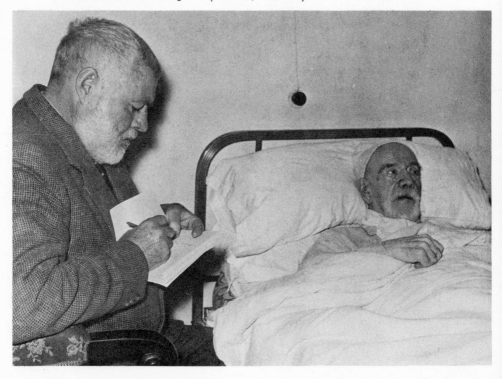

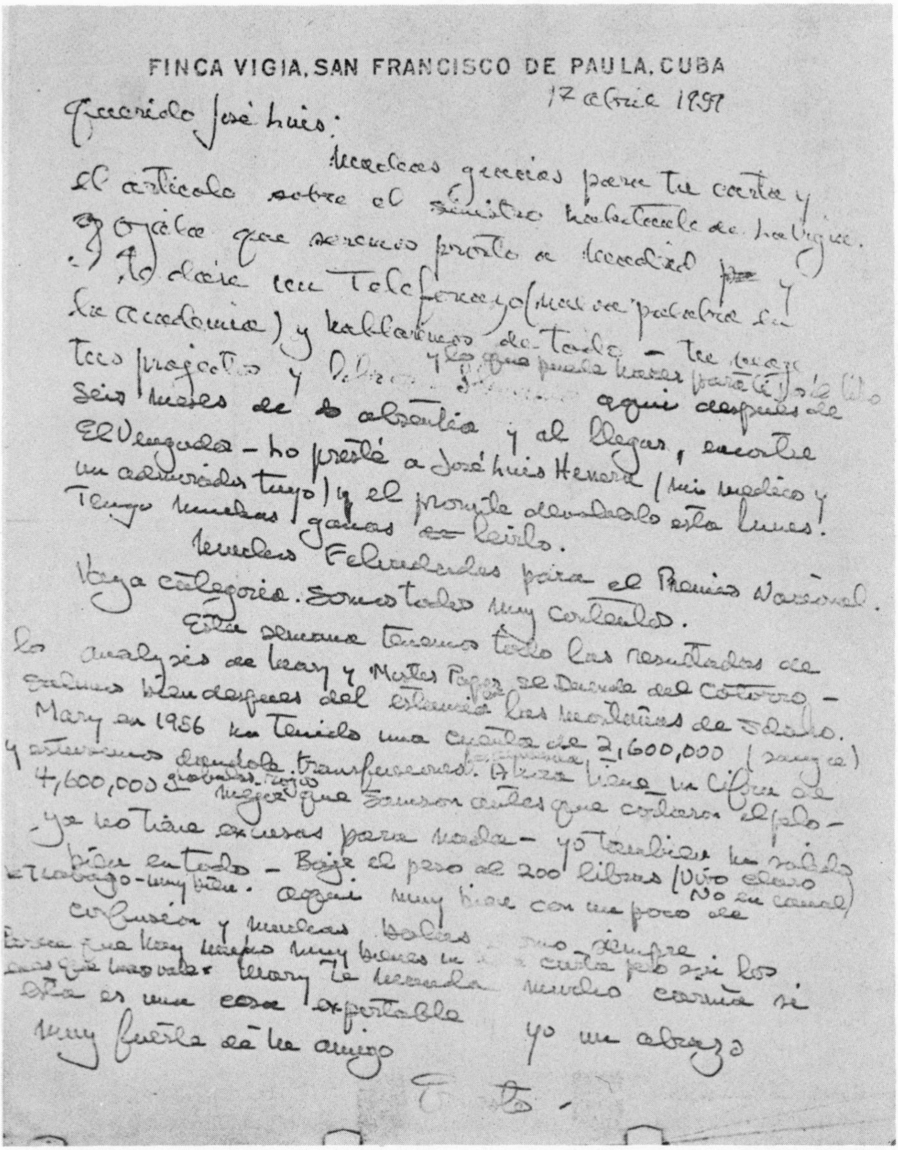
FINCA VIGIA, SAN FRANCISCO DE PAULA, CUBA

17 abril 1959

Querido José Luis:

23. Final paragraph of one of Hemingway's last and most revealing letters. (EDICIONES DESTINO)

24. Hemingway and I are standing in front of the famous painting "La Masía," by Joan Miró. (EDICIONES DESTINO)

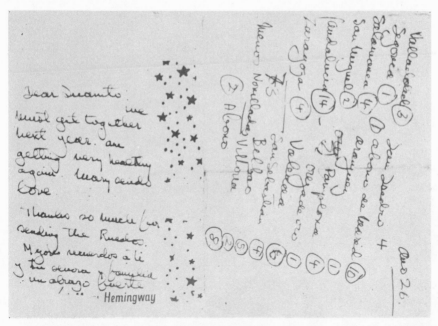

25. A fragment of a card Hemingway sent to Juanito Quintana. The card contains notes on the bullfights that took place in 1926. (EDICIONES DESTINO)

26. Ernesto Hemingway walks around the streets of Pamplona in the early hours of the day. On his right is Castillo-Puche, and on his left is Mr. Davis, whom he jokingly called "the nigger"—an ironic reference to Davis' blondness. (CANO)

27. This photo shows Ernesto and his wife with "Miss Valerie" and the other "kidnaped" girls at the Irati River. (MASPONS, BARCELONA)

28. The author of this book chatting with Hemingway just as they are about to take a dip in the Irati. At the foot of the tree is the picnic basket, full of treats for our lunch on the riverbank. (MASPONS, BARCELONA)

29. Ernesto licks an ice-cream cone in the middle of the summer heat at Pamploma. The city is burning hot at this time of year and you just have to cool off before enjoying the running of the bulls. (MASPONS, BARCELONA)

30. Many American tourists had their best opportunity to meet the Nobel Prize winner of their country at the Pamplona fiesta. These two American students were part of the group of girls "kidnaped" by Ernesto during the "dangerous summer" of 1959, who traveled all over Spain with him and his wife Mary and "Miss Valerie," the "kidnap victim" closest to the Hemingways. (MASPONS, BARCELONA)

31. Although under tremendous psychological strain, Ernesto remained to the end a grown-up child. Here he is bending over to play with a pair of parakeets bought for "Miss Valerie's" enjoyment. (MASPONS, BARCELONA)

My friend Pérez hadn't said a word as yet. The thick lenses of his glasses always seemed to isolate him from a conversation, and thus far he'd simply sat there, like a clam with its shell shut tight, not uttering a peep. But finally he spoke up and said, "Why do you think he killed himself?"

It was stupid to keep raking over the dead coals again and again, when Ernesto had forever passed into the realms of mystery. But Pérez at least had not asked me that out of mere vulgar curiosity; he was the sort of person who seriously ponders what life is all about.

"He killed himself because it was all too much for him," I replied.

"Did you hear what Edgar Neville said?" Luis said in his pompous know-it-all way. "I'm quite sure Neville knew him quite well, and I read that when he heard the news he remarked: 'I wonder what went wrong? They got there too late this time!'"

"Neville didn't know Ernesto very well at all, but what he said is nonetheless quite true: they got there too late this time," I replied, even though I knew that Neville had been referring to all of Ernesto's many close brushes with death.

"Listen," Pérez said, leaning over to me and lowering his voice, "do you really think Ernesto had been trying to kill himself those other times?"

"I've said many a time that he was on the most intimate terms with that sort of death."

"But why was that?" Pérez asked.

"Why was that? You might say that it was because that was the only important tenet in his very simplistic metaphysics," I said.

"Don't tell me you think Hemingway was a philosopher with a systematic credo!" Luis butted in again.

"That's not what I was trying to say at all. I merely meant that suicide is a sign of some sort of enormous weakness and a terrible spiritual poverty, and when you've been haunted by the thought of killing yourself day after day after day, it becomes a sort of strength. I'm convinced that Ernesto had thought about it so much that he'd narrowed the gap separating him from death tremendously . . ."

Pérez, who was sincerely interested in trying to get to the bottom of what had really happened, spoke up again and said, "That's all well and good, José Luis, but you were on very close terms with him and I'd really like to hear *your* explanation of why he killed himself."

"I think he took his own life because he was bored," I replied.

"That's no explanation at all!" Luis objected. "Boredom! What kind of a reason is that?" he said scornfully. "I'm certain he killed himself because he wanted to leave this world in a blaze of glory, to die a death that would be a sort of grandiose Wagnerian apotheosis . . ."

"It seems to me that that's too literary an explanation," I said. "As

I see it, Ernesto had hoped all along that 'the Great Bald Lady' would embrace him at a moment when he was enjoying life to the fullest, that is to say, that she would creep up on him without his noticing, that he would die a dramatic, so-called 'accidental death.' But he was not at all prepared for an 'accident' in the form of the sort of lingering illness that slowly destroys both the man and the writer, both a person's life and his work, as he lies on his sickbed dying by the inch. If he had been killed eight years ago in the African jungle, it would have been the death of a man at the height of his powers, the sort of death he had always hoped for and always sought. But as it turned out, that wasn't what was in store for him at all; the only death he could see in the cards was a disgusting sort of death, that of a senile old man slowly wasting away. Blowing your brains out can free you from terrible thoughts haunting your mind . . ."

Hortensia came over to our table just then, a faded beauty who had once been a splendid peacock but was now a drooping matron. Not so long before, she had been a voluptuous marble statue, but now she was merely a plump, blowsy, middle-aged woman you were almost inclined to make fun of. In the old days, there had been an air of innocence about her even though she was a lady of the evening, but now she was simply an obviously overripe fruit.

"What'll you have, Hortensia?" I asked her.

"Are you offering me a drink?" she replied.

"Sure, whatever you like."

"Can I have some cigarettes too?"

Luis offered her one, but she said she'd like a whole package. She looked the four of us up and down then and said:

"Well, quite a few of you oddballs are hanging out together here tonight, aren't you?"

"What do you man by that, may I ask?" I answered jokingly.

"Oh, nothing really—I just noticed you're all sitting around trading tall stories," she replied, striding off with an air of great dignity to a table by herself and calling the waiter over.

Pérez plainly wanted to go on with our discussion about Ernesto. "So you really think Hemingway was fed up with everything, despite the fact that he seemed to be living the life of Riley?" he asked.

"There's a certain sort of boredom that lends itself to the creation of works of art and even to a search for a more interesting way of life, but the boredom that Ernesto was suffering from was like a kind of blind alley," I replied.

"But what about his scandalous life as a great womanizer, a famous adventurer, a fabulous drinker, a front-line combatant, a world-renowned sportsman—were they all signs of utter boredom, too?" Ramón asked, siding with Luis.

226

"All that was just Ernesto's way of hiding his boredom from the prying eyes of the public," I answered.

"Like every artist, he liked to hog the spotlight. He couldn't stand it when he wasn't surrounded by a whole crowd of reporters," Ramón said.

"I think you're wrong there."

"He was the number one publicity hound of all time."

Pérez spoke up again then, still trying to dig deeper. "You were saying, José Luis, that Ernesto had found himself trapped in a blind alley, that he'd discovered that his life was completely empty . . ."

"What I meant was that Ernesto had died many times over before he finally shot himself. He was haunted all his life by the thought that he'd kill himself. He was a born suicide, and in his mind he'd pulled the trigger countless times."

"So it wasn't just that he'd gotten terribly bored with life recently, as you were claiming a minute ago," Luis said. "You can't deny that there were times when he was out to live life to the fullest."

"Living life to the fullest was like the safety catch on his rifle," I answered. "But once he realized that he had become the mere shadow of his former self, he was terror-stricken, and as he had so often dreamed of doing, all he had to do was to release the safety catch. I still insist that taking his own life was an idea that had long haunted him, one that he was on the most familiar terms with."

"Why didn't you say so in the first place?" was Luis's rejoinder. And then he added, "As a matter of fact, why didn't you call in the reporters and tell them so? It would have made you famous."

"I did say precisely that, in my own way. I didn't say so in so many words, because I pitied him."

"I don't remember having read your article. So the reason why he killed himself is as plain as day, in your opinion?"

"Not at all. It's still a mystery, because however you explain a suicide, it's still only a possible explanation. It's just that I always had a premonition, or rather I was almost certain, that that was what was going to happen in the end."

"You could have written to his wife, or done something to prevent it . . ." Luis argued.

"As a Catholic, I felt that all I could do was pray, but apparently my prayers weren't very effective," I answered.

"You were praying for a great atheist," Luis said in his usual flippant way.

"I wouldn't go so far as to say that. An atheist is seldom as tragically tormented by his lack of faith as Ernesto was. The skepticism of the atheist is a very comfortable sort of philosophy, whereas Ernesto's radical lack of trust in God was peopled with ghosts that eventually killed him."

"You're not going to tell me, I hope, that he obeyed the ten commandments: thou shalt not commit adultery; thou shalt not kill—or kill thyself."

"You're being unfair, Luis. No writer simply inserts bits and pieces of his own autobiography here and there in his works. An author reveals himself unintentionally in what he writes, and the basic rhythm of his works betrays the sort of spiritual life he is leading."

"All this talk of spiritual things is making me sick to my stomach," Luis remarked nastily.

"Let José Luis have his say," Pérez begged.

"I don't mind his saying what he has to say," Luis replied. "He really pisses me off, though, when he starts shoving communion wafers down our throats as though we'd swallow anything. I've always suspected Hemingway of being a little bit queer—I've seen a photograph of him making calf's eyes at Ordóñez where it's as plain as day that he was more or less a fairy. But José Luis keeps trying to pass him off as an absolute angel who worshiped bulls and their balls, not to mention sharks and rhinoceroses and hyenas and meek little sparrows, as God's own creatures . . ."

I started to get up from my chair and leave, but Pérez and Ramón made me sit down again, and as though trying to patch things up between Luis and me, Ramón turned to me and said, "You mustn't pay any attention to Luis. He likes to needle people just to stir up an argument. Everybody has his own way of getting his kicks."

Monchi came in the back door of the bar just then—a whore who was a frustrated "philosopher," in much the same way that Hortensia was a frustrated mystic; Monchi was a Castilian who'd become a Madrileña, and Hortensia was an international Galician. The two of them were always together, even though they both maintained they disliked each other intensely. Hortensia knew very well that I wouldn't leave without going over and talking with her for a few minutes, even though I'd avoided her thus far. She'd come over to our table a while before, which wasn't at all like her, because usually she just sat by herself in a corner somewhere, playing the role of the *femme fatale*. But that wasn't Monchi's way at all: the minute she sat down at the bar, she motioned to me to come over and take the empty bar stool next to her. I saw my chance to get away from the three men, excused myself by saying that Monchi seemed anxious to talk to me, and went over and sat down on the edge of the bar stool next to her, to make it clear I only wanted to chat with her a minute. Monchi was naturally trying to steal a march on Hortensia that night and take me off to bed with her. Nonetheless, I was eager to get away from those old "buddies" of mine, Luis especially. I hoped Hortensia wouldn't come over to talk to me too.

"What brings you here?" Monchi asked me.

"I just dropped in for a while."

"I haven't seen you in ages, and when you finally do turn up, you hang out all evening with those boring friends of yours. . . . They're all as dull as ditchwater. What were you having such an argument about, anyway? . . . I'll bet two cents you were talking politics."

"You lose your bet."

"I can't stand your pal with the thick glasses. He never looks you straight in the eye."

"If that's the way you size up people, you'll be wrong most of the time. If a bull doesn't look the bullfighter straight in the eye, is that any sign he's not a noble *toro?*"

"Absolutely."

"Maybe bulls like that just have defective vision."

"That's precisely what I mean: if there's something wrong with them, they don't look you in the eye. You can always tell. And the ones that have tender horns have a way of looking at you too. That guy just coming in the door for instance—a month ago he asked me to marry him and I turned him down. It was such a put-down he wouldn't dare look me in the eye."

"If you're going to sit here spouting nonsense, I'm leaving."

"You know what? I've been wanting to get really potted for days now. If you want to really live it up, you have to get plastered and let yourself go a little. You can't do crazy things till you've gotten quite a few drinks under your belt—and I'd sure like to do something a little bit crazy, you know what I mean?"

"Sure I do."

"Hortensia certainly looks unhappy, doesn't she?"

It was true: Hortensia had a sad, faraway look in her eye. How different the two of them were! They were mortal enemies, and at the same time they were very concerned about each other. They were exact opposites: Hortensia had taken up prostitution because she was anxious to keep her whole family going, her mother and all her brothers, who were grown men, not little kids; she was devoted to them, and was doing her utmost to see them get ahead in life. Monchi, on the other hand, was a crazy, wild girl, the black sheep of her middle-class family, with two sisters who'd married well and a father who had plenty of money.

"I never could understand why you were so crazy about Hortensia," Monchi said.

"Well, don't try, then . . ."

"What's more, you're not the only one who's mad about her. . . . I hear you once asked her to marry you . . ."

"Did she tell you that?"

"Admit it: you're still sort of crazy about her."

"That may be sort of true."

"You look awfully down in the dumps—like a railway clerk who's got nothing to live for."

"Maybe so."

"You're not at all like you used to be; you've got no spark left in you, and you're getting as fat as a *picador*."

"Maybe so."

"You're not the life of the party the way you used to be—you're just sitting here like a bump on a log. You're no fun at all any more. Do you remember that night you grabbed some guy's hat and put it on and gave him a big kiss on the forehead—and the look on his wife's face? Do you remember promising to buy me a plastic raincoat when they first appeared in the stores? Well, it's rained a lot since then."

Monchi was happy as a lark now, and several of the other girls came over to talk to us. They were rather nice girls, and even though they all kept coaxing me to buy them a drink or give them some cigarettes, they weren't at all pushy or impolite.

"I think you're going to have to do something to shake off the bad mood you're in," Monchi said. "We can go somewhere together if you like. Is there anything I can do for you?" she hinted.

"No, not really."

"Everybody knows what's the matter with you."

"I suppose so."

"You're a funny guy."

"I'm doing okay; really I am."

"Who would ever have imagined it!" she exclaimed.

"Imagined what?"

"You a married man and the father of a family and all that. I just can't get used to the idea."

Damn! A friend of mine, Rafael, a real boozehound, was motioning to me from the other end of the bar to come join him. Since it would make matters even worse if he came over to sit with Monchi and me, I decided I'd go have a word with him. It gave me an excuse at least for not talking to Monchi any more. But just as I was saying good-by to her, I noticed that Rafael had strolled over to my old buddies' table and was talking to Luis. For some odd reason, Rafael wasn't plastered to the gills tonight.

I went over and joined them. "José Luis had a fight with us—how about that?" Luis said to Rafael. "He went off in a huff."

"I don't believe it," Rafael replied.

"I didn't go away mad at all," I retorted. "You just pulled a little too hard on the bridle and I bolted."

"It was really nothing," Pérez said.

"Everybody has a right to his own opinion. When you come right down to it, it's only the dead who know the real truth, and they don't do much talking," Luis said. "We were talking about Hemingway," Ramón explained. "We were wondering whether he'd committed suicide, and our novelist friend here says he did, and he should know, but he also claims that Hemingway killed himself out of boredom and Luis wouldn't swallow that."

"Have you read the four or five editorials on Ernesto's suicide?" I asked. "The people who pretend to be the most shocked by it are the very people who are living the rottenest, the most disgusting sort of lives. In a certain sense, I consider it much more moral to blow your brains out in the middle of a 'dark night of the soul,' as Saint John of the Cross calls it, than to go on living a miserable, contemptible life, trusting that at the end the priest will come running to give you the absolution you're suddenly in such a hurry for as you lie there on your stinking sheets. What's more, there are many ways of committing suicide, and one of them, a very slow way of killing yourself, is to assume the cheerful mask of a man who believes in the goodness of life when behind the mask you're living in an absolute hell with every breath you draw. None of the people who wrote about Ernesto's suicide, either in yesterday's papers or today's, has the slightest compassion, either for him or for others, despite all their pious words about divine compassion. Would you like me to mention a few names, so you can see if there's any comparison between the decent life Ernesto led and the sort of lives those corrupt charlatans are living?"

Rafael turned to me and said amiably, "That priest, Father Félix, who wrote about Hemingway's death, may be the one that said that Ernesto wouldn't have killed himself if he'd come to Spain. You knew him very well, José Luis. Do you think it's true he wouldn't have killed himself here, if according to you he'd had a crazy urge to kill himself almost all his life?"

"It wasn't a crazy urge at all," I said.

"Well, what the hell would you call it, then?"

"A constant, morbid obsession, a pathological inclination, a weakness of the spirit."

"What the fuck, then—it was a crazy urge, like I just said. You've just put it in different words. But to go back to my question: Do you think he wouldn't have killed himself if he'd come to Spain?"

"He always maintained that Spain was 'the best country in the world to live in,' and when the wire services reported that he'd died at his friend Davis's estate in Málaga, he repeated once again that Spain was no place to die in. As I remember, Father Félix didn't say that Ernesto wouldn't have killed himself here in Spain. He's a priest who's visited many intellectuals and artists on their deathbeds and heard many of their last confessions, so he disagreed with Ernesto and maintained, as I recall, that Spain is not only a good country to live in but a good country to die in. But as I've said before, I for my part am one of those who believe that once Ernesto had begun to undergo that crisis brought on by premature senility, it was almost a foregone conclusion that he would die by his own hand."

"In a word, he was bound to fuck up."

"Wasn't there anything that could have saved him?" Luis asked.

"Only a sort of miracle . . ." I murmured.

"Let me think a minute," Rafael said, and sat there for a moment not saying a word, almost as though he was quietly meditating. Then he spoke up and said, "It seems to me that even though Ernesto had certain suicidal tendencies all along, he killed himself last Sunday because he was suddenly more depressed than he'd ever been before in his life."

"Born suicides don't consider killing themselves just one time; they flirt so often with the temptation that it becomes a sort of dangerous game, one that involves great risks that are terrifying, but at the same time one that gives them a certain curious sort of thrill," I replied.

Monchi had disappeared. Had she gone off with some john? I hadn't even noticed when she left her seat at the bar. But Hortensia was still sitting there at her table, with the same implacable, indifferent, faraway look in her eye, like a sort of oracle almost. On seeing me stare at her so intently, Luis said to me in a very serious tone of voice:

"There's somebody who's going to kill herself, too, someday, right?"

I didn't say anything, but Pérez asked in a puzzled tone of voice, "Why in the world do you think she's going to kill herself?"

"Isn't it obvious? She's bored stiff. She's going to hang herself any day now," Luis remarked.

Remembering my theory about Ernesto's killing himself out of what I'd called "boredom," they all laughed, even Pérez. Seeing that his little joke had gone over pretty well, Luis said, "She's obviously a born suicide."

"Don't talk nonsense," I said.

"It's not nonsense!" Luis retorted. "Whores are like creative artists—when they don't work, they're bored stiff and decide to do themselves in and that's the end of it," he said, pretending to tighten a noose around his neck.

I sat down again, on the very edge of my chair, wanting at least to give Luis, that high-and-mighty cock of the walk, his comeuppance before I left. I turned to him and said, "What's really tragic is not knowing God's reasons for allowing the purest and most generous spirits to be overcome by such tedium and boredom that they can no longer face life, while frivolous good-for-nothings and flighty social butterflies are never overcome by any sort of fear of anything and don't have the remotest idea what the emptiness of utter desperation is like. . . . That's really sad."

"You see, you see?" Luis exclaimed. "He's changing his tune. He's talking about desperation now, not boredom."

"There is a kind of gnawing, continuous, exhausting desperation that steals over certain people the moment they first draw breath, and sometimes it lasts their whole life long. It's a sort of desperation that's much more terrible than the personal dialogue with God about all the evils and depravities of life that we imagine the suicide entering into. What do we know about the last months of Ernesto's life in that clinic he went to several times, including once when he was admitted under a false name, lying there in that hospital bed surrounded by ghosts that were destroying his very soul? Do you think this was the first time Ernesto had ever tried to kill himself?" I said to Luis. "I must go."

"I hope we haven't upset you," Rafael said.

"And if we have, I suppose we should apologize," Luis said. "Apologize because Ernesto Hemingway, the purest and most saintly and most courageous man the world has ever seen, has humbly blown his brains out. . . ."

"He was a tragic figure, a truly tragic figure."

"Or a great tragic actor."

I couldn't bear it another minute, and got up from my chair; nobody dared say a word as I left the table. But as I stalked off I heard Luis say: "As far as I know, José Luis wasn't named Hemingway's literary executor." And I could also hear Pérez arguing furiously with him, which was most unusual, because in the days when all of us used to pal around together and throw dice to see who paid for coffee and get into heated arguments, we used to call Pérez "the gentle lamb."

I headed for the door, elbowing my way through masses of perfumed flesh.

I walked down the Gran Vía toward Alcalá, thinking I'd drop in at the Gijón, just to have a look around and see what was doing on the terrace before going home, when suddenly I heard somebody whistle at me from a taxi slowly cruising down the street.

It was Hortensia. She poked her head out the window and said to me, "Come on, hop in, you tramp. You look like a bum who's got no place to go."

I just stood there, making no move to get in the cab with her, and the taxi driver sat there smoking a cigarette with a knowing look on his face. Finally Hortensia said impatiently, "Come on, get in, and make it snappy. If people see a taxi parked here like this, and the two of us talking together, who knows what they'll think?"

"I don't care what they think," I said.

"Where have you been lately?" she asked.

"Where do you think? At home, of course."

"But you've got quite a tan and you're awfully fat. You're a different person altogether these days! I thought maybe you'd been spending a quiet summer with your family somewhere."

"Why not?"

"Who would ever have thought it!"

"Thought what—if I may ask?"

"I can't explain—it's just that I can't understand the change in you at all."

"There's nothing very mysterious about it."

"But I just can't picture you as a married man, and the father of a couple of kids besides."

"Well, how *do* you picture me, then?"

The taxi driver had turned the radio on but he wasn't listening to the music. He was just sitting there quietly smoking his cigarette, obviously enjoying this whole scene between Hortensia and me.

"Are you going to get in or aren't you? I only wanted you to take me home. I don't feel well."

So I got in, and the minute I sat down next to her, I felt like making a pass at her, just to impress the taxi driver. But at the same time, I didn't feel any sort of passionate desire for her, as I had in the old days when I was crazy about her.

"Take us to Ventas," she said to the cabbie.

The whole thing was ridiculous, and she kept saying, "You're being absurd."

"So are you," I kept saying.

The whole night was absurd, for that matter. As we were driving past the statue of Espartero, I asked the taxi driver to stop for a minute.

"What's the matter?" Hortensia said anxiously. Then she took my hand and said in a kittenish, childish, pleading tone of voice, "I'd like a drink. I don't feel very well."

Two old women were sitting on the terrace of the Domingo with their husbands, fanning themselves.

All Hortensia really wanted was to see how far she could go with me. Domingo came over to our table himself to take our order, but he very discreetly pretended not to be at all surprised to see the two of us together. Discretion was one of his greatest virtues, though perhaps not the most important one. He was prosperous but very tired these days, spending all his time walking from one table to another, helping customers choose from the menu, making out the checks, joking with people, pinching the pretty girls, scolding his whole troop of waiters.

"I haven't seen you around for a long time," he said to me.

"I've been out of the country," I replied.

"What will you have?" he asked us in a very deferential tone of voice.

"I'd like a pitcher of *sangría* and an aspirin," Hortensia said.

"Is the *gazpacho andaluz* good today?" I asked Domingo.

"It's delicious," he replied.

"I'll have a cup too," Hortensia said.

Domingo went off, doubtless totally disapproving of our being together. My worries and anxieties about Ernesto, living and dead, seemed to be over for the moment. Hortensia wasn't the same as in the old days, when what counted most between us was sex. I'd had great times in bed with her, but here I was, sitting right next to her, feeling quite cold and indifferent, and even though I was trying my best to stir up the coals, all that seemed to be left was dead ashes.

Domingo brought the cups of *gazpacho* and a pitcher of *sangría* with lots of ice in it. But he, too, appeared to be in a very odd mood, a strange mixture of condescension and grouchiness. He seemed to be doing his best to be polite, but it was quite obvious that he was worn to a frazzle and very ill at ease.

"It seems to me you've changed," I said to him.

"We all seem to have changed," he slyly retorted.

At that, Hortensia burst out laughing and exclaimed, "That's for sure! You've hit the nail right on the head!"

I was thinking about my almost empty wallet, and said to Hortensia, "Don't you think I should pay the taxi driver and not have him wait for us any longer?"

"I thought you already had!" she replied.

I went to pay him and made a few rapid calculations. I was going to be able to squeak by, but with only pennies to spare. I remembered again what Ernesto had said to me one day: "I know of no other country in the world, José Luis, where people get as much pleasure out of spending money as you Spaniards do."

"Yes, we're becoming a good country to invest in."

"Well, it's better to be a good country to invest in—to invert in, as you Spaniards say—than a country full of inverts, like certain others I might mention. But seriously, I'm more interested in spending money than in investing it, and I know of no other place in the world where you get as much fun out of spending money . . ."

The taxi driver said to me with a sly wink: "Even the best of broads ought to be thrown to the buzzards," but when I made it clear that

235

such talk wasn't to my liking, he stopped in midsentence and then immediately added, "Is she feeling any better?"

I went back to our table. There was another mystery in Ernesto's life that I would have to think about when I was in a calmer mood: his failure with women. I am not referring, to actual physical impotence, though there were times when he suffered the most painful sort of inhibitions when he tried to have sexual relations with women, nor am I referring to his almost total lack of self-abnegation, which to my way of thinking is a necessary and perhaps even the most characteristic quality in any true love relationship. Three marriages that had ended in divorce were more than sufficient proof of Ernesto's inability to love, especially if one also takes into account the fact that Ernesto was not a great Don Juan or even a skirt chaser in the usual sense of the word. As I tried to unravel the mystery, I would take it as a sort of basic premise that women mattered very little to him, that both in his marriages and in his occasional passing affairs it was the women who fell in love with him first and that he simply followed wherever they led him.

With Hadley, his first wife, he had more or less realized his youthful dreams of love and romance, getting married, and fathering his first son. But he soon discovered that he felt no deep attachment to his little family: the baby cried constantly and interfered with his writing, and his wife kept making terrible scenes, accusing him of being a selfish brute. The breakup of his marriage with Hadley was inevitable, for love could not fill the great emptiness in his heart. He sought out women—or rather women sought him out—the way he sought out wars to fight in, game to kill, adventures. But like wars and adventures, women in the end also proved to be a vast disappointment, so painful a one that, in order to heal the wound, he turned to art as the one possible remedy.

If Ernesto had ever felt any deep attachment to anything in his entire life, it was to art. He was married to it, intimately bound to it, almost shackled to it. He had lived with his second wife, Pauline, a Catholic and an intelligent person with a very strong personality, for some twelve years, and she had been the woman who had had the greatest influence on his life, quite apart from the fact that she was also the mother of two of his sons, one of whom, Patrick, was always Ernesto's favorite. If Pauline had not been an American, she might have been able to make their marriage last, but American women, even Catholic ones, seldom have the intellectual background and the spirit of self-abnegation, or the cleverness that Mary, his last wife, had, for example, qualities that were absolutely necessary to understand and above all to live with a man as difficult as Ernesto. Ernesto's affair with Martha Gellhorn had begun in Spain during the Civil War, and he married her a year later; but you might say that this third marriage of Ernesto's never was anything more than an affair. And then there was Mary, that marvelous person, who'd been married to him for fifteen years—of all Ernesto's wives the one best able to cope with this willful but weak man, this child who had never grown up, this fiercely selfish artist. If he had met Mary before, would things have been any different? Probably not. His inability to communicate with women made him seem almost a stranger to his other wives. Had he seemed a stranger to Mary too? He was very generous to all of them, and at times he was very tender and affectionate toward Mary; but for all that, he was basically a pathetically lonely man. Could Mary have possibly prevented Ernesto from shooting the bolt home with that great bang as she lay there sleeping in their house in Ketchum?

Mary was able to prevent many things, because she was almost as amazing a person as Ernesto, the colossus with the feet of clay. She was able to keep his tender idyl with the Irish girl he had met at Pamplona from going any further later on, by joking about Ernesto's having "kidnaped" her and all the rest. The Irish girl was a fiery, spirited creature, and so worshipful an admirer of Ernesto's that she might well have turned his head and persuaded him to prove that he wasn't the wreck of a man he'd been diagnosed as, especially on such a sentimental occasion as the San Fermín fiesta, the first time he had been back in Pamplona in fifteen years, and his reunion with Ordóñez. He was very smitten with this Irish girl, as a sort of decorative creature to have around, as a pretty member of his court who made him feel young and carefree again; but no one will ever know how far their mutual infatuation might have gone had it not been for Mary, as always an intelligent, discreet, understanding woman, who succeeded in turning what might well have been a frantic senile passion for the girl into a paternal, protective affection for her.

Hortensia was peering at herself in a pocket mirror, putting on lipstick and combing her hair very slowly and deliberately. She was more or less attentive to me, trying no doubt to prove to me and everyone else, including herself, that she cared about me, but her mind was far away as she sat there staring at the moths flying back and forth from the lanterns to the branches of the trees or watching the convertibles roaring down the streets full of joy riders out for a night on the town. The truth was that she was bored to tears, so bored that it was like living in a world apart. But it wasn't the sort of boredom that would lead her to take her own life—far from it.

"I'll take you home whenever you like," I said.

"You mean you'll walk me home," she answered, just to needle me a little.

Even though the night was still sultry, the shadows beneath the acacias were a dark leafy green that made it seem almost cool. How many years had it been since we'd walked together arm in arm? But I walked beside her without experiencing any sort of excitement at being with her, feeling as distant and indifferent as she appeared to be, or perhaps more so, as though I were strolling down the street with her as a sort of act of self-discipline. But I nonetheless couldn't help thinking to myself, "Admit that you liked arousing this woman's passion."

The Taurina would ordinarily have been an ideal place to stop by for a drink, but I knew that it would bring back painful memories, so I didn't even suggest going in.

"I'd like a few drinks tonight," Hortensia said.

"We'll go out drinking tomorrow night or some other time," I answered.

"But it's tonight that I need a couple of drinks."

"Why is that?"

"Just because. There's no use explaining—you're such a cynical person. You'll admit, though, won't you, that you get along marvelously well with Monchi, with that awful girl who's so stupid and vicious? I suppose you think I didn't notice the way you were cozying up to her. I know exactly what's with you two."

When we reached the corner and were about to cross Torrijos, I said to her, "Okay, let's go have a drink."

"I wouldn't think of having a drink with you."

"Alcohol's a pretty good thing."

"You said it. It helps you forget."

"Do you know what a friend of mine who's just died used to say about alcohol?"

"That he wanted them to use it to embalm him?"

"No. He used to say, 'This is what kills the worm that's eating us.'"

"What worm?"

"The one that's eating us."

"Heaven knows what that means."

"*He* knew. When he came back from one war and was about to go off to ano___ ___ ___rt drinking his whisky neat and say, 'This is what ___ ___ating us.'"

___ ___worm was it that was eating that guy—who must ___ ___lman if he was a friend of yours?"

___ ___ eating him: before he went into battle he may ___ ___th remorse because he would be obliged to kill."

"Every time he came back after a battle or had seen awful things behind the lines, he was always very depressed and would get dead drunk remembering those who had died."

"What was your friend's name?"

"Oh, he went by many names," I replied. "Sometimes he called himself Pablo, or Robert, or Anselmo . . ."

"And he was a murderer, you say? I think you're just trying to scare me."

"I didn't say that at all. He never killed anybody."

"A minute ago you said he killed people. Did he or didn't he? You're not making any sense at all."

"You don't understand. My friend grieved for all the people he had to kill, and would have gladly brought them back to life again if he possibly could have."

"Well, why did he kill people, then, to go on to the next reel of this crazy serial?"

"He killed other people so as not to kill himself; he killed people in his imagination, so as not to kill them with his bare hands. He once wrote . . ."

"Oh, he was a writer, was he?"

"Yes, he was a writer."

"A madman like you, in other words."

"We resembled each other only superficially."

"It's just as I thought. You're absolutely nuts."

"So are you, you know."

"Who, me?"

"Sure. If you weren't, you wouldn't be here with me this very minute. We're all crazy. I remember that this friend of mine used to get his outsize shoes shined every day by a bootblack in the plaza, keeping up a running coversation with him the whole time, asking him all sorts of questions about himself and his family and his job, and always leaving him a big tip. It was all very straightforward and friendly. But then, one day, several foreign girls, a man with a goatee, an American in a flowered shirt, and a priest in a beret came up to him as he sat there getting his shoes shined and asked him for his autograph. He didn't seem to mind at all, and cheerfully signed his name for all of them. And then the bootblack, who was also an admirer of his, said to him: 'Would you please autograph my shoebrush for me?' That made my friend furious, and he got to his feet, swore at him, and called him all sorts of dirty names. The bootblack dropped all his rags and ran down the street, with my friend chasing after him . . ."

"Your friend obviously had a violent temper. He should have known the bootblack was only joking."

"No, he wasn't joking. Neither were all the people who used to ask my friend to autograph their handkerchiefs, their hats, and even their shirts . . ."

"Was the bootblack the only one he ever got mad at?"

"No, he also got mad once when a peasant who was very drunk shoved his rope sandal in front of him and asked him to sign it."

"Let's go in here," I said, and dragged her into a place in one of the little side streets, a terrible dive that looked as though it was about to cave in.

"You've changed a lot—and all for the worse," she said.

"It's not a bad thing at all to change."

Ernesto had written, in *The Dangerous Summer*:

> The faces that were young once were old as mine but everyone remembered how we were. The eyes had not changed and nobody was fat. No mouths were bitter, no matter what the eyes had seen. Bitter lines around the mouth are the first sign of defeat. Nobody was defeated.

Not even Ernesto, the total wreck, the most tragically defeated man in the world, had felt defeated in Pamplona two years ago, just two years ago now . . . And I said to Hortensia:

"Things can change a great deal in two years. But the change is only apparent. Nothing ever really changes."

"What do you mean, nothing ever really changes? I was right: you're a real nut."

"All of us are."

"Let's get out of here."

We walked on down the street.

" 'To go to bed at night in Madrid marks you as a little queer,' " I said, citing Ernesto.

"I can't get used to the idea of your living in a stodgy family apartment."

"I can't, either."

"Not to mention having a couple of kids. And working."

"I can hardly believe it myself."

"I just can't get over it."

"All I do is go to bed early and get up early and do a day's work . . ."

"You're no doubt the most cynical man in all Madrid."

I laughed and so did Hortensia; she was obviously flirting outrageously with me, but it left me cold. Or perhaps it was flattering to another person, the self that I had once been but could no longer be, however much I would have liked to.

We got to Hortensia's place finally, a new building in the newest section of town, a housing development in the heart of the old Madrid.

No doubt she was not only feeling down in the dumps for some reason, but was also ill. Or so it appeared. That was why she had knocked off work so early, taken some aspirin, and was spending the evening thinking and remembering instead of trying to pick up customers. I had been able to see more of the real Hortensia tonight than other times, but I still didn't understand her. Spending the evening together this way had made me feel much closer to this woman than sleeping with her or waking up next to her in the early morning or taking her out dancing or writing her letters or telephoning her or even shedding tears over her. How many nights it had been since I had last seen her!

"I don't suppose you'd let me come upstairs with you for a while," I said.

"You're as welcome as anybody else."

"I don't much like the way you put it."

"You're very cynical." Women like Hortensia have a pitifully meager vocabulary. The minute they latch onto a word that catches their fancy, it pops up practically every other sentence. "I wish I hadn't seen you again," she said.

"I know you really mean that."

"What's more, I've told myself over and over: the next time I see him, no matter who he's with, I'm going to slap his face."

"I'm glad you didn't. Thanks."

"But now I don't mind telling you that if you want to come up you're welcome to, but this time you're going to do things my way and pay cash on the line."

"You're making me feel terrible." I wasn't joking. I was feeling very ill all of a sudden, and grabbed the door handle to hold myself up.

"Don't put on a big act. I can see right through you. I've been very nice to you, or rather, I've been very stupid, but it's all over between us now. Life's taught me a great lesson."

"It's got a lot to teach people."

"I've been unhappy all my life."

"I'm certain that's true; you don't deserve what you get, and other people don't deserve what they take from you. But that's just one more of the lessons life teaches you."

"Don't give me any more of your fancy speeches, because this time you're not coming upstairs. I don't care to have you make any more passes at me. I only like the kind in the bullring . . ."

"Please, Hortensia, don't remind me of the bullring."

"Are you scared of the bull's horns?"

"No, it's just that sometimes rival matadors are meaner than Miuras."

"The same thing always happens every time you get a few drinks in you. You start raving like a madman and then . . . It's obvious you don't care much for horns."

"I care even less for *toreros*. I prefer bulls' horns to the other kind. There's nothing worse than a *torero* who gives other men horns because he's gotten gored himself. . . . Bulls are angels with horns by comparison."

"You've had too much to drink."

"Maybe so."

"You have no idea what you're talking about."

A taxi stopped at the corner. I heard the night watchman coming down the street, clapping his hands, calling out all's well, and pounding his pike on the pavement. Hortensia hid inside the entryway. She was doing her best to be cold and distant, but her next words were spoken in a soft, apologetic voices: "You're such a cynic, the most cynical man . . ."

"I seem to have heard that before."

"I don't want to start all that old business over again."

"Neither do I. Nor any new business either . . ."

She held out her hand to me very politely and I kissed it even more politely, and before I knew it she had disappeared. It was best that way. I had proved to myself that I was capable of letting the last burning embers die. It was nothing heroic, but it was certainly unexpected— at least as far as I was concerned.

I walked slowly on down the street toward the Ventas subway stop across from the plaza, laughing at everything and everybody in the world except Hortensia, and laughing loudest at myself.

How many times we say: "It's a small world!" And it's true: it's as small as a handkerchief. Sometimes it's a folded handkerchief, sometimes a handkerchief laid out flat, sometimes a clean one, sometimes one so filthy you can't stand to look at it. There were lights on in the window at a place down the street, and I went in.

Ernesto and I had dropped in at this tavern on the corner many a time. One night as we were sitting there the owner had piped up all of a sudden and said to him, "You don't wear the same sort of leather jacket you did back in the old days, during the war."

"Back in the old days?" Ernesto was wary and suspicious, as he always was when anyone brought up the Spanish Civil War, but when the man began telling us some of his unforgettable wartime memories, Ernesto forgot his fears and his eyes sparkled. As we were leaving, the owner said to us, "I wonder when we poor Spaniards are going to be able to read that book that there's been so much talk about . . ."

"He'd like a copy of *For Whom the Bell Tolls*, Ernesto," I said.

"An autographed one," the tavern keeper hastened to add, being a pretty smart man.

The other people in the tavern that night had gathered around

Ernesto in a circle to watch him drink. But tonight the atmosphere in the place was quite different, and people barely nodded when I said, "Good evening," as I came in. The whole tavern seemed plunged in gloom, almost as though they were all holding a wake.

"I wonder if you remember me," I said to the owner.

"Of course I do," he replied, without raising his eyes from a strip of cheap paper that he was writing a whole string of numbers on. Then, after a while, as he was serving me a "palomita" (a white, anis-flavored drink), he said to me in a rather gruff voice, as though he disliked even mentioning the subject, "I thought about the Great Man several times today, and even more often yesterday . . ."

"Do you remember how we sat here one night right here at this very table?"

"I remember it perfectly. It was right after that famous episode in Murcia, when he'd had his money clip stolen, just as the bullfight season was ending. He was wearing a leather jacket—a really elegant one, not the kind he used to wear during the war. And if I remember rightly, he had a silk scarf around his neck. I'm certain at any rate that he was wearing a cap, a corduroy cap with a bill. He'd gotten a terrible paunch, as I recall."

"You'd known him for a long time, I take it."

"I knew him slightly, only slightly," he replied evasively.

"The way it all ended was terribly stupid," I said, downing my palomita in one gulp.

"When I first knew him he used to wear a big gabardine trench coat with lots of buttons, and sometimes a deerstalker cap and a leather jacket, not the kind we wear here in Spain but the kind the Russians used to wear."

"Did you first meet him in Madrid?"

"Near Madrid, in Guadalajara. He was a militiaman fighting for culture," he said, lowering his voice as though he were in a catacomb.

"That's not a bad thing to be," I answered.

"Yes, it's quite a good thing; I was a school superintendent myself, and yet I've spent the past ten years here in this tavern peddling cheap, rotgut red wine."

"I'll try a glass of it."

"After an anisette?"

"Sure, why not?"

And after that, we were friends again, as in the old days.

"I saw him after the victory at Brihuega," the tavern keeper went on. "He visited the front lines and gave everybody a big bear hug—the top officers, the political commissars, the men in the ranks, everybody. And I could see he had tears in his eyes. And when he saw the Italian prisoners being led away, do you know what he said? I'm merely repeat-

243

ing his remark word for word: 'I've shed my own blood for Italy, and it doesn't deserve to be plagued with riffraff like that.' Then somebody said, 'We ought to shoot every last one of them.' 'We ought to take their pictures and show the world what the army that claimed to be the "saviors of Europe" really look like,' he replied. Those were his very words. I remember it very well. And I also remember that one night when the two of you were sitting here, before I came over to the table, he leaned over and whispered to you, 'Do you think those two guys over there are tailing us?' And you said, 'No, I don't believe so.' 'They look like cops to me,' he replied. And you answered, very firmly, 'I think you're wrong there.' And he was, because they were two guys who had lived in the neighborhood for ages—petty thieves and pickpockets that everybody around here recognized."

"They were doubtless trying to pinch his money clip," I said. "How odd it seems that Ernesto's famous money clip, which always had plenty of bills in it, had the words 'I will keep thee safe' engraved on it, beneath an image of Saint Christopher. I was very upset when it was stolen in Murcia, because it made me feel ashamed for my country. I wrote letters to the mayor and the municipal council that were later published in the newspapers, and the nine thousand pesetas turned up at Ordóñez's, just after Camorra (do you know him?) had tried to reimburse Ernesto for the money he'd lost. What a laugh! Ernesto would never have accepted it. He didn't regret losing the money at all, but he felt very bad about losing the money clip, because it had been a gift from his son Patrick."

"Isn't it possible that the whole business of the stolen money clip was a publicity stunt or something? There's so much of that these days that I'm always suspicious!"

"I suppose people will keep accusing Ernesto of that sort of thing forever, but the fact of the matter is that he was a terribly naïve man, a great, big innocent child . . ."

"Do you honestly think so?"

"I believe that Ernesto was a big innocent child his entire life, including the moment that he looked into the barrel of that shotgun and pulled the trigger," I replied.

"Do you think his remarks about Manolete were all that innocent?" the tavern keeper asked me, and realizing that this was a subject to be talked over man to man, he came out from behind the bar counter with an anisette-and-seltzer in his hand, and to my surprise, sat down there with me at the very same table that Ernesto and I had sat at. "Nobody can convince me that he was being fair when he wrote all those nasty things about Manolete. All the other *toreros* were great enemies of Manolete's. He had cast such a giant shadow that naturally they were all jealous and prepared to go to any lengths to ruin the dead man's reputation, in the most spiteful sort of way. And that's not right. To claim that the great Cordoban matador was a master of cheap tricks in the bullring was both untrue and unfair."

"I admit he went too far when he wrote that."

"What happened to that English writer . . ."

"He wasn't English, he was an American."

"Okay, then, that American writer—you should know. But as I was saying, what happened to him was that he got to be like one of those very religious women who only believe in one saint. If they believe in saints, they should believe in all of them. And the same thing is true of that writer-mister; there were all kinds of idols around, but the matador from Ronda was the only one he cared to worship."

"If you claim to be any sort of a bullfight *aficionado*, I'm sure you'll admit Antonio's a good matador."

"He's a good one all right, an expert one, but he's not the one and only. But to your writer friend, there was no one who could touch him, neither Dominguín, nor Ostos, nor Paco Camino, nor even Joselillo if he were suddenly to come back to life again, nor Belmonte if he were ever to put on a suit of lights again. . . . To him there was only one absolute master, and that's not right . . ."

"All of us have our own personal preferences."

"That's quite true, but according to what I've read, which I admit isn't very much, and according to what I've heard, which is quite a good bit, your writer friend not only was gaga about his idol, but also didn't care much for any of the other matadors and in fact more or less despised them."

"Real *aficionados* have always been very rough on bullfighters they didn't like," I said.

"But have they spoken that harshly about dead bullfighters? I can understand why he might pick on Dominguín, but was there any reason for him to attack Manolete? If you ask me, I think he went too far, even though I always liked him."

I sat there remembering a conversation about Manolete that Ernesto and I had had one day. "You got to know Manolete rather well, didn't you?" he had asked me. "In a manner of speaking," I answered. "Tell me, what was he like?" he asked. "He was a sad person," I said. "A sad person?" he muttered several times, and then said: "I don't understand." "That's right, he was a very sad person, with some sort of complex, but deep down he was a very serene person," I replied. "What kind of a complex?" Ernesto asked. "Manolete was a very sad person—I think he suffered from severe melancholia." "But what made him so sad?" Ernesto asked. "Life in general," I answered. "You say you got to know him fairly well?" Ernesto asked again. "In a manner of speaking," I was obliged to answer again. We sat there talking about other things for a while, funny things mostly, trading jokes back and forth, but then he asked me again: "Tell me, what made him a sad person?" "I told you—life in general, and himself and everything around him in particular." "In short, a wet blanket and a jinx," he said, trying to be funny. But he sat there scowling for a long while, lost in thought, like a doctor trying to make a diagnosis, and then he said: "Tell me, did you ever see him when he wasn't sad?" "Oh yes, I occasionally saw him shake off his melancholy mood, but at such times he was sadder than ever." "Like one of those people who reek of death even before they kick off," Ernesto said. "I saw him just a few days before he died and he reeked of sadness, not of death; and I assure you I'm quite familiar with the smell of corpses and the smell of dead people who haven't died yet." Ernesto took off on another tack then and asked me, almost offhandedly: "Did you like seeing him in the bullring?" "On certain afternoons I liked it so well I was almost moved to tears," I answered. "Did you think he was a *torero*-god?" "All I know is that the day he died I wept." "People have shed tears every time a *torero* has died in the bullring." "It was something more than that in Manolete's case: I think even the bull would have wept if he could. And many people shed tears; the whole country wept." "I've seen *toreros* die in the bullring myself." "I don't think it will ever be the same again." "People in Spain always weep bitter tears for something they've lost forever, but only after they've lost it; you Spaniards also shed a great many tears for Alfonso XIII, but only after he was dead." "Alfonso was a sad, pathetic man too," I said; "you might almost say he was the Manolete of kings." Then Ernesto shook my hand and said to me: "We may not have the same thoughts on the subject, but it seems to me that something more is involved than just mourning the death of a sad man, though that's what people who are still alive tell themselves to console themselves . . . isn't that right?" "Yes, that's right," I replied, and then the subject was dropped and we went on drinking, in that very special way that was an art with Ernesto.

I repeated a few snatches of this conversation to the tavern keeper, who said to me, "I'm very surprised. I always thought that whole business about Manolete was some sort of publicity stunt, or something the bullfight people your friend palled around with put him up to . . ."

"It was also partly that, because Ernesto was more naïve than most people think. And when he finally realized how gullible he'd been, it was too late. That was why he had no illusions left in the end. Do you know what I think? I think one of the most naïve things he ever did was to allow himself to get involved in rivalries between *toreros*, and even worse, to begin inventing them—the great duel between Ordóñez and Dominguín, for instance. And it was all because he was so easily taken in: he wanted so much to believe that it was all true that he eventually even fooled himself, and as a result certain people took advantage of his good faith, his generosity, and even his affection, and got a whole lot of free publicity for themselves."

"You're probably right there. He was a great man. I first met him in Brihuega, and you can't imagine what a great man he was in those days . . ."

"He knew a lot about bullfighting in the days before the war, and when he came back to Spain years later he didn't realize that everything had changed, that publicity gimmicks were ruining bullfighting as he knew it and *toreros* were being promoted like detergents."

I stood up and tried to pay for the drinks I'd had, but he wouldn't hear of it and even accompanied me to the door.

8   I was at the newspaper office by eight-thirty the next morning.
I had trouble getting my check at the cashier's window, and went to
the business manager's office to get things straightened out. I finally got
my money, but only after the editor-in-chief had intervened in my behalf. The business manager had been blue in the face at first and bright
purple at the end of the argument, but now he was clapping me on the
back and saying: "Glad to help whenever I can."

Then they asked me if I would like to go to Rivadelago to report on
the dam disaster there. But I hadn't lost any old friends in Rivadelago.

Ernesto had once visited the *Pueblo* office in Madrid. Though he
had practically lived in the offices of newspapers and magazines for
many years, he had recently tended to avoid them as much as possible
and was almost surly when editors approached him. He had accepted
assignments only when it suited him and the things they asked him to
report on seemed really important or likely to earn him a pretty penny.

He had visited the office of this Madrid evening paper for other
reasons, however. For a long time it seemed likely that he wouldn't
show up at the *Pueblo* office even though his visit on the eighteenth of
August, 1960, had all been arranged. At the last minute, when I
dropped by to pick him up, he suddenly announced he wasn't coming.
He had often unexpectedly changed his mind like that in the last days
of his life, and it wasn't easy to come right out and tell him that that
was no way to behave.

"I've never visited any other newspaper office in Madrid, so why
should I drop by the *Pueblo* office?" he said to me.

"But going there is a different matter. You've put up the money for the Hemingway Prize that the *Pueblo* is going to offer."

"I know, but I've since been told that it is a worse Fascist rag than the others . . ."

"Neither you nor your prize has anything to do with politics. And the *Pueblo*'s one of the papers that has always been very decent to Ordóñez and always will be. Remember Marino Gómez Santos's series of articles about him?"

"Yes, but as you know very well, I've gone out of my way to show my appreciation."

Bill Davis spoke up then in his cautious way and said, "Isn't there a chance that the other papers will take it amiss if Ernesto visits the *Pueblo?*"

"Why should they?"

"They might boycott Ernesto and he'd suffer the consequences."

"I don't think I should go," Ernesto said.

"Do as you like," I said. "But you're going to look bad if you don't go, because they're waiting for us."

"But wouldn't it be more or less the same thing if the editor-in-chief or somebody like that came here? We could have a drink or two together and that would be the end of it," Ernesto replied.

I was between the devil and the deep blue sea, because from the very first moment that Ernesto had hit upon the idea of offering a prize, I had been the one who had taken it upon myself to set up the machinery for awarding this generous prize. And since I had managed to get my own paper, the *Pueblo*, to sponsor the prize competition, I couldn't believe that Ernesto would go back on his word now.

"I'll go along with whatever you decide, but it seems to me that visiting the *Pueblo* office can't possibly get you into any sort of trouble," I said.

"They'll be out for my neck and say that I'm playing footsie with the Falangists."

"Nobody's going to say any such thing. The newspapers in this town are quite naturally all more or less the same. The only difference is that the *Pueblo* is the spokesman for the Spanish labor unions. In some ways that's a disadvantage, but in other ways it's also an advantage. It's a paper that lots of working-class people read, and its views as regards literature are much more liberal than those of other papers . . ."

"I don't think Ernesto's decided one way or the other yet . . ." Davis said.

"The idea of a Hemingway Prize has gone over very well with Spanish writers. And that's only the beginning. It will attract some very original entries, and I'm certain that it's going to be considered a great honor to win it. It'll be a prize worthy of your name," I said to Ernesto.

Bill didn't know what to think, and was afraid to contradict Ernesto.

"Why don't you phone them, José Luis, and tell them to come and hold their ceremony here? Tell them I'm . . . tell them anything you like. You might say I have to leave town on a trip, which is quite true."

"I don't think that's going to set very well with them. The editor-in-chief, Emilio Romero, isn't a man who's easily taken in."

Bill was nervously waiting Ordóñez's arrival, because Antonio was supposed to go with Ernesto to the *Pueblo*. We called him at his house, but he'd already left.

I don't know why Ernesto was so concerned about the whole thing, but whatever the reason, he kept popping in and out of his chair, going to the bathroom, peering at himself in the mirror, picking up envelopes full of bullfight photographs and putting them down again, checking one phrase or another in his manuscript and asking Bill and me countless questions. The moments ticked by one by one, yet Ernesto paid no attention to how late it was getting and seemed not to notice how uneasy Bill and I were. Apparently he felt that he had already done his part by putting up the money for the prize, and that was all he should be expected to do. I called Emilio's office, and he came on the other end of the line immediately and said, "Has something gone wrong?"

I tried to explain, but as often happened when things weren't going right, he cut me off in the middle of a sentence. If Ernesto wasn't going to be able to come to the *Pueblo* office as he'd promised, I was to tell Ernesto for Emilio that he hoped he would be feeling better soon and have a nice trip, because Emilio was too busy to come to the hotel.

I hung up and told Ernesto what Emilio had said. He was even more upset then, but managed to control his temper.

"Well, what do *you* think I ought to do?" he said to me.

"I'll go along with whatever you want to do, but I really think you should go," I replied.

"And what'll happen if I do go?"

"Nothing at all. It'll just be a nice, friendly, cordial get-together. We really ought to go. Do you honestly think I'd set any sort of trap for you? Don't you trust me?"

"Of course I do. I trust you absolutely."

"Well, then, get ready and we'll go."

"Will anybody take photographs?"

"Not if you don't want them to."

"And I don't want to go if there's going to be any kind of speeches."

"All right, no speeches—I promise."

Bill was still his usual, quiet self, but he was nervous. Ernesto started getting ready to go, but every once in a while he'd think of something else he wanted to do and would start rummaging through his papers and his suitcases. And every so often he'd start checking with Bill about his reservations for the trip he was going to take.

Ordóñez showed up then, and it was thanks to him that Ernesto finally decided to go to the *Pueblo* office. I explained briefly what was going on, and Ordóñez leaped into the breach. Turning to Ernesto, he said to him in that intimate, impudent tone of voice that always made Ernesto melt like butter, "Okay, let's get this show on the road, Papa. They're waiting for us."

"So you agree we should go?" Ernesto said to him.

"Why not?" Antonio answered.

"We've just been asking José Luis whether he thought all this might get me in trouble later."

"Let's go," was Antonio's only reply. "Emilio's waiting for us."

"Okay, let's go," Bill said.

"Right," Ordóñez chimed in. "It'll all be over in a few minutes. We don't have to stay long, but we really have to go. Manuel Escudero's going to come with us."

"Okay, let's go," Ernesto said, as though it were the most natural thing in the world.

We were all relieved, and on the way to the *Pueblo* we all kept teasing Ernesto about how scared he was.

We hadn't planned any sort of celebration there at the newspaper office, and the only people who were going to be there were members of the staff, Gómez de la Serna, Luis Pérez Cutoli, and as a special guest, Marino Gómez Santos, the author of the series of articles about Ordóñez.

I went into Emilio's office and he came out in his shirt sleeves to receive the others. He immediately invited us into the editorial department, and the first thing he did was bring out a set of galley proofs of the announcements of the prize, and then in a few brief words he assured Hemingway the journalist and the writer that he personally, and all of the staff, were at his entire disposal. Ernesto then said a few brief words in reply, thanking him politely. In order to liven things up a bit, Ordóñez kept making little jokes the whole time, and I began writing a rough draft of my article describing his visit:

> . . . Since he had been invited to appear in the literary bullring and since *toreros* ought to have a chance to see how writers fight a *corrida*, Ernesto had brought that first-class expert at cape and sword work, Antonio Ordóñez, with him. . . . A person doesn't really begin to respect bulls until he is on intimate terms

with a *torero* like Ordóñez. The bull and the bullfighter are two parts of a single mechanism; if they interlock smoothly, everything is fine; if they don't, it's not so good. Ordóñez, like other good *toreros* yesterday, today, and tomorrow, is a dark-skinned, impudent cherub who keeps tickling that old hag, the Great Bald Lady whose first name begins with a *d*, in the ribs and all the other places where it gives her the most pleasure: the tailbone, the crotch, and even the belly button, if my readers will pardon these specific anatomical references. . . .

With Emilio leading the way, we visited the entire building, and at one point Emilio said in his usual rapid stutter, "All this is just a bunch of scrap iron. We're going to have a new building and new printing presses soon."

"Congratulations," Ernesto said, as though this were the first time he had ever been in a newspaper office.

I kept jotting down more notes for the article I later wrote.

Bill Davis was very pleased at how things were going and stood there taking the whole scene in like a delighted sheriff or a referee at some sort of sports event. This was one of the very few times I had ever seen him in a dark suit, as though this were a formal reception.

The linotypers were amazed not only at Ernesto's enormous bulk, but also his air of great simplicity, his quiet composure that at the same time was a sort of shyness, as though he were being deliberately self-effacing so as not to disconcert other people.

The ceremony had thus been a rather intimate one, and fortunately several of the regular reporters on the *Pueblo* who had recently begun to write outrageous things about Ernesto were not present that afternoon—the same reporters who a year later were to write the most despicable things about the dead man before he was even laid in his grave. Perhaps his fiercest detractor was Eugenia Serrano, a reporter who after Ernesto's death wrote an article entitled "For Whom the Bells Ring," in which she called Hemingway "a second-rate Blasco Ibáñez," "a novelist in the realist tradition of not nearly the stature of Don Passos, Steinbeck, Sherwood Anderson, Bromfield . . . ," ". . . as if tomorrow I were to write a novel that would also discuss at length the Kingsley [sic] report or the strange tendencies of the Elia Kazan school. Or one that contained flowery passages hailing the Chicago Mafia, a bunch of bloodthirsty killers. Or a *Gone With the Wind* describing the savage excesses on both sides. . . ." She had once written enthusiastically about Hemingway ("Please, please introduce me to him"), but in a later article, entitled "For Whom the Whisky Tolls," a story full of spite and venom, she had complained that she had felt like telling Ernesto a few truths "to his face." If she had presented herself as a candidate for the Hemingway Prize, it would obviously not have been for the money or to honor his name. I had no idea why she had attacked Ernesto so viciously.

What Dámaso Santos, the literary critic of *Pueblo*, had written about Ernesto was also unfavorable, but it was not a malicious piece, and he had a perfect right to his opinion. What he had said about him seemed quite within reason: "Our war, which he did not understand . . ."; "After all, I admire Manolete more than I admire Hemingway . . ."; "I confess I've never been a Hemingway-worshiper." The nastiest comments had come from people who had never read a single book of Ernesto's and had always disliked him: "Do you really think there's nothing between Ernesto and Antonio?" they would ask me. "What do you mean by that?" I would answer; "of course there's something between them." "I'm sure there is. There's bound to be," they would say. "But what is there between them exactly?" they would then ask me in a furtive whisper. "Well, confidentially, what there is between them is a noble friendship, and an intimate association that's more or less useful to both of them, though much more so for Antonio the *torero* than for Ernesto the writer," I would reply. "Is that all?" they would comment. "That's quite a bit, wouldn't you say?" "But they seem to spend all their time together," they would remark. "That's only natural," I would retort. "I don't mean just around the bullring; they're always together in some hotel room too," they would insist. "They're very fond of each other. They're good friends," I would answer.

I had this sort of conversation with people constantly, both in the *Pueblo* offices and elsewhere.

Ernesto's visit to the *Pueblo* was turning out very well, as I had been quite certain it would. Although Emilio had told me many times that he didn't care at all for Ernesto's writing, he was being the perfect gentleman, and even unbending enough to laugh and chat with Ernesto. We all had a few drinks then to celebrate his visit. There were no toasts or speeches, only a few friendly words of thanks, and a few photographs. I hastily scribbled the final paragraphs of my article entitled "Invitation to the Bullfight." In it I said:

> . . . that huge man, at once burly and frail, that great hulk of a man with the elegant beard known as Ernesto Hemingway, the Nobel Prize winner, by the grace of God and his pen, visited the *Pueblo* offices with all the reverence of a pilgrim come to leave an offering. . . . He came to deliver an invitation to young Spanish writers in search of a subject—be they Andalusians, Castilians, or even Galicians, be they short-story writers, novelists, essayists, or reporters (which is no sin if they write well)—to arm themselves with their pens, to enter the arena,

to write about bulls and bullfighting, blood and sand, horns, and safety screens. Do we Spaniards still have a passionate love for the art of killing bulls at the risk of one's life? What does the heart-rending trumpet blast that made gentle Franciscans out of many rabid romantics sound like to young people today? Isn't the *torero* fated to die on the horns of the bull?

(If Ernesto were still alive to read that paragraph, he would surely immediately knock on wood.)

I then went on to say in my article:

The contest is open now, and the *plaza* is still empty. The bullfighters who are to appear have not been chosen yet, and as yet there are no scalpers hawking tickets for the fight at exorbitant prices. An *espontáneo* may dart into the ring any moment now. All a contestant need do is pick up his pen and write about bullfighting. That is absolutely the only requirement.

Everyone approved of this announcement of the contest that I had written, because I had tried to formulate it in such a way as to reflect the spirit in which Ernesto had offered this generous prize; the contest was to be entirely open and aboveboard, there were to be no hard-and-fast rules so long as the contestants' submissions had to do with bullfighting, and everyone would have an equal chance to win.

"Let's hope they submit some good pieces," somebody commented after I had read my rough draft of the announcement.

"I'm leaving the whole thing entirely up to you," Ernesto remarked immediately. Then, pointing to Emilio, Ordóñez, and me, he said, "It's entirely in your hands."

I was very optimistic about the modest but prestigious prize that Ernesto had offered and assured him it would be a great success. There were many good bullfighting subjects to write about, and all that Spanish writers needed to do, if only to honor their profession, was to sit down and write. But, as usual, Ernesto was less inclined to be carried away by enthusiasm, and said, "If there are no good pieces submitted the first year, don't award the five hundred dollars—save the money for another year."

We were all pleased to hear him say that, since it meant that he intended to continue sponsoring a Hemingway Prize for a long time to come.

Ernesto had visited the shabby old *Pueblo* offices less than a year before, on August 18. He had spoken very confidently of the years to come, yet today he had passed into that undiscovered country from whose bourn no traveler returns, as his favorite author, Shakespeare, had put it, or was pushing up daisies, as they would say in my home town. We would learn nothing more about him, save from his books and a few unpublished manuscripts that would turn up from time to time. The reasons for his death would remain a matter of conjecture, because not even those of us who had seen him depart for his homeland and slowly slide downhill into madness really knew why he had killed himself, though we had had a vague premonition of what was going to happen. Ernesto's life was only a memory now, like the ash of a Havana cigar left half smoked on one of the seats in the bullring on a gray afternoon.*

I left the *Pueblo* office, and as I walked down the stairs I kept muttering to myself: "Please, Lord, tell me why I don't have twelve thousand *duros* so I can fly to Ketchum." But I had done everything else I possibly could. What pained me the most was realizing, after the fact, how badly Ernesto had been duped, misled, and exploited by the bullfighting crowd, for though tauromachy is an art, it is also a cruel, pitiless world. How obvious it now was that the whole *Dangerous Summer* affair had been a snare and a delusion, a cheap trick, a farce that had been a major factor in precipitating Ernesto's ultimate fatal fit of depression and his utter disgust with everything.

I went into the Rafa bar and asked them to wrap up a slice of ham for me to take out, as though I were setting out on a long, perilous journey. And luckily, several journalist pals of mine on the *Pueblo* staff came in just then and asked me if I wanted to play a little game of dice with them. I not only won enough to pay for all my drinks, but two hundred pesetas besides, which I immediately spent buying everybody

*The first Hemingway Prize was awarded to Alfonso Martínez Berganza for his article "El Desolladero" ["The Skinner"], and the second to Pedro de Lorenzo for a brief biography of the American Nobel Prize winner published after his death. The Hemingway Prize was then taken over by others, and eventually forgotten. This was only to be expected. Even though it had been Ernesto's intention—as was evident both from what he told me and others and from what he had written in letters composed just before his death that are a sort of last will and testament—that I was to be closely associated with the awarding of the prize, *toreros* and publicity agents attempted to interfere and naturally they disregarded my own wishes in the matter altogether. When Ernesto first began making arrangements to establish this prize, a gesture that was yet another proof of his sentimental attachment to Spain, he tried several times to appoint me the head of the project so as to ensure that it would be properly administered and fulfill his intended purpose. I told him then that Ordóñez would be the best possible person to see that his wishes were carried out. But once Ernesto had died, the Hemingway Prize was eventually dropped, both because I had left the staff of *Pueblo* and because Antonio Ordóñez had such a heavy bullfighting schedule that naturally he was inclined to forget that the prize had been left in his hands as a more or less sacred trust. Ordóñez might well have continued to sponsor it, since the sum involved was a quite modest one, and, among other compensations, it would have at least served to perpetuate Ernesto's name among young Spanish writers. Even though I eventually had nothing to do with the prize, I would have been very pleased to see it continue to be awarded, especially if Ernesto's original intentions in offering the Hemingway Prize had been faithfully respected.

midmorning whiskies. When somebody telephoned that the boss was on his way up to his office at the *Pueblo*, it broke up our little party and I left and caught the first taxi that came along.

"Take me to the Calle Ruiz de Alarcón," I said to the driver.

Among all the places of pilgrimage in Madrid that should be sacred to admirers of Hemingway was the home of Don Pío Baroja. I felt a sudden, irresistible urge to pay my respects to Ernesto at that place where he had given me something more than a friendly handshake and a few cordial words. There in the apartment of a shy, retiring, terribly lonely man, a pact had been sealed attesting to our mutual admiration of a literary style, if not of a way of life.

"Go straight on up," the concierge said to me.

Don Pío's nephews weren't there. Julio, a scientist, was off traveling again, heaven only knew where, and Pío was probably in America.

Around 1956, Ernesto had kept plying me with questions about Don Pío, obviously half in awe of him and at the same time genuinely concerned about him. Ernesto had always taken up the cudgel in Baroja's behalf whenever anyone mentioned his works, and had proven to be a fervent admirer of Don Pío as a person once I had told him how Baroja was facing death with enormous courage as he rounded the last bend on his life's journey.

"Why don't you go visit him some day?" I finally said to him.

"Do you think there's any possibility he'd see me?" Ernesto answered.

"Of course he would. And it would please a lot of people both inside and outside Spain if you called on him," I said.

From that moment on, it was clear that we'd eventually visit the *viejo*; but I knew I'd have to make all the arrangements. Ernesto was not only timid, but actually shied away from such things. He would immediately start worrying about what people would say—or pointedly fail to say.

A few days later I remarked to him, "If you don't go see him soon, it'll be too late."

"You think it's the right thing to do, don't you?"

"It seems exactly the right thing to do, since that's the way you feel about it," I replied.

"Well, then, we'll go visit him whenever you say."

So I made arrangements for the visit with Don Pío's nephew Caro, making it a point to mention that Ernesto had asked me specifically to ensure that there wouldn't be any sort of publicity; all he wanted was a simple, intimate meeting with Don Pío, without a whole bunch of curious onlookers and big spreads in the newspapers.

We had arranged to meet in the Cervecería Alemana, on the Plaza de

Santa Ana. I had also invited Miguel Ruiz Castillo, Baroja's publisher, who at the time was also my publisher, to go with us. Mary had a package in her hand. "Do you think it would be all right if we bring Don Pío a little present?" she asked me, undoing the little parcel, which contained a very nice wool sweater and some beautiful socks. "They're real cashmere," Mary said.

"I'm sure he'll be pleased," I said. "He's always been very cold-blooded, a man who's fond of a nice warm fireside and a cozy armchair and a lap robe."

"Great," Ernesto said, and called his chauffeur over, gave him a thousand-peseta bill, and told him to go out and buy Don Pío a bottle of whisky as well.

Ernesto thereupon ordered big double Pernods for himself and me, and coffee for the others. Then Basabe, the photographer, arrived. I phoned Don Pío's nephew, who reported that everything was all set.

On the way to Baroja's house, I noticed that Ernesto seemed nervous. When he had said good-by to Mary, he had remarked to her, "I never met Baroja when I was young, and it's only right that I should go see him now."

Then he had put his huge paw on my shoulder and said, "And you must be very frank with me, as always. If there's anything I can do for him, anything he needs, you must tell me."

"Don't worry—I promise I'll do exactly that," I said.

I was a little nervous myself. The visit was important, because it was like the encounter of two giants, one of them a fierce, forthright battler and the other a scoffer sitting on the sidelines; one of them a triumphant victor, the other a great skeptic apparently defeated by life.

But they were not such total opposites as they might have seemed. Despite his aggressiveness and his irascibility, Don Pío the Basque was a shy man at heart, just as Ernesto's violent and adventurous life was not at all in keeping with his real nature. The one had dreamed of wars and the other had lived them, but both shared the same basic inner chaos, the same romantic impulses, the same spiritual emptiness, the same fear that sometimes expressed itself as blustering truculence and sometimes as very middle-class misgivings. They were much more alike than was apparent at first glance, and even their works were like two sides of the same coin.

"That old man ought to have been awarded the Nobel Prize twenty times over," Ernesto said.

"It doesn't matter now; he's dying," I replied.

"I confess he was one of the few authors I could ever stand to read, and one of the few I've continued to read . . ."

257

"I've seen his books at your house—you've read them so often they're dog-eared, and they're covered with your notes."

"I've learned a lot from his novels, a whole lot."

"Don Pío has said hundreds of times, 'They'll never give me the Nobel Prize. They'll never forgive me for having stayed here in Spain to live with my people. But it was the only thing I could do.' And since he was such a timid man, despite his reputation as a 'man of action,' he would always add: 'I wonder what would have happened if I'd been able to go to America?'"

"And how does that poor old man manage to make ends meet?" Ernesto asked.

"When some publisher happens to give him five thousand *duros* in royalties, he's flabbergasted. 'That can't possibly all be for me, can it?' he says."

"That isn't right, that simply isn't right," Ernesto exclaimed in the same irascible, cutting tone of voice that was so typical of Baroja.

I told Ernesto then that he would have to more or less shout in Baroja's ear, since the penicillin Don Pío had been taking had left him very hard of hearing, and told Ernesto how a big standing wardrobe had fallen on him one day when he was alone, and how one day the parish priest had dropped by unexpectedly, and Don Pío's nephew had refused to let him in, because several times when Don Pío had taken a turn for the worse he had said: "I don't want any priest poking his nose around here. . . ." Don Pío may have been so insistent because when his brother Ricardo had died, the press had made him out to be more or less a great sinner or an outspoken heretic who had returned to the bosom of the Church on his deathbed. There were many other things that I would have to explain to Ernesto, but not just then.

"Here we are," I said.

The man in the seven-league boots who was famous throughout the world was about to visit the writer in slippers who was dying in almost total obscurity in his own country. But the two of them were both great dreamers, two disillusioned idealists who had seen all their hopes dashed, two scathingly critical spirits, two rebels, two men overcome with a mortal tedium, two artists whose works were both different and yet one and the same.

We went upstairs in the elevator and I saw Ernesto look in the mirror and run his hand through his beard and then smooth his hair down, so as to appear as neat and tidy as possible. He was dressed more formally than I had ever seen him before. And in his suit-coat pocket was a copy of *The Sun Also Rises*.

Don Pío's nephew opened the door; and I noticed immediately that two other people were present, the journalist Rodrigo Royo, who had visited Ernesto at El Escorial, and his brother, a United Press correspondent. Ernesto had intended this to be a private visit, but it was unfortunately not going to be nearly as private as we had hoped.

We went into Don Pío's hushed study, a room that served both as his library and as a reception room, with balconies overlooking the silent street adjoining the Prado Museum. Don Pío's study was full of little statues and paintings, all very much resembling the man himself, a pilgrim cloaked in a dull gray costume concealing a proud, rebellious spirit, a poet of the quiet quarters of the city.

Caro stepped into Don Pío's bedroom to make sure that everything was ready. Miguel Ruiz Castillo immediately followed Don Pío's nephew into the bedroom and said to Baroja, "Do you know who's here to see you?"

Baroja apparently didn't hear him.

"You've a visitor—it's Hemingway, no less."

"Who?" this old, old man asked.

"Ernesto Hemingway, the Nobel Prize winner."

"I'll be damned!" Don Pío exclaimed. "How come that fellow's come to see me?"

I went in then and shouted in Don Pío's ear: "Hemingway would like to come in—he's very anxious to see you . . ."

"Why is it he's come?" Don Pío asked.

"He just wants to see you. . . ."

Don Pío looked more lonely and at the same time more haughty than ever, as independent as a beachcomber but at the same time as dressed up for the occasion as a village mayor, with his white nightcap perched on his head, seemingly not at all impressed by any of this but in fact as keenly interested as always in what was going on around him.

When he came back to the study, Caro showed Ernesto some of Don Pío's things, and when he pointed to Baroja's favorite armchair, noticing how eager the photographers were to get a good picture of Ernesto I ventured to say, "Why don't you sit down in it for a minute, Ernesto?"

"No, no, I couldn't possibly," he answered in a genuinely humble tone of voice.

"Please, please, sit down," they all chorused.

And as though to please them, but at the same time fully aware of the symbolic significance of his gesture, he sat down in Don Pío's favorite armchair. He stayed in it only a few moments, but his gesture was quite unforgettable, because the Hemingway who had refused at first to take that chair, claiming it was an honor he didn't deserve, sat there very stiffly, embarrassed and discomfited. Though I tried to make him feel more at ease as the photographers took his picture, it was plain to see that he was deeply moved.

For once, I had caught a glimpse of the real Hemingway, without any sort of mask, a humble man with all his defenses down.

We went into Don Pío's bedroom then, a room farther toward the back of the apartment, overlooking a rather noisy courtyard. As we walked down the hall, Ernesto said to me, "How is he?"

"He's all right," I answered. "Better than I thought he'd be."

Don Pío's nephew went over to the left side of his uncle's bed, and I stood there with Ernesto on the right, at the head of the bed. The white sheets and the silence in the room made it seem as though death was close at hand, practically on top of poor Don Pío. This old man nonetheless still had the penetrating look of a predatory eagle in his eye. He glanced briefly at those of us who were familiar visitors at his bedside, searching for the face of his famous fellow writer, that man who had lived so many of the things that he himself had only dreamed of, but who did not in the least resemble the man the newspapers had talked so much about, for Ernesto was standing there with a terribly sad look on his face, as though he too had been, if not destroyed and defeated by life, at least brutally punished by it.

It was a shame, a real shame, that this meeting had not taken place before, even just a few years before. At that moment, I saw Don Pío look down toward the floor, as though searching for something under the bed. Was he perhaps looking for his cat? His love of cats was another thing he had in common with Ernesto. Or was he perhaps searching for some of the cookies or one of the little bottles of sweet wine that he often hid under his mattress? Despite his curiosity, which was obviously still as lively as ever, what we saw before us was the last physical remains of an indestructible human spirit, but Baroja the writer unfortunately was no more. Fortunately for all of us, however, he was the living proof of words that Ernesto had once written: "A man can be destroyed but not defeated."

From the very first, Ernesto had been subdued, like a wayward student about to be subjected to an oral exam. Or at any rate it was obvious that he was trying very hard to accept the fact that Don Pío was suffering from a very ordinary sort of disease—he looked like a penniless old man who might have been found lying ill in some rather shabby hotel room. The walls of his bedroom were completely bare, and although everything was very clean, it also had the air of a kind of temporary shelter. One unconsciously found oneself looking for Don Pío's boots under the bed.

"He's brought you some presents," Don Pío's nephew, Caro, said to him.

Don Pío looked at him with a puzzled expression on his face.

"To keep you from getting a chill," Caro said.

"And something to warm you up a bit, too," he said, setting the bottle of whisky down on the night table. Don Pío stared at it with a bewildered look on his face. But the *viejo* nonetheless still had an air of great dignity about him. As he lay there helpless on his sickbed, that rude, sharp-tongued, mordant-humored, difficult man suddenly appeared to be a very simple, very humble person. The bare, spare room did not seem so much the cell of an ascetic monk as the sickroom of a dying man.

Ernesto, who was standing there in the corner to the right of the bed, suddenly leaned down so close to the sick man that he seemed almost to be kneeling at his bedside. Though his demeanor throughout this meeting had been extremely modest and respectful and more or less shy, he nonetheless still seemed a majestic figure by comparison with this gravely ill man, especially when he held out his hand to him. With his usual lordly air of a great aristocrat, Baroja lay there gazing into the eyes of his visitor.

Ernesto said only a few brief, clipped words to him, but his voice was trembling with emotion. As I remember, what he said was something like: "Don Pío, I've been wanting to come see you for a long time, because I feel I owe you a great debt of gratitude. I've never forgotten how much I owe you, how much all of us who have read your books owe you. . . ."

Don Pío listened respectfully to this great giant towering above him, who seemed to be making a heartfelt confession.

"To us younger writers, you were our master, and we learned so much from your works and from the personal example you set us. . . ."

Don Pío looked at all of us, one by one, as if he were watching a theatrical performance.

"I'm convinced that you deserved the Nobel Prize much more than many writers who won it—myself first of all, for I am more or less just another of your disciples—because you have set us all such a marvelous example, and both your works and your life have taught us so much. . . ."

Ernesto spoke these words in an admirably grave, even tone of voice, but it was obvious that he was terribly moved.

The sick man apparently found this meeting tiring, because he turned his head the other way and lay there staring at the wall.

"You and many other writers deserved to win the Nobel Prize much more than I did," Ernesto went on, murmuring the names Unamuno and Valle Inclán and several others as though to convince his audience of the truth of his words.

This half-whispered list apparently was not to Don Pío's liking, because without actually uttering the words "that's enough of that," his gesture said as much. He was suddenly no longer a humble old man, but a proud, imperious genius who disliked having to share his fame with all these other writers Ernesto had mentioned. It was as though he had suddenly ceased to be curious as to why his visitor had come, or as if he were suddenly furious about something. But Ernesto went on in the same vein, like a meek student who is scared to death in the presence of his great master. . . .

All of a sudden things livened up a bit, because Ernesto took a copy of *The Sun Also Rises* out of his pocket and began writing a very brief and very polite dedication in it:

To Don Pío Baroja, from a respectful disciple.

Ernesto Hemingway.

That made Don Pío perk up a bit, and he lay there staring intently at Ernesto with his knowing eyes. He glanced at the book with a pleased expression on his face, and then stared down at the other gifts spread out on the bed as this great tall man stood there at the head of his bed leaning over his white pillow. Don Pío's beard and mustache trembled slightly just above the top of the sheet and his white nightcap made him look like a slightly comical old patriarch.

The meeting between Don Pío and Ernesto was nearly over now, and we all muttered a few polite phrases: he looked fine, and would doubtless be up and around soon; his name was admired and cherished all over the world, as this visit from Hemingway the Nobel Prize winner proved. Don Pío gave a weak little wave of his hand. Doubtless the word Nobel had reminded him of Echegaray, Benavente, Cajal, and Juan Ramón Jiménez, all of them men he had more or less ridiculed both in public and private.

A housemaid began humming a popular song in the courtyard. Then the telephone rang in a neighboring house and we heard voices arguing. When he saw that we were about to leave, the old man sat halfway up in bed, as though making an effort to be as courteous and gracious as possible. Ernesto stood there for a moment, staring at him intently. Neither of them had been at all effusive, and no phrases for posterity had been exchanged. It had all been very simple and straightforward and heartfelt, and very touching.

We all shook hands with Baroja one last time, and his feeble handshake seemed a sort of symbol signifying that his life's work was now forever over. Then his hands fell back limply on his belly, like the hands of a dead man who has not had the strength to cross them before breathing his last. As his nephew Caro walked back down the hall with us he said, "He's in bad shape, very bad shape. He hasn't been his usual self for several days now."

Ernesto was very pleased at how his visit with Don Pío had gone, even though it had moved him almost to tears.

"He's exactly like his books," he said.

That was one of the first times that I noticed the angry red streak and the flaky white patches extending from the bridge of Ernesto's nose to his eye. In this respect, too, he had come to resemble Don Pío, whose skin we had noticed gradually peeling away on the bridge of his nose and on his cheek. But whereas in Don Pío's case these pasty chafed spots seemed to be the result of a lingering cold, in Ernesto's case they seemed more like deep claw marks that life had left on his face.

As we started down the stairway, Ernesto said to me, "What enormous dignity that old man has. He must have been a great person."

"Yes, he was a marvelous man," I replied.

"I only wish I'd visited him earlier."

"Well, you at least met him before he died."

"I'm very happy we went to see him, and very glad that it all turned out so well. But this visit has also hurt a lot right here," he said, stopping on the stairs and putting his hand over his heart.

And as we went on down the stairs, he said to me rather hesitantly, "Do you think it was the right thing to do to bring him those little presents?"

"I think it was exactly the right thing to do," I replied.

"It occurred to me several times up there that I ought to give him a more personal sort of memento," he said. "I would have liked to give him my watch. It's one I've worn for a long time—through thick and thin."

"Your watch?" I said. "I don't really think you should have parted with it. If the saying *Omnes nocent, ultima necat* is true, if it's true that every tick of a watch sends you to your grave, the very last tick is very close at hand for poor Don Pío. Whatever his last hours are like, he's got very few of them left. And I'm sure he'll remember your visit."

"That old man must have been as solid as a rock in his day," Ernesto said.

"He really was, and he had a spirit that even bombs couldn't destroy," I replied.

"What swine so many Spaniards have been! Imagine him dying like that . . ."

This meeting between the misanthrope practically breathing his last and the fearless adventurer had taught me not only something about life but about art.

There in the street outside Baroja's apartment (where I was standing this very minute), Ernesto had said, "Come eat with me. I feel such a great weight on my shoulders after meeting that old man. Mary's waiting for us. And why don't we invite all the rest of these people? It's as though I were carrying a great burden on my back that I want to get rid of. It's not right that that old man should die such a lonely death," he said, smacking the palm of his left hand with his right fist.

And that is how this simple visit, almost like the blind meeting the blind and the deaf meeting the deaf, had ended, though there was a great deal of talk about it later.†

Seeing how depressed and upset Ernesto looked as he stood there on the street after his meeting with Don Pío, I realized that he had been utterly horrified, and knew that the horror he had felt had been not so much a physical revulsion as a psychic revulsion at the sight of that old man wasting away there on his deathbed, at glimpsing what it is like to die leaving one's shroud soaked with the last few drops of sweat one ever sheds, on seeing that ridiculous nightcap that Don Pío had donned for his trip to the very end of the line, or the adhesive tape that would be used to affix syringes to his body, dripping fluids into him that would do no good whatsoever. Would Ernesto allow himself to die such a lingering, disgusting death? Probably not. He would prefer to think of himself as dying by accident, killed by a buffalo or a leopard he was tracking, devoured by sharks in the Caribbean, burned to a cinder in a rented airplane, or the victim of a fatal crash along a curve on some highway. Though still under the care of several doctors, Ernesto had begun drinking again. To drink was to forget the very real possibility that he would go to pieces altogether; to drink was to raise a glass to toast the possibility that he would not have to resign himself to giving up the things he loved best; to drink was to defend himself against attacks both from within and from without.

I went into the pastry shop across the street and had a comforting glass of Río Viejo, a wine for tottering sick people. I sat there staring at Baroja's doorway through the big plate-glass windows, remembering what had happened at Don Pío's funeral as clearly as though it had been only yesterday—another unforgettable memory of Ernesto.

On the night Don Pío had died, I stayed with Ernesto till the wee hours of the morning. As we parted company, Ernesto said, "I'll come pick you up at your house early tomorrow morning."

And he arrived exactly at the hour he had said he would. Ernesto always appeared right on the dot when he had arranged to meet someone

† There were many subsequent versions of what transpired during this meeting between Hemingway and Baroja, circulated, naturally, by people who had not been present. According to some accounts, written half in jest and half with a sort of mooning sentimentality, Ernesto had brought Don Pío a nightcap as a gift. Someone else who had been very touched by their meeting had reported that this American tough guy had planted a kiss smack in the middle of this dignified Basque's forehead, confessing at the same time that he himself had been a mere adventurer all his life. . . . A kiss on Don Pío's forehead? Even if Baroja had been certain that he was dying, he would never have permitted such a thing.

somewhere. We arrived at Baroja's half an hour before the funeral, walking up the stairs to his apartment this time instead of taking the elevator.

"How did he die?"

"Gasping for breath, like a fish out of water."

The crowd at the door had recognized Ernesto the moment he appeared. They were awed at seeing him in person, a living legend.

As we went in, he said to me in a low voice, "There are many fewer people here than there should be."

"But there are more than I expected there would be," I replied. "A non-Catholic funeral and burial in a non-Catholic cemetery seem very strange to Spaniards."

After extending his condolences to Caro, Ernesto headed straight for Don Pío's bedroom, since this time he knew the way. We went in, and there Don Pío was, his body laid out with only a sheet over it, looking as though he were shivering from a chill that was not of this world. There were no signs of suffering on his face, but at the same time his expression was far from beatific. It was the weary but serene look of a traveler who has reached the end of his long journey at last. Lying stretched out there, he looked taller than when he was alive, but the only thing about him that reminded one that Don Pío had once been one of Spain's most imposing men of letters was his hands, those hands now forever empty that would go to the tomb like fearful talons destined never again to seize upon a victim and tear him apart, hands now as beautiful as those of an exiled prince, a prince of poverty and loneliness.

Lined up outside the door were many so-called *barojianos*, a school of writers who mechanically copied their master rather than sharing his sensibilities or learning from his style. One could better understand now why Baroja had had such scorn both for his admirers and for his enemies, dismissing all of them as a bunch of circus clowns, and why the bombastic flattery of these fervent devotees had sent him into fits of rage more often than any other thing. There they all were, a whole raft of second-rate Baroja imitators, buzzing about like pesky gnats. Fortunately, among all these failed writers there were one or two *sobresalientes*—topnotchers—to use a bullfight term.

It seemed very cold there in the dead man's room. I felt as though not only an illustrious, exceptional man, Pío Baroja, a man who had always tried desperately to be merely a humble man of the people without ever succeeding, had died here within these four bare walls. To our great loss, something equally precious had died here: the Spanish novel.

The moment Ernesto had entered the room, he had gone over to Don Pío's bedside and crossed himself.

"That's Hemingway," somebody there in the room said.

"How could it be Hemingway? Can't you see the man's praying?" another Baroja disciple said.

Ernesto went on reciting the Our Father in a barely audible whisper. I heard him and was deeply moved. But Don Pío lay there, as indifferent as a statue now to our prayers for him. Baroja was a mummy now, his face a mere mask of flesh frozen in an inscrutable expression, perhaps an ironic, impassive smile at his own death.

Perhaps the only real revolutionary in the room, the only one to have truly come to grips with both life and death, with and without faith, with and without hope, but always with enormous love, was Ernesto, that man so close to death himself.

The hour for our last farewell was at hand. But who was bidding whom good-by forever? Several people came over to Ernesto and announced that it was time to go downstairs; it had not been Don Pío's nephew, certainly, who had sent them, but rather all those publicity-conscious mourners who had climbed out of bed very early that morning so as to be sure to have their faces appear in the photograph that was bound to be on the front pages of all the newspapers.

Ernesto had to duck his head again in order to pass through the doorway. The great adventurer had met the great dreamer just in time. Lying there in the cheap coffin in the room Ernesto had just left were the remains of an art and an ethic that neither rust nor worm could ever corrupt. Ernesto went on down the hall, and the disciples who were eventually to destroy whatever was left of Baroja's once-glorious reputation did their best to get him to stay. But Ernesto shook them all off, quietly but firmly. He realized immediately that they were trying to use him, in a cheap way that was an affront to the dead man.

"Let's go," he said to me.

"They want you to walk in the funeral procession," I said.

"No, I don't want to," he answered.

"Shall we go, then?"

"Yes, I think we should. Do *you* think I ought to stay?"

"It's up to you."

"All right, then; let's go."

Among that crowd of mourners whose reputations would doubtless fast fade now that Don Pío was no more, Ernesto seemed one of the very few who was genuinely grieved at his death, and he walked slowly down the stairs with a very pensive look on his face. But then we found ourselves surrounded again by people with messages from Don Pío's nephew and other of the mourners, pleading with us to come back upstairs.

"They all want him to be one of the pallbearers," they said to me.

Ernesto stood there looking very aloof and haughty, but when he finally answered, there was a note of genuine humility in his voice: "It's too great an honor."

"Try to convince him that it's only right that he should be one of the pallbearers," someone said to me.

"Camilo's upstairs, and he wants you to be one too," someone else said.

"Hemingway's going to agree to be one!" someone else shouted.

There was lots of commotion on the stairway, and Ernesto suddenly became very nervous and said very firmly, "This is an honor that properly belongs to Spanish writers; they're the ones who should be Don Pío's pallbearers."

"And you should be one too," an intermediary said, grabbing him by the arm.

Ernesto jerked his arm away and repeated: "They're the ones who should serve as pallbearers." Then, turning to me, he said: "You should be one of them, Castillo."

And having categorically refused to serve as a pallbearer, Ernesto headed on down the stairs. I knew that he had not refused out of any sort of false pride, but only because they were trying to turn Don Pío's funeral into a kind of *cause célèbre* that would have greatly offended the dead man.

But they sent a third message down from upstairs; the tone of this one bordered on the insolent. And then, as though to settle any possible lingering doubts in anyone's mind, Ernesto grabbed me by the arm and said, "Let's get the hell out of here."

"You really could have accepted—it would have pleased people."

"This funeral is none of my affair. And I don't like this sort of three-ring circus."

"They asked you with the very best of intentions," I said.

Someone else was eager to persuade him to change his mind, but didn't dare approach him. And Ernesto, who by this time was a little angry, said to me, "If they keep making such a big fuss, I'll go up there and carry him off to the cemetery all by myself."

When we reached the street, he said again, as though trying to convince himself that he had done the right thing, "You deserve to be one of his pallbearers, but I don't."

"Maybe it's not just an honor but a duty," I answered. "But it's too late now."

We walked across the street and stood on the sidewalk opposite, watching the crowd of people streaming in and out of Baroja's building and the curious onlookers lined up along the street. We waited for some time, but the coffin did not appear, and Ernesto said, "I hope they're not having trouble finding pallbearers."

Ernesto's Italian chauffeur, Adamo, was standing there watching the whole scene with a rather puzzled look on his face. The dead man was obviously a celebrated figure, but there was little sign that people were grief-stricken.

The funeral procession turned out to be a very simple, very short one, with very few people marching behind the coffin. We joined the mourners for a short distance as the cortege made its way down a quiet side street. Then we joined the line of other cars heading toward the Cementerio del Oeste. For a long while Adamo kept directly beside the coffin. The flowers of the month of November, which blossom on all the graves on All Souls' Day, had bloomed a bit early for poor Don Pío. The whole scene was straight out of one of his novels: everything was gray, vague, fuzzy, confused, dreary, dull, pointless.

Ernesto commented on the fact that there were no priests and no cross in the procession, as though it were a matter of some concern to him. His reaction was thus quite the opposite of that of certain fanatical admirers of Baroja's who proudly boasted of the fact that Baroja's funeral had not been conducted according to the rites of the Church.‡

As we approached the cemetery, some traffic policemen blocked off the road leading directly to it and we were forced to take a long, roundabout route. Ernesto said to me in a furtive whisper, "It seems to me that there are lots of police at this funeral."

"There naturally would be some."

"I can smell a cop a mile away, and I'm certain there are a whole bunch of them here."

Since it was the day before All Souls' Day, there were many people all along the road bringing flowers to the cemetery. Few of us had ever been in the "civil" part of the cemetery, and the fact that it was an entirely separate plot of ground seemed very disturbing to many of the mourners, because even among Baroja's disciples there were a number of persons who had religious inclinations. There were great bunches of chrysanthemums and dahlias, those sad flowers that seem to bloom only so that they may be placed on graves, on almost all the tombs. One of the ones with the most bouquets of these autumn flowers was that of the Spanish Socialist leader Pablo Iglesias, more of a doctrinarian than a courageous champion of the rights of the people, but nonetheless unquestionably the guiding light of the workers' movement; I have heard it said that there are wreaths of roses on his tomb the year round.

Some of the mourners were wandering about that flat plot with no crosses, reading the very disconcerting, extremely unconventional in-

‡ There were rumors later (which apparently had some basis in fact) that one of the persons who had insisted most adamantly that no priest was to be allowed to set foot in Baroja's house died a short time later, after having sought on his deathbed absolution from a priest.

scriptions and quotations on the gravestones. But there were also emblems and symbols that made you feel more like weeping than smiling, since the things that they stood for had perished long before the bodies of the dead whose memory they were meant to perpetuate had turned to dust. There was something grotesque about these outlandish gravestones, and those who were easily shocked were simply aghast.

About fifty or sixty friends of Don Pío's, most of them men of letters, were gathered around the yawning grave where that once-fierce Basque rebel, now forever tamed, was to be laid to rest. No prayers of any sort were said at the graveside either, but as before at Don Pío's house, Ernesto withdrew a few steps, bent his head, and began to pray silently.

Once the coffin was covered with dirt, Don Pío's friends dispersed, and though Ernesto, too, wanted to slip quietly away, I detained him long enough to introduce him to Camilo José Cela, Julián Marías, Dionisio Ridruejo, Gaspar Gómez de la Serna, and many others. A number of illustrious professors and then several young writers such as Sastre, Aldecoa, and Pilares tried to arrange a meeting with him later; it would have pleased me very much had he agreed to meet with them, for they would then have had a chance to get to know him better. But as we were getting into the car, Ernesto said:

"We'll see if maybe some day we can arrange for me to get together with those young writers and talk with them; but I don't have the least desire to meet with university professors or critics or sacred cows in the world of letters. And especially not today of all days."

This was his usual reaction to people from the Spanish literary world. One day when he had dropped in at the Café Gijon, he had been equally standoffish, but this was nothing unusual, because in the United States he behaved in much the same way toward old Yankee pals of his who were writers, and in Havana he was often quite distant to both old and new friends of his who were writers. What literary figures had he palled around with in Paris, London, or Rome? Very few of them, and always ones he himself had chosen as intimate friends, never those who toadied to him.

Ernesto felt satisfied, as though he had honorably repaid the debt he owed Don Pío by attending his funeral. On the way back, he said several times, "I only wish I had met him sooner, when I was young." And then, once, he added, "But everybody said he was such a ferocious, blustering, unapproachable man. . . ."

"Who, Baroja? He was the most courteous, the most gracious, the most human man of letters we've ever had in Spain," I said.

"Were you really fond of him?"

"Quite fond of him. There are so many things I can't forget. Have I ever told you that Don Pío, who hated ever bothering anyone, sent a letter in his own hand to Victoria Ocampo in Argentina recommending my first novel to her, thereby paving the way for its publication in Argentina when the authorities refused to allow it to be published here?"

Ernesto sat there not saying a word for a long while. I knew him well enough to realize that he was pondering something of great concern to him. But, as usual, I didn't ask him what was on his mind.

Ernesto had had Adamo stop the car at the door of the Church of San José. Ernesto had clapped me on the shoulder and said, "It's plain to see that you were deeply moved."

"What's that? Deeply moved by what?" I said, my thoughts suddenly returning to the present. I had been sitting there so absorbed in my memories that I had almost forgotten that we had just come from a funeral—not a first-class or even a second-class but a third-class one. The ceremony had not lacked solemnity, but I did not feel that Don Pío had been paid the homage he deserved.

"You seem annoyed about something," Ernesto said.

"I'm absolutely furious."

"How come?" he asked.

"I can't explain."

"You're all worked up about something—that's obvious enough."

"This world is a crock of shit, as Don Pío would put it: as he lay in state there today, I saw the deformed image of his bare, spare philosophy, his vast humanity, his magnificent style reflected in the eyes of good-for-nothing people so nearsighted they can't see their own noses in front of their faces, in the eyes of his narrow-minded disciples, pitiable skeptics who only know they're alive because they've got cramps in their belly. And above all, I saw that those who make the biggest show of being 'the heirs of Baroja's philosophy' are the most inane phrasemongers in the entire country."

"Don't let it get you down, José Luis. I know exactly what you mean, and I agree with you one hundred per cent. I also saw lots of well-known faces there today, or rather lots of barefaced publicity hounds, and I'm quite sure that if you and I had each made a separate list of that sort of Baroja disciple, the very same names would have appeared on both our lists."

He took his flask out of his hip pocket then, offered me a drink from it, and took a few sips himself. Then he asked, "How do you think other writers are reacting to all this?"

"The older generation of writers are scared stiff. The younger writers are delighted by Don Pío's defiant refusal to be buried as a Catholic, but basically they couldn't care less about him. Except for a very few writers who were real friends of Don Pío's, the rest are just second-raters who were eager to be seen marching in his funeral procession."

"Don't tell me this country has lost its balls altogether."

"For years now."

Ernesto gave Adamo instructions as to where to pick him up, and then took me by the arm and said, "Would you like to walk around for a while with me?"

"Of course."

"I've been taking up a lot of your time lately, I'm sure."

We walked on down the street, and after a moment, he said to me, "Look, wait here for me a few minutes, will you? I don't think I'll be gone long, but there's something I have to do today that's really ridiculous. I've got to see the doctor—mostly to reassure Mary."

That was the first time he had mentioned his health. And I was so surprised to hear him say he was going to the doctor that I thought it was some sort of a joke that he'd explain later. But this was neither the first time nor the last that Ernesto was to visit Dr. Medinaveitia, one of the few physicians whose advice he paid any attention to.

"Wait for me right here, if you don't mind. I'll tell you all about it later."

"Of course. I don't mind waiting at all."

"It's just a routine checkup. But Dr. Medinaveitia's expecting me, and I really have to go see him. It'll set Mary's mind at rest."

"Don't worry about me. I'll be right here."

"Nothing's wrong with me, you know," he assured me several times. "But I don't mind telling you I'm not the man I used to be—do you know what I mean? You get somebody to check to see how the old motor's running and then you do whatever the hell you feel like. . . ."

In 1959 he had visited Dr. Medinaveitia again, and this time it was for much more than a routine checkup. He had come out of the examining room convinced that something quite serious was wrong, something he was quite sure was the beginning of the end.

For the first time that year, I had seen Ernesto searching for something in Spain that was not simply the excitement of rushing here and there and seeing everything, something that was not simply the urge to experience and enjoy every sort of intense passion, including the passionate urge to write. In a certain sense, he had come to Spain to recapture his passion for life, or rather, to renew his passionate struggle against death. What a strange coincidence that his visit to the doctor was taking place on the very same day that we had seen Baroja to his grave!

He was not gone long, or so it seemed to me at least. I remember that when he came back, I was sitting in the bar where he'd left me, scribbling my last farewell to Don Pío on several paper napkins, an article that began: "Don Pío is gone now. He always had an enormous hunger to see new places and meet new people. He had the piercing look of eagles in his eye and the soaring spirit of the skylark in his breast. . . ." The remainder of the article went on in this vein, and it would have to be published just as I had jotted it down, with scarcely a word changed, because such articles in memory of the dead are always like champagne corks—you think they're never going to come out, and then all of a sudden they come out very easily, with a loud pop. I was sitting there writing:

> . . . You traveled the world's highways and byways, with your jacket slung over your shoulder, humming or singing a joyous song. . . . But roads, like men, eventually come to an end.

Today I was still sitting there in the pastry shop staring fixedly at the building across the street, and the waitress finally said to me, "Are you waiting for someone?"

"No. Why do you ask?"

"Oh, nothing. I just saw you sitting there staring out the window . . ."

That afternoon when I had been waiting for Ernesto, I had filled a whole pile of paper napkins with my scribblings, though my ball-point pen had several times gone right through the very thin paper. I kept on writing as I waited for him:

> You were the first writer to realize that literature is not some sort of mystical, otherworldly pursuit. Why make such a fuss about writing? You simply sat down and wrote, because that was all you felt you could do. You merely tried to describe things on paper, to recount what you had seen, as barely and sparely, as vigorously, and as spontaneously as you possibly could. What a bore grammar is!
>
> When all is said and done, life is a story to be told. Everything in life is strange and wonderful, everything is worth writing about. But alas, there is never time to tell the whole story! Naturally there are many people who will say—as they have already said—that you were merely a good reporter. But what do you care now what they say?

"Miss, would you please bring me another of the same?" I said to the waitress in the pastry shop.

That day in the bar as I sat scribbling while waiting for Ernesto, the waiter stared at me as though I were a madman. Whatever was I doing with all those napkins I kept asking him for—eating them? I went on filling one of them after the other.

> Your role was to observe, to penetrate the spine-tingling mystery that serves to conceal human misery, tragedy, crime, treason.

And in the end you yourself were seized with an immense, chill fear, a sense of utter panic. . . .

How awful! These words that I was writing in memory of Baroja, who had been in his grave scarcely an hour and a half, were also a perfect description of my friend Ernesto, who was still alive, very much alive, but had gone off to have a chat with an old and good friend who also happened to be a doctor. What I was writing about my friend who had departed also applied to my friend who had not yet arrived. And it had been on that long-ago day that I had first begun to ponder the fundamental resemblances between the two of them, despite their apparent dissimilarities and above and beyond their superficial similarities of style.

I went on writing:

> May you rest in peace, Pío Inocencio Baroja. You have not traveled that road you took in vain. You have left us your books, the one consolation for those of us who have lost you forever; an incomparable master among Spanish men of letters, you have shared your genius with us, and set us an awesome example of what it means to be a writer.

"Waiter, another rum, please," I said.

"That's a good thing to be drinking on a sultry, rainy day like this," he replied.

I went on scribbling:

> I would have given anything to be able to place my rosary on your coffin in exchange for your slippers or your beret, because they would have been the best possible mementos for anyone setting out to be a serious writer. But the image of Christ is ultimately too crucial, too profound a symbol for me to question what it meant to you or for you to answer.

Ernesto still hadn't shown up, so I got up out of my chair and wandered around the bar for a while and then went outside. I spied him coming down the street with a very odd look on his face, and though he was trying his best to appear to be his usual tough, hearty self, it was plain to see that he was badly shaken. The minute he met me there on the street, before we went back into the bar, he took his silver flask out of his hip pocket and said in as cheery a voice as he could muster, "Let's celebrate the good news about my blood pressure and my liver."

"What kind of a report did you get from Dr. Medinaveitia?" I asked.

"He says I'm in great shape, though I may have a touch of diabetes."

"Diabetes?"

"He was mincing words. What he really meant was cirrhosis of the liver."

"I don't believe a word of it. You're as strong as an oak."

"I don't believe a word of it either," Ernesto answered, offering me his flask, which I noticed had very little vodka left in it. Then he ran his hand through his beard, a gesture meant to show that he didn't give a damn, but one that betrayed how upset he was, and said, "All the advice doctors give you about taking care of yourself is such a bore: they keep telling you that you should lose weight, that you shouldn't eat this or that, that you shouldn't drink, and shouldn't fuck at all of course, or at most once a year, that you should avoid any sort of emotional stress and not get into any heated arguments, and be careful not to travel too much and live as regular a life as possible . . . in a word, to straighten up and fly right no matter what's troubling you. . . ."

He was doing his best to pass it all off as a joke, but there was a bitter, almost sardonic edge in his voice. I thought he was just getting a load off his chest, however, and didn't pay much attention.

My memories of the remainder of that day are very fuzzy. As I remember, we finished off Ernesto's flask of vodka and then went back into the bar and drank more than either of us should have. I do seem to recall, however, that this was one of the very few times I ever heard Ernesto openly criticize Spain, making insulting remarks about people whom he obviously had no respect for but whose names he had never mentioned before. And, as I remember, he also brought up the subject of religion, for both of us were very moved by the thought of Don Pío lying in his grave, unable now to voice any sort of protest about anything, no longer aware of who was attacking him and who was defending him; Don Pío would now turn to dust, with no expectation that his utter simplicity of spirit would be a silent message that would one day cause the dry earth of Castile to blossom again, and he would never know that the final, overwhelming silence that had overtaken him in that sordid, pathetic plot of ground in the Cementerio del Oeste would also engulf his early novels.

That day when we had gone back to the Cervecería Alemana after visiting Baroja, Mary had grabbed me by the arm and said, "Ernesto doesn't seem like his usual self at all . . ."

"Yes, I think you're quite right," I said. "That visit meant a great deal to him."

"It made a deep impression on him—I'm certain of that," she replied.

Meanwhile Ernesto had wandered over to the bar, and was standing there pounding his fist on the counter saying, "It's just not right!"

"What's not right?" the waiter had asked politely.

"Nothing, never mind," Ernesto had replied. "I'm really going to tie one on now, though."

Alcohol had become Ernesto's way of fighting off his serious fits of depression. And Mary was beginning to be very concerned about his taking to drink to ward off his anxieties, because she was convinced he was fighting a losing battle against acute alcoholism.

Liquor those days made him fall into long, moody silences. He never became talkative or rowdy when he was drinking. He never seemed to be spouting pure nonsense, because he always spoke in a very quiet, cryptic tone of voice, so that one never quite knew what he was saying exactly, and every once in a while he would make some surprisingly bright remark that sparkled like a pearl that a deep-sea diver had suddenly brought up from the depths of the sea.

We headed down the street then to the Callejón de la Ternera, a restaurant where we had often eaten together, although during the last days of his visit to Spain in 1960 it had been the scene of a memorable row. Words kept pouring out of him as from an uncorked bottle. Speaking of Baroja, he said to Mary, "That old guy was really something."

"Did he look like you thought he would?"

"Yes, but I didn't think he'd be that impressive."

"What do you mean?"

"I never imagined he'd be such a courtly, dignified old man."

From time to time we would stray back and join the others. At one point when the two of us were alone, I said to him, "I consider Baroja the greatest Spanish writer since Cervantes, because Galdós . . ."

"Galdós smelt slightly of piss, like an old man confined to his wheelchair, even when he was very young. . . . But he was quite a guy nonetheless. But the most screwed-up Spanish writer I know of was Blasco Ibáñez. I've always thought he chose altogether the wrong career; he should have gotten a great circus together and gone on a world tour with it. He would have raked in piles of money and earned just as great a name for himself."

"What about Azorín?"

"Azorín always impressed me as being stuffed with sawdust."

"And Valle Inclán?"

"His writing was like good bagpipe music—it sounds gay at first but then it gradually begins to sound sadder and sadder. It's as though it gave him more pleasure to write of cruelty than of beauty. And the worst part is that from time to time he used it as a sedative."

"Used what as a sedative?"

"That sort of piously melancholy, deceptively simple bagpipe music. He resembled Don Pío in that respect."

I was dumfounded, and wondered what he was going to say next.

"Goya should have founded a college in this country to wean writers away from that sort of drug . . ."

I wanted to distract his mind from his gloomy thoughts, and more to cheer him up than to satisfy my curiosity, I turned to him and asked, "Where exactly was the bridge you described in *For Whom the Bell Tolls?*"

"We'll have to see the spot some day," he answered. "And some other day we'll also have to take a trip to Guadalajara."

Sitting there next to the windows of that pastry shop where I had so many times bought tarts and perhaps a bottle of sweet wine for Don Pío, little treats that he stole bites of, like a child, during my visits, often leaving crumbs on his mustache and beard, the place seemed like a sort of quiet aquarium. If a tiny fish had been swimming around and around in there, it might well have taken itself for a denizen of the deep.

I paid the waitress and left. Once outside on the street, I looked up at the balconies on the fourth floor of the building opposite. Baroja's apartment was still shut up tight, and there was a very gloomy air about the whole place. Don Pío's nephew Julio might be almost anywhere, at Oxford or in the Sahara, at Vera or in India, searching for stones, bones, tools, bits of pottery. His other nephew, Pío, a very nice person, was doubtless kicking around Europe or America with his professional movie camera over his shoulder.

9

I walked on down the street toward the Hotel Ritz and hailed a taxi. I told the cabbie to take me to the El Lago swimming pool, but as we passed the Prado, I changed my mind and said to him, "Will you let me off here please?"

"Do you want me to wait for you?"

"No, I'll pay you what I owe you and you can go on."

He took my money, looking daggers at me because it had been such a short haul.

I hadn't planned on this at all, but there I was outside the Prado Museum. The esplanade and the stairways were crawling with the usual picturesque throng of tourists, and there was a long line of them waiting to get in. Ernesto had often given the crowd lying in wait for him in the lobby of the Hotel Suecia the slip and taken refuge among the horde of tourists waiting to get into the Prado. We often used to sneak out through the back entrance of the hotel, and he would say, "I really enjoy these early-morning visits to the Prado—but please don't let the news get around."

"Don't worry—your secret's safe."

He would halt in front of the museum, and his description of it written so many years before would suddenly seem as fresh and perceptive as ever:

> The Prado, looking like some big American college building, with sprinklers watering the grass early in the bright Madrid summer morning.

These words seemed as true now as then, and as I stood there in front of the stone balustrade, I could almost see him there among the crowd of tourists. And as I remembered more of this passage I was so fond of, I found it as striking as always:

> If it [Madrid] had nothing else than the Prado it would be worth spending a month in every spring, if you have money to spend a month in any European capital.

That was what Ernesto had done, whenever he possibly could. Had anyone really realized how hard it had been to get him to leave Madrid the last time he had been here? Davis and Hotchner had had an epic struggle on their hands getting him aboard the plane for the States. He had canceled his reservation any number of times, making the wildest sort of excuses for staying on. He simply would not—or could not—leave Madrid. He had been like a bull stubbornly standing his ground in his *querencia*, as though he had had a premonition of what was in store for him.

He had so resisted returning to America that it was almost as though he felt he was being sent off to prison or into exile; he loved Spain so much that it was like being uprooted from his real homeland. Apparently even the prospect of being with Mary again was not enough to make him want to board the plane. I remembered now the rest of that passage of Ernesto's that had suddenly popped into my mind.

> But when you can have the Prado in the bullfight season at the same time with El Escorial not two hours to the north and Toledo to the south, a fine road to Avila and a fine road to Segovia, which is no distance from La Granja, it makes you feel very badly, all question of immortality aside, to know that you will have to die and never see it again.

I lingered about there at the entrance to the Prado, trying to decide whether I should go in. Why not? I really ought to. I would wander about the galleries as though Ernesto were there at my side, breathing in deeply, as though trying to absorb everything to be seen in every last gallery.

I went over and stood in line for a ticket, and we went in—and I say *we* even though all those boorish Americans wouldn't have had the least idea what I meant if I had told them that Ernest Hemingway was there at my side.

Ernesto had hit the nail right on the head. I wondered what in the world these tourists had expected to find there in the Prado.

> The colors have kept so wonderfully in the dry mountain air and the pictures are so simply hung and easy to see that the tourist feels cheated. . . .

It was quite true. The tourists had no idea what they were looking for. As Ernesto had put it:

I have watched them being puzzled. These cannot be great pictures, the colors are too fresh and they are too simple to see.

I had only to let myself float on the tide of my memories: the day, for instance, that Ernesto and one of the guards had bantered back and forth:

"Please keep in line, all of you," the guard said. "You'll all get your chance."

"But what if someone steals the painting I want before I can make off with it?"

"We'll get right to work and paint another one for you."

"As good as the one I want?"

"As good or better."

"I rather doubt that."

And then Ernesto turned to me and said with a laugh, "It's marvelous. There's no place in the world anything like this."

Whenever we visited the Prado together, we always headed straight for the galleries with the Goyas. Ernesto couldn't wait to return to one of the prime sources of his own violent metaphysics, of his own passion for life: Goya's battle scenes, his dramatic sketches of action in the bullring, his fiercely satirical drawings of court life peopled with grotesque princes, his mystical frenzies, his pathetic orgies. . . . As Ernesto strode along that wooden floor and stood enraptured before one canvas after another, he was as beside himself with joy as on those afternoons when he sat in a front-row seat watching top-flight matadors in action. Here in the Prado, too, he couldn't have been happier, though it was a different sort of happiness.

Sometimes he would stand for some time looking intently at a Velázquez, because a canvas by that master was the entrance to a world that later, in Goya's paintings, would become a question that sent shivers up your spine, often an unanswerable question that created a great metaphysical emptiness, a total numbing of the senses.

"Velázquez believed in painting in costume, in dogs, in dwarfs, and in painting again," he had written in *Death in the Afternoon*.

To Ernesto, Velázquez's paintings were the gateway to a whole style of life.

"What sort of person do you think he was?" I once asked him.

"I think he was very masculine, but also a bit too eager to please."

And if we lingered before an El Greco, he would say much the same thing: "I'm still convinced El Greco was something of a pansy, though I'm sure he was also a visionary who lived in a world all his own. That's why his paintings are terribly disconcerting."

I saw little reason to dispute that.

Then we would suddenly come upon Goya, Ernesto's "*señor padre*," as he used to call him, and at that point he was unable to conceal his emotion. He would stand there very quietly, as though intoxicated by this world of Goya's, this Spanish world so close to his heart.

There was a very strange resemblance between Goya the painter and Hemingway the writer. Both were at once fanatics and agnostics, capable of killing others or allowing themselves to be killed for an idea; men who made anarchism their ideal, who made the pleasures of the senses a toast to life tinged with sadness, and death an exciting reality; two hearts who between the first bright light of dawn and the waning light of evening burned themselves out in furious fits of frenzy or passion, like moths consumed by a flame or blind nightingales whose hearts burst in a last great outpouring of song. . . .

Ernesto found Goya invincible, or at any rate a tireless warrior who had fought to his last breath. He clenched his fists, and I remembered what he had written in *Death in the Afternoon* about this painter who so resembled him:

> Goya did not believe in costume but he did believe in blacks
> and in grays, in dust and in light, in high places rising from
> plains, in the country around Madrid, in movement, in his own
> cojones, in painting, in etching. . . .

Row upon row of Goyas lined these walls. At first sight these many works seem hastily improvised, set down on the canvas on the spur of the moment, but as one looks more closely, one realizes that these great paintings required a great deal of thought, an over-all vision, a perfect harmonizing of fiery emotion and cool reflection.

Ernesto had learned from Goya to be obstinate, relentless, beautifully precise, to search endlessly for exactly the right touch, to use shockingly vivid patches of color, to capture reality so forcefully that it sent a shiver up one's spine. Ernesto had learned from Goya a style of draftsmanship that was at once disconcertingly bare and spare and simple and extremely subtle and complex. Goya's style strikes one at first as being very facile and disjointed and dazzlingly spontaneous and at the same time quite monotonously sardonic, when in reality each and every one of his works, from the smallest sketch to the largest canvas, is the product of much reflection, much patience, much careful planning. Goya lived life with white-hot intensity, and his paintings are the ashes that were left. The journey that took him from the pale blues and rosy pinks of his early paintings to the somber grays and blacks of his late works was a journey that cost him many tears, many days of bitter loneliness, though I suspect that on reaching the end of this road he did his share of carousing to celebrate, possessed to the very last of that biting, wicked sense of humor that so often is a form of innocence, the spark that burned brightly to the very end of that amazing career of his, which had taken him from simple poetry to philosophical parable, from picturesque touches of local color to vast sweeping frescoes, from little popular sketches to epic masterpieces.

"This is painting that cauterizes and cures, José Luis. It's painting that's a health cure for those who don't want to live with poison in their veins, for those who don't want to die amid the rosy colors of what goes by the name of a happy life," Ernesto said.

"I understand perfectly," I replied.

Of course I understood! It was not simply a theory; it was a philosophy he had lived all his life. As he had written in *Death in the Afternoon*:

[Goya believed] in what he had seen, felt, touched, handled, smelled, enjoyed, drunk, mounted, suffered, spewed-up, lain-with, suspected, observed, loved, hated, lusted, feared, detested, admired, loathed, and destroyed. Naturally no painter has been able to paint all that but he tried.

The hours were ticking by, but this was the one place where Ernesto was never in a hurry. He would move along from one canvas to another very slowly, devouring every detail, making each of them his very own flesh and blood, so to speak, and when we left, he would always start talking a mile a minute, scribbling down notes or telling me what he was going to write—a furious outpouring, inspired by an ideal that compensated for all his inner ambivalences.

Goya's works were a perfect fusion of life and art. One ought to be able to write as Goya had painted: cartoons, engravings, canvases, and even tapestries capturing immediate realities, mingling the crudest experiences and the most lofty dreams; one ought to be able to learn from Goya the secret of that mysterious lyricism capable not only of ennobling the most debauched individuals but of dignifying the most vulgar speech by using it to discuss the most transcendent truths; what on first sight might seem to be a rhetoric of drunkards would become a sort of transparent vision of manly angels struggling for perfect purity of soul. Goya's paintings were like bullrings where men confronted death with great pride and great grace, and in them this great painter had approached the very threshold of eternity. . . .

This had been Ernesto's impression of Goya from the very first. The great Spanish artist had painted as his mind and heart dictated, just as Ernesto wrote as he lived, creating out of his very own flesh, his own life, an art and a style.

Even more than at the bullrings, it was when Ernesto stood rooted to the spot, gazing intently at a Goya, that he seemed most one of us. In war and in peace, Ernesto had come to be a living part of the Spanish people, and I am convinced that from the very first it had been Goya who had been the strongest link in this unbreakable chain binding Ernesto to Spain and its people. Both in his life and in his work, Hemingway had taken as his model this rough, pagan Aragonese peasant who had become supercivilized in the sophisticated atmosphere of Madrid. Ernesto was eager to write as Goya had painted, and therefore he based his style primarily on visual impressions, on a language that becomes a vision of the world, that fuses the passing event of the moment and the fundamental pulse of life, history and myth, carnival and ecstasy, a canvas painted in the most vibrant, slashing brush strokes, but at the same time a canvas capable of communicating a profound sense of peace. And how many times Ernesto had said: "If only I could stay here forever."

Ernesto would also sometimes go have a look at Goya's serene religious paintings; but it was obvious that what he was most addicted to, as though they were a drug, were those canvases blocked out in great furious brush strokes, so much like those shocking, dissonant, crude words in Ernesto's books, words so powerful that they sometimes numbed one's senses.

Muttering indignantly, Ernesto would allow the hordes of tourists to elbow their way past him, and slowly go on from one canvas to another in this great collection of paintings depicting everything from bloodless court scenes peopled with pale infantas and kings to bloody massacres by an enraged rabble.

We were about to leave when suddenly he went back for a last look at the war paintings.

What a divinely diabolical thing war is, with its blaring bugles and its tolling bells, its gallantry and its devastation, its lusty vitality and its abominations, its passions and its resignation, sex and hunger, strong wine and bloodshed, an inspiration and a punishment, the warm embrace and the chill kiss of death!

"Paintings like this are rather convincing proof that it's better to hunt animals than to let other men hunt you," he remarked.

But to Ernesto, war was something more than a bloody spectacle. It was refusing to wear mourning as convention dictated, laughing and singing when by all rights you should be reverently silent; it was a force of will as sharply honed as a blade of steel, the delirious fear of oneself become a death-defying bravery.

And Goya was the burning flame, the sublime example that turns human carnage into a school that teaches a man honor. Palaces, gallows, masquerades, brothels, tribunals, visions and nightmares, hideous plagues, eerie secret meetings, confessionals, plaster saints touted as models of piety, inspired buffoonery—all these things were as nothing compared to the blood of heroes. And thus, since war was not only a great gaping horn wound, a bull as relentless as an inquisitor, a bullring with a frenzed crowd of spectators, along with the *toros* and the *toreros*, Goya had depicted the more salutary arena of revolution, the hand-to-hand combat in which individual cowardice and terror are miraculously transformed into a collective epic and perhaps a personal victory over one's own weaknesses.

To Ernesto, Madrid without Goya would have been an unfinished ode, a desert island.

I once asked him, "Have you ever come to Madrid without visiting the Prado?"

"Never, except during the Spanish Civil War, because in those days you didn't go to the Museum to see Goya—you went out on the streets."

He even had a copy of a Goya* in Havana, hanging there on the wall of his *finca* presiding over his entire life: hunting expeditions, fishing trips, wars, bullfights. . . . That canvas was the symbol of the genius that had transformed Ernesto's own art. By comparison with a Goya, a Picasso or a Miró was mere dust, mere lines and colors that meant nothing.

Ernesto heaved a deep sigh and continued on down the gallery, still not ready to leave.

He stood in silent meditation before each of these Goyas—all of them different and yet all the same—not merely to study yet again a concrete style that had greatly influenced his own but also to allow himself to be overcome by the spell that Goya never failed to cast over him.

Hearing Ernesto's heavy footfalls on the wooden floor—despite his every effort to tiptoe about as quietly as possible—I was reminded of passages of his works I could never forget, phrases that were like flashes of lightning in the darkness. I suddenly remembered a paragraph, for instance, in "The Natural History of the Dead":

> He looked at the man twice; once in daylight, once with a
> flashlight. That too would have made a good etching for Goya,
> the visit with the flashlight, I mean.

And the unforgettable impact of the war on him, or rather the irreparable wound he had suffered in that massacre, the stretchers strewn about everywhere and the stinking little hospital rooms, were an

---

* I readily admit that I had always believed that this painting was an original Goya, and even described it as such in a piece I wrote, and Ernesto never bothered to inform me otherwise. It was Mary who told me after Ernesto's death that it was only a copy, albeit an excellent one.

experience that later seemed to him to have borne Goya's own special imprint, for the Spanish painter's works were the only breath-takingly convincing things he had seen after he had begun trying to decant this bloody reality he had lived through.

He was to say many times in his books: "It was a scene that would have inspired Goya."

This sort of phrase usually occurred in the midst of a scene that was apparently cruel, bloody, and gruesome, though beneath the surface there were always pathetic, tender undertones. Ernesto had first learned from Goya secrets of the flesh, and then secrets of the spirit.

We had now halted before one of Goya's paintings of Christ. I watched Ernesto intently. He ran his hand across his mouth and his forehead and scratched his beard.

Ernesto yearned to be a true believer. Or rather, he was a sincere Christian, but had never found a way to formally bear witness to his faith. Generally speaking, sincere religious beliefs should find expression in certain specific forms of worship, certain clear-cut patterns of behavior, but just as Ernesto refused to bow to the usual social conventions and was to remain a wayward rebel all his life, so he refused to participate in conventional religious rites. But the look in his eyes was very revealing, as were his quiet words, the hesitant words of a believer trapped in a spiritual desert. Could it possibly have been otherwise?

"You have to visit the Prado at the same time of day that you meet with God or your mistress; either very early in the morning or just as night is falling," he said with a deep sigh, taking off the pair of glasses that made him look like a learned professor.

We walked on, contemplating one Goya after another in that vast collection that was such a startling mixture of religion and paganism, mysticism and sensuality, tyranny and anarchy.

It has always seemed highly significant to me that Ernesto had prefaced his first novel with a Spanish background, *The Sun Also Rises*, with a passage from Ecclesiastes. And what a passage it was! One that summed up all of Spanish philosophy: its profound stoicism and its disenchantment with the things of this world; its essential pessimism and its faith in the consolation of religion—a sort of giant water wheel or hourglass or carved catafalque that illustrates the rise and fall of our history, as the inexorable rising and setting of the sun in the end cancels out all the differences between the joy and the despair of living, between the fear and the hope of dying. These verses attempting to cast a ray of hope in men's hearts in the face of the grim swatch cut by the sickle of the Great Reaper (which Ernesto used as the epigraph of his novel) always leave me with the impression that he did not learn them in Sunday school or hear them recited in his home or come across them as he idly leafed through the Bible; it seems, rather, as though he first heard them on the lips of one of those rough-spoken, sad-eyed, sardonic Spaniards that one still meets these days in our country's trains and in little inns; men who use the crudest language, betraying both the cruelest sort of skepticism and incredible resignation. I am inclined to think that these Old Testament verses are a sort of summary of Ernesto's philosophy, and find it really striking that a writer of the so-called "lost generation" should regard them as a sort of promise of salvation for his art.† The text from Ecclesiastes that Ernesto used as an epigraph for *The Sun Also Rises* reads:

> One generation passeth away, and another generation cometh; but the earth abideth forever. . . . The sun also ariseth, and the sun goeth down, and hasteth to the place where he arose. . . . The wind goeth toward the south, and turneth about unto the north; it whirleth about continually, and the wind returneth again according to his circuits. . . . All the rivers run into the sea; yet the sea is not full; unto the place from whence the rivers come, thither they return again.

Even though Ernesto was referring to the biblical notion of the fleetingness of life, when he quotes these verses about the generations that come and go, we must also remember that when Ernesto first visited Spain there was much talk in literary circles of "generations," especially the so-called Spanish "generation of '98." This epigraph did not appear in Spanish editions of *The Sun Also Rises*, for apparently his Spanish publisher took what was an inborn, classic pessimism in Hemingway for a vague attempt on his part to give his novel a picturesque Spanish flavor. But this epigraph should not have been omitted, for as Hemingway knew, these verses from Ecclesiastes have been a constant source of inspiration for Spanish literature, and always will be, for in them we find reflected the essential Spanish world view: a scorn for the things of this world, a profound awareness of the ravages of time and the eternal mutability of all earthly life, the painful yearning for the eternal, an unshakable faith in the divine—an aspiration, a compensation, and a drama running like an unbroken thread through all our literature from Jorge Manrique to Antonio Machado, by way of Cervantes.

Goya not only moved Ernesto to the very depths of his soul; this great Spanish artist also set Ernesto's mind to whirling madly, like the

† What is more, I later found out that Father Waldman, a Catholic priest, quoted these very words as a prayer for the eternal rest of the worn-out body and the tormented soul of Ernest Hemingway, the globe-trotter and seeker of salvation.

sails of a windmill in a great gale. To Ernesto, Goya's painting was a sort of strange magic caldron, in which blasphemy was intimately blended with veneration. In Goya's canvases saints and highwaymen, angels and witches mingled together; the ephemeral glory of kings and infantas existed side by side with the frenzy of the rabble; and great multitudes of people proved to be heroes and saints, but died the deaths of unsung martyrs.

As I watched Ernesto gazing at these Goyas, I could understand why the Spanish painter was his muse, and why the dramatic clash of the barbarous and the festive, the blustering and the tenderly affectionate, the human and the exotic that he had first become aware of during his earliest visits to Spain, around the year 1922, had eventually proved so fertile. We will not have a true picture of Hemingway's work if we fail to take into account how important a part Spain and Spanish themes played in his life and his writing, and by that I mean not only Spanish places but Spanish people, not only stories of Spain but meditations on Spaniards' moral and aesthetic values.

I became a little tired of standing there watching Ernesto contemplating all these canvases, and waited impatiently for him to decide we had been there long enough. He was ready to leave, finally, and we walked down the stairs and out the door. In front of the Prado is a blackish-green statue of Goya, which makes the great painter look as though he had passed through the fire and brimstone of hell. Fortunately it was a cool, brisk morning, so the sober frown on the deaf genius's face seemed less gloomy than usual. Redeemed by the truth of his paintings, his fingertips appeared to be touched with fire, and I was sure I could also see bright sparks of love in his fierce eyes and the trace of a loving smile in the corners of his tightly pursed lips.

Many people recognized Ernesto, but looking neither right nor left, he walked over to the statue, took his cap off, and bade Don Paco good-by:

"So long, Maestro. I'll be back to see you again soon."

We walked down the street. As I recall, that was when he said to me, "Why are you shouting at me like that?"

"I didn't realize I was shouting," I replied.

"Mary complains that you talk very fast, but my complaint is that you talk very loudly."

"I'll try to talk more slowly, then."

"No, more softly; I'm not deaf, you know."

He was always very polite to ordinary Spaniards who approached him. Sometimes taxi drivers and even flower vendors would stop him on the street to have a few words with him. He liked talking with them, though he was always a little edgy and quite reserved. I suddenly remembered what he had written in "The Capital of the World":

. . . decorum and dignity rank above courage as the virtues most highly prized in Spain. . . .

It always unnerved him when admiring crowds surrounded him. We often used to stroll through the great iron gates of the Retiro and walk about inside, and I never dared tell him that he had confused the Retiro and the Botanical Gardens in *For Whom the Bell Tolls*. He would often walk along for minutes at a time, not saying a single word. Mary, who spent a lot of her time "doing a bit of shopping" in Madrid, would usually join us later and immediately begin questioning Ernesto to see what sort of a mood he was in and what the rest of the day was going to be like. His eyes would still have a dazed look in them after seeing so many incomprehensible things, and in order to get himself out of his mood of awed bewilderment he would immediately head for a bar, his one way of forgetting both his defeats and his triumphs.

We would sit in some bar drinking, neither of us saying a word. Life is exciting but also a great destroyer. It is beautiful, but it is also cruel if one lives every moment of it as intensely as possible. Art is a source of enormous satisfaction, but also a source of bitter disappointment. Man is the victim of this duel he cannot resist fighting. And even if he is the victor, in the end all that remains is the acrid taste of his own destruction. But what if you start from absolute zero, what if you have refused to believe in any sort of illusion from the very beginning? Then life, art, love can help a little. There was another phrase in "The Capital of the World" that had always impressed me, and as I stood there by myself beneath the statue of Goya, without Ernesto's great bulk towering over me, without his big paw on my shoulder, I was even more struck by the childlike, biblical words he had written in that story:

He died, as the Spanish phrase has it, full of illusions.

Full of illusions? Ernesto had destroyed all his illusions, or perhaps they had destroyed him, one by one, a whole great heap of frustrated illusions, most of them typically Spanish.

I walked on down the street, and on reaching the National Lottery Building, I hailed a taxi and told the driver to take me to the Norte Station.

It was just past 10 A.M. when I walked through the door of the Norte Station. Many years before, Ernesto had written, in *The Sun Also Rises:*

The Norte Station in Madrid is the end of the line. All trains finish there. They don't go on anywhere.

That sentence had always struck me as very funny. If the trains went straight on to Estremadura or to Levante, for instance, they would have to go along the Cuesta de San Vicente, the Plaza de España, the Gran Vía, the Puerta del Sol, and then Cibeles or Atocha. Had the Spanish leader Indalecio Prieto's plans for what everyone called "that insane tunnel" ever been carried out, they would have crossed the city underground.

Seriously probing the wound that Spain had inflicted on Ernesto had now become a sort of obsession with me, an adventure I could no longer postpone. With his hunters' infallible sense of smell and his keen nose of a pursued animal that sniffs the wind and knows exactly what and whom to expect, how was it possible that Ernesto had fallen into the trap of his own imagination and his own mental processes?

I bought a round-trip ticket to the Escorial. The only baggage I took with me was my copy of *For Whom the Bell Tolls*, because I was returning to the very source of Ernesto's most unforgettable memories, to the war, leaving behind all his other works. It was as though all his other writings, even *The Sun Also Rises* and *Death in the Afternoon*, were explorations of a past that was now forever dead, whereas his Civil War novel was his only enduring message to posterity, because it is one of the very few books he has left us that show with blinding clarity how sensitive he was to human pain and suffering. In other works, from his very first pieces for the Kansas City *Star* to that marvelously energetic novella *The Old Man and the Sea*, we would discover the hand of a great writer, a prose unlike anyone else's, an absolute mastery of the nuances of language, a simple but powerful style. But what enduring values were there in a work such as *To Have and Have Not*? What was there that was worthwhile in *Across the River and into the Trees*, outside of a few glimpses of Ernesto himself? I didn't quite know why, but ever since I had heard the news of his death, I had felt a greater attachment than ever to *For Whom the Bell Tolls*, that passionate novel documenting the Spanish scene, in which the adventures of the hero are not only an overwhelming self-confession on the part of the author but a monumental indictment of injustice, deceit, falsehood, futility, tyranny, disloyalty—every aspect of a civil war that is an unpardonable vice. What a school for learning courage, and what a smithy of the soul!

The Escorial brought back many memories of Ernesto. He had been staying there at the time of his visit to Don Pío, in 1956, and we had returned there after seeing Baroja to his grave. It was also where Ernesto had unexpectedly extended to me an invitation to visit the United States, after phoning the American Embassy. And most importantly of all, it was where we had taken long walks together in the pine groves on cold, snowy days, in the course of which I had learned a great deal more about Ernesto than what I had already discovered in his works.

"What do you mean when you say that the process of literary creation is based on the iceberg principle?" I had once asked him during one of our strolls.

"I've explained it a number of times: only one seventh of what you're saying should show above the water."

"In other words, you leave the most important part concealed below the surface . . ."

"That's right. The part that is clearly visible must be very intense and ring absolutely true, but it must not give the reader the feeling that it has been laboriously polished and repolished. The underpinnings that give a work solidity and strength must be hidden beneath the surface."

"Which of your works meant the most to you, and which of them was the hardest to write?" I asked him.

"*For Whom the Bell Tolls*, I think. I was trying in that novel to communicate something more than the momentary anguish of a dramatic encounter with life. I wrote it quite quickly, but at the same time I spent countless hours going over it afterward. It wasn't meant to be an entertaining popular novel, but a personal testimony. After it came out, a lot of critics wrote that I was obviously washed up. They'd said the same thing when "The Snows of Kilimanjaro" was first published, because the writer in it is dying and everything that meets his eye, including the woman he loves, gives him the feeling that he's been forsaken and abandoned. So the critics all leaped to the conclusion that almost all of it was autobiographical and applied word for word to me."

"Does it upset you very much when people say you're a character out of a novel rather than a novelist?"

"It doesn't upset me one bit, and I care even less about what the academic scholars and critics say about me—they're great ones for sucking the juice out of everything, all in very fancy prose, of course. The things they've said about Jake Barnes in *The Sun Also Rises*! That he betrays the streak of puritanism in me that makes me want to castrate myself! But there's a key to all this sort of criticism that's infallible: people who are stupid idiots always talk about complexes, whereas people who have something inside here see symbols," he said, pointing to his head. "But why bother talking about all that nonsense?"

"You don't ever want to look back, is that it?"

"I don't want to be turned into a pillar of salt. I've still got quite a few years ahead of me before I'm washed up."

A fair number of people were coming back from the mountains. Despite the fact that it was still very early in the morning and a weekday, the atmosphere in all the train stations along the way was quite festive and relaxed, almost as though it were a Sunday.

I was still unwilling to give up the idea that *For Whom the Bell Tolls* was Hemingway's best book, or at least his best book with a Spanish locale. He had written very humbly:

You learn in this war if you listen. You most certainly did.

And he had added with great pride:

He never felt like a foreigner in Spanish [sic] and they did not really treat him like a foreigner most of the time.

I would have to search for this Ernesto, at once a stranger to me and an intimate friend. And I would have to look for him in that landscape of stunted pine trees, naked rocks, little brooks that were mere trickles of water but nonetheless had a most melodious murmur. Today this landscape looked as peaceful and picturesque as a postcard, but Ernesto had seen it when it was completely torn to pieces, pitted with shell holes and crisscrossed with trenches, devastated by machine-gun fire, disfigured by parapets and fortifications. In later years he had loved strolling about in this mountain setting, surveying the entire scene, as though he were reconstructing his own past. But at the same time, far from making him feel tranquil and serene, his visits to this onetime battlefield that now resembled a print of some idyllic Arcadia had awakened all sorts of ambivalent memories within him—memories of the bravery and the disillusionment, of the soaring ideals and the crushing defeat, of the rightness and the failure of a cause that had been the very fabric of his life in Madrid during the Civil War. As we walked about the countryside or drove along the highway from Madrid to the Escorial, I had never once heard Ernesto give voice to any sort of hatred. Often, however, he made comments that betrayed his feelings of puzzlement and bewilderment. Returning to this scene seemed to plunge him into the same mood as after the defeat of the Loyalists. Robert Jordan asks himself at one point:

What were his politics then? He had none now, he told himself.

But being his usual wary, wily self, like Ernesto himself, Jordan immediately adds:

But do not tell any one else that, he thought. Don't ever admit that.

Are these the words of an author who had compromised himself or those of an author who is uncompromising? I believe them to be the expression of the true writer's sort of compromise: forthrightly condemning hypocrisy on the one hand, and chanting a hymn of praise to the ideal on the other, following the example of the great masters who have fought a hand-to-hand battle with life. The ideal and ideology are two quite different things. But Ernesto's communion with the ideal in no way detracts from the value of his personal testimony, recorded in his own magnificent, inimitable fashion. He describes abuses and scenes of sheer horror during the Civil War that he himself had not actually witnessed, but at the same time he gives the most rigorously accurate account of the slaughter in the war zones he visited as a correspondent. Could he possibly have been more honest? What there is in this work is grandeur—a grandeur of the mind, the spirit, and the heart. Ernesto succeeded in placing himself above any and every sort of narrow ideology, for his goal was to record history itself in the making.

This part of Spain was the region Ernesto liked best of all: lofty pines or stunted ones, both an image of man; hills that had been at once strategic targets and beloved vistas, with stones that could be used for many things: official monuments, façades for urban buildings, hiding-places and shelters for spies, or for lovemaking in the few remaining moments of a person's life—an ideal site for a battle long dreamed of but destined to end in crushing defeat. Doubtless Ernesto's ultimate goal had not been simply to report on this or that battle of the Civil War; the task he had really set himself was to study how a collective heroic will is forged, how an entire people, including outlaws and cowards, wage their fight for justice and truth.

The train was delayed at Villalba. I got off, had a glass of *cazalla*, the strong anisette railway workers drink out of an unlabeled bottle, bought a newspaper, and climbed back on the train. The obituary of Ernesto in this paper was in the same vein as all the others, and again most of it was devoted to *For Whom the Bell Tolls:*

> The man's book was deliberately biased in favor of Red Spain. . . . The few sketchily portrayed Nationalist characters in the book are all made out to be villains, and at the same time he did his utmost to justify and to ennoble those Spaniards whose cause he espoused.

But in a paragraph farther on, the author of this obituary had also been obliged to add, in all fairness:

> However, this scene is described so vividly and so truthfully that not even those writers who were the most fervent supporters of the Nationalists have ever written as compelling an episode.

The scene referred to was, of course, the *corrida* in the village square of the little mountain town. César González Puano, the author of this obituary, had written:

> There is one chapter, which takes place in a small village, that is the most breathtakingly outspoken accusation possible of that particular moment and that particular political régime.

And yet he had pontifically concluded this obituary of Ernesto with the words:

He only half understood us.

But how else could Ernesto have understood us, since we Spaniards only half live, think, and love? I grant that Ernesto may only have half understood us Spaniards, but he understood us far better than we understood him.

Ernesto's critics were not so much buzzards (an image that was now fading in my mind) as a pack of stray dogs, jealous of another writer's fame and glory, pitiless, cruel, scornful detractors of their better. I threw the newspaper out the train window in disgust, and this slanderous obituary, full of pious pronouncements like all the others, fluttered down onto the tracks:

> In all truth, Don Ernesto never really understood Spain. Our Spanish world is not at all what he took it to be. . . . He heard bells ringing somewhere, but never knew quite where. . . .

Such pieces had of course been written more or less in good faith, as a tribute to something or someone, and most of them were simply penny-a-line free-lance articles. But what colossal nerve it takes to dismiss universally recognized geniuses in a few words, with one sweep of an ordinary household broom! The howitzers and the mortars were long gone from Spain now, and the great majority of the prisoners and those who had not died on some battlefield or other had returned to everyday life believing that their experiences in the front lines had been a glorious dream, and their lives in concentration camps or prisons a cruel nightmare. And the leaders had been the most self-deluded clowns of all.

Everything was different now, however. Life had gone on, and Spaniards were complacently enjoying themselves and prospering. The bullet holes in the little houses in the mountains had all been plastered over, and today all these dwellings once again looked very comfortable, if not downright attractive.

Every war he had had a part in had been yet another wedding ceremony for Ernesto, but the war in Spain had been like the discovery of true love. His youthful innocence around the year 1938 had been truly touching:

> Don't ever kid yourself about loving some one. It is just that most people are not lucky enough ever to have it. You never had it before and now you have it. What you have with Maria, whether it lasts just through today and a part of tomorrow, or whether it lasts for a long life is the most important thing that can happen to a human being. There will always be people who say it does not exist because they cannot have it. But I tell you it is true and that you have it and that you are lucky even if you die tomorrow.

And that was why he had built his love nest here in this ideal site out of the wispiest of conjectures and surmises and presuppositions. On the eve of battle his love affair with Spain had been a romantic attachment, and after the war it had been a peaceful tryst.

There was María, his most famous Spanish heroine: a rather conventionally drawn figure, the daughter of Loyalists murdered by a firing squad and subsequently raped, who nonetheless prays to "the sweet Blessed Virgin" in moments of great danger, like any other simple country girl.

Ernesto had returned to this very spot with Mary, his fourth wife, and I remember very well his saying to her as he once again trod these paths that now only goats and mules used: "Mary, you can't imagine the things that happened here!" He was so eager to relive the past, to relive his romantic dreams with the woman who was now his one true love, that everything he had written now seemed the gospel truth, including those parts of his novel that had been pure figments of his imagination.

He felt so close to an old woman like Pilar, the guiding light of an improbable band of guerrillas that included both Castilian peasants and wandering gypsies, that he has her cuttingly remark to her husband, a supplier of horses for the bullring, a coward, and a criminal: "Mother of God . . . Even here one man can make a bureaucracy with his mouth." And at another point she says to him, even more bitingly, "We are in possession of thy opinion." And with even more shocking directness: "And today there is not enough of you left to make a sick kitten. Yet you are happy in your soddenness."

Pilar says all this to the man once her lover and now the head of a band of guerrillas, though it is most unlikely that a vulgar ruffian such as Pablo would ever be a leader of anything in a small village in Castile.‡

‡ Arturo Barea's comments along similar lines, which reached me after writing the above, serve to confirm the impression I had had since first reading *For Whom the Bell Tolls*: the character Pablo simply does not ring true.

The novel takes place within a setting of early-morning fogs, bright sunlight, melting snow, with planes flying over the mountaintops and roaring down to drop their bombs, pink-cheeked enemy troops picking their way carefully and cautiously through pine groves and across clearings, the sound of water falling down the dam below the bridge. . . . Ernesto chose the mountain vastnesses of the *sierra* around Madrid as the background of this novel that was to be the repository of everything he knew about Spain and Spaniards, bulls and bullfighters, love and death, life and his few brief thoughts about life after death. His rare intimations of immortality did not amount to very much, but they nonetheless counted for something. . . .

Even at very high altitude the *sierra* around Madrid is warm, the air clear but stifling. Ernesto liked Madrid best in summer, but he loved Spain at any season of the year, both by day and by night. As he once said to me: "When you are intimately involved in something, you discover you are able to write less and less about it with each passing day. It's the same as with a mistress. What sort of youngster is it who writes the kind of letters that melt the hearts of the women who read them? Young men who are in love with themselves."

And Ernesto was in love with Spain.

From the time he first climbed the Cantabrian mountaintops when he was a young war veteran barely out of his teens to his last frenzied visit to Andalusia; from his earliest fishing trips along the Irati to his last whirlwind visits to La Mancha and La Alcarria; from his sojourns in later years in the Hotel Suecia in Madrid to his rediscovery of Valencia, everything he had said and written about Spain had been like a carefully composed, artfully crafted treatise on love. He had not come by his knowledge of Spain easily; he had earned it the hard way, violently wringing the last drop of truth from his experiences in our country, with a certain brutal directness and at the same time an immense sensitivity. The birds he found most beautiful at first were the storks perched in the bell towers of our towns; later he grew very fond of the dusty-winged partridges along our roadsides; and then, toward the end of his life, our proud falcons and intractable eagles became striking symbols to him.

When we took to the open road, heading for the countryside, his voice would become tinged with emotion, and an excited rush of words would come pouring out. Usually Ernesto did not say very much, but at times such as this his voice would ring out like a hunting horn opening the chase or a trumpet signaling for the door of the bull enclosure to be opened. When something touched him deeply, he would ordinarily try to contain his emotion, and would communicate his feelings in a very quiet, offhand, almost ingenuous way. This wary, understated manner of speaking was part of his personal moral code.

In his writings there are examples of this particular tone that the casual reader might never notice, yet they are like psychological manifestoes. This bit of dialogue from *The Dangerous Summer*, for instance:

"This town is dead," he said, "except on market days."

"How will the wine be this year?"

"It's too early to know anything," he told me. "You know as much as I do. It's always good and always the same. The vines grow like weeds."

"I like it very much."

"So do I," he said. "That's why I speak badly of it. You never speak badly of anything you don't like. Not now."

"Being here is going to do Mary lots of good. She's only just arrived and she's already a different person," he said to me.

"You seem to be in great shape yourself," I said.

"I'm unbeatable," he said, pounding his chest with his fists.

When you were with Ernesto, you had to be careful not to express your feelings too openly. He studiously avoided any sort of effusive or enthusiastic outpouring as he would the plague, and I had noticed more than once how disapproving and stern-faced he became when he was around someone who was plainly wearing his heart on his sleeve. "Sentimentality makes me a little sick to my stomach," he would say to me.

Times had changed a great deal, of course. My visits to the Escorial as a youngster had been quite different. I had always gone there with a whole bunch of my pals from school, and then after I had left school, with other groups of friends who were more inclined to kick over the traces, but even so, we had never felt as free and easy or behaved as rowdily as the youngsters I could see piling in and out of the trains going to and from the Escorial, emancipated young people who obviously did more or less as they pleased. I remember how shocked we were back in my day when on one of our weekend house parties at the Escorial we had come upon our hostess sleeping with a man in an antique bed that was a treasured family heirloom. . . . And I also remember that later I stole off with one of the girls to a little abandoned shepherds' hut. The others began calling to us, trying to find us, the girl's sister in particular—and it was perhaps a good thing that they had begun shouting our names just when they did, for at that very moment I was on the point of going all the way with the young lady right there on the ice-cold stone floor of the hut. But young people nowadays didn't have that sort of problem: the boys wandered all over with their guitars and the girls wore trousers; all of them had knapsacks on their backs full of bottles of wine and Coca-Cola and perhaps a flask or two of Chinchón as well, not to mention perfumed Japanese condoms and pills to keep from having a baby, whereas our friend of those days had had to marry the girl when he discovered he was about to become a father.

The first time we had come to this *sierra* together, wandering all over on foot or in Ernesto's car, I had warned him of the effect that our country would have on him. Spain to Ernesto was not only a taste he had acquired long before and a source of pleasure in more recent years. It was also a sort of guilt and pain that he would be obliged to purge himself of. The color of the sky, words exchanged along the roadside, people's attitudes, the silences of the countryside, the smell and most of all the taste of things Spanish were unbreakable ties binding him to our land and our people.

It had been in Spain, in fact, that he had first come really face to face with himself, and there was one thing about his death that would always remain a mystery: the fact that he had chosen to kill himself on the very day when all of Navarre had begun to sing the song whose echo would soon reach every corner of Spain, the song that Ernesto himself had sung so many, many times:

> Uno de enero,
> dos de febrero,
> tres de marzo,
> cuatro de abril,
> cinco de mayo,
> seis de junio,
> siete de julio:
> San Fermín.

> [The first of January,
> the second of February,
> the third of March,
> the fourth of April,
> the fifth of May,
> the sixth of June,
> the seventh of July:
> San Fermín.]

Therein lay the great mystery, or at least part of it. Why had he come to Spain so many times (though fewer times than he had wanted to or planned to), and why was 1961 the one year that he had failed to come to the San Fermín fiesta when he had promised his friends he would be there for certain?

I had *For Whom the Bell Tolls* in my hand, and I could have brought all the rest of Ernesto's books with me. But I could recall the passages

cano

32. In this picture, Hemingway is kneeling before the San Fermín religious procession through the streets of Pamplona. This rough man, who at times thought kneeling was a sign of weakness, was humble and sincere enough to do it on certain occasions. (CANO)

33. A quiet moment between Ernest Hemingway and the author at a bar on the Pamplona square—one of the many bars where Hemingway had taken refuge since his earliest visits to Spain. (CANO)

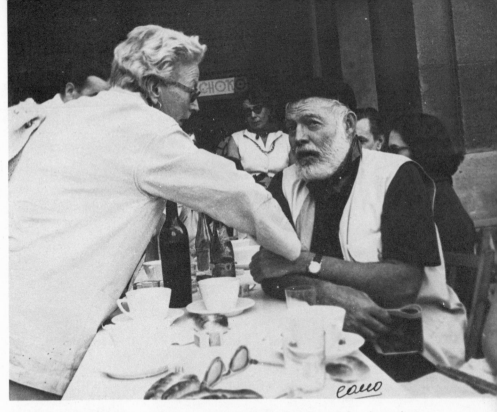

34. Hemingway and his wife Mary, with "Miss Valerie" at right. (CANO)

35. Hemingway and "Miss Valerie." (CANO)

36. Ernesto and a beautiful señorita, at Pamplona. (CANO)

37. Ernesto with Juanito Quintana—on the right—who put him in contact with many bullfighters in the 1920s. On the left is the photographer of bullfighters, Cano. (CANO)

38. Both Spaniards and foreigners would ask him for his autograph. Here he is in the Plaza del Castillo in Pamplona, patiently signing his name on a tourist's fan. (MASPONS, BARCELONA)

39. Hemingway in a reflective mood. (EDICIONES DESTINO)

40. Hemingway and Mary at a bullfight. (UNITED PRESS INTERNATIONAL)

41. Ernesto's widow, Mary, attends the unveiling of a monument erected to her husband's memory by the city of Pamplona. The city wished to express its gratitude for Hemingway's interest in the famous San Fermín fiestas. With Mary Hemingway are the mayor of Pamplona and his wife. (UNITED PRESS INTERNATIONAL)

about Spain in them just as well by simply lifting my eyes and gazing at the countryside through the train window or staring at the stippled floor of the compartment, for I knew almost all of them by heart. I could remember word for word, for instance, a passage in an early story of his, "Wine of Wyoming":

> We were through the town and out on the smooth road beyond, with the stubble of grain-fields on each side and the mountains off to the right. It looked like Spain, but it was Wyoming.

And when Jake Barnes, the hero of *The Sun Also Rises*, announces that he is planning a visit to Spain, he does so with such high hopes and such dreamy-eyed expectations that the passage seems like something straight out of Goya: "Won't it be splendid . . . Spain! We will have fun," Ernesto has Brett Ashley say.

Ernesto had said almost exactly the same thing in his last letter. He had not written those words in order to flatter us Spaniards who were his friends, but because he realized that a visit to Spain had become an absolute necessity to him if he was to go on living. It was in Spain, at the very beginning of his career as a serious writer, that he had first grown confident of his ability to describe the struggle for existence, a discovery that made such a deep impression on him that he never forgot it. During his visit to Spain in 1956, as the date of his departure drew closer and closer he became very irritable and withdrawn, and on occasion was very short-tempered even with Mary. And one day during one of our heart-to-heart talks, he said to me:

"This country is an inexhaustible mine, José Luis."

"That may well be true," I replied.

"You Spaniards have no idea what an inexhaustible mine it is."

"Oh, I'd say we have something of an idea."

"But there are times when I simply can't understand why such a rich vein should be clogged up with so much disgusting, worthless rubbish."

Very early in his life, Ernesto had discovered a powerful, deeply human symbolism in our Spanish rivers, our country inns, our mountains, our taverns, and he did not like the thought that it might all disappear some day. He had been a mere nobody when he had first arrived in our country, but at the same time he had been enormously sensitive and sharp-eyed, and everything he saw and heard and experienced and loved and suffered in Spain became a precious, unforgettable part of his life, "an inexhaustible mine," as he called it. In our arid, dry landscape, peopled with men and women whose faces delighted him because they looked as though they had been carved out of the very earth itself, as he often used to say, his somewhat fuzzy youthful dreams of becoming a writer were to take definite shape and become a firm vocation, and it was here in our country that he first discovered those powers of concentration that were to sustain him almost to the very end of his career.

Many of the youngsters in the corridor of the train were singing and clapping their hands and tapping out flamenco dances on the wooden floor. But not all of them. Some of them were kissing furiously.

Ernesto's first visit to Navarre, with its vineyards, its ancient stones, its picturesque villages, had made such a deep impression on him that in his very first novel he had his hero Jake Barnes say on arriving in Bayonne:

> We went out into the street again and took a look at the cathedral. Cohn made some remark about it being a very good example of something or other, I forget what. It seemed like a nice cathedral, nice and dim, like Spanish churches.

In other words, even before arriving in Spain Jake Barnes is anticipating what it will be like, contrasting the scene before him with the scene in his mind's eye. And that is also why he goes on to say:

> In the morning it was bright, and they were sprinkling the streets of the town, and we all had breakfast in a cafe. Bayonne is a nice town. It is like a very clean Spanish town and it is on a big river.

All this belonged to a world of long, long ago. But I did not need to go back that far to discover what the Spanish earth, these mountaintops in the *sierra*, the region he had made the setting of his heroic feat of imagination, of his fictional distortion of reality not so much for ideological as for sentimental reasons meant to Ernesto:

"What are people here in Spain saying about my visits to this country?" he had asked me.

"They aren't saying anything."

"You're my eyes and ears, and you've got to help me: if you should happen to hear anybody say that I've come here to turn over a new leaf and forget the past or that I've put my stamp of approval on something that's against my principles, you must tell me."

"I will—I promise."

"I'm sure you'd be the first to tell me. You know how I hate lies and injustice, and you know very well what my real reasons are for coming to Spain."

"You mustn't worry."

"I'm not worried, but I don't want anybody to think I've turned up here for political reasons, when my real reason is that I desperately needed to come back again and be with my Spanish friends."

"I understand perfectly."

"I want to forget the past, but I also wish Spaniards could let bygones be bygones. If anybody thinks I'm happy to see the U. S. Army setting up huge bases here in Spain, they're very much mistaken. But let's drop the whole subject, shall we? It makes me sick just talking about it."

Living at the Escorial was a sort of sedative for Ernesto. It was part of Madrid, and at the same time it was outside the city proper. He could visit the sites of long-ago battles round about whenever he liked, and withdraw to the peace and quiet of the Escorial whenever he pleased, like a patient taking a leisurely rest cure.

He looked upon these mountains as something that belonged to him personally, by right of conquest, even though he had been just another of the vanquished in our Civil War. Because this conquest had been a spiritual one, the word defeat did not apply to him.

"It's a shame that writers like you weren't in Madrid during the war," he said to me one day as we were climbing the Cuesta de las Perdices.

"The two of us lived the war years in very different parts of the country, but I can assure you that the war was just as terrible an experience for me as for you: I lost my entire family, and my spirit has been broken ever since, you know."

Ernesto didn't utter another word during all the rest of the climb.

The train had finally arrived at the Escorial. I immediately grabbed a cab, as though I were late for a funeral, and told the taxi driver to take me to the Hotel Felipe II. I had spent many happy hours there with Ernesto during his various stays in Spain, much happier hours, usually, than during his last visit, when his mood would shift in the most disconcerting way: one minute he would be very friendly and expansive and cheerful, and the next he would suddenly fall silent and sit there brooding, so withdrawn and reserved that it seemed almost a deliberate slight. However, once the ice had been broken and he no longer felt the need to keep his distance, he had received journalists and writers there in the hotel. He was still drinking as much as ever. But what a great change there had been in him in the three years since I had last seen him! He had been in a glowing mood then, but now he seemed very gloomy and depressed; the last time I had seen him he had been positively exultant, but this time he was almost sullen. I could see him in my mind as plain as day, standing at the window of the Hotel Suecia on a foggy afternoon when his gaze was so piercing it was almost painful.

We had walked in these mountains many a time, and I remembered how he always used to sing Civil War songs under his breath. The memory of him humming these songs he had never forgotten was so vivid, in fact, that it was almost as if I could hear him that very minute.

His attachment to Spain was something that went much deeper than a mere literary style. It was also a style of life. With his huge hands like the great mitts of a rustic woodcutter or a mountain guerrilla fighter, Ernesto was a new breed of knight-errant. His plaid shirts, his wide, leather elephant herder's belt, his outsize hiking boots of a latter-day crusader, his booming laughter of a mountain bandit, his icy silences of a creature from another world made him a legendary figure.

The moment I arrived at the Felipe II, I headed straight for the bar. Someone came over to me and offered his condolences as though a member of my family had passed away. But wasn't that exactly what Ernesto was?

Ernesto's words were still ringing in my ears:

"I haven't come to Spain for a vacation, you know," he had said to me.

"I'm sure you haven't," I replied.

"If I can turn out just five hundred words a day, I'll have it made."

To Ernesto, Spain was a welcome respite and a sort of salvation, but it was also the kind of arduous test that is very exhilarating, the sort of violent contradiction that allows you to get both your thoughts and your feelings in sharp focus. Why is it that Ernesto's critics have always described him as one of those terribly repressed, tyrannically self-disciplined authors who kept too tight a rein on his emotions, and have consistently failed to realize that he was a very sentimental writer full of self-doubts, a radiant but painfully wounded romantic?

I had a vivid mental picture of Ernesto standing there in that very bar, surrounded by a whole crowd of headwaiters, barmen, and bellboys. His towering bulk, at once like that of an imposing university professor or a great, hulking vagabond, a testy Yankee tourist or an exuberant sportsman, had been truly awesome.

"I'll be here at the Escorial and in Madrid. We'll see each other both places—almost every day," Ernesto had promised.

Telling passages concerning Spain that he had set down in his books were still running through my mind—the words he had written, for instance, in "The Capital of the World":

Madrid is where one learns to understand.

And also that other blinding flash of intuition he had summed up so succinctly in that same story, words as cutting as the whiplash of a politician furious at his country's inertia:

Madrid kills Spain.

I asked for a Pernod, the drink Ernesto and I had so often ordered there in the bar of the Felipe II. I remembered, however, that on the very last day I had ever seen him, the day we met at the Hotel Suecia to say good-by to each other, he had drunk wine diluted with water. Ernesto drinking wine diluted with water? That one small thing should have alerted all of us to the fact that our great captain's long voyage was swiftly drawing to a close. In a certain sense his death should not have come as such a surprise. When Ernesto had arrived in Spain in 1956, he had come trailing clouds of glory. Like the simple fisherman in his great novella, he was still dizzyingly intoxicated by the very pulse of life. He had earned the highest honor that can come to a writer, and winning the Nobel Prize had made him as giddy and lighthearted as a schoolboy. He had come bearing *The Old Man and the Sea* in his hands, and had left bearing on his back the heavy burden of the whole vastly irritating, stupid, disgraceful *Dangerous Summer* episode, an ugly business that had ended with Ernesto being not the skillful wielder of a sharp-edged sword but a huge hunk of tender meat for ambitious, unscrupulous, selfish, sly scoundrels to feast on. Wasn't this the real truth of the matter, or at least a part of the truth?

Ernesto the born rebel, the great battler, had been gored to death by a treacherous bull. But as his Spanish friends stood by watching him buying hundreds of photographs, scribbling notes there in his seat in the bullring, tearing them up and starting all over, trying to please some people and subtly knife others, driven half out of his mind with anxiety at being forced to cut whole paragraphs out of a text that he was being paid for by the word, at an astronomical rate, which of us would have dared to speak up and tell him to his face that he ought to go back to what he was best at, to that marvelous directness and simplicity of his fisherman in *The Old Man and the Sea*?

Ernesto was like a volcano: the fire within smoldered far beneath the surface. His tough outer shell completely concealed the diamond-hard mother lode below. Writing was a tiring task, as monotonous (and as beautiful) as the ebb and flow of the tides, and the rhythm of his prose was like the steady but majestic tread of oxen—of biblical oxen, I am tempted to add—and as imposing and lofty as those oaks and spruces he had chosen as the overarching roof of his tomb there in Ketchum, rather than the Guadarrama pines he had been so fond of and so often dreamed of.

Ernesto had always been his own worst critic, a pitiless critic who was never satisfied, and perhaps it was for that reason that in the end he could not keep himself from falling into the black pit of despair and giving up everything. By sending Ernesto home from Spain in an attempt to rescue him from his despondency when he had instinctively insisted on staying, his friends may well have pushed him past his limit, driven him to an insane criticism of his own criticism, plunged him into the terrifying vacuum of ultimate nothingness. Because the bull-fight crowd had played sly tricks on him, the very last *corrida* of Ernesto's life had been a dismal failure.

"I've never lost a moment's sleep over what the critics have had to say about me. And I'm not about to lose any now," he said to me there in the bar.

"Don't pay any attention to them."

"Critics are like gentle bulls—they're always much easier to handle than the brave ones. What a fighting bull with real spirit wants to find out is what the center of the bullring and the picador's lance are like, what a good sword thrust feels like. But above all, what the brave bull is most eager to discover is why he has horns; what he wants most is to test his own weapon, to see if it can really rip and tear—even though he may be scared to death. . . .

We drained our glasses of Pernod, and then Ernesto said in a jovial tone of voice, "But *toros* are very peaceable, very well-behaved when they're castrated—don't you think so?" Then, after a few moments' silence, he said very softly, "Listen, what people are saying is quite true, you know: Spain's changing a lot."

"Oh, that's just a commercial for the country," I answered.

"No, it's really true: Spain's changing a lot." And then he went on, in an even softer voice: "There are quite a number of people who are determined to save this country."

"Bunches of them."

"Well, let them have a go at it, I say. All those people who are out to save Spain ought to be given a free rein, and when they've saved it and handed it back to us alive or brought it back from the grave, we'll take a turn at saving it too—but in our own way. . . ." He took a big swallow of his second Pernod and then went on: "Listen, if I'm somewhere far away when this country is finally saved, you'll let me know, won't you?"

"Of course—I promise I'll get word to you."

It was as though he had renounced his own political convictions from the very beginning in order to be absolutely fair, to propound a brand-new ethic, to arouse in his readers the greatest possible sympathy for his characters' undertaking. But he was also extremely perceptive, and the moment he fell into conversation with almost any Spaniard—a doorman, a waiter, a taxi driver, a tavern keeper—he could instantly understand the man's innermost motives, his most heartfelt desires, his mental outlook on things; he could tell you exactly what the man's life had been like in the past and could often predict what lay ahead for him in the future.

Returning to Madrid after so many years, to his beloved *sierra*, to the very front he himself had seen action on made him even more exuberant than usual; he was in such good spirits that his mood was very contagious. He was like one of those birds who sing as they have never sung before, just before they die.

"Five hundred words a day," he said again, very softly. Then he leaned over and whispered in my ear, very paternally, "Never join a political party."

"I've never been a joiner," I answered.

"That's the best policy, to my way of thinking. The only bearable sort of party would be one made up of honest, just men. It would be a tough job to organize a party like that, though, because it's not simply a question of rounding up men who *want* to be honest and just, but men who actually *are* honest and just already. And then they would have to be given the chance to . . ." He stopped in midsentence, took another long sip of his drink, and then went on: "Do you know what was most disappointing about that war that was lost?" And without giving me time to answer, he said: "The fact that immediately afterward real democracy became impossible in America as well. Americans have turned into a bunch of bums!"

This was the first time Ernesto had ever spoken to me about his own country, and even this time he had appeared to do so only with a certain reluctance. Every time he made any sort of reference to the Spanish Civil War, the memory of it seemed to reawaken in him a sense of integrity and spiritual maturity. Despite the fact that his presence in Spain had been misconstrued both by Loyalist leaders who thought that he had come to our country to write a great lyric paean to revolution and by Nationalist leaders who admired him but nonetheless called him an impostor who had sold out to anarchists, it was as though the struggle as a whole had given him an infallible standard against which to measure people's values, including his own. He had not only been a witness but a judge; he had not been so much an enthusiastic commentator as a stern inquisitor in the manner of Quevedo.

"Sometimes it's better to fight monsters than to fight men," he remarked.

"Do you say that because of *The Old Man and the Sea?*"

"I say it for all sorts of reasons. A crocodile is better than a hypocrite, a lion better than a demagogue, a tiger better than a cop or a spy. . . ."

Guests who had just arrived and others who already were settled in their rooms upstairs kept coming into the barroom and heading immediately for the outside terrace, for even in the bar it was stifling hot.

I went out on the terrace too, with my glass in my hand.

Ernesto had done lots of drinking and eaten many a meal out there. I remembered one lunch in particular, when the maitre d' and all the waiters had crowded around to watch the great spectacle. It was the first time that Ernesto and I had eaten out on the terrace alone together, for Mary had eaten her lunch as the two of us were having a few whiskies, and then after sunning herself for a while out there on the terrace with us, she had gone upstairs to her room. It was always an unforgettable sight watching Ernesto eating and drinking. All his repasts in taverns and restaurants were giant meals, but in this quiet, rather stuffy middle-class hotel the lunch he had ordered beforehand seemed even more of a Lucullan feast. They first brought him a huge *turmix* full of shrimp, crayfish, bits of lobster, and heaven only knows how many other things, all so subtly blended that it was impossible to tell what ingredients had gone into it. After offering me a taste, Ernesto grabbed his soup spoon and began downing this first course, washing down every second or third mouthful with a whole glass of Las Campanas rosé. He was eating with such great gusto and enjoying this *turmix* so much that all the dining room personnel stood around marveling at his lusty appetite. He went right on eating, laughing and joking with all of them, and as there was still a bit of juice left in the bottom of the tureen, he put a couple of slices of bread in it, stirred them around with his spoon till they'd soaked up the last few drops, downed them, and with a satisfied smile finally allowed the waiter to take the tureen away. Then he turned to the maitre d' and asked him how he looked to him, and the maitre d' said he thought he looked pretty good, and immediately set a huge pot of stew in front of him—a hearty, spicy, dark-colored bean stew with slices of sausage, blood pudding, eggs, and a pig's ears, feet, and tail in it—hardly a dish for an invalid. Ernesto served me, filled his own plate to the very brim, dug in, and ordered the waiters to leave the pot on the table. He downed the bits of meat with the greatest gusto, and the look on his face as he raised the spoonfuls of juice to his mouth was positively beatific. The waiters were all delighted to see how much he was enjoying his meal, and he kept them on the run, bringing bottle after bottle of wine to the table, with two cold ones ready and waiting in the ice bucket at all times. Ernesto was in an especially good mood that day, because he had finally persuaded the American Embassy to grant me a visa for a stay of at least a month in the United States, thus allowing me time enough to visit a fair number of states, Idaho for one—the place where he would one day kill himself. It had seemed like such a happy day then, and words cannot express how sad it made me feel looking back on it.

I sat there remembering every moment of that marvelous lunch when he had seemed so cheerful and carefree. "Madrid always gives me a monstrous appetite!" he had exclaimed. As a matter of fact, however, it had been after Ernesto had been put on a fairly strict diet by Dr. Medinaveitia that we had had that lunch worthy of a Renaissance prince. But

Ernesto had naturally decided to disobey doctor's orders that day, and the time had not yet come when the only alcohol he was allowed was one small glass of wine with each meal. I suddenly remembered that he had held his glass of wine up to the light that day and said, "I'm sure the water here in the Escorial is very good, but this is better."

I leaned back in my chair there on the terrace, trying to revive the past. I could see the very table we had eaten at, and perhaps the very chair Ernesto had sat in that day—like a sort of breakwater awash with all my memories of moments I had shared with him in Madrid, among them the day he had gone with me to see how Don Pío was, and that other day when the two of us had scattered a handful of dirt on Don Pío's coffin lying at the bottom of the grave hollowed out of the dry, hard earth. . . . But even though I was gazing at it through a cloud of memories, the terrace was still there before me, looking exactly the same as always in the bright, clear mountain air.

The bean stew had not been the last course Ernesto had downed that day, because afterward he had had a main dish, a plate heaped full of huge slices of meat, also cooked peasant style, plus a bit of salad to clear his palate, and some fruit to finish the meal off, all this washed down with copious quantities of wine, sipped very slowly, savoring every drop. And when we finally got up from the table, he told me to grab one of the cold bottles that were left (the tenth one they'd brought us, as I remember—seven or eight of which Ernesto had downed, for I had drunk only two or at the most three of them myself) and take it up to his room with us.

"If we sip it very slowly, it'll help us digest our lunch," he said, taking off the pair of glasses that made him look like an elder of the Presbyterian Church and mopping the sweat from his forehead with a courtly flourish of his handkerchief.

Once upstairs in his room, this Herculean giant collapsed on his bed and talked on and on like an old warrior still eager for battle. As the words tumbled out, it seemed as though a strong sea breeze had suddenly begun to blow through the room, and the curtains might have been a mainsail unfurled in mid-ocean. A mountain wind was rising outside, and the branches of the pine trees suddenly stirred, as though a storm were about to break at any moment.

He rambled on and on in a low murmur. No, he was not an ox in harness, and he never would be one. No, he would never be a slavering, lustful, dirty old man. No, he would never play the clown in the sort of farces staged by politicians and diplomats. No, he would never, ever accept the infamous kiss of death without dignity, a death that would leave him shorn of his pride as a man. No, he would never become the intellectual mentor of anyone, not even himself, nor would he allow himself to be devoured by the bitter pleasures of sex, nor would he . . .

305

Mary gave him a kiss on the forehead, just above the bright red blotch on his cheek, and he shut his eyes and began to drowse.

"He'll be snoring in a minute," Mary said.

"You'll be the one who'll snore," he replied, and suddenly we heard him make a noise that was more like the wheezing of a great bellows than a snore, his great bulk heaving as though shaken by an earthquake —a great life force bubbling over, and at the same time something like the low moan of a dying man.

"He's dropped off to sleep," Mary said, and I tiptoed out of the room.

10

Traveling with Ernesto from Madrid to the *sierra* always meant returning, either directly or in a roundabout way, to the theme of our Civil War. He kept coming back to this battle site again and again, but at the same time, like the *toro* in the bull enclosure, he was also returning to the gateway that had led him to the illusion of freedom.

Here at the Escorial, where he had stayed at the Felipe II in 1956 and come on occasional visits both in 1959 and 1960, we had taken many a stroll along the quiet, deserted little paths circling the adobe walls of the monastery or climbed the many pine-covered slopes leading to the crestline of the *sierra,* and after walking along for some time without saying a word, he would inevitably bring up that usually taboo subject, the Spanish Civil War. Though his wartime experiences had deeply moved him, he never tried to embroider his memories and make a great epic tale of them; it was more as though he felt the need to make a personal confession. He never pretended he had been a great hero fighting for justice, but neither would he allow anyone to dismiss his participation in the struggle as simply another of his many adventures.

He would point to the verdant mountainsides sloping down to Madrid and say: "That was where I fought as fiercely as a wild boar."

"Did you ever actually go so far as to fight the enemy hand to hand?" I would ask him.

"I went all the way—just as everybody else did," he would reply.

Then he would usually clam up and not say another word about the war the whole rest of the way. I knew very well that he had never really fought with the Loyalist troops; the closest he had ever come to the actual line of fire was when he accompanied some general of the International Brigade to the front on an inspection tour. He himself had assured me a number of times that he had never borne arms in Spain. But these mountain vistas moved him so deeply that he would start telling me things that had happened only in his imagination. Then he would change the subject and say, "When you breathe this mountain air up here, it clears more than your lungs."

"Yes, it's as sharp as a knife."

"It clears your head, too."

I was trying to thread all my memories together now.

"I hope you don't think that the Loyalists lost the war only because Russia and the Communists intervened," he said once, as though weighing his words very carefully. "They also lost because . . ." His voice trailed off then, right in the middle of his sentence.

I thought he had probably been about to say that the Loyalists had also lost because of Spanish anarchism, that charge that has so often been leveled against them. But Ernesto took off on another tack entirely.

"There were others who were also to blame, beginning with my own countrymen. When Americans start acting like filthy pigs, they're unbearable."

Then, after a moment, he said in a furious tone of voice, "It makes me laugh to hear people say that there are as many Don Quixotes running around loose among the Russians as among the Spaniards; but it strikes me even funnier when they insist that my country is saving the world. . . ."

He went on talking then, in a very soft voice, about Madrid in the days of the siege.

It was obvious that the war in Spain had not been just another adventure for Ernesto, but a test of his maturity and his integrity.

"What was the most painful moment for you during our war?" I asked him.

"What hurt the most back then, and has continued to hurt the most, was all the lies we were told about our war, as you call it."

I had been careful not to mention so much as the title of *For Whom the Bell Tolls*, but he for his part seemed to be actually afraid to mention it. I did my best to avoid the subject, but I was quite sure that some day the dam would burst and Ernesto would feel he had to talk about it.

One cold, snowy day in 1956, he had suddenly said to me, "We'll have to visit the bridge one of these days."

I was just about to ask him, "What bridge?" when I realized he obviously meant the one in *For Whom the Bell Tolls*, and immediately said, "Oh, I'd like that so much."

And again, in 1959, he had said several times, "Some day we'll visit the bridge and the whole countryside around it."

"Any time you like," I had replied.

And then, one other day, as we were coming back from Guadalajara, he had suddenly exclaimed, rather apologetically, "We've passed by the site of the bridge so many times, but we've never stopped to have a look."

We had gone on trips to Ávila and Segovia together, but for some reason we had never gone to see this bridge that was one of the central symbols of his novel.

I had finally decided that the bridge he described in the novel had never existed, nor had there ever been any fighting around such a bridge that might have changed the entire course of the war. The bridge in *For Whom the Bell Tolls* had been a figment of his imagination: he had first constructed it, and then destroyed it, entirely in his mind.

I had heard him refer to the heroic feats that had taken place around this bridge and the tragic failure of the entire operation many times in conversations with non-Spaniards, both Americans and people from other countries. But even though he helped draw up very precise battle plans during the war, he had never told a soul exactly where this bridge had been. Moreover, I had noted that his descriptions of the bridge site varied considerably from one conversation to another. But I hadn't said a word, and I never would, because in the final analysis the fact that such a bridge had never existed didn't lessen the value of the novel at all; in a certain sense, it might even enhance it.

There were a number of bridges in the region that might very well have been a target of a demolition team, but none of them could possibly have had the strategic importance or the symbolic import of the one in the novel, which was to be destroyed in order to halt a great Nationalist offensive. There are a few small bridges here and there in that part of the country, but none of them could have been the vitally important bridge in the novel. Moreover, there had been no guerrilla forces, either large groups or small isolated bands, operating in this sector during the war. There had been a few breaches in the lines and a few minor infiltrations by the enemy, but no bridge in this region had been a key point in any sort of military operation.

I had often questioned forest rangers, highway workers, peasants in little villages in the *sierra*, men who had fought on both sides during the war, and none of them could recall any situation even remotely similar to that in the novel. Even during the Republican offensive against San Ildefonso and La Granja, neither the big bridge along the main line of advance nearby nor the smaller bridges round about had been key strategic points.

But when the subject came up in conversations, I had more than once heard Ernesto talk about this operation as though he had personally witnessed it.* Doubtless he had seized upon some minor heroic episode he had heard about, and decided to use this simple test of courage, rather than a great, full-scale battle, as the climax of his novel. He often received reports from the front at the Gaylord Hotel, and used them as strands to fill out the fabric of his superb narrative between the two great scenes of carnage. But didn't the fact that a number of the scenes in his novel had been more or less modeled on episodes that had taken place in other parts of Spain make his novel perhaps a little less authentic from the strictly literary point of view? And might not the fact that the bridge episode was a historical distortion detract somewhat from the otherwise admirable realism of the book? But doubtless no one could have convinced Ernesto that this was so, and he kept saying to me:

"Some day we'll have to go camping by the bridge."

"Great! Whenever you like," I would reply.

But we never did go have a look at it, of course. This imaginary episode had merely been a way of bringing the guerrillas' activities to a dramatic climax. But here again, Ernesto had overemphasized the role the guerrilla band had played. Soldiers and officers of every rank on both sides had all agreed that there had been no such infiltration and sabotage by small bands of guerrillas in this sector. There had been a few episodes of this sort, but not in this particular part of Spain, and such bands had never had whole herds of horses at their disposal as in Ernesto's novel.

As time went by I became more and more convinced that *For Whom the Bell Tolls* contained a number of errors of this sort, but I no longer questioned people to try to ascertain the real facts. Would the precise truth have made Ernesto's story any more valuable as a human document and work of literature? By and large, Ernesto's novel had been admirably true to life. What did it matter if some of the details were not quite accurate? The real impact of his book, its magnificent powers of revelation belonged to a much higher order of truth. To my mind, the most important thing was Ernesto's noble idealism, which had been strikingly evident throughout the struggle, and equally evident twenty years after the war had ended.

But still, in my mind the bridge had taken on something of the proportions of Kafka's castle, mainly because it still amazed me that Ernesto had stubbornly insisted to the end that the bridge actually

---

* I have since discovered that Ernesto was not even in Spain at the end of May 1937, when this minor attack on La Granja was launched from the *sierra* above Madrid.

existed and that the skirmish that had taken place there was a historic fact. What an author invents very often becomes part of himself, and I quite understood that, once Ernesto had written his novel, he could have sincerely persuaded himself that all the facts related in it had happened in the particular region of Spain he had chosen as the background of the book.

Episodes such as Ernesto describes in *For Whom the Bell Tolls* had admittedly happened during the war, though not in that particular sector. Nor had they been as strikingly and starkly dramatic as in his novel. But, for me as a writer, and for all the other Spaniards who had lived through the war, wasn't the story he tells a sort of allegory of what had happened in each and every one of the Spanish towns where the revolutionary struggle was waged by a mob led by vulgar village bullies?

I had been offered a ride to Segovia, and we drove on through this wild countryside, bare crags dotted with occasional clumps of pine. The tiny mountain hamlets and even the larger villages we passed through seemed most unlikely settings for the bloody, criminal mass slaughter described in *For Whom the Bell Tolls*. Events such as Ernesto depicted in his novel simply could not have happened here, not even twenty or twenty-five years ago amid the bitter passions of a civil war.

There had been frightful atrocities certainly, but not in this particular area. It had not been the townspeople of Castile who had proven to be the most vengeful and the most hate-ridden—far from it. There had been terrible acts of savagery all over Spain, but it was precisely in this part of the country that there had been the least brutality. In several regions—Estremadura, La Mancha, Andalusia, Levante, and Asturias of course—where the reasons for waging a revolution had been most compelling, there had been a number of instances of collective slaughter when the dam had burst and people were no longer able to contain their wrath; but no such thing had occurred in the zone that Ernesto portrays in the book, an area of very small villages inhabited only by peasants and shepherds and simple day laborers, with no militant urban proletariat, very little real poverty, and no great passion for revolutionary change.

Moreover, even though Pilar and Pablo, the husband and wife who are the leaders of the guerrilla band, are characters who are very vividly described, Ernesto's portrait of them is a fairly serious distortion of reality. It is simply unbelievable that an entire village would follow their lead, and even less believable that they would be the guiding light of a romantic band of guerrillas, having begun their struggle against the enemy not by a baptism of fire but by a baptism of blood, the sinister, brutal, bloody carnage in the village square.

Even granting the fact that the townspeople in this imaginary village may have been fearful of the vengeance their enemies might take upon them at any moment and panic-stricken at the thought of the revolutionary struggle they would be forced to wage, it is most unlikely that such decent, dreamily idealistic villagers would agree to follow the lead of a man as evil and cowardly as Pablo. It was possible, of course, that they might have forgiven him for urging them on to deeds of fierce violence in the very first days of the uprising, when all the simple people in the village were terror-stricken and overcome by a passionate collective rage, but once the bloody liquidation of their enemies was over and done with, they would never have accepted Pablo, even as a military strategist, in the battle against their enemies. It was impossible to believe that such humble, decent supporters of the Republican cause would ever have agreed to carry out to the letter the orders of an outright murderer. The events that Ernesto depicts in his novel may well have taken place in some other sector, but locating them in the *sierra* above Madrid was an error of fact, for such things had never happened, nor could they have ever happened, in that particular area.

These peasants and shepherds do, of course, eventually consider getting rid of Pablo as their leader, and even Robert Jordan begins to realize that Pablo is damaging the Republican cause and the revolution and is seriously hindering the project of blowing up the bridge. Nonetheless, it is most unlikely that an entire Castilian village would have obeyed his orders and turned the execution of their enemies into a macabre *corrida*. Once one has come to know these mountain people intimately and lived with them or at least become thoroughly acquainted with the social, political, and economic patterns of their lives, it is simply beyond belief that half-breed gypsies, or even full-blooded ones for that matter, the majority of whom were mere horse traders or horse thieves, could ever have become revolutionary leaders in these little mountain hamlets.

I suppose that the many acts of barbarity committed during a civil war eventually came to seem all more or less the same to Ernesto: bloody deeds that were all quite similar, adding up to a great, collective slaughter. But, in one respect at least, the Spanish Civil War had been unusual: the nature of the struggle had been quite different from province to province and from sector to sector, and the behavior of people on both sides had been determined by their geographical origins, by their particular ideological persuasions, and even by the particular psychology of the region in which they were fighting. It strains belief that there would be so many red and black flags—the anarchist colors —proudly waving in a little Castilian village such as the one in Ernesto's novel, for anarchism and the various workers' movements more or less allied with it, such as the CNT and the FAI and the labor-union extremists of the POUM, never had such widespread support in this particular area.

Ernesto's epic novel had an impressive scope and sweep, and he had, of course, never deliberately falsified or distorted the facts or consciously concealed the truth. At times, however, realism and verisimilitude may be two quite different things. Would a gypsy, for instance, ever utter the words:

"It is to this we have come with so much inaction"?

And when there is talk among the guerrillas of the son of "La Pasionaria," whom that great Loyalist firebrand has sent off to Russia while simple peasants and workers are having a rough time of it in the front lines, the reader is quite taken aback when one of the mountaineers, a man who has never had a day of schooling in his life, exclaims:

"He is studying dialectics."

As the peasants are preparing for battle, Ernesto makes them sound like Renaissance poet-warriors. And old Pilar, that bawd reminiscent of our famous Spanish Celestina, asks María very discreetly and delicately whether she and Robert Jordan have "made love."

The reader is aware that all this is meant to be more or less symbolic, but even so it seems to me too eloquent and high-flown to seem true to life. This dialogue is intended to show how revolutionary ideals have filtered down into the speech of humble folk. But it is not merely the fault of the dreadful Spanish translation that in many passages of the novel the characters as Ernesto portrays them and the spiritual climate they are meant to symbolize simply do not go together, despite all his efforts to make his novel as realistic and as authentic as possible.

Curiously enough, it is in this Spanish Civil War novel that Hemingway appears to feel the greatest need to give the emotion of love the tenderest and most romantic of shadings. Nonetheless, in a number of passages there is a sort of artificiality about the dialogue that makes it sound most incongruous. On the eve of Robert Jordan's heroic exploit, for instance, María whispers to him in the sleeping bag:

". . . I am ashamed. I do not wish to disappoint thee but there is a great soreness and much pain. I do not think I would be any good to thee."

We all know what María is referring to, but a girl from a remote mountain village would never describe what has happened to her so shyly and delicately. Ernesto may have decided that he had used too many crude words in other parts of the book, and was trying to compensate for it by occasionally using overly polite words and phrases. He may have deliberately employed this grave and solemn style to counterbalance the frankness and outspokenness of some of the other dialogue in the book, but I found the effect nonetheless disconcerting.

313

But aside from these romantic interludes, Ernesto had forthrightly called the Spanish Civil War "murder on a grand scale," and in this respect at least he was not mistaken. As time had gone by, this had become increasingly obvious, and even though every time I reread this novel I discovered errors of fact, I also became more and more aware of how absurd and barbarous the war of Spaniard against Spaniard had been.

We were back at the Escorial by six that evening.

I walked down to the station. Without Ernesto, even the Escorial was no longer a sure cure and a creative inspiration, a lesson in discipline and a place that through some mysterious power always set me to dreaming the loftiest dreams. The Escorial this time seemed to be nothing but a place for cheap exhibitionism and vulgar promiscuity, a tourist trap, a key that unlocked no mysteries, a stage for the most tasteless sort of behavior. The experience had left me with a very bad taste in my mouth, and I found I couldn't bear it a moment longer. I got on the train feeling fed up with the whole scene and out of sorts at having wasted my time making such a sentimental journey.

Madrid fortunately glowed brightly in the distance—like a bonfire lighted in the middle of a village square to celebrate some midsummer fiesta.

The moment I arrived at the Norte Station, I hailed a taxi and told the driver to take me to the Hotel Suecia. What I needed at that point was a marvelous session in the hotel sauna. If I was beginning to highhandedly criticize the texts of Ernest Hemingway, that author so close to my heart, it was because something was physically wrong with me.

Without a word, the barman—a man from my part of the country, and what was more, a fervent admirer of Ernesto's—poured me a giant double scotch. Then, after a while, he said, "I knew you'd turn up here sooner or later."

"I knew I would too," I answered.

There was no denying one thing: Ernesto had swaggered into this very bar in 1959, puffing out his chest, aggressively sticking out his chin, clenching his fists, and filling the room with his booming voice.

Ernesto Hemingway, for years and years an irreducible, impenetrable fortress, had already begun to fall to pieces, but the cracks were not yet noticeable from the outside. It was during this visit that Ernesto had begun visibly falling apart. His powers of concentration, which had so impressed me when I had seen him in 1956, were declining, slowly but surely. Fortunately, attending bullfights and writing about the *fiesta brava* up in his hotel room had served as a sort of cathartic and a kind of catalyst that had counterbalanced his failing powers of will.

One of the things I was most anxious to question Ernesto about during his 1959 visit was the situation in Cuba, since I had spent some time with him at his *finca* outside Havana during the last tragic days of Batista's regime, in 1958. All in all, he was quite unhappy about what was happening in Cuba. When I quizzed him about the Castro regime, his reply was, "It was wonderful in the beginning, as you know, but it's started to take a very nasty turn lately. I'm afraid the whole thing's going to go down the drain."

It was probably his own temperament rather than the realities of the situation that were responsible for his disillusionment, and doubtless he also had grave misgivings as to whether the Cuban people would be capable of carrying out the revolution their leaders had planned. Although Ernesto had the warmest affection for the Cuban people, it was quite obvious that he had many reservations as to their ability to shape their own future and develop their country.

It was as though something or someone had suddenly begun to "rub him the wrong way"—one of his favorite expressions. Though I carefully forebore to mention the firing squads, the on-the-spot executions, and the kangaroo trials in the sports stadiums in Cuba, I asked him once again:

"Tell me, what do you think of what's been happening in Cuba?"

"The situation's still a bit confused, it seems to me, but the whole thing's turning into a big bore as far as I'm concerned. . . . The Batista regime was a disaster, and the worst part of what's happened since isn't all the wholesale bloodshed. There's something that scares me much more—all the fancy language they've been spouting." And then, trying his best to be fair, he said: "But Fidel's a youngster with a good head on his shoulders and lots of balls . . . he's inexperienced and a little bit crazy, but he'll keep the country moving ahead all right. . . . The Cuban people deserve to make a go of it, because they're a very decent lot, for the most part."

Neither of us said any more about *barbudos* or the revolutionary "purge" in Cuba. Ernesto hadn't come to Spain because he was fleeing Cuba, and he hadn't yet lost all hope in Castro. But there would come a time when he would become completely disillusioned by the outcome of the Cuban revolution.

Though Ernesto did his best to pretend he was having a good time hunting and fishing in Ketchum, his last days there could almost be described as a sort of self-exile in his own homeland. He was eager to go somewhere else, to visit a country where he would be more or less in control of the situation, where he could satisfy his curiosity and his passion for living and at the same time remain politically neutral. Spain could offer him all of this, and if in addition he could find something to write about, the expenses of his trip and his stay there would be more than repaid. Spain was no longer a thrilling new discovery, but it was still an enormous stimulus.

When I saw him arrive with so much baggage—he always brought heaps of luggage, but this time he had even more than usual—I wondered whether he might not be coming to settle down permanently in Spain. He had thought of doing so several times before, and, each time, the possibility of his coming to Spain to live had been like dreaming with his eyes wide open, like a nightmare that had suddenly turned into the happiest of dreams.

I had noticed that he never lost sleep, even after receiving disturbing letters from intimate friends and members of his family. He did not find it at all hard to forget almost anything that momentarily worried him.

It was quite obvious, however, that every once in a while he was troubled by his financial situation. He spent money like water, but did his best to convince himself that the dollars would continue to flow in. When with friends, he had always been the first to reach for the check, and would continue to do so. Up until the very end, he wanted people to think of him as an incredibly generous person. Though the truth of the matter was that he was inclined to be a bit of a penny pincher about certain things, he always managed to give outsiders the impression that he was as lavish as a prince. If Ernesto had learned anything at all from life, it was to put up as splendid a front as possible, to be generous to the point of prodigality. It was almost as though he kept saying to himself: "Are you trying to spoil me? Why try? I've got enough money to spoil all of you." This was one of his very characteristic ways of satisfying his ego. And many times his marvelous shows of hospitality and generosity were really a cover-up for his shyness, a way of feeling secure and at ease with other people.

But this time he seemed to feel closer to all his Spanish friends than ever. And he also seemed more excited than ever, as though Spain had turned out to be even more of a marvelous surprise than usual. Everything else in his life was a known quantity, and therefore boringly predictable. But there was always something unexpected in store for him in Spain. The words Ernesto had written long before, in *The Sun Also Rises* when he first arrived in Madrid, still applied:

You can never tell whether a Spanish waiter will thank you.

Ernesto's beard had been perfect that last trip. It was not only a noble beard—it was beginning to be a majestic one. The pair of glasses that made him look like a retired colonel or a country doctor like his father or a Protestant theologian on vacation had never entirely hidden the injury to his left eye, and on this visit the lesion was even more noticeable. And the red-and-white blotch on his face, between his nose and his cheek, worried me even more than it had in 1956. It was much

316

larger now and a much angrier red, and the pasty-white flakes that kept peeling off it were clearly visible amid the flowing locks of his beard.

It was clear to all of us that this visit in 1959, and the one almost immediately afterward, in 1960, were not like the other times Ernesto had come to Spain. When he had first arrived he had been in real fighting trim, bubbling over with excitement and eagerly anticipating getting to work on his great piece of reporting (which he was already planning to publish in book form as well, a definitive book far superior to everything he had already written about bulls and bullfighting). But when he left in 1960, his departure was as pathetic as that of a *torero* who has failed in the bullring and knows that he will never return to the *callejón* again. In the space of a single year, Ernesto's outlook on life had changed completely: he was no longer the triumphant winner at the very peak of his success but a man tasting the bitterest sort of defeat. On one of the very first days after his arrival, when he was still bursting with enthusiasm and confidently expected to write an absolute masterpiece, he had said to me: "I've come to do some serious work and take my pulse."

And when he left the country, very much against his will, he had said: "What in hell do they expect me to do? Commit hara-kiri like a perfect samurai? That'll be the day!"

I don't know why, but I was certain from the very first that Ernesto was "running out of gas," as he would put it, both physically and mentally. When he first arrived, he was eager to visit all his old haunts in Madrid, though he was not the least bit interested in seeing any of the new sections of town. But little by little be began spending most of his time in his room in the Hotel Suecia, as though shutting himself up in a cage. Fortunately he sometimes ventured out on trips here and there, and seeing bullfights made him feel as dauntless and intrepid as in his raw youth.

I think the fact that Mary was with him on this last trip was what reassured him the most. I am convinced that with the exception of Pauline, Ernesto's second wife, Mary was the woman who had the greatest positive influence on him. It was more or less for her sake, in fact, that he had come to Spain in 1956, to give her a chance to recover her health and cheer her up a bit. But in 1959 it was as though their roles had been reversed, for this time it was Mary who was eager to see her husband's health restored.

It was very hard to fit together all the Ernestos I had seen on these various visits—the hospitable and outgoing Ernesto of 1954 and 1956, the rather cold and withdrawn Ernesto of 1959, and the frankly inattentive and childishly absurd Ernesto on the eve of his departure in 1960. Mary was well aware of the difference between a spectacular but momentary fit of depression and a morbid, dangerous, obsessive self-preoccupation. Only a woman like Mary could have put up with those two ridiculous figures who hung around Ernesto every minute: Davis the jealous watchdog of his fame and fortune and Hotchner the exploiter of his reputation. Only Mary knew that Ernesto's real riches were intangible, and therefore she allowed him and Davis and Hotchner to do as they pleased. It is possible that his two American friends may have sincerely thought they were looking after his interests and protecting him. There was no question but that Ernesto's worship of Ordóñez as an ineffable and unsurpassable idol had made him an easy prey to a whole swarm of buzzards from the bullfight world, and in the end they were to do him incalculable harm, not only seriously damaging his prestige as a writer but also playing havoc with his most intimate feelings. . . .

What had happened to Ernesto became clearer and clearer to me as I sat there in that lonely downstairs bar of the Hotel Suecia, a place that had not been the least bit lonely in the past and doubtless would be the scene of other lively doings in the future.

Despite Hotchner's warmly enthusiastic predictions that *The Dangerous Summer* was going to be a rousing success, I for my part had clearly foreseen that the entire affair was going to be the ruin of Ernesto—from every possible point of view. I was very well aware that bullfighting was his fount of wisdom and the source of his most penetrating metaphors, his symbol and his reality, his basic image and the key to his style, but only when he kept a certain distance between himself and the bullfighter confronting the bull. Tauromachy could well serve as the ideal model of the writer's art, but only so long as Ernesto succeeded in viewing it from the perspective of the artist. As soon as he started eating up bullfights the way he would down a slice of wedding cake, we were lost and he was lost. And more than once I even went so far as to try as best I could to get that point across to him.

"I don't know why it is you dislike bullfighting so much," he would answer.

"You're wrong, Ernesto. What I dislike is horns—of any size, shape, or description. You have to know when to quit. . . ."

He admired and respected my frankness, but my remarks rubbed him the wrong way. He had proudly staked his reputation on this piece of bullfight reporting, and I think it was to play a large part in driving him to suicide, for it is quite clear that one of the reasons for his serious depression and his mental illness was the difficulty he had encountered trying to write something entirely new about bullfighting. I had seen him—and still had a vivid mental picture of him—up there in his hotel room that was almost like a prison cell putting sheet after sheet of paper away in his files and then taking them all out again, pages only half finished, pages so full of corrections that they were scarcely legible. For the first time since I had known him, I saw him get all confused, tear up whole sections of his manuscript, rip up photographs or fling them across the room in a fit of temper, swear at those present in the room and others elsewhere, and swear at himself. For the first time in his life Ernesto had made a mess of what he was writing.

Fortunately, when Ordóñez visited him he was able to cheer Ernesto up and get him out of his sour mood. There were times when Antonio would also take a few sly digs at him, but since Ernesto was convinced that Ordóñez was an absolute angel with the very best of intentions, he didn't even notice, or at least pretended not to notice.

"Listen, Ernesto, I don't doubt that your writing's getting better and better, but I must say I find this part just a little bit boring," Ordóñez would say.

And Ernesto would immediately reply, "Okay then, let's try to liven it up a little. Does it seem to you that it's a bit short on adjectives? If so, we'll swipe some somewhere."

"I'm sure that'd do the trick. And since 'Freckles' is selling your product at a thousand pesetas per comma, two thousand pesetas per accent, and a thousand duros per ellipsis dot . . ."

"I don't care much for ellipsis dots," Ernesto would chime in.

"How would it be if I found you a subject?"

"*You* find *me* a subject?"

"A really good one, I mean. Then the two of us could live for the rest of our lives on the profits."

"I'm all ears. Go ahead—tell me what I should write about."

"What percentage of the profits are you going to give me if I suggest a subject?"

"It all depends. If it's a really fantastic one, we'll split the profits fifty-fifty—the same as we do with the money you get fighting *corridas.*"

"Well, I'll have to think about it," Ordóñez would say jokingly, pretending to be holding out for a better price.

Ernesto wasn't afraid of being laughed at as long as he had the situation well in hand and felt at home in the bullfight world. Nobody in that world took anything very seriously—it was all a big joke. That crowd scarcely even suspected that Ernesto's love of bullfighting was something more than play-acting and grandstanding. It would be a long time before most of them realized that Ernesto's artlessness, his unfailing good humor, his earthiness, his genuine popularity concealed a mystery—and more than a mystery, a tragic inner drama. Of all of them, only Ordóñez began to understand, little by little, what tortures

Ernesto was suffering. But since Ernesto seldom confided in him, all Antonio could do was crack the same tired old jokes. I remembered one of their typical conversations:

"It's my guess that you pay that 'nigger' of yours quite handsomely," Antonio remarked to Ernesto.

Davis smiled expectantly.

"That's for him to say," Ernesto replied.

"Well, in any case, I suspect he's got a little something to fall back on," Antonio replied.

"I think he's getting a fair slice of the pie. And I think it's a pretty good idea for you and me to split fifty-fifty, don't you?"

"What about 'Freckles'? What would you do without him?"

And Hotchner flashed 'Papa' a sly smile, playing the game with him along with the rest of them. Ernesto looked Antonio up and down and said, "You're right—what would I do without 'Freckles'? But if he's unhappy working for me, you can sign him up as one of your assistants. Maybe he's just now discovering his real vocation—he's thinking of running with the bulls, you know, and maybe he'll turn out to be a serious rival of yours some day."

"We'll try him out, shall we?"

In the last months of Ernesto's stay in Spain, they all joked with him about the girls he had "kidnaped" at Pamplona.

"How are the kidnap victims? Are you treating them right?" somebody would ask.

"Oh, very well!" Ernesto would exclaim. "They're receiving the best possible treatment."

"I've heard that the Irish girl especially is looking a little pale these days and has big dark circles under her eyes."

"That's just idle gossip—a pack of lies," Ernesto would say, pleased as punch that everyone was still talking about his now-legendary "kidnaping," a little adventure that had never amounted to anything more than a childish prank.

Ernesto had not withdrawn from the outside world—far from it. He was still very much concerned about what was happening in faraway places, and always made sure that the leading newspapers and magazines reached him wherever he was. He did his best to conceal his avid interest in the printed word, but I often noticed that he read not only the pieces on politics and sports, but also searched through all these publications to see if there were any reviews of his works, though he stubbornly maintained he couldn't care less what the critics said. More than once, however, I had seen him throw a paper or a magazine on the floor in a fit of pique and exclaim testily, "Why is it the press always tells such outrageous lies about me no matter what I do?"

"It's the price you pay for being rich," Antonio or someone else who wanted to needle him a little would reply.

"The whole lot of them keep sniffing around like stinking, starving hyenas. And they've got their obituaries of me all written up already," he would answer.

The cables and letters he received from his agents, publishers, magazine editors, and television network executives were not always to his liking, and when things weren't going his way he would sit sulking for hours. It was common gossip that his price for a piece kept going up all the time, but the higher the rate went, the more nervous it made him. He spent hours going over his accounts, and what worried him most was the bite taken out of his earnings by the U.S. tax authorities. He kept telling us how they were sucking him dry: did we know, for instance, that out of the $150,000 paid him for the film rights to "The Snows of Kilimanjaro" the Internal Revenue Service would leave him only $50,000?† And how much were they going to take out of the money he was going to be paid for the television rights to a number of his short stories, for the *Dangerous Summer* pieces in *Life*, for the rights to one of his other works that another film producer might buy?

As he sat there at a table littered with hundreds of bullfight photographs, every few minutes or so he would get up out of his chair, go into the bathroom, and peer intently at his face in the mirror. What he probably was staring at was the terrible blotches on his face beneath his beard, because he would come back from the bathroom looking depressed or out of sorts, but it would seem that at times he also spied something else in the mirror, for occasionally he would come back looking quite relieved. When the phone rang, it was always Davis or Hotchner who answered, because Ernesto hated talking on the telephone.

The *Dangerous Summer* assignment was driving him literally out of his mind, plunging him into a sort of paranoia very different from his usual marvelous brand of antic madness. He thought and felt and wrote the entire series of articles as though they were up-to-the-minute news bulletins, an approach to the assignment that was bad both for his literary style and for his nerves.

Personally, that whole mess—the supposed "duel of the century" between two famous bullfighters and Ernesto's no less fictitious tales about his young Irish "kidnap victim"—had begun to make me ill, but I didn't dare speak up and tell Ernesto how disgusted I was, because he took even such basically trivial things as this very seriously. It was almost as though he could not go on living without the excitement of the dramatic battle between Ordóñez and Dominguín, a summer-long

† Paramount had also paid him approximately $150,000 for the film rights to *For Whom the Bell Tolls*, and if I remember correctly, all he had left of this sum after paying the taxes on it was $60,000.

mano a mano that for the most part was merely a publicity stunt. I couldn't bear to see him getting more and more deeply involved in such a stupid affair, but there was nothing I could do to prevent it. Moreover, I didn't want to play any part whatsoever in the whole insane project.

Might Ernesto not have been a kidnap victim himself from the very beginning? "Kidnaped" by friends who had greatly influenced him—Gertrude Stein, for instance—by this or that band of rogues and scoundrels, by hunters, fishermen, guerrillas, *toreros*? And weren't all his marriages more like a kidnapping than anything else?

One day I said to Mary, "He's going to go all to pieces some day if he keeps this up."

"You're wrong there—he's a very strong man," she replied.

"I know he is, but I don't understand how he keeps going."

"More or less the way a bull keeps going."

"But there comes a time when bulls reach the end of their rope too."

"He's even stronger than a bull."

She said this in an awed tone of voice, but at the same time she also saw what I meant, and was undoubtedly even more concerned than I was about this new stage Ernesto seemed to have entered, an odd combination of the worst sort of dissipation on the one hand and the most intense concentration on the other.

Mary was an expert at defending her own terrain, but this period of traipsing from bullring to bullring, from fiesta to fiesta, must have been even more wearing and more unsettling to her than Ernesto's deeds of derring-do in the days of the invasion of France and all the traveling she had had to do to be with him in London and Paris. She was jealous only of Ernesto's time, and concerned only about his work, and seeing him dashing frantically about and wasting his energies on subjects that were beneath his talent and his own ambitions must have been a very trying experience for her.

"When this whole business here in Spain is over, I'll see that he stays on a strict diet, and he'll soon be as good as new," she remarked. And then she said with a sigh: "We've given up so much."

I am convinced that Mary was referring to something more than the house in Ketchum or the one in Havana. It was no doubt Ernesto who felt that everything was going down the drain—his health was ruined, his nerves were shot, and he had lost whatever peace of mind he had once had. But it was largely his own fault: the hectic life he had led from 1959 to 1960 would have been enough to kill a thoroughbred who has won every race imaginable.

But Mary had never let him down. She was with him every moment—whether actually there on the spot with him or not. She knew where

322

her duty lay, and instinctively looked after his best interests and did her utmost to keep him from harming himself. Though she had more and more reason to fear for his life, she never nagged him; she simply watched over him night and day, tactfully and unobtrusively.

It seemed as though I could see Ernesto there before me that very minute, lazing on the terrace at twilight, with a glass of wine in his hand, gazing out over the rooftops and the chimneys and the towers with the sharp eye of an expert navigator.

Almost every day, he received not only books with personal dedications, but also a great many letters from Spanish writers, most of them young authors, but also a number of older ones. I was amazed at his critical acumen; he could instantly single out those books that were the most important and the best written. After reading only a paragraph or at most half a page, he could immediately tell whether a work was ripe wheat or worthless chaff.

It was no easy task to persuade him to attend any sort of formal gathering, much less a literary one. He very cleverly sidestepped the personal homage that the writers of the younger generations were eager to pay him. He would often remark: "I'm sure good writers are going to be appearing on the scene both in Spain and in America in the next few years. But we must let them alone and allow each of them to develop his own aesthetic and his own set of values. Don't you agree? Letting others pay you homage, even in the most personal way, is something that only writers past their prime go in for. But I haven't reached that point yet: I'm still in there fighting in the front lines."

As a general rule, Ernesto was very much averse to expressing a definite opinion about almost anything having to do with literature, and disliked being asked to pass judgment on novels in particular. He would leave the books he was sent lying on top of his file cabinet for a time, and then he would take the ones he found most intriguing—usually works dealing with the war, bulls, boxing, fishing, or picturesque new folkways in Madrid—off to his bedroom and leave them on his night-stand to leaf through at his leisure. Then he would eventually send the bulk of them off to his *finca* in Havana.

Like sex and religion, literature, in Ernesto's eyes, belonged more or less to an intimate, secret, very personal world. Almost everything that commentators wrote about his works annoyed him, for as he saw it, they had either failed to grasp how sound his philosophy of life was, or had seriously distorted the meaning of his words.

Sitting there at the downstairs bar in the Hotel Suecia, I found the place very gloomy and depressing. Since it was the middle of the summer, it was not nearly as lively as at other seasons of the year, when it is a favorite hangout for lovers and friends and casual acquaintances dropping in together for a drink. Ordinarily the Suecia bar is very crowded, because there is also a sauna and a restaurant in the hotel, but today the barman and I were the only people in the place.

"I knew you'd take the news of his death very hard," the bartender said to me. "The minute I heard what had happened, I said to myself, 'Señor Castillo-Puche must be terribly upset.'"

"You're quite right. I just can't believe it, even though I'm quite certain his life couldn't have ended any other way," I said.

"Have you seen the afternoon papers?" the bartender asked.

"No, why?"

"Nobody seems to know what's going on. One of the foreign papers says that Ordóñez has gone to the U.S.A. to attend the funeral, and the Spanish one reports that he left this morning for Pamplona. Heaven only knows what the real story is."

"We'll soon find out," I replied.

I went to the phone booth, and when I finally got through to Ordóñez, I discovered that he hadn't gone either to America or to Pamplona, but would be leaving in a few hours for the San Fermín fiesta.

I wasn't sure I understood why he was going, but perhaps that was what Ernesto would have wanted him to do.

I went back to the bar and just sat there, as though I were waiting for a train or very important news, something that might change the entire course of my life.

I walked over to the elevator and went up to the top floor. It was very quiet and peaceful up there. Ernesto sometimes used to leave the door of his room open, so that Hotchner, his financial adviser, and Davis, his major-domo and bodyguard, could come and go as they pleased. And waiters would pop in with bottles and ice every few minutes too, and sometimes bring Ernesto snacks as well, since he didn't like to take time out for a full meal when he was working.

During his last stay in Madrid, Ernesto's close friends and drinking buddies and the women he'd taken into his intimate circle kept wandering in and out of his room too, like mother hens and chicks in a poultry yard. And it was at this point that Mary began to be seriously concerned about him, though she never said a word. Ernesto was obviously going all to pieces. Every once in a while, for instance, he would come back from peering at himself in the mirror in the bathroom or turn back toward us after gazing out the window with a very strange look in his eyes, as though he felt some terrible curse hanging over his head—a wild, desperate look and at the same time an indescribably sad, forlorn look. How many times I wished that he would fall into a tantrum or lash out furiously at all of us—anything to get him out of that dark tunnel he found himself in, that obsessive mood that seemed on the surface to be a childish sort of sulking, but was really a mood of blackest despair.

Of all the visitors he received, it was probably Ordóñez who cheered him up the most, but after Antonio had left, Ernesto always seemed more depressed than before. Once he was gone, Ernesto would first become restless and then terribly bored. He would force himself to go back to work, and would sit there in his room all by himself, feeling relieved that everyone had gone, concentrating on his writing, searching for the precise word he wanted, choosing exactly the right photograph from the many hundreds he had on hand. Davis was an enormous help to him in preparing his text, and Hotchner was always close at hand to help him settle urgent business matters in the States. I believe Ernesto may have been a little bit hurt when he saw that I wasn't as enthusiastic as he was about his bullfight articles and not at all excited about the supposed duel between Spain's two leading *toreros*. Things would have been entirely different if what he had allowed me to read had been another book like *The Old Man and the Sea* or some of his unpublished works he had occasionally discussed with us.

He phoned me one afternoon after lunch and said in an urgent tone of voice, "Come on over here as soon as you possibly can," and hung up.

When I arrived at the hotel, I ran into Carlitos Barral, a highly regarded Catalan publisher and first-rate poet, in the bar.

"I'd like to talk to Hemingway," he said to me.

"I'll see what I can do," I answered.

"I know he's staying here at the hotel."

"Yes he is, but he's given us strict orders not to let on to anyone that he's here."

Barral didn't pursue the subject any further. I presumed he wanted to propose publishing Ernesto's works, an offer well worth considering, since the only Spanish editions of Ernesto's principal works had been very bad Chilean or Argentinian translations. I knew that Carlitos would tactfully offer to do better by him.

As I was about to step into the elevator I thought better of it and went back to the bar and asked Carlitos, "How long are you planning to be here?"

"The reason I wanted to see Hemingway was to invite him to the Formentor round-table discussion and ask him to present our International Publishers' Prize," Barral replied. "What do you think of the idea?"

"I really don't know what to tell you; my guess is that it would be very hard to persuade him."

One of Barral's friends, Salinas, who was there with him, said, "He'd have a great time."

"We'll hold a special ceremony in his honor."

"The trouble is that Ernesto doesn't like that sort of thing at all," I said.

"Well, in any case we'd like him to come to Formentor, and bring his wife, too, if she's here with him. They're both invited—and so are you."

"I'll pass your invitation on to him and do my best for you."

I stepped into the elevator and went up to Ernesto's room. The minute I came in the door, I could see that he was terribly angry and upset about something.

"What in the world is the matter?" I asked him.

"Nothing, nothing, I'm clearing out of here, that's all," he answered, choking with rage. And by way of explanation he added, "They not only turn this hotel into a whorehouse whenever they please—it's also getting to be a hangout for queers."

Davis was trying to calm him down, but Ernesto kept popping in and out of his chair, swearing like a trooper.

I couldn't image why he was so distraught, but once he had quieted down a little, he told me what had happened. As he was coming upstairs in the elevator, a guy with a little goatee had stared and stared at him, as though trying to work up the nerve to speak to him. And when he stepped out of the elevator, he noticed that the guy followed him. He'd been tempted to give the man a kick in the balls, but instead he'd rushed down the hall to his room, and the moment he'd closed the door behind him the guy had slid a note underneath it.

"Have a look for yourself—where did I put that damned note anyway?"

I almost burst out laughing, but Ernesto was still so angry that he'd gone to the telephone and was about to complain to the hotel manager and tell him he was sick and tired of being accosted in his establishment and was going to leave immediately, and what was more, he was going to spread the word far and wide that his hotel was a den of iniquity. I asked to see the note—and discovered that it was simply a very respectful and very cordial invitation from Carlitos Barral to visit Formentor.

Ernesto gradually cooled down when I explained what the note was all about. But he always refused on principle to accept any invitations of this sort, and the more I stressed the fact that Barral was a brilliant publisher and a rather highly regarded intellectual in Barcelona, the more adamant Ernesto became: "I only allow people to extend me invitations. What's more, it's only certain people who get invitations from me. And that's it, period."

But that wasn't the end of the affair, after all. Just a few minutes later, Ernesto received a telegram from Camilo José Cela, couched in the most cordial and the most flattering language, urging him to accept the invitation to Formentor. Knowing Ernesto as I did, and knowing also that there were going to be numerous round-table discussions on the objective novel and other such subjects, I was certain that it was absolutely useless to try to persuade him to attend. Deep down, Ernesto was a very timid man who went out of his way to avoid such gatherings. I tried to convince him that it would be a good chance to visit a very picturesque spot, and that all the rest of it, including the awarding of the Formentor Prize, would be a rather enjoyable experience for him. But since the invitation had mentioned the names of some of the honored guests who had been asked to attend, among them writers who were both practicing novelists and authors of essays on the novel, plus several critics, from a number of European countries, Ernesto grimaced and said: "I wouldn't attend an affair like that even if they sent mules to drag me there, the way they drag bulls out of the ring."

Then he sat there for a while with a rather thoughtful look on his face, and since he was always extremely polite, he asked us to draft a courteous telegram declining this kind invitation. He liked the way I phrased it and Davis immediately went to the phone to send it off. When Ernesto saw that it was on its way, it was as though he'd rid himself of an enormous burden. He sat there then, reminding us over and over how much pressing work he had to do. What was more, he kept pointing out, he was about to go out of town and couldn't possibly postpone his trip. Since I was going to attend the Formentor conference, I would surely be able to explain why it was impossible for him to come and smooth any ruffled feathers. And then he remarked:

"Camilo ought to know me better than that. Why does he keep trying to back me into a corner like that?"

"He had only the very best of intentions, I'm sure," I answered.

"I know, but that whole business of sitting around chewing the fat about the novel of the future strikes me as downright asinine. And yet he has the nerve to tell me, 'We'll have a great time.' I can't abide that sort of pretentious nonsense."

I said good-by to Ernesto for a few days, and if I remember correctly, just as I was going out the door he called me back and asked me to stay and have dinner with him. As Davis tidied up everything, Ernesto tried to prove to me that he was intimately acquainted with Spanish literature but didn't like to discuss it or deliver fancy speeches on the subject. He could sum up what he had to say about our literary tradition in a few words: At times, what Blasco Ibáñez most resembled was a fairgrounds barker with a microphone in his hand; Azorín was a stonemason who had ended up being the justice of the peace in a delightful little town; Valle Inclán was a bagpiper playing haunting tunes for a nation of religious pilgrims; Unamuno, that sad-faced man who looked like a widowed gravedigger, had tried to preach felicity but had ended up

327

being a pitiless prison warden, a deadly castrator, a proponent of suicide, or at least mental suicide, in short a ghostly shadow of his former self. And Ortega y Gasset? Well, it was quite true that he had made himself a reputation as the illustrious spokesman for Spain's most famous *toreros*, but he had spent the latter part of his life as a rich cattleman, a mentor who had tired of preaching to deaf ears and taken to giving oboe concerts as a hobby. And Machado might have become a sort of reformer of Franciscanism in the West if there had been the slightest chance of reforming it.

"And Baroja? What do you think of Don Pío now, four years after that visit you paid him?" I asked.

"I think of him as a doctor who chose the wrong profession. He was always cold, and liked nice warm ovens so much that he should have been a baker. But he tried very conscientiously to autopsy the Spanish soul, and partially succeeded. There's never been a Spanish writer who was anywhere near as good as Don Pío, except maybe Galdós, with his thick woolly scarf; and the windmills of the imagination, any of the windmills that are going to grind out the fiction of the future, aren't going to turn unless they catch Baroja's gusts in their sails."

I hailed the waiter and said, "Bring me another drink please, but not so much ice this time."

Remembering Ernesto made me feel like drinking, because that was the only way I could relive certain moments; alcohol either brought to mind everything he had ever said, word for word, or reminded me of other painful words, bearing his own inimitable stamp, that he himself might have uttered.

Yes, he had been marvelous that night, and I seem to recall that it was that same night, or perhaps one a little later on, that he had gone on at some length about what was rotten and what was sound in Spanish literature, and drawn me up a list of writers exemplifying both tendencies, a list that I shall keep an intimate secret and carry about in my heart for the rest of my life. The sound writers, according to him, were those who helped a person to live and to die, and the rotten ones those who wrote piles of shit because they were corrupt and afraid to speak up, crap that fuzzy-minded critics and publishers positively ate up. He mentioned a few names and then said in a very firm tone of voice: "Don't read them; all they do is spread panic like a disease."

"Would you please send someone out to get me the afternoon papers?" I asked the bartender, an old friend who's from my part of the country.

"Sure—right away."

"And I'll have another of the same."

"On the rocks?"

328

"No, no ice, just a little bit of lemon juice."

"The way Ernesto used to like his drinks?"

"That's right."

"I bet you can't guess what Ernesto liked most about Madrid," I said a while later.

"The wine."

"No."

"The women."

"No."

"The water."

"Are you kidding?"

"The sky."

"You're getting warmer."

"The bulls."

"You're even warmer, but you still haven't guessed."

"I give up, then."

"Okay: what Ernesto liked most about Madrid was the air."

"What do you mean, the air?"

"Just that—the air—the air you breathe, the air that lifts young girls' skirts, the air that makes the muleta stir very slightly, the air that makes the acacias murmur secrets . . ."

The waiter stared at me in wide-eyed amazement. "It's as though I could see him this very minute, right here at the bar!" he exclaimed.

"Me too—I can see him just as plain as day, sitting here at the bar, or rather half sitting on the edge of his stool and half standing here at the taprail with his glass in his hand, staring at the rows of bottles and the mirrors with a faraway look in his eye and a fierce scowl on his face."

"Yes—he almost scared you sometimes."

"But I'm sure you've also seen him sitting right here looking as though he had a great weight on his conscience, drinking steadily but never getting plastered, though the more he drank the more serious, the more gloomy, the more lonely and sad he became. Wasn't it plain to see that he was drifting like a shipwreck victim on a sea of alcohol?"

A strange look came over the waiter's face.

"He must have really been suffering," I said.

"Suffering!" the waiter exclaimed incredulously.

"Yes, suffering terribly. All the truths he had discovered in Spain, the things he'd loved best—war and bullfighting—were either a dead letter or were slowly dying in the most ignominious way. And do you know what caused him the worst pain of all?" I asked.

"His liver?"

"No, what pained him most was his lost youth, because the very thing he had loved the most, that he had lived and written about so truthfully, so beautifully, so courageously and honestly, at the cost of such great sacrifice, was becoming the grossest sort of travesty, an empty spectacle and a trivial popular amusement."

"I don't believe for one minute that he was suffering. He really lived it up here in Spain. I know that for a fact—I saw him out on the town many a time."

The waiter must have noticed the annoyed look on my face, because he shut up and respectfully stole away, leaving me sitting there by myself. But he came back a few minutes later and said: "We were all very sorry to hear he'd died. I remember the day he made such a fuss about that man from Barcelona, the guy with the little goatee. Señor Hemingway was like a hurricane—or rather, like an earthquake."

"You're quite right. He was a force of nature, a force that was not as blind as might have appeared to be the case, but nonetheless an uncontrollable one. That's becoming more and more clear to me as time goes by," I replied.

In one corner, I spied a couple necking passionately. But I couldn't work up the nerve to turn around and stare openly at them. Two older-looking foreign couples came into the bar just then. I climbed down off my stool, paid the check, and said good-by to the bartender.

"See you again soon."

I went out onto the street. It was as hot as a bake oven out there. When I reached the Puerta de la Tabacalera, I tossed a coin. If it came up heads I would go to Pamplona, and if it came up tails I would go back to Benicasim and rejoin my family. It had been only a few days since I had left them there, right in the middle of my summer vacation, but it seemed as though I had been gone for ages.

It came up tails, and I immediately hailed a cab. If the driver stepped on it, I could just barely make my train. What was I doing in Madrid anyway? If only the editors I worked for had felt generous and handed me the money to go to Ernesto's funeral! But nothing of the sort had happened; the dead man was being lowered into his grave and the live one left standing there empty-handed, dredging up his memories for free.

Oh what a marvelous train, what a miraculous train, jam-packed with vacationers headed for Levante, on a July day that made you sweat and drowse; the excitement and the bone-weariness of a midsummer day, caramels, fruit, wineskins, ice-cream cones in the stations along the way, oranges, melons, Coca-Colas, orangeade, tomatoes dripping with juice, one cigarette after the other . . . and piles of suitcases and hordes of kids, not to mention countless transistor radios, that intriguing, enjoyable, educational, nerve-grating, irritating, outrageous device. . . .

I was headed for the seashore again. What had I been doing in Madrid in the middle of July, that time of year when there is always talk of an imminent crisis? The fact that I was heading back to the sea again seemed somehow to cleanse my very soul. The moment I reached the water's edge I would dive into the waves and not even come out to eat.

Madrid was behind me now. The stifling heat there, or possibly my growing awareness of my own identity, made it seem a foul, corrupt, rotten place in retrospect. How could anyone possibly feel healthy and whole and vigorous in that inferno, where your blood flowed sluggishly in your veins and you felt the bile clotting in your throat, where your sensibilities atrophied and sounded as hollow as a badly cracked brass bell.

I had simply had to leave the city, and was absolutely amazed that I had been able to stay there as long as I had, wandering up and down the streets in a state of utter confusion. Would I have eventually decided to go to the fiesta of San Fermín, in Pamplona? Probably not.

As the train sped along through the dry stalks and faded flowers along the tracks, the steady clack of the wheels seemed very reassuring. I even found the crowded compartments, full of noisy families in a holiday mood, not only bearable but rather entertaining.

My memories of Ernesto were less disturbing now, as though nothing out of the ordinary had happened at all. And his words describing his travels had a pleasant ring to them that lifted my spirits:

> . . . days on the train in August with the blinds pulled down
> on the side against the sun and the wind blowing them: chaff
> blown against the car in the wind from the hard earthen thresh-
> ing floors; the odor of grain and the stone windmills.

Ernesto had not journeyed from one end of Spain to the other the way other writers had done, storing up experiences and noting down the moods of the moment in order to fill a book with intimate personal reactions. He had loved every moment of his travels in our country, sometimes enjoying them to the fullest and sometimes feeling the deepest pain, at times protesting vigorously and at other times applauding wholeheartedly, but unfailingly living the experience to the hilt. He had not come to our country as a missionary, a spy, a sociologist, or a journalist reporting on his fleeting impressions of Spain. There were more profound reasons for his close association with Spain, and it may well be many years before Spaniards realize how great a service Ernesto rendered our country. His readers, and his American readers in particular, ought to be grateful for the life-restoring blood transfusion that Hemingway's message represented, for the invaulable Spanish treasures of wisdom passed on to them in his books. Among the many words of praise uttered in honor of Ernesto Hemingway, Salvador de Madariaga's strike me as particularly significant: "Without his meaning it, Hemingway thus revealed to his country and to the world many Iberian aspects until then badly misunderstood, which he was able to do possibly because of his familiarity and almost obsession with those essentials of the Spanish ethos: love, death, and eternity; and in so doing he revealed to the Iberians that lesser-known aspect of American life: a capacity for direct approach to the life of others without distance, prejudice, or reprobation, which may well turn out to be the chief asset of the United States in this period of inevitable American leadership." (*The Saturday Review*, July 29, 1961). How sad it made me feel that journalism, that profession that is so exploitative, so humiliating, and so sterile, would not permit me the time to write a rational, carefully thought-out piece about Ernesto! But the phone calls, the special assignments, the trips, the whole complicated machinery for grinding out stories— everything that Ernesto had criticized me so many times for wasting my time doing—would be beginning again soon.

Except for all those transistor radios blaring and occasional earsplitting hand clapping from a group of Marine recruits on leave, the train trip was far more bearable than I had thought it would be when I climbed aboard. Everything around me still bore Ernesto's special stamp, that particular Spanish light that he had discovered in so many things, that noble profile, even of the humblest of people, that he had so often remarked on, the enormous pleasure he had found in describing the simplest scenes that met his eye. What he had written in *Death in the Afternoon*, for instance:

> If I could have made this enough of a book it would have had everything in it . . . eating the cheese later up in the room; it would have had the boy taking the wicker-bound jugs of wine on the train as samples; his first trip to Madrid and opening them in enthusiasm and they all got drunk including the pair of Guardia Civil and I lost the tickets and we were taken through the wicket by the two Guardia Civil (who took us out as though prisoners because there were no tickets and then saluted as they put us in the cab). . . .

Could anything be more colorful, and at the same time more penetrating? No, Ernesto had neither raced through Spanish towns like a greyhound that has lost its sense of smell, nor wandered aimlessly about at a snail's pace like those stupid tourists too blind to catch even the slightest glimpse of the real character of a person or a nation. How well he captured the very feel of Spain when he wrote in *Death in the Afternoon:*

> . . . the smell of olive oil, the feel of leather; rope soled shoes; the loops of twisted garlics; earthen pots; saddle bags carried across the shoulder; wine skins; the pitchforks made of natural wood; the early morning smells; the cold mountain nights and long hot days of summer, with always trees and shade under the trees. . . .

What gratitude for the shade of a tree, of a little clump of trees, as he journeyed halfway across Spain! He had described the feelings aroused in him by his stay in Africa in the most glowing words. What, then, would he say—and leave unsaid—about the country that had penetrated his heart like a great spike driven through it? Giving his readers an image of Spain, an absolutely lifelike image and at the same time one painted with a light touch, seemed an almost impossible task. Even wine was no help in such an undertaking, as again in *Death:*

> It should have the smell of burnt powder and the smoke and the flash and the noise of the traca going off through the green leaves of the trees.

Ernesto's first glimpse of Spain had been of the northern part of the country, but little by little, in an offensive mounted in several successive stages, he would journey to the center of the country and then to the eastern and southern provinces.

> . . . and it should have the taste of horchata, ice-cold horchata, and the new-washed streets in the sun, and the melons and beads of cool on the outside of the pitchers of beer; the storks on the houses in Barco de Avila and wheeling in the sky and the red-mud color of the ring; and at night dancing to the pipes and the drum with lights through the green leaves. . . . [*Death in the Afternoon*]

In this word picture there is something that transcends the immediate, that is more than a mere description of the scene before him, because Ernesto has managed to penetrate below the surface—something that suggests a perfect communion between the artist and his subject, something that communicates the pain and the pleasure he feels as he ponders what everything we have seen and loved will be like when the thread of life has been severed and we have passed on to that undiscovered country from whose bourn no traveler returns:

> I found that if you took a drink it got very much the same as it was always. I know things change now and I do not care. It's

all being changed for me. Let it all change. We'll all be gone before it's changed too much and if no deluge comes when we are
gone it still will rain in summer in the north and hawks will nest
in the Cathedral at Santiago and in La Granja, where we prac-
ticed with the cape on the long gravelled paths between the shadows, it makes no difference if the fountains play or not. [*Death
in the Afternoon*]

Spain, to Ernesto, was a powerful nostalgia, an enormous temptation,
an inescapable vacuum. It was like the measuring rod of his desires, like
the satisfaction of a promise fulfilled that for many long years would
shower him with an abundance of gifts:

We never will ride back from Toledo in the dark, washing
the dust out with Fundador, nor will there be that week of what
happened in the night in that July in Madrid. . . . [*Death in the
Afternoon*]

As a young man, he wrote of what he would feel as an old man; and
as an old man, he tried to write of what he had felt as a young man—
that vicious circle cherished by the artist, that incurable sickness:

We've seen it all go and we'll watch it go again. The great
thing is to last and get your work done and see and hear and
learn and understand; and write when there is something that
you know; and not before; and not too damned much after. . . .

If bullfighting was the cradle and the peak of the particular art that
fascinated him and served as his model, why did he use his knowledge of
it for the wrong purposes and betray his vocation, in *The Dangerous
Summer?*

"I know this whole thing is turning out very badly," he said one day.

"What can I say? . . ." I replied.

"Do you think there's any chance of its ending without one of them
getting killed?" he asked, and then sat there aghast at the sound of his
own words.

"I don't think the duel between them will go that far," I answered.

"One or the other of them is going to end up the lord and master of
the bullring."

"Both of them are good matadors—each of them has his own particular style and grace."

"There's no comparison between them—and one of them is going
to be crowned king of the art of bullfighting."

"They're both expert *toreros*."

"But Antonio's mastery of the art of bullfighting is something out of this world—his style's the very essence of every sort of beauty imaginable," Ernesto said.

"Luis's technique is excellent too," I replied. "He's got it all right there at his fingertips, and on afternoons when he's calm and cool and collected, he provides marvelous lessons in the art of bullfighting."

"Luis's art is still a thing of this world, however, whereas Antonio is a *torero* with supernatural gifts. Antonio's already attained immortality, and his art belongs to the realm of eternity," Ernesto answered.

"But does that mean he's going to get killed?" I said.

"When a *torero* becomes something more than a man, he's gone as far as he can possibly go. The only thing left is an ideal. . . ."

Ernesto both hoped for Antonio's death and feared it, and for that very reason he found it more acceptable to think of him as some sort of superhuman or legendary being, rather than a mere mortal whose lucky star may suddenly fail him. Ernesto had restlessly flirted with tragedy many times in his life, but I think he felt that only he had the right to deal with the "Great Bald Lady" on such familiar terms. Since he constantly talked about death without ever mentioning the word, I often remembered the story of what had happened when the galleys of *Death in the Afternoon* came back from the printers' with each sheet slugged "Hemingway's Death," the typesetter's shorthand for the full title. Ernesto was so livid with rage when he noticed, that he immediately demanded that the compositor be fired! The editor had had to swear that the poor man had not meant anything by it and persuade Ernesto that he didn't deserve to be punished.

"The way *torero*s kill themselves is the most beautiful way of all," he said that day.

"I don't know of any *torero* who doesn't unobtrusively draw back a fraction of an inch or so at the very last moment," I remarked.

"Antonio's different—he's not anything like the rest of them."

"But he doesn't want to die. Particularly when each of his *corridas* is a greater triumph than the last."

"He's killed off every one of his rivals," Ernesto said finally in a trembling voice, obviously annoyed at the turn our conversation had taken.

How can you ever get used to traveling by train again, once you have become accustomed to flying all over on planes or driving hither and yon in a car that at least gives you a few glimpses of the countryside as it eats up the miles? You don't see very much from a plane, but at times traveling by air creates a sort of special awareness of the countryside below and an urge to embrace the whole of it. And a car gives a person a certain sense of communion with the people and the landscapes glimpsed through the windows, even though this feeling of identification may be an entirely illusory one. But travel by train, which in days gone by was a means that permitted a person to enter into closer contact with people and places, has today become more or less a kind of semivoluntary kidnaping, like being shut up in a prison cell on wheels, like being both literally and figuratively "taken for a ride" that isolates you from your surroundings. As I sat there, comforted at times by my philosophical reflections and at other times with my mind a total blank, I kept looking at my watch and wondering where we were, as if knowing exactly how far we'd come would relieve my boredom.

In Alcázar de San Juan I bought several more newspapers—and discovered to my amazement that the most outlandish rumors were still going the rounds. A couple of the papers carried detailed stories on the role that Ordóñez was playing as Ernesto was being laid to rest, supposed on-the-spot reports that Antonio was going to be one of the pallbearers bearing Ernesto's coffin to its final resting place, which some of the stories described as a hillside covered with flowers and others a cemetery. The whole thing was front-page news—like Ernesto's visit to Palma de Mallorca.

I went into the little bar in the station, trying my best to swallow this colossal lie. The news stories on the front pages of these papers—and in the foreign ones as well—flatly contradicted stories on the inside pages describing what was happening in Pamplona, where Ordóñez was reported to have attended a private mass for Ernesto. Not only Ernesto's Spanish friends, among them Uncle Matías and Juanito Quintana, but also such figures as Orson Welles, along with almost everyone in Pamplona and many of Ernesto's lifetime acquaintances in the world of bullfighting, from humble attendants to fervent *aficionados*, had also been present. Gonzalo Carvajal, the bullfight critic who had followed every step of Ordóñez career, had written a very moving, carefully detailed account of the ceremony.

I had a vivid mental picture of the whole thing. The peasants from nearby Navarrese villages had doubtless said to each other:

"It's odd, isn't it, that that *inglés* with the beard didn't come this year."

"He wasn't an *inglés*, you know; he was an American," others would doubtless say.

"You mean that guy with the beard who wrote all that stuff about the 'fiesta brava'? Haven't you heard?—he killed himself."

"Killed himself!"

"Yes, that's right—he did himself in."

"He must have been out of his head. . . ."

The first one to express his regrets at Ernesto's death had been old Matías, that innkeeper for gentlemen, with his great Basque beret as round as a bullring and the apron he never took off, though when the time came to go to the church for the mass he had probably changed into a white shirt or at least a striped one, and since he was virtually a member of the deceased's family, he had doubtless worn a black necktie, and may even have turned up in a new black beret.

"Poor Ernesto!" I would have said to old Matías had I been there.

"Poor Ernesto!" he would have replied.

"Was Hemingway ill?" a reporter had asked Matías.

"The last time he ate here, two years ago, he told me he'd given up shaving because he had skin cancer and had running sores all over his body from the disease. He also told me that if it hadn't been for that, he would have preferred to be clean-shaven."

Old Matías had doubtless ended the interview by exclaiming in a sad voice: "Poor Ernesto!"

Old Matías had always been very grave and dignified in his dealings with Ernesto, whereas Juanito Quintana, no doubt the best friend that Ernesto had ever had in his life, was as familiar as an old shoe with him. Ernesto used to like to sit down at a table way off in a corner and whisper his sins in old Matías' ear, as if to an aged confessor ("Oh, what a marvelous man!" he always used to exclaim afterward), whereas he would unburden himself to Quintana in quite a different way, relaxing with his old pal and basking in his friendship ("He's very courtly, a real gentleman of the old school," Ernesto would always say). He never forgot him; from the very first, memories of Spain and Juanito were closely linked in Ernesto's mind. Perhaps Juanito Quintana had been the only one at the mass who had shed tears, because that was the sort of person he had always been and always would be.

I could see the whole memorial service vividly in my mind after reading the newspaper accounts.

Dressed in his very best, Juanito had no doubt hurried to the chapel of San Fermín on the eleventh, three days after Ernesto had been laid in his grave, worried that he might be late, and on entering the church immediately joined Ordóñez, who had been the first to arrive and was already on his knees praying for his dead friend.

The next to arrive was Orson Welles, swaying like a freighter loaded to the gunwales with a precious cargo. He was making a film entitled *Sancho Panza in Pamplona*, a movie full of both roguish humor and cool irony, youthful high spirits and lechery, savory popular wisdom and mysticism—realism in the Navarrese manner, in short, a dish very much like Navarrese trout in that it is always hearty and satisfying if prepared correctly.

The bells were tolling now—there was no doubt of that. Tolling for Ernesto. Instead of trumpet blasts, all of Pamplona was echoing with the eerie sound of every church bell in town tolling his death knell. Pamplona owed Ernesto a great deal, and only this year the mayor had decided to honor him by naming him an official guest of the city when he came for the Sanfermines. But it was too late for that now.

Other friends had arrived and were standing there in front of the chapel together: Nicole, Orson Welles's constant companion; Alexandra Steward; Alfredo Pickman, a champion fisherman. Many ordinary townswomen had also gathered, not knowing exactly who this requiem mass was being held for; for all they knew, it might be for some youngster gored to death by a bull some other year, or some unknown young *torero* who had died in some bullring heaven only knew where, or for all the bullfighters who had died in all the many years of *encierros* and *corridas*. . . .

It was a short mass, but a very moving one. Ernesto's good friends of bygone years, so many years of delirious happiness and joy, had all come to honor him on this sad occasion. The townswomen in mourning were praying fervently, knowing that someone or other had died a tragic death, but many of them had no idea who it was that the mass was being said for.

One of them thought she knew, and said: "I'm quite sure it's for Ordóñez's father."

In his own way, Ernesto had indeed been a father to Ordóñez, and in a manner of speaking, a father to Ordóñez's father, Niño de la Palma, as well.

Ernesto's "double" had suddenly appeared at the entrance to the church—the ubiquitous Mr. Vanderford, who may or may not have turned up as a sort of sardonic joke on the dead man. In any case, there had always been something grotesque and macabre about this bearded "double" of Ernesto's who had so often fooled even those reporters who knew that there was a "real" Ernesto and a "fake" one. How many times one or another of them had called me from some place in Spain and told me: "Listen, Ernesto's just arrived here." "Ernesto, you say? Which Ernesto?" I would ask. "Ernesto Hemingway, of course," they would say. "Well, take another look and you'll see the difference between the real article and a fake, between a fascinating human being and a dull clown." "What's that again?" they'd reply in a puzzled voice. "A stupid clown, I said." "I don't know what you're talking about," they would answer. "Never mind, I'll explain later," I would say.

Quite possibly this "double" of Ernesto's had come to pay his sincere respects to the dead man, but just as he was about to step into the chapel Orson Welles flew into a rage and stopped him.

"Now that 'Papa' is dead, your little joke isn't one bit funny," he roared.

"It's downright offensive," several other people chimed in.

"Why don't we cut his beard off?" Welles suggested in his great, rumbling voice.

"Let's get the guy!" somebody else shouted.

But whatever his intentions, the impostor escaped unharmed. Ordóñez couldn't bear the thought of Vanderford's being there at the mass for Ernesto, but at the same time he wasn't in favor of doing the man any sort of violence. Antonio doubtless believed that he had not yet entirely fulfilled his obligation to Ernesto, and was planning to appear in the bullring at his next *corrida* wearing a black arm-band on his gold and purple suit of lights, and ask the spectators to observe a minute of silence in memory of Ernesto. That was doubtless what was on his mind just then, not lopping off the beard of that ridiculous prankster.

I got off the train for a moment to stretch my legs, but since the ham they sell travelers in the station at Albacete appears to have come from a bull rather than a pig, and even if you order three different kinds of wine you'll never be served the claret you need and have your heart set on, I was back in my seat again in just a few minutes. There were not nearly as many people on the train now.

It must have been in the station at La Encina that I was again painfully reminded of Ernesto, thanks to one of those transistor radios. And the program being broadcast this time was the real *coup de grâce*. After the chorus of the famous San Fermín song:

> *Levántate, pamplónica*
> *y da de la cama un brinco*
> (*Wake up, pamplónica*
> *And hop out of bed . . .*)

the commentator delivered a great long speech in praise of *The Sun Also Rises*, though everyone in Spain knew that it was fiesta time in Pamplona and the Sanfermines scarcely needed publicity in the form of quotations from a novel by a foreigner. Fortunately the passage the commentator quoted was one of the best in the book, and was recited in a soft voice tinged with sadness:

"The fiesta was really started. It kept up for seven days. Then dancing kept up, the drinking kept up, the noise went on. The things that happened could only have happened during a fiesta. Everything became quite unreal finally and it seemed as though nothing could have any consequences. It seemed out of place to think of consequences during the fiesta. All during the fiesta you had the feeling, even when it was quiet, that you had to shout any remark to make it heard. It was the same feeling about any action. It was a fiesta and it went on for seven days."

It was as though the events of the novel were being played out again in real life. But nobody seemed to have connected Ernesto's death with the San Fermín fiesta, though I for my part firmly believe that Ernesto may well have suddenly been so overcome by memories of happy Sanfermines of the past that the thought of not turning up at Pamplona, and therefore being taken for a coward who didn't have the nerve to show his face after *The Dangerous Summer* had appeared in print, may have hastened his violent end.

The memory of him was again as painful as a fresh wound. My eyes filled with tears, and I turned away and looked at the wine sellers and the reapers and the mules so that no one would see how grief-stricken I was, standing there trying to dredge up every last memory of the past, a past that did not seem at all remote, for its very echo was still ringing in my ears. . . .

The morning of the first day of the fiesta had been very moving. Only a little after dawn, we were already out in the streets, walking up and down, greeting the sleepy-eyed, nervous youngsters who were going to run with the bulls. The groups of young lads were already choosing the places along the streets where they would confront the bulls. Even the sleepiest of them, huddling along the sidewalk like big, inert bundles of rags, were ready and waiting for the bulls to appear.

It was like the beginning of a battle, that moment when the combatants are at once scared to death and almost lustfully eager to meet the enemy face to face. The sky was growing lighter and lighter, like a foamy sea bearing us from one corner to the next and gradually revealing the most dangerous spots. Every street along the route was crowded with excited onlookers and delirious white-shirted youngsters eagerly awaiting the thundering bulls, all singing:

Levántate, pamplónica. . . .

It was mostly strong, lusty, male voices singing, but every once in a while we could also hear the higher-pitched voices of women and even children joining in.

One image in particular haunted my mind: the sight of the bulls in their pens the night before, when we had gone to have a close look at them. One minute I felt very brave and was sure I wouldn't beat a cowardly retreat when the bulls came running after me, and the next moment I had my doubts and could just see myself falling on the ground or being cornered by one of the beasts and crushed to death against the board fencing.

I was amazed at how calm Ordóñez and the rest of them, including the women, all were, standing there coolly cracking jokes, and it was plain to see that Ernesto was as excited as a kid.

We had a couple of drinks in a terrible dump, and Ernesto turned to me and said:

"Let's see you spit."

I spat, and he said:

"Let's see you do it again."

I spat again.

"Once more!" he exclaimed.

I felt like a fool standing there spitting like that, and the *cazalla* I'd drunk was churning in my guts.

"You're a little bit scared, but not all that much," he said to me. "Some of the others are feeling much more panicky."

Ernesto firmly believed that if you were scared your mouth would be as dry as dust, and therefore, if you could work up enough saliva to spit, it proved you weren't afraid.

We went over the whole route of the *encierro* again, picking the spots where there would probably be the most excitement. Ernesto was carrying his silver flask in his hand and offered me a swallow.

Then he delivered a little lecture: The important thing was not only to run with the bulls, but to run well, keeping ahead of them, but not too far ahead, and not falling, being very careful not to let the others trip you in the mad scramble, and if you got into trouble and weren't an expert hurdler (as was most probably the case), the best thing to do was to throw yourself down on the ground, if you could manage to do so without breaking you neck. As a theory of bull-running, that wasn't bad; but it all depended on how it worked out in practice, and practice was precisely what I hadn't had, of course.

If you thought about it, it wasn't really very risky. Moreover, the *encierro* was only part of the fiesta—an important part, to be sure, but there was also much more to come. As the fateful hour approached, my legs began trembling a bit, and despite the vodka my voice sounded a bit unsteady.

Time was flying by and I would have to decide where to wait for the bulls. On the corner by the city hall? No, that was a place for experts, and only a fool would have advised me to make my stand there.

"They'll come thundering by in just a few seconds, and you won't even have to run," Ernesto had reassured me.

I decided the best place would be in the Calle de la Estafeta, just around the corner from the Calle Doña Blanca de Navarra. There were hundreds of *pamplónicas* there, and I thought I might as well join them and be just one more in the crowd. If I waited for the bulls there, all I'd have to do when they appeared was run like a madman, do my best not to get trampled on or stumble over anybody else, and keep out of the way of the drunkest bull-runners.

There were only twelve minutes to go now—twelve long minutes. I found myself wishing that the bulls were already off and running.

I tried to station myself as close as I could to the wide end of the street leading to the plaza de toros. Ernesto and Mary had picked a choice spot from which to watch the *encierro* and would be able to see everything, despite their having turned down several invitations to watch from the balconies reserved for special guests. They planned sometime to watch the end of the *encierro* in the bullring. There was no use looking at your wristwatch. The signal to let the bulls loose would be the clock on the chapel of San Fermín striking seven, so softly that no one would hear, because the minute the first stroke sounded and the rocket went off in the pearl-gray sky, the great, black thundering herd of bulls would be heading down the hill, a fascinating, terrifying sight, huge, beautiful animals reminiscent of deadly tanks advancing. The route they would follow measured just a few inches short of 823 meters, according to the San Fermín experts, but the *toros* would easily cover the distance in about a minute and a half.

If the *encierro* wasn't over within two minutes, it would be because some sort of incident had occurred that had held them up. Sometimes these incidents were hilariously funny, and everyone would swap stories about them for the rest of the fiesta; but at other times they weren't funny at all, leaving at least one *pamplónica* weeping bitter tears, and not a word was said about them.

Ernesto wasn't able to run with the bulls any more and was casting envious, nostalgic glances at the *pamplónicas* waiting for the *toros* to appear. Mary was standing there watching the liveliest groups, camera in hand.

There was only five minutes to go now.

It was definitely time to pick a spot, as safe and easy a one as possible. At this point, you calculated your strength for the very last time and tried to figure out exactly how much of a head start you would need when the bulls appeared at the top of the Calle de la Curia.

The bands of musicians who had been wandering about the streets since five that morning, making it impossible for anyone in Pamplona to get another wink of sleep, were beginning to gather in the plaza now. Many of them must have collapsed on the sidewalks for a short nap at some time during the night, with nothing to pillow their heads but their instruments.

"What would happen if for some reason the clock on the tower of that French saint's chapel didn't strike seven this year?" I asked a young peasant lad.

"Don't worry, that's never happened. San Fermín's always as punctual as the hangman."

342

The hangman? I didn't care much for his answer, and moved away from the fellow before he brought me bad luck.

I was afraid to let Ordóñez see how little talent I had as a bullfighter, so I didn't want to be anywhere near him either; a big crowd had gathered around him, and I was sure Antonio and all the rest of them would die laughing when they saw how clumsy I was. Moreover, there were hordes of *pamplónicas* eager to show the great matador how brave they were, and there would doubtless be a lot of pushing and shoving and tripping and falling over, there where he was.

Standing there along the sidewalk, looking about for nearby iron gates to climb or holes in the wooden planking along the route to dive through if the need should arise, we were all restlessly waiting for the clock to strike and glancing apprehensively over our shoulders. But I wasn't quite so scared now, since many of the others, especially the foreigners, had obviously never run before the bulls either. But even the old hands at it couldn't hide the fact that they were just a little bit nervous.

"Have you ever run before?" an older man, about my age, sitting on the sidewalk near me asked.

"No, this is my first time," I replied.

"Well, in that case keep a little bit ahead of the rest of them and run like hell down the middle of the street as soon as you hear people shouting."

"Okay, I will," I said, tying the laces of the rope-soled sandals I'd bought the afternoon before even tighter.

I hoped the few remaining seconds would fly by—there was only a minute and a half to go now. Doors were slamming shut all along the street, and the guards had disappeared as if by magic. There was such a deep silence now that it seemed as though the rocket would never be able to break through it and explode in the sky above to signal that the gate to the bullpen had been opened and the herd of *toros* was on its way down the hill, like a sinister locomotive moving along without rails, prepared to sweep aside any and every obstacle in its path.

At that very instant, for some inexplicable reason I suddenly felt perfectly calm and sat down on the sidewalk. Men about to be executed by a firing squad at any moment must feel much the same. And as the *pamplónicas* scrambled to their feet and looked back over their shoulders, called to each other, shouted up to the balconies, and whistled, and then suddenly fell totally silent, like a great chorus following a magic baton, I simply sat there, quietly and calmly . . .

It all happened very fast. As the first rocket burst went off, many of of *pamplónicas* began running, myself among them; but then I realized that the roar I had heard was not bulls thundering down on me, but

343

others along the route snorting and stamping their feet and trying to scare us. I didn't hear the second rocket go off, because I was already off and running, like just another bull in the herd, except that *toros* probably don't feel as though their hearts are leaping out of their mouths.

What worried me most at that moment was the huge crowd collecting right in front of me. The avalanche descending on us from behind was sure to crush us all, it seemed to me. How could all of us—men and bulls alike—ever get through that dense, roaring mob blocking our way like a solid wall?

I was running rather well, I thought, skillfully managing not to trip over any of the *pamplónicas* who had fallen and deftly slipping through any sudden gaps in the crowd that I spotted. It would have been just as dangerous to run along the sidewalks as down the middle of the street, for they were packed with men who looked even fiercer than bulls. Despite the many white-shirted *pamplónicas*, the crowd seemed to me to be one huge, solid, dark mass.

I had hoped to wave to Ernesto as I ran by, but it was impossible. The only thing I could think of was the bulls, roaring down upon me in a deafening thunder of hoofs. Every once in a while, the women on the balconies would all scream in chorus, as though some bloody accident had just occurred below them. And the furious pounding of hoofs was coming closer and closer, a great, mad din mingled with great sighs and bursts of laughter, advancing down the street like a huge tidal wave.

I could see the bullring gate, and the spot where I would be out of danger at last. I had only to make one last mad dash and enter the bright sunlight of the arena. Despite my terror, I was feeling very proud of myself, terribly excited, and almost radiantly happy. I was just another of the *pamplónicas*, and my legs were faithfully obeying my bidding. It never once occurred to me to turn and look back to see how close the bulls' bristling horns were. The furious metallic tinkle of the bells around their necks was quite enough to tell me that they were very close indeed.

If I could remain cool and calm and collected for just a few seconds more, it would all be over and I would be safe. I realized that it was not only my own force of will propelling me, but also the whole great throng of *pamplónicas*, breathing and running as one, all joyously sharing the same experience, a force even stronger than the mad onrush of those great beasts pursuing us.

Many youngsters had flung themselves to the ground along the curbing and were lying there piled one on top of the other. On seeing that tangled heap of bodies, you were tempted to throw yourself on top of them, but suddenly it seemed less frightening simply to go on running and leaping over these excited *pamplónicas* who had taken a nose dive and seemed to be more happy than sad to be out of the running, and glad to have bodies piling up on top of them to protect them.

How could all of us *pamplónicas* and those bulls with their great horns have made our way through that dense crowd and all those sprawling bodies lying on the ground like a grove of felled trees without leaving a trail of blood in our wake? I still can't get over it, to this day.

I was so excited as I dashed into the bullring that even though the entrance was jam-packed with crazy, drunken fools (that was when I realized that all of us were more or less intoxicated, and not just because we'd drunk a lot), I frantically pushed and shoved my way straight through to the *barrera*, and just as I reached it, a great, almost savage roar suddenly filled the entire plaza and I leaped over the barricade, so awkwardly that I almost fell headlong on the sand in the *callejón*. It could have been a very nasty fall, but fortunately it was merely comical, and everybody laughed.

Everything that happened in the bullring then was so farcical and good-humored that it would have been fun to stand there watching the hilarious sight of harmless calves sweeping drunks off their feet as though they were dominoes. But during the entire circus there in the ring, I simply stood there hugging the wooden fence, my mind a total blank.

And then I heard someone say, "Ordóñez was injured."

"Ordóñez the *torero?*" I asked.

"Naturally. What Ordóñez did you think I meant?" was the answer.

"Where is he?"

He wasn't hard to find. He'd refused to go to the infirmary and was still cavorting in the streets with the youngsters. He'd gotten grazed by the horn of a bull from Pablo Romero's ranch—one of the six that were to be fought that very afternoon—because he had tried to divert the beast as it was about to attack a hapless youngster, and was as proud of the wound he had received as he would have been had he been gored going in for the kill.

But Ernesto made a terrible fuss about this little scratch, and finally dragged Antonio off to have it attended to. He kept asking Antonio to show him the wound, and wouldn't be content till he had personally seen to it that the wound was disinfected and bandaged with the help of his friend the American doctor from Idaho. Since Ernesto was so superstitious, he regarded this little scratch as an ominous sign; he didn't dare say so in so many words, but he was nonetheless convinced it was bad luck.

"But it's just a tiny little nick!" Antonio kept saying.

"I know—it's nothing, but you have to have it attended to. You've got to be careful."

Ordóñez went right on dancing, and Ernesto said to him in an affectionate but reproachful tone of voice, "You might have been hurt worse, you know."

As the saying goes, it never rains but it pours, because Mary, who had been so concerned and so solicitous when Antonio was hurt that we had hardly realized that she'd been hurt too, also needed medical attention, for she had begun to limp very badly. At first we thought she'd merely twisted her ankle, but it began to hurt her more and more, and finally the doctor had to put her entire leg in a light cast. The poor woman had broken a toe and was in terrible pain. She could hardly get around, but she didn't want to miss the fun, and even more importantly, she didn't want to leave Ernesto by himself, so she spent the rest of the San Fermín fiesta limping about very slowly and clumsily, leaning on one or the other of us for support. I was surprised to see that Ernesto worried constantly about Antonio's little scratch, which required no more than a strip of adhesive tape, yet dismissed Mary's really painful injury as nothing at all, or rather regarded it as a nuisance that would force him to change his plans and interfere with his trips back and forth between the city and the country and his outings on the river. It wasn't that Ernesto was callous or no longer loved Mary; he was simply inclined by temperament to attribute epic proportions to everything having to do with bullfighting, whereas the little everyday realities of life seemed dull and unimportant. He kept saying jokingly, "I've said more than once that women have no business attending *encierros*—your own wife especially."

There was no doubt about it: not only had Ernesto shown signs of all the manias that were now an old familiar story to all of us; he had also begun to behave so strangely that we were all worried about him. He needed Mary and couldn't get along without her; nonetheless, for days at a time he would play the role of the sentimental and romantic swain to the hilt, and we were all flabbergasted to see him approach one of the "kidnap victims," usually the little Irish girl, even though she was no great beauty, with a flower clutched in his hand and present it to her with all sorts of high-flown compliments. With her curly hair, her delicate skin sprinkled with freckles, her obvious willingness to begin a serious affair despite her blushing innocence, the Irish girl was like a sort of toy or a distraction for Ernesto the world-famous writer, or at any rate she served him as a handy reason for straying off from the rest of us and an excuse for being unfaithful to his own true self.

The two American college students who for a time were members of the chorus of "kidnap victims," were really were decoration, young

346

women whose company pleased Ernesto more than it excited him. Anyone witnessing the whole affair from afar would doubtless have concluded that Ernesto was sleeping with all three of these girls; but in actual fact, it was all very open and aboveboard and rather dull. He had taken up with them on the spur of the moment, and the entire escapade was completely harmless until the innocent habit of being together all the time began to create a vague climate of guilt—not only in Ernesto's mind. It was no more than to be expected that women who in the beginning had been merely a decorative element would end up clinging to him like ivy to a wall. Perhaps Ernesto needed that escape route by way of tender affection in order to break out of the forbidding walls of madness that were already beginning to close in upon him.

At times, amid all the innocent merrymaking, he would become very distant and unapproachable and depressed, as though he had already suffered a wound that would eventually prove fatal. He would often appear to be quite drunk—but even though the *feria* served as a handy excuse for excessive drinking, it was sadness and loneliness, not alcohol, that had gone to his head.

The San Fermín fiesta had become the ideal background for his little love-adventure and his art. It was as though the Sanfermines that year had suddenly crystallized time past, as though it were only there in Pamplona that his feelings could bloom and flower, only there that his imagination was capable of carrying on its work within his mind and heart.

Once the *encierro* was over, the remainder of the morning was spent drinking coffee and eating doughnuts in the Plaza del Castillo, spiced with endless stories about the bullbaiting, the leaps, the headlong dives, the falls, and the gorings in the streets of the town.

Next came the hours-long offensive against the person of this genius, as Ernesto welcomed some of his admirers and pointedly ignored others, exchanging cordial words with certain of them and giving others the cold shoulder once they had fought their way into his unforgettable presence. Then the river of wine would begin to flow, though little by little in recent years I had seen him drink both lesser quantities of it and weaker vintages. When I had first met him, he had most often drunk very strong wines from La Mancha, Riojas and clarets, but gradually he had taken to drinking rosés.

Drinking was more or less *de rigueur* in Pamplona: all the townspeople and all the outsiders consumed enormous quantities of liquor. It was as though the Sanfermines gave you an unquenchable thirst—or a feeling of deepest sorrow—that could only be drowned in alcohol, endless floods of alcohol. The characters in *The Sun Also Rises* had long since given us ample proof of how a person, even without drinking to excess, can catch a glimpse of the truth or the mystery of death, a truth or a mystery so close at hand that one breathes it in with every breath during the Pamplona fiesta. Everything about the fiesta in Pamplona is ritual, culminating in a sort of sacrifice that may be bloody and cruel—from the *encierro* shortly after dawn to the *corrida* in the bullring in the late afternoon.

We always planned our day there in the Plaza del Castillo, and would then go directly to Casa Marceliano, where we would have a delicious lunch consisting of spareribs, eggs, fried peppers, ham, sausages, and fresh-picked fruit from neighboring orchards. However, if the word seafood was mentioned, the meal might be quite different. This huge midday repast sometimes went on till dinnertime; but, more often, Ernesto would spirit all of us off to the banks of the Irati after lunch. He was always beside himself with joy whenever he visited the province of Navarre, and everything he loved best was right there, including lots of talk about the bloodlines and the look of the bulls that were to be fought in the late afternoon.

That first day, he stayed with Ordóñez till the very last moment, trying to get him to rest. The slight horn wound in his leg was a trophy that Antonio was proud of, but Ernesto wanted to make sure he took proper care of it.

"Don't be a fool," Ernesto said to him paternally. "You'll be fighting *mano a mano* with your pal in the Puerto de Santa María next week, remember."

"Okay, Papa—I'll do as you say," Antonio replied.

The food baskets had been packed and bottles of wine iced for our picnic in the country, but Ernesto couldn't tear himself away from the world of bullfighting.

The past and the present had become one. Of Cayetano Ordóñez, Ernesto had written:

> . . . in his first season as a matador, promoted in the spring after some beautiful performances as a novillero in Sevilla, Malaga and some incomplete ones in Madrid, [he] looked like the messiah who had come to save bullfighting if ever any one did.

Yes, he had said that and many other things about the father and very soon afterward had had to correct them and qualify them, almost shamefacedly. But nothing of the sort could possibly happen in the case of the son. His feelings and his thoughts about Antonio Ordóñez would never change; as he wrote in *The Dangerous Summer*:

> The first time I saw Antonio Ordóñez I saw that he could make all the classic passes without faking, that he knew bulls, that he

could kill well if he wished to, and that he was a genius with the cape. I could see he had the three great requisites for a matador: courage, skill in his profession and grace in the presence of danger.

Ernesto had come to believe that Ordóñez stood in need of his lucky star, if not of his advice. He would bring Antonio luck, he would protect him, he would assure him a position above every other living *torero* and perhaps establish him as a guiding light for every future matador. What had happened to the father, a talented bullfighter but a failure in the end, could not possibly happen to the son. His words about Antonio's father in *Death in the Afternoon* had been heartfelt but also very humiliating:

> I was present the day of his first presentation as a matador in Madrid and I saw him in Valencia in competition with Juan Belmonte, returned from retirement, do two faenas that were so beautiful and wonderful that I can remember them pass by pass to-day. He was sincerity and purity of style itself with the cape, he did not kill badly, although, except when he had luck, he was not a great killer. He did kill several times *recibiendo,* receiving the bull on the sword in the old manner and he was beautiful with the muleta. . . . At the end of the season he was gored severely and painfully in the thigh, very near the femoral artery.
> That was the end of him.

As we sat there in the car waiting for Ernesto, Mary said:
"It's crazy, the whole thing is crazy. The streets are full of madmen, madmen who don't even know what a bull is, yet that *toro* headed straight for the only man who knew what a bull was and how to fight one. I just don't understand it. And he might have hurt Antonio . . ."
Ernesto turned up eventually and we started off. It was no longer possible for him to sit out on the terrace of any of the bars in Pamplona. Foreigners, townspeople, and tourists immediately congregated by the hundreds, lining up in front of his table, presenting him their hat or their blouse or their silk scarf or their fan or their shirt or their bare flesh to sign, or fishing personal papers or family photographs out of their wallets and shoving them at him to autograph. And Ernesto would sit there signing his name, patiently and politely and calmly. Every so often there would be some sort of commotion, and Ernesto would say, "If you don't behave, I won't sign another one."
The waiters had a terrible time serving the customers amid all the hubbub. And then one wave of photographers and foreign reporters after another would descend upon him, and more than once Hotchner or Davis would have to intervene and send them packing.

349

"We only want to ask him a few questions," they would plead.

"Just a couple of shots of him, sitting there drinking and fondling that pretty girl . . ."

"He's come to see the fiesta and you're pestering him to death. It isn't right," the "kidnap victims" would say, mostly in sign language, but nonetheless getting the message across that they didn't approve at all.

Ernesto would suddenly get tired of signing his name and say sternly, "Okay, that's all now. I'll sign some more later on today, or tomorrow."

It was time to steal away to the remote little spots he loved so much, many of them described long before in *Death in the Afternoon:*

> In the morning there we would have breakfast and then go out to swim in the Irati at Aoiz, the water clear as light. . . .
>
> But when the wind is from the south Navarra is all the color of wheat except it does not grow on level plains but up and down the sides of hills and cut by roads with trees and many villages with bells, pelota courts, the smell of sheep manure and squares with standing horses. . . .

There was nothing that made Ernesto more furious than having his privacy violated. And it was always at Pamplona that his patience was most sorely tried. One asinine Swiss journalist had asked him, "Which of the women you've made love to do you have the fondest memories of?" and Ernesto had first muttered under his breath in Spanish, *"De la puta de tu madre"* (your whore of a mother), and then said aloud, "A black girl, I think, whom I never got around to making my lawfully wedded wife." "As an expert on bulls, what do you think of the ones for this afternoon's *corrida?"* the reporter then asked him. Ernesto turned to us first and said out of the corner of his mouth, "They're all shitty," and then looked the sobersided interviewer straight in the eye and said, "It's a bullfight card I'd be very pleased to hang over the head of my bed." Then came another question he'd been asked a thousand times before: "Why didn't you go to Sweden to receive the Nobel Prize in person?" Ernesto again turned to our little group first and murmured, "This guy must think I like showing my ass in public," and then said to the dutiful reporter: "Was I supposed to go to Sweden? I was sick in bed at the time, it seems to me." "After you'd been injured in that accident?" the newsman asked. "No, I'd come down with the mumps, as I recall," Ernesto replied. "Had you been looking forward to receiving the prize from the King of Sweden in person?" the reporter persisted. "I've never been one to sidle backward like a crab; I've never had any practice at it—not even during the wars I've taken part in; but the fact that my dinner jacket wasn't pressed may also have kept me from going." "Were you pleased at having received the Nobel Prize?" "I'm always very happy when tax-free dough comes my way, and to prove it, I invite you to have a drink on me—anything you want—seeing as how you're such a nice, intelligent, persistent sort." The reporter ordered a Coca-Cola, and after politely asking his permission, Ernesto poured a big slug of absinthe in it and the fellow heroically downed the terrible-tasting concoction. Ernesto wasn't always that polite by any means, and would sometimes leap to his feet, shouting like a madman and kicking the reporters in the shins. He must have scared a number of them so badly that they turned tail or ran for cover whenever they saw him. If he was in a good mood when they started asking him questions about the war in Spain, he would tell them one tall story after another, each more incredible than the last, but he would never say a word about his real experiences during the war.

"You keep staring at her all the time," he said to me, referring to the Irish girl.
"She's a pretty little thing."
"She might like it if you tried to make out with her."
"Sometimes it's more fun to invent a story than it is to live it in real life," I said, feeling it advisable to bring the conversation back around to writers and writing.
"But you're not going to run away, are you?"
"No, I'm not. But neither am I one of those dashing fellows who leap over the casement singing at the top of their lungs."
"I hope you're not expecting that nice girl to fall into your arms."
"No, she might hurt herself."
"You're not exactly a Spanish cavalier, it seems to me."
"You're right there—I'm probably not your typical Spanish cavalier."
Ernesto had tended recently to be more and more testy and coarse and crude, but in surroundings such as this, he became much mellower. Those changes for the worse were no doubt a reflection of the sort of world he usually frequented; they may very well have also been a sort of armor to protect him from that other world, of thinkers and intellectuals and critics, that he both frankly detested and unconsciously feared. Everything he did in Spain was at once a kind of play-acting and an absolutely genuine response; partly a frivolous pastime and partly a profound, moving experience: a way of life that suited him perfectly, a sort of style he had created for himself to prove that he was both a revered sovereign in the kingdom of the meek and humble and the imperious lord and master in the decadent world of the bullring.

People who thought of him as a leftist revolutionary politically or an unscrupulous and lustful man in private were dead wrong.‡ This was the image of him that the press was pleased to put before the public, and most Spaniards would have found it an amazing sight to see him, as I did that day, completely naked both bodily and spiritually.

We were lazing about there on the riverbank, stripping for a dip before lunch, with cans of this and that open and bottles of beer, Cokes for the girls, gin and whisky uncapped. . . . As Ernesto undressed there in the sunlight, I was able to see what terrible shape he was in. It was a tragic sight, for his once-magnificent body was now fat and crisscrossed with scars, and I suddenly felt a boundless pity for the man. It was quite apparent that physically, if not spiritually, Ernesto was a martyr, a man who had sacrificed both great patches of living flesh and a part of his soul in his effort to survive the great manhunt that life is for each of us. His noble head was covered with round, puckered scars and the traces of fine surgical stitches, a reminder that he had suffered terrible injuries that would have shattered any one else's skull, wounds that had seemingly had little effect on him, other than causing him to indulge in one minor vanity—combing his hair forward in bangs that made him look like a grown-up schoolboy—in order to conceal some of the scars. His back was majestically broad, though his shoulders were surprisingly narrow and his upper arms, which were neither as massive nor as robust as might be expected, seemed quite out of proportion to his great girth and his enormous torso. His one shoulder was furrowed with several enormous scars and countless smaller ones, like traces in living flesh of the cruel refinement of the surgeon's art. His great swollen belly made me think of a beautiful thoroughbred that has taken on elephantine proportions with the advent of old age; his thighs, all his life too slender to allow him to go in for any sort of horseback riding, had now turned to flab; but it was his calves and bowed legs that were the most cruelly scarred, the calves and legs of a slave forced to do hard labor and frequently horsewhipped, or a soldier sentenced to death and branded, or a prisoner tortured a thousand times for a hundred crimes. His entire body was a lacy, zigzag network of scars and scratches and bites and pricks and cuts, slices removed from the living flesh, a sacrificial offering made by the enthusiastic adventurer who dared to enter into carnal embrace with life itself, often at the risk of his own life, in the jungle and the desert, in the forests and the trenches, in hotels and on the shores of rivers, on the ocean and along the world's highways

‡ I find confirmation of my description of Ernesto's political beliefs in Gabriel Jackson's *The Spanish Republic and the Civil War, 1931–1939,* Princeton Univ. Press, 1965, page 352. Though not supporters of either rightists or leftists, certain misguided Spaniards with axes to grind have attempted to prove that Ernesto was a spokesman for one or the other of the contending factions in the Civil War. But Ernesto was really one of the very last liberal romantics, a generous idealist with far loftier ends in view.

and byways. His huge feet and powerful hands were the most striking proof that he was still a strong, vigorous man. But it was a forbidding and terrifying experience to look him straight in the face: his eyes that had once flashed like lightning as the storm raged within now had only the feeble glimmer of a dreamer who had ceased to dream; they were now eyes with a vacant, faraway look in them, the downcast eyes of a man no longer able to squarely confront life's onslaughts. His once-burning lips had been consumed by the fire; an unquenchable thirst masked the fury within; they were faded, tired lips, a mouth that kisses, more imagined than real, had left as dry as dust; lips left cracked and parched as the wellsprings of his inspiration ran dry, as mortal tedium overcame him, like a spiritual drought, on finding himself forced to draw upon his real-life experiences in his writing when the life he was leading was so different from the life he dreamed of; lips that had set in a grim line at the disappointment of hopes for a peace of mind long dreamed of but never attained in the course of his deliberate pursuit of risk and adventure; wooden apathy in the face of fortune, be it good or bad, and the numbing realization that death is inevitable, though no man can know for certain when or where he will die; a bone-deep weariness of soul that his body was merely a complacent witness to; a spirit terrified by its lack of responsiveness and its insensitivity to anything above and beyond the five senses. . . . More than the creator of characters whose life might spur others on to fight for an ideal, Ernesto was a famous personality who had gone down to defeat because he had ceased to live for an ideal. There under that oak tree, naked to the waist with his billed cap perched on his head, he was the living image of the fisherman in *The Old Man and the Sea,* except that his heroic struggle had not taken place on a stretch of ocean made of the stuff that dreams are made of, but rather the hard, cold ground he walked on—a last-ditch struggle, like a beautiful animal caught in a trap, or a soldier pinned between two trenches by artillery fire, for he had been a man trapped between life and death since the day he was born. . . .

Ernesto's wife and the three young girls he had taken along on this outing for company were all there on the riverbank; love and sex were both on hand; and two friends as well, Davis and I, respectively representing a loyalty that had nothing to do with art and a friendship whose very cornerstone was a shared aesthetic.

"And how are your other projects going?" I asked Ernesto.

"I'm fed up," he replied, and then he added: "Gypsies are absolute angels compared to lots of people in my country."

I wasn't sure what he meant by that. Perhaps he was hinting, as he so often did, at the problems he was having with people who were making television or film adaptations of his works, or the tyrannical highhandedness of certain of his publishers, alongside whom bull-fighters' agents and bullring impresarios were also more or less angels, despite the fact that the latter were notoriously hardhearted. Projects such as these were sometimes a form of relaxation for Ernesto, though more than once I noticed that he later found ironclad agreements of this sort very irksome.

Often it was Ordóñez's presence—or his absence—that explained Ernesto's bad moods. Putting up with Antonio's sudden whims made Ernesto as frantic as a bull trapped in a very awkward position between the bullring fence and the matador's cape and unable to fight back.

It was time now to take our dip in the river and then have lunch. Instead of picnicking together as a group, each of us picked an isolated spot to eat in, or else we wandered back and forth exchanging idle chitchat. Our conversations couldn't have been more trivial, but this outing was nonetheless very relaxing and we all felt better.

Mary let us in on a little secret and told us what had happened that morning. Just as it was getting light, Ernesto had awakened her by shaking her till she opened her eyes and said, "Listen, darling, see if you can do something about this cramp."

"What cramp?" she had answered.

"The one that's hurting me like crazy!"

"What's the trouble?"

"I'm going to have to go out on the street, and it hurts so much I can't."

"What is it exactly that's wrong with you?"

"I just told you—I can't move, that's what's wrong, damn it!"

"Well, what do you want *me* to do?"

"Stop asking so many questions. Help me get rid of this cramp and then we'll talk."

Ernesto frequently began the day by waking up with a cramp somewhere or other, and often after he had gone to bed at night he would complain of peculiar sensations of some sort, and Mary, as always the most patient and imperturbable of nurses, would do her best to calm him down. He very often suffered severe attacks of anxiety or had terrifying nightmares, and acting as cross as a bear and swearing a blue streak were usually simply his way of asking for help. Mary was unable to work miracles, but fortunately she knew exactly how to handle Ernesto and could usually get him back to sleep again.

"To hell with you and your nightmares!" she would exclaim. "I need at least a little bit of sleep, you know."

"What are you bitching about now?"

"I'm complaining because I've fallen into the hands of savages from the North."

354

"No, you're complaining because I'm complaining."

"Why should I complain if we're spending our time with the nicest madmen in the whole world?"

"Rub right here."

"Like this?"

"No, you're hurting me."

"Like this, then?"

"Damn that cramp! It's killing me!"

"Just relax."

It was a lovely day. A hot July sun was beating down there at the bend in the river, but fortunately there was also a nice, cool breeze blowing. On a number of our trips out into the countryside, there had been a flurry of rain and it had looked as though a furious storm would put an end to our outing, but now the sun was really warm, and after two or three days down by the river we would have as dark a tan as though we'd been out separating the wheat from the straw on the threshing floors in the fields.

The ladies were the first to dive into the river, with Mary as the leader of the group of "kidnap victims," looking as slender and lithe and regal as always. She immediately waded out into deep water, while the other three splashed around in the shallows and cavorted about Ernesto as he strode into the water, looking for all the world like a statue of Saint Christopher. Having ventured out waist-deep in the ice-cold water, Mary then made her way back to Ernesto's side like a faithful, affectionate pussycat. Ernesto was very fond of Mary as a person: she was unfailingly good-humored and helpful; she constantly hummed cheery little songs, gave him sound advice, settled accounts, scolded him, and let him know when something displeased her, but always with enormous discretion and tact, choosing exactly the right moment and the right words. Her youthful high spirits and her infectious good humor, plus exactly the proper dose of tender affection, delighted this touchy, distant *viejo*, though there were times when these very same qualities of Mary's rather irritated him.

After we had had our dip in the river and drunk our apéritifs, it was time to get down to some serious eating, and nobody said a word until the last bite was gone. These picnics there on the river's edge were a liberation from the routine of eating formal meals in such restaurants and taverns round about Pamplona as the Casa Marceliano and the Casa del Marrano. There would be plenty of time to try other places, such as the Príncipe de Viana, the Hostal del Rey Noble, the Hostería del Caballo Blanco, and the Hostal de Aralar, or drop in at some modest little place on the Calle de San Nicolás, though we would have to have reservations if we wanted to have a meal at Las Pocholas. We ate with gusto, and after lunch all of us half dozed off under the shade of a tree, though we could hardly wait for the afternoon's *corrida* to begin.

Ernesto would never have enough of bullfights. Bullfighting to him was not a temporary diversion, much less an amusement, but rather a total concentration on a contest possessed of a classic perfection and an incomparable artistic purity.

The girls in their swimsuits kept appearing and disappearing, making this rustic scene along an isolated bend in the river seem like some sort of pagan ecloque. After splashing joyously about in the water like an enormous whale and downing more than his fair share of our picnic lunch consisting of a couple of chickens, some country sausage, other cold meats, slices of beef and pork, cheese, fruit, and great quantities of wine, Ernesto stretched out on the ground. But the moment any of the young nymphs happened to walk by, he would say, "Look, be a good kid, will you, and scratch me right here?"

"Sure," the girl would reply good-naturedly and apply herself wholeheartedly to the task.

"A little lower down, please," Ernesto would say.

"Here?"

"Yes, but scratch just a little bit harder—don't be afraid."

And if the girl did it just right, scratching vigorously in precisely the right places, Ernesto would exclaim, "That's just about perfect."

"Shall I do it some more?"

"No, wait a second till I turn over."

And then, finally, he would say very gratefully, in a solemn tone of voice: "I can't thank you enough. You're an almost ideal odalisque."

He nonetheless kept looking at his watch every few minutes. It was impossible to be with Ernesto very long without the words *toros* or *toreros* being mentioned. The mere words *pase de pecho* or *matar recibiendo* were more intoxicating than wine to him.

We drove back to Pamplona at breakneck speed then, to find the entire city in an uproariously festive, carnival mood, and Ernesto prepared himself for that afternoon's *corrida* by thoughtfully sipping at his drinks, sitting there as though lost in a world of his own, identifying both with the matador and with the bull thundering into the bullring and halting in confusion in the middle of the arena. As the crowds thronged through the streets shouting and dancing, Ernesto tried his best simply to sit there quietly amid all the excitement, with a very solemn look on his face, overcome with a sacred respect for the word *bullring*. He enjoyed all the merrymaking, but was attempting to remain as serene as possible, as though immersed in spiritual meditation.

Ordóñez turned up then, seemingly more eager than ever to show everyone—though it had long been more than obvious—that this old man idolized him and all he need do was allow Ernesto to worship the very ground he walked on. Antonio kept joking and kidding around with him, but it was plain to see that he was quite aware that he was the object of the admiration of one of the greatest writers in the world, even though "Papa," like all geniuses, was a bit of a nut. Nonetheless Antonio always had a great time when he was with Ernesto. Like all *toreros*, Ordóñez was quite certain that he was the best bullfighter in the world, and the fact that he was not going to appear in the bullring that particular afternoon made him seem even more of a fantastic, legendary idol. In the next few days he would be fighting some of the most important *corridas* of his life—and we had only to wait and see what a terrific bullfighter he was.

Ernesto was brimming over with enthusiasm that afternoon, and his exuberant mood was catching. Before we knew it, Antonio and I had joined one of the most talented and most fervent groups of dancers, with huge Havana cigars in our mouths. As soon as we fell in with this joyous group of musicians and dancers, who were not professionals— that would be much too fancy a word for them, but they were none- theless a wonderful ensemble—we were immediately caught up by the rhythm the drums were beating out and began to cavort about like jungle savages, making fantastic leaps in the air and wildly clapping our hands over our heads, inventing our own improvisations, winding through the streets forming circles, separating from the group and snaking in and out of the crowds, and then joining the others again and dancing all over town in marvelous long, sinuous chains.

We were dripping with sweat, but it was a glorious feeling to have let ourselves go for once in our lives at least. Antonio and I leaped and cavorted our way to our seats in the bullring, on the sunny side of the arena, forming our own little trio there, for Alvario Domecq had joined us. We were so excited we simply couldn't stop dancing, and even after we'd taken our places in our seats, we kept jumping up, joining hands, and dancing round and round, shouting like madmen the while, till our voices were so hoarse we could scarcely whisper.

I was having such a great time that I hardly noticed that there was a *corrida* going on below us in the ring, though Ordóñez and Domecq both paid close attention from the moment the bull first appeared. But the minute the matador dispatched the beast, the three of us began cutting up again; we grabbed the musicians' instruments and made an absolute spectacle of ourselves there amid the laughing, shouting, ex- cited crowd. I would never have suspected that my arms and legs would prove to be so incredibly agile.

Between bulls, Antonio and I kept madly waving our handkerchiefs and shouting "Papaaaa, Papaaaaaaaa!" And Ernesto and Mary kept popping up out of their seats there in the official box on the shady side of the ring and waving back at us—with more decorum than enthusiasm, however, since the other guests in the box were frightfully respectable dignitaries of the town and the spectacle we were making of ourselves there on the opposite side of the arena made us look like madmen.

I watched Ernesto closely, and noticed that he kept surreptitiously sliding his flask out of his pocket and sneaking a swig out of it every few minutes. And I suddenly recalled what he had written in *The Sun Also Rises*:

> "You're cockeyed."
> "On wine? Well, maybe I am."

The one difference was that what Ernesto was swigging was not wine but vodka, or perhaps whisky. The three of us on the other side of the ring were the ones who were downing enough wine to make us cockeyed.

The *corrida* hadn't been a very moving experience for us. It was more like a kind of therapeutic bath and a form of heroic self-discipline, and on the following day, after spending an entire night without a wink of sleep, we would once again run with the bulls in the streets and all the rest of it. And the fiesta would go on like that for seven whole days and nights.

As we left the bullring, we linked arms again and joined up with that sort of careening, dancing chariot, a chariot without wheels, made of living flesh, which delightful young girls would climb aboard every so often, as though to ensure that it would be properly lubricated.

The hours after the afternoon *corrida* were always a pleasant relaxation. Ernesto was often tired, but never exhausted, and would simply sit quietly somewhere, allowing the world of inner emotions crying out for expression to take possession of him.

This was the proper moment to sip one's drinks slowly and philosophically, to relive images not so much actually seen as dreamed of. The crimson blood shed in the bullring would be followed by dust clouds tracing marvelous outlines of castles and great towering walls against the sky. The *riau-riau* groups were still wandering the streets, but as we sat enjoying our charcoal-broiled cutlets and our trout stuffed with savory slices of ham, it seemed the right moment to discuss what Ernesto had already written and sent off to *Life* magazine, with little chance now to change a single word. There were certain things that had upset him so much that they had served as a sort of inspiration.

"Do you really believe all that stuff about the bulls' horns being shaved?" he asked.

"Sure—and they've been doing even worse things than that."

"Did you know that they've been loading heavy sandbags on bulls' backs before a fight so that they'll be as gentle as seafoam in the ring?"

"Anything's possible in the bullfight world."

"Listen—did you really actually see Manolete fight?"

"Of course I did—I've already told you that."

"Did you see him lots of times?"

"Quite a few—I saw him in the ring more often than any other bullfighter, it seems to me."

"What did you think of him?"

"Sometimes he was sensational, and other times he had a terrible afternoon. I've told you all that already, many a time," I answered.

"It's pretty easy to doctor a brave bull, and it's also quite easy to castrate an entire people, to the point that none of them would even recognize their own father," Ernesto replied.

It was plain to see that Ernesto was beginning to be tormented by the thought of the trap he had allowed himself to fall into, but it was too late to try to free himself from it. The only remedy left was drinking—to forget and to try to come to terms with himself for having played the part he had in the whole sorry *Dangerous Summer* business.

He would often put his hand on my shoulder and ramble on and on in the most incoherent way, making very little sense. If you paid very close attention, you could see that there was some sort of inner logic to what he was saying, but it was very hard to follow his train of thought, because Manolete and the Spanish Civil War were all mixed up in his mind, and he would frequently become so distraught that he would start bringing up subjects that ordinarily he refused to talk about. More than once, his violent outbursts were so bitter and so irrational that they seemed almost sadistic.

"Okay, on your guard," he would say, clenching his fists like a boxer and pretending to punch me in the jaw. And then he would say, "We're going to have to settle this whole thing man to man. Don't tell me you're too yellow to fight back!"

I was sick at heart at the thought that Ernesto had been so badly taken in by people who had only the most questionable intentions and would no doubt make him a perfect laughingstock all over the world. And what upset me most was that it had been people who were supposedly intimate friends of Ernesto's who had led him so far astray as an artist, when he had always been such an extraordinarily honest writer. But did he really have any close friends? When you came right down to it, was he a man capable of ever having intimate friends?

The *peñas y comparsas*—the groups of musicians and dancers—were still joyously roaming about the Plaza del Castillo, and more than once

359

we were almost swept off our feet by the boisterous crowds of young-sters following the *chistu* and *gaita* players.

The girls in our group were dripping with sweat, and all aglow—from the hot sun beating down on the plaza, the fresh country air, the excite-ment of the great throngs of people dancing in every street in the city, and the whole aura of frank, orgiastic sexual passion surrounding the fiesta.

We went upstairs to dress for dinner. The first to come down again was Hotchner. Then Mary arrived with the other girls, all of them look-ing very pretty and as fresh as daisies. Then Bill Davis appeared, and as Ernesto's chief of public relations, began getting the whole show on the road for the evening. Being Ernesto's number one major-domo, he had naturally planned everything in advance. Meanwhile Ernesto was hav-ing a private consultation with his family doctor, the friendly physician from Ketchum, and chatting with the latter's wife, also a very outgoing sort.

Before we got up from the table, Ernesto noticed that I seemed to be a little bit out of my element and feeling somewhat ill at ease, so he grabbed my glass and thrust it in my hand, picked up his own glass, and linked arms with me. We drained the two glasses with our elbows crooked like blood brothers, a bit of affectionate horseplay that made me feel even more flustered, and Ernesto burst out laughing on seeing the embarrassed look on my face.

He had waited for Ordóñez till the very last minute, but Antonio had made other arrangements for the evening, and I could tell that Er-nesto's feelings were hurt. This was not the first time that his idol had disappointed him by seemingly forgetting all about him and leaving him in the lurch. Though Antonio kept giving him friendly pats on the back and pretending to be a bosom buddy, Ernesto always felt bad when Ordóñez took off with his own cronies. It almost seemed as though Antonio was convinced that the only purpose Ernesto served in his life was to trumpet his triumphs in the bullring, that both Ernesto's art and his life were merely something good for a laugh, for joking and kidding around—as a sign of an affection that Antonio perhaps did not really feel at all, or at any rate was incapable of demonstrating in any other way.

He behaved very peculiarly all that evening, and I shall never forget how he kept restlessly popping out of his chair, all set to pick a fight, as though he thoroughly mistrusted both himself and all the rest of us. I also remember him standing there in a corner pointing to a little picture-map of Pamplona, showing among other things the site of a statue of Saint Ignatius Loyola, who had been wounded within the walls of the city.

"Now there was one of the great ones!" he remarked.

"Yes, there was a man who fought the good fight," I agreed.

"A man like that can save an entire nation," he said, and then crossed himself in the most reverent way and added: "Even though a country touches absolute bottom, as long as there are guys like that, it's sure to be saved eventually." I noted that his lips were moving, and was certain that he was praying.

That was Ernesto all over. You might think that you had found out everything there was to know about him, yet there was always a surprise in store for you, at some moment when you least expected it.

After dinner that night we sat in the Plaza del Castillo watching the fireworks display, and to this day it is almost as though I can still see him there among the townspeople, oohing and aahing and applauding like the humblest peasant in the crowd, whistling in admiration when the final burst of skyrockets lighted up the whole sky, and winking slyly out of the corner of his eye when some local expert on bullfighting struck up a conversation with him.

But what I was trying hardest to recall just then was exactly how it had been when we had bid each other good-by there in Pamplona. I remembered that he had taken me aside and said, "I'll give you a call just as soon as I get to Madrid. And I'd like you to do me a favor if you will."

"Of course—anything you like," I'd said immediately.

"It's something that means a great deal to me, and you're the only one I trust to see that it gets done," he had replied.

"It's a promise," I'd said. "I'll see you soon in Madrid, then."

"Right: see you in Madrid," he had answered, giving me one of those enormous bear hugs of his.

I had left Pamplona behind, with its grainfields on the high plain and the transparent waters along which we had had our outings, with its rosé wines and the sad bellowing of the *sobreros*—extra bulls shipped off to the bullring but never used; that city where all of us had been gratified to see that Ernesto's spirit was still burning with a bright flame and that he was still apparently seriously pondering themes that went much deeper and were much more vitally important than the whole ridiculous *Dangerous Summer* business. In actual fact, that summer had been no more dangerous than his tender idyl with the Irish girl, a chaste affair that appeared to be an attempt on Ernesto's part to revive the romantic dreams and desires of his first days with Mary, a summer that in the end proved to be the one he would look back on as the happiest of his life.

I had left many things behind: the convent towers of Pamplona and the turrets of the city's battlements, its vineyards and threshing floor, the little shops with their strings of garlic cloves or farm tools hanging from the ceiling, the walks along the highway where boys and girls were gathering the flowers of their youth, hand in hand. And more besides: the pealing of the bells and the brass bugles sounding so early in the morning, the *comparsas* and their merrymaking, the bursting of skyrockets and the braying of the bulls. What I was leaving behind were hours I would never forget, hours that the clock on the chapel of San Fermín had struck one by one, joyously devouring them, sounding a bit like the delightful jingling of a cowbell in the early morning and the late afternoon.

"We're pulling into Valencia," someone in the compartment said.

"I can hardly believe it!" I exclaimed in amazement.

"It's true, though—we're pulling into the station this very minute," the others assured me.

And they were quite right. There was Valencia, before my very eyes, with its chalk-white houses blindingly bright in the broiling sun.

Good old Chano, a Galician lumber dealer with a very sound and healthy curiosity about all things literary, drove me to Benicasim. I had been away exactly nine days. Chano was a Hemingway enthusiast and was eager to find out more than I could possibly tell him about Ernesto's death. He was very upset and drove very erratically, plying me with one question after another as we bounced from one side of the road to the other.

"Why in the world did he kill himself?" he asked me.

"I think he killed himself because of Nick," I answered.

"Who's Nick? That girl that everybody says he was having an affair with?" he asked.

"Don't be silly! I mean Nick Adams. You've read 'Indian Camp,' haven't you?"

"I'm not sure whether I have or not."

"Well, that story explains everything. You really ought to read it. The whole thing is as plain as day in my mind now," I told him.

But even though my very first flash of intuition had gradually come to seem more and more of an objective, proven fact as far as I was concerned, it was not going to be an easy task to explain my theory to other people. "Indian Camp" was simply Ernesto's fictional transposition of his brutally sudden discovery of violence and death as a youngster, but how could a single impression, the mere witnessing of a tragic, bloody scene in his earliest years forever undermine a constitution as strong as his, when all his life he had appeared to be a vital man capable of overcoming all odds? Yet it was obvious, to me at least, that he had never been as strong or as vital a man as almost everyone had thought.

Ernesto's life had been a continuous series of sufferings that he had kept carefully concealed but had lacked the moral courage to overcome.

362

Suicide had been merely the natural outcome—as though a bull, once having entered the arena, could retreat to the dark bullpen and with no one watching kill himself by butting his head against the wall.

Ernesto's highly suspect "accidental" death is already prefigured in this early story, and young Nick Adams is the prophet of Ernesto's tragic death. The scene that Nick witnesses in "Indian Camp" was a lesson that was to haunt Ernesto his whole life long. His many adventures, the wars he fought in, the bullfights and the hunting expeditions and the cruel encounters with denizens of the deep were all the natural consequence of this bloodcurdling vision. The Indian who slits his throat because he cannot bear his wife's moans of pain during the brutal Caesarian operation with a jack knife left a great, yawning hole in Ernesto's sensibilities that only a lead bullet could fill. Not many years after this incident, Ernesto's own father had also remembered what a rifle bullet might be used for.

The words with which the Catholic chaplain in Ketchum had buried Ernesto had had something of the mysterious sound of waves eternally breaking, for they were the same words that Ernesto had taken from Ecclesiastes (Chapter I, verse 4) as the epigraph of his very first novel, *The Sun Also Rises:*

> One generation passeth away, and another generation cometh,
> but the earth abideth forever. . . .

The story of a man's life is at once everything and nothing. Yet the earth abides, perhaps as God's witness to His creatures that the earth is something more than earth and nothingness more than nothingness, that between the very first breath of life and the final chill of death there is an emptiness, and the drama of man's existence the fact that he does not know how to fill this emptiness, is unable to fill it, or sometimes does not want to fill it.

It was quite clear that Ernesto had killed himself for reasons known only to himself, but he had also taken his own life in the name of all the characters in his books, for all of them had experienced this same terrible temptation, and although some of them had been able to resist it, in the end this enormous burden that his characters had borne had been too much for the author who had created these fictions.

"I'm going to have to read 'Indian Camp,' I guess," Chano said.

"Yes, read it and you'll see that it explains a lot of things. The whole truth is right there—and he wrote that story very early in his career, in 1925, just after the slaughter he had witnessed at the front and his first encounter with bullfighting."

"What I can't understand is how an American could be so crazy about bullfighting."

"He wanted to be a soldier, and eventually became one. He also wanted to be a *torero*, but he never got to be one."

There were many nuances I was going to have to try to get across. What underlay this crucial episode in the life of young Nick Adams, the name Ernesto gave himself in many of his autobiographical stories, was not so much a dramatic narrative tension as a terrible personal shock that Ernesto was never to recover from. From early adolescence onward, that cruel slit in the throat of the humble Indian lying dead in his crude bunk bed was to represent to Ernesto the absurdly thin line separating living and dying, the unthinkable step over the threshold between life and death.

It was going to be necessary to remind people that this youngster's sudden, brutal encounter with death had occurred at much too early an age, and all the remainder of Ernesto's life would be much the same: precocious sexual experiences while still a lad in his teens, a pleasure that left a taste of ashes; the sudden breaking off of the ties that bound him to his family, a liberating experience at first, but later a source of the most haunting nostalgia and of many memories that nourished his art; an unequal combat in the name of an ideal that he believed in with all his heart, ending in deep disappointments for which there was no possible cure; a total embrace of everything life had to offer and a no less total despoiling of everything he touched; a love that resulted in no sort of enduring affection; passing affairs that began as casually as they ended; wounds that healed without being bandaged, yet kept oozing . . .

All this was what his life had added up to, and more besides: a Caesarian operation he had performed on himself with a jack knife, without an anesthetic; an attempt to find himself by fathering children whose death was unthinkable but who would nonetheless surely die one day. And who knows how many times he himself had died during his lifetime, in all those many beds he had lain in—in hospitals and bawdy-houses and hotels and rest homes.

A pool of blood on a bunk bed in an Indian camp, a squalling newborn babe, an old, straight-edged razor, a jugular vein still pumping like a bellows, an overwhelming urge to flee this bloody scene and try to forget it forever . . .

And later on, a repetition of this scene, another piercing cry from the throat of someone other than the victim this time too, brains spattered all over the place, his father lying there dead on the floor, an inert mass of flesh, and the death-dealing rifle still smoking . . .

So many things in his books resemble the scenes he saw as a fearless but impressionable youngster in the endless corridors and the long line of butchering rooms in the slaughterhouses of Chicago: heavy, dull blows, the bodies of animals collapsing on the tile floors, trembling and heaving and twisting and writhing in terrible contortions as the knife blade enters; it is no easy job for the butcher to penetrate the animal's thick hides, but eventually the knife goes in and pierces a hole in the creature's flesh, entering and leaving the animal's body like a greased key, leaving pools with trails of blood both as it goes in and as it comes out; blood spattering all over the walls, foaming crimson blood slowly flowing into the drains in the floor with a melodious gurgle, as the animal continues to shudder and tremble all over, as everything turns the color of blood, even the soft white wool of the lambs and the shining hides of the steers . . .

Blood. That first blood that young Nick Adams ever saw and kept seeing for hours afterward, the blood covering the newborn baby, the blood spattered all over his father; Ernesto's first wife's blood, his own blood. He had seen so much blood, so many times—as though it were not so much a liquid as a cry and a voice, as though this blood that he could see on his back, beneath his feet, on his hands were the secret vocabulary of the great temptation.

Life hanging by a thread, as with men dangling from barbed wire or a noose, as with men badly wounded in the legs or the spine, or as with bulls, so brave half an hour before their death.

There was no other philosophy possible for this fear-haunted, driven man who nonetheless spit in Death's eye and earned the whole world's plaudits for his courage.

How can we live, seeing we have to die? That was what he asked himself all his life, and the answer he found in the end was as chillingly empty as the question.

That was why Spain with its inescapable triptych of bullfighting, war, and death—embraced mystically or defied with a roguish wink or lived with blind rapture out of a love for what one accepts totally, with a romanticism that stems not from the senses but from the spirit—had to be the homeland of his hopes and desires.

They should have buried Ernesto with a canvas by Goya as a shroud.

There was nothing left to do now. This disconcerting, enigmatic man who had sought eternity amid the fleeting, empty joys of the moment had at last found safe shelter in our mother earth, the bosom of God, as Unamuno had called it, and the plot of ground that was now a resting place for his weary limbs would also mark the spot where his lifelong loneliness had at last ended. He would understand now that he was not alone, that he had never been alone.

Not even writing about him would be any sort of solace to me, unless what I wrote was as moving as a prayer—one of those prayers voiced in the respectful silence that reigns between God and His creature.

My wife came over to the deck chair I was lying in.

"Are you absolutely certain he took his own life?" she asked me.

"My dear, to each his own—even though it may seem the most tragic death imaginable. It's far worse to die like a rabbit shivering with fear or be crushed to death underfoot like a cockroach."

"What in the world are you talking about?" she said.

"I'm merely saying that it was a foregone conclusion that Ernesto would never die between a pair of white hospital sheets amid the reek of medicine. And if he put up with such things in those last months of his life, it was surely because they would serve as yet another argument in favor of taking his own life and putting an end to the whole business."

"He was crazy, then."

"He was always crazy, but toward the end he was just a little crazier than usual.

"But haven't you often told me he was a Christian and a God-fearing man?"

"Yes, I did tell you that, more than once, and it was the truth. But Ernesto just couldn't die in bed. He had to die with his suit of lights stained with blood, the way *toreros* die."

"It seems to me you're a little crazy in the head, too."

I said no more. I would have given anything if Ernesto could have died as he had so often said he wanted to—a sudden death on some battlefield, in a war where trumpets sounded and bells tolled, a war you went to with a light heart and didn't care to come back from if all your dreams were shattered, a war that would have given him a feeling of indomitable courage and perennial youth. The worst thing was not the hushed silence surrounding the dead man, that silence that is so vulgar, but the pious rustle of black silk and crepe, the funeral elegy, and the trivial chitchat as one bids one's friend good-by for the very last time. At the very moment that the suicide puts the fatal bullet through his temple or his heart, he may feel perfectly sane and joyously happy as he hammers furiously on the gates of eternity. But Ernesto had arrived at the gates of paradise feeling very resigned, or to put it a better way, overcome with humiliation and a total wreck of a man. He was not a man still sound in mind and body, but a grotesque mountain of cruelly battered flesh.

My wife went off then without saying one word about life in the hereafter, and I silently thanked her for sparing me that.

I went to my room and started pulling on my swimming trunks. A nice long dip in the ocean would do me lots of good. There was no use thinking about Ernesto's death any more. When all was said and done, I had circled back to the very point I had started from the morning I had left Benicasim for Madrid, as though going off on a trip might explain everything.

"Why is Daddy acting so funny?" one of my children asked.

"A friend of his has died and he's feeling sad," my wife replied.

"Why don't we say prayers for Daddy's friend so he'll go to heaven?" the children asked.

"Yes, let's pray for him. He was such a good man—that's why Daddy's feeling so sad."

I headed for the beach and the children followed me, shouting, and kicking a big orange rubber beach ball.

Although I was tired, I plunged into the white surf and sank into its foamy refuge. It was as though I had an imperative need to rid myself of an oppressive, overwhelming weight. As I splashed about, I thought of the times I had gone swimming with Ernesto, like a young dolphin alongside a whale.

The pounding of the waves gradually lifted the weight from me a bit until, once I was out in calmer water, I felt a strange serenity come over me. Ernesto's words in *Death in the Afternoon* came to me as if they had dug a furrow in my consciousness:

". . . the dead are tired too."

CHRONOLOGY

1899   (July 21) Ernest Hemingway is born in Oak Park, Illinois, a residential suburb of Chicago. His father, Clarence E. Hemingway, a doctor, is fond of outdoor sports, and will teach him at a very early age to hunt and fish. His mother, Grace, a domineering, puritan woman, will try to no avail to interest him in music. He is the first of six children; he will have a brother, Leicester, and four sisters.

1902   His father gives him his first fishing rod.

1909   His father gives him his first shotgun; he is allowed to shoot three shells a day, during vacations. The Hemingways spend their summers on a farm they own at Horton's Bay, on the shores of Lake Walloon, in northern Michigan. These vacations spent hunting and fishing in the wilds with his father are the happiest days of Ernest's childhood and no doubt of his entire life, and he will often mention them later, in his works.

1913   He enters Oak Park High School, and is an outstanding student. He goes in for a variety of sports, in particular football and boxing. While training, he fractures the bridge of his nose and receives an injury to his left eye that leaves him with a slight squint and a vague, strained facial expression for the rest of his life. Although he studies hard, he is already something of a rebel and runs away from home and school twice.

1916   He is editor of the school newspaper, *The Trapeze*, and has many articles printed in it. A number of his teachers discover his literary gifts and encourage him.

1917   He graduates from Oak Park High School.

1917   (October) He decides not to go to college. He wants to enlist as a volunteer in the Army to fight in Europe, but his father will not permit it. An uncle gets him a job on the Kansas City *Star*, and he moves to that city to begin the apprenticeship that will eventually make him an outstanding reporter. The editors of the *Star* will not tolerate florid writing, and young Ernest learns to write in a bare, spare style, with short, declarative sentences and a minimum of adjectives.

1918   (April) He and his friend Ted Brumback hear that the Red Cross is recruiting volunteers to serve as ambulance drivers with the Italian Army. Both of them sign up and leave for Europe. (Ernest has twice tried to enlist in the American Army despite his father's opposition, but has been turned down both times because of his bad left eye.)

1918   (May) He arrives in Paris with his friend Ted, on a night when the city is being bombarded by the famous German "Big Bertha." He is very excited about the war adventures in store for him.

1918   (June) He arrives in Milan and helps evacuate dead and wounded after an explosion in a munitions factory.

1918   He is seriously wounded in the Italian front lines near Fossalta, on the shores of the Piave River (July 8). He remains in the Military Hospital in Milan for three months, and receives a silver Medal of Valor and a Medal of Merit.

1919   The war over, he returns to the United States and convalesces at home, in Oak Park. He suffers from terrible nightmares and insomnia, and spends most of his time reading and drinking.

1919   (Summer) He holes up in Petoskey, near Horton's Bay, recovers somewhat from the shock of the war in his lonely forest retreat, and begins to write articles and short stories.

1920   He resumes his career as a newspaperman and contributes to the Toronto *Star Weekly* and other publications. He meets Sherwood Anderson and other writers of the Chicago Group. His short stories and articles are turned down by a number of editors, but Anderson encourages him to continue writing and bolsters his confidence in his talent. But Hemingway soon frees himself of Anderson's tutelage.

1921　　He is married in September to Hadley Richardson, a pianist he met several years before, while vacationing with his family at Horton's Bay. At the end of the year, in December, he gets a job as a roving correspondent for the Toronto *Star Weekly*, working out of Paris. The same month, he boards ship for Europe with his wife.

1922　　He lives and writes in Paris. He meets Gertrude Stein and other expatriate American writers there, among them Ezra Pound, Archibald MacLeish, and John Peale Bishop. He travels all over Europe as a roving correspondent: Switzerland, Spain, Turkey, Greece, Italy. He covers the war between Turkey and Greece, interviews a number of famous people, among them Mussolini, and has articles accepted by a number of Canadian and American publications.

1922　　(Summer) On his previous trip to Europe, he has passed through northern Spain on his way to Paris. He now goes to that country for his first real visit. He attends the San Fermín fiesta, in Pamplona, for the first time and sees his first bullfights. He is so overwhelmed by the experience that he is unable to write anything about the fiesta until the following year. But he already has plans to write a book about bullfighting, and begins taking notes, attending *corridas*, and digging up all sorts of information about bulls and bullfighting. (He does not begin *Death in the Afternoon* until 1925, however.)

1922　　(November) A disaster befalls the Hemingways. As Hadley is leaving Paris to join Ernest in Lausanne for the International Peace Conference, in the Gare de Lyon she loses a suitcase containing all his manuscripts. Ernest is thoroughly disgusted and angry with her.

1923　　(February) He and Hadley go to the Italian Riviera (Rapallo) to visit his friend Ezra Pound. There he meets many European and American artists and writers.

1923　　(Summer) He goes to Pamplona again for the fiesta of San Fermín. Bullfighting is now like meat and drink to him, and for the rest of his life he will attend the Sanfermines, in Pamplona, and other Spanish *ferias* as often as he can. He sends his first bullfight story to the Toronto *Star*, describing the *fiesta de toros* as a "tragedy."

1923   (Autumn) He goes to Canada with Hadley. His first son, John, whom he and Hadley nickname "Bumby," is born in Toronto in October. His article on bullfighting is published in the Toronto *Star* on October 20.

1924   (January) He returns to Paris with his wife and baby. After heated arguments, Bumby is baptized in an Episcopal church in Paris, with Gertrude Stein and Alice B. Toklas as godmothers. Ernest has quit his job as correspondent for the Toronto *Star* and is now writing for the *Transatlantic Review*.

1924   (Summer) He returns to Pamplona for the fiesta again this year, accompanied this time by his wife and several American writer friends, among them John Dos Passos, Robert McAlmon, and Donald Ogden Stewart. Not content to be mere spectators, they participate in the running of the bulls. On the second day, Ernest's friend Stewart is badly gored by a bull and Hemingway rushes to his aid. He saves his friend's life, but he, too, is gored. The versions of this story in American newspapers are greatly exaggerated.

During these years when he comes to Pamplona for the fiesta, he always stays at the Hotel Quintana (the Hotel Montoya of *The Sun Also Rises*). The owner of the hotel, Juanito Quintana, a great bullfight fan, introduces him to Maera and other matadors and becomes both Ernest's mentor and a close personal friend. Ernest writes of him in *Death in the Afternoon*: "The best *aficionado* and Spain's most loyal supporter." The Hotel Quintana is a hangout for everyone in the bullfighting world.

He follows the bullfight calendar and visits other Spanish cities: San Sebastián, Zaragoza, Valencia, and Madrid, of course. When he visits Madrid during these years he stays in a *pensión* in the Carrera de San Jerónimo (the Hotel Montana of his novel), most of whose guests are people connected with bullfighting, plus a few students. Here he picks up both the special vocabulary of the bullring and a great deal of information about bullfighting, and continues taking notes for *Death in the Afternoon*. He sees every *corrida* he possibly can. He meets Chicuelo, Villalta, Lalanda, Belmonte, and other matadors. Between *corridas* he has a wonderful time fishing for trout in the Irati River in Navarre and the Tambre in Galicia.

1925   This is the great year of Cayetano Ordóñez, known as "Niño de la Palma." Ernest meets him in Pamplona and comes to greatly admire him both as a person and as a bullfighter. He follows him about on the bullfight circuit as far as Valencia, and in that city on July 21, his twenty-sixth birthday, he begins writing *The Sun Also Rises*. Pedro Romero, the bullfighter in the novel, is modeled on Niño de la Palma. He goes on writing, "to the point of exhaustion," in Madrid, San Sebastián, and Hendaye, and finishes his novel in Paris on September 6 of this year. He then revises it from beginning to end, and on April 21, 1926, sends the manuscript off to Scribner's for publication. During this year he also sees Rafael El Gallo, who is now forty-three years old, fight.

1926   He visits Pamplona, Valencia, Madrid, and San Sebastián once again. He sees Manuel Baez ("Litri"), Zurito, Niño de la Palma, Nicanor Villalta, and others fight in the bullring. He continues work on *Death in the Afternoon*.

During this summer, a very important event in his personal life takes place. His wife Hadley and a friend of theirs, Pauline Pfeiffer, an American reporter who has been working for the Paris edition of *Vogue*, plan to join Ernest in Madrid, but when "Bumby" comes down with whooping cough, Hadley is obliged to stay behind in Antibes, and Pauline goes on alone to Madrid. Ernest and Pauline begin to have an affair. Since Pauline is Catholic, they go to mass together. The closest bond between them is the fact that they are both writers. When Ernest returns to Paris in September, his marriage to Hadley has broken up.

1927   Hadley divorces Ernest in March, and he marries Pauline in the summer. From this point on, Hemingway is a practicing Catholic.

He goes to Spain with Pauline and sees Belmonte and Lalanda gored in Valencia. He continues work on *Death in the Afternoon*.

1928   Pauline and Ernest return to the United States and move into a house that Ernest has bought in Key West. *The Sun Also Rises* has brought him a lot of money, and he begins his life as a great sportsman. He fishes in the Caribbean, and hunts partridge in Arkansas and big game in Wyoming. He helps start *Esquire* magazine and becomes one of its principal contributors. He begins writing *A Farewell to Arms* in Key West. He does not visit Spain this year, because his second son, Patrick, is born by Caesarian section in June and Pauline's health is delicate.

In December of this year, a tragedy occurs that affects Ernest deeply: his father, Dr. Hemingway, commits suicide.

1929   He comes to the *feria* of San Isidro in Madrid and sees snow fall on the fifteenth of May. He becomes a great fan of Marcial Lalanda's, whom he considers the top matador in Spain now that Belmonte has retired.

1930   He visits Spain again and continues working on *Death in the Afternoon*. He sees Manolo Bienvenida work in the ring, but still regards Lalanda as the number one bullfighter. He also sees Cagancho, Gitanillo de Triana, and other *toreros*.

A *Farewell to Arms*, published the year before, is an enormous success. Lawrence Stallings adapts it for the stage, and the play opens in New York on September 22; it is not a success, however.

In the fall he goes to Wyoming on a hunting trip. Driving back home in his yellow Ford convertible with his friend John Dos Passos, he has an accident and badly fractures his right arm.

1931   He spends the months of May, June, and July in Spain with his son "Bumby." As in previous years, the Brooklyn-born bullfighter Sidney Franklin, who has helped Ernest a great deal with the bullfighting terminology in *Death in the Afternoon*, is also with him. When he visits Madrid this time he stays in the Hotel Florida in the Plaza del Callao, rather than the *pensión* in the Carrera de San Jerónimo. He again sees a number of *toreros* fight: Cagancho, Gitanillo de Triana, Félix Rodríguez, Chicuelo, Manolo Bienvenida. In Aranjuez he sees the first fight of Domingo Ortega, a *torero* who has been deeply involved in politics now that Spain has been declared a republic. On May 31 Ernest sees Gitanillo de Triana gored to death in the ring.

He finishes *Death in the Afternoon* during this year, after having witnessed more than fifteen hundred *corridas*.

At the beginning of the year, he has high hopes for the new Spanish Republic, but during the year he becomes very disappointed at the course events are taking, and discusses and notes down his thoughts on the subject. The prinicipal reasons for his disillusionment are the anticlericalism of the 1931 Constitution, the empty rhetoric of the politicians, and the increasingly pointless, proliferating bureaucracy stifling the country.

1932   His third son, Gregory, is born. *Death in the Afternoon* is published by Scribner's. His daily life in Key West is divided among fishing, hunting, and writing.

374

1933   An important year, full of exciting events and activities. He organizes his first safari in Africa. He and Pauline board the *Queen of the Pacific* in New York and sail directly to Spain, where he spends the months of July, August, and September. He goes on several hunting trips in Extremadura as the guest of the artist Luis Quintanilla, who paints his portrait. He attends almost all the *corridas* of the season. In November he and Pauline go to Paris for two weeks, spending most of their time there buying equipment and provisions for the safari. Later this same month, they board ship in Marseilles bound for Africa. In Port Said, Ernest comes down with dysentery and is in bed with a fever for several weeks. He feels much better once the hunting in Africa begins, however, and bags four lions, a buffalo, a rhinoceros, and other game. He and Pauline then travel to the east coast of Africa, where he goes out after the great game fish in those waters. They fly over Mount Kilimanjaro, and despite the fact that he is still suffering from dysentery, he refuses to give up hunting. The stay in Africa five months. His articles on the safari are later published in *Esquire*.

1934   He returns to Key West from Africa in April. He is still suffering from the severe dysentery he has contracted in Port Said, and is obliged to undergo medical treatment. He nonetheless works very hard on the first draft of *The Green Hills of Africa*. The money he earns from the safari articles allows him to fulfill one of the greatest dreams of his life: buying a large boat for deep-sea fishing. The moment he arrives in Key West, in fact, he orders it from the Wheeler Company, and it is delivered a few months later. When it arrives, he behaves like a child who has just received the perfect toy. He christens it *Pilar*, after the Virgin who is the patron saint of Spain, the same name he will later give one of the most moving characters in his great novel *For Whom the Bell Tolls*.

His fishing trips aboard the *Pilar* are more exciting and more dangerous than ever. He fishes the waters all around Key West, going as far as the Bahamas. In this same year, he catches a record fish, which he presents to the Miami Deep Sea Fishing Club, where it is still on display.

In November he and Dos Passos arrange for an exhibition of the engravings of Ernesto's Spanish friend Luis Quintanilla, paying all the expenses and taking care of all the details personally. He writes an introduction for the catalogue, and gets Dos Passos to write something for it too. (When the show opens, Quintanilla is in prison in Spain, charged with having participated in the October revolt.)

1935   Fishing expeditions on the *Pilar* continue to be his great passion; nevertheless he still writes every day. Many American guests come aboard the *Pilar*: writers, newspapermen, editors, and above all deep-sea fishermen who are as fond of the sport and as good at it as Ernest. He has experiences that he will later incorporate in *The Old Man and the Sea*. He takes a great liking to Havana, and often stays at the Hotel Ambos Mundos. He also often visits Bimini to fish. He invites ichthyologists out with him on the *Pilar*, and on one expedition they catch an unknown species of porpoise, which they name after Ernest, *Neoreminthe Hemingway*.

He helps found the International Game Fish Association, an organization sponsored by the American Museum of Natural History.

On one of his fishing trips in the *Pilar* he accidentally shoots himself in the foot while trying to kill a huge shark he has just boated. Several bullet fragments have to be extracted from his leg, and he is forced to stay in bed for several days.

In September of this year, a great hurricane levels the towns along the Florida coast and wreaks enormous damage in Key West, destroying, among many other buildings, a camp for veterans of World War I, more than two hundred of whom die in the hurricane. Hemingway joins the first volunteers evacuating the dead and makes an admirable contribution to the rescue efforts.

All his articles on fishing are published in *Esquire*.

1936   While on a fishing trip to Havana, he receives the news that the Civil War has broken out in Spain. He is very excited, and though he continues to fish and write, he follows developments closely. From the very first, he regards the Spanish Falange as a Fascist movement and is openly against it, for he has had a close look at Fascism in Italy and is an irreconcilable enemy of this system of government.

He spends the summer in Montana, and on his return home sends a personal donation of forty thousand dollars to the Spanish Republicans for the purchase of ambulances and medicine. His commitment to the Republican side is more humanitarian and sentimental than political.

• Hemingway meets Martha Gellhorn in Key West in December.

1937   Seeing that the Spanish conflict gives no sign of ending soon, he decides to go to Spain. He contacts the North American Newspaper Alliance (NANA) and signs a contract as a war correspondent attached to the Loyalist Army. He is thus only a correspondent and never a combatant in Spain—a man lending moral and material support to the cause of freedom.

He sails from New York on February 27 aboard the *Paris*. He arrives in Barcelona on March 18, by plane from Paris. This is also the day of the Italian forces' disastrous retreat from Guadalajara. He goes directly to the Guadalajara front via Valencia and Alicante and covers the battle of Brihuega. He then goes to Madrid and sets up headquarters in the Hotel Florida, where other well-known writers and intellectuals are also staying.

On April 9 he covers the great Republican offensive at University City and the Nationalist counteroffensive, during which Madrid is bombarded for twelve days and more than thirty shells fall on the Hotel Florida.

One of his most important activities, aside from sending stories to the NANA, is hunting up food and raising funds for the combatants, especially the wounded. All witnesses agree that he was extraordinarily ingenious at scouring up whatever was needed. When they run out of food, he goes to the Pardo, a large park in Madrid, with a shotgun and brings back rabbits he has killed, or wangles tins of caviar from the Russians. The Hungarian general Mate Zalca Lucasz, commander of the Twelfth International Brigade, gives a banquet for him, attended by a number of newspapermen, intellectuals, and cultivated militants.

On this first trip to Spain during the Civil War, he meets the young Dutch film director Joris Ivens and his cameraman John Ferno. The three of them begin to shoot a film on the war, entitled *The Spanish Earth*. Several other American writers, among them Dos Passos and Archibald MacLeish, also collaborate on the film.

In May, Ernest returns to the United States; his main purpose in doing so is to raise money for the Republican cause. Sparing himself no effort and no sacrifice, he begins his fund-raising campaign by arranging showings of *The Spanish Earth*. The premiere takes place at the White House, where Ernest and Joris Ivens are guests of President Roosevelt. He then raises large sums of money among his millionaire deep-sea-fishing pals. Sufficient money is raised to buy twelve ambulances, but because of the American Government's neutrality policy, the ambulances never arrive in Spain.

He now does what he has never done for himself: he asks favors, he begs for money, and for the first and last time in his life, gives a lecture, even though he detests the thought of speaking in public. But impelled by his deep love for Spain and his passionate concern for what is happening there, he delivers a speech on the Civil War and the dangers of Fascism, in Carnegie Hall, under the auspices of the Association of American Writers.

In August he returns to Spain, remaining there until November 1938. On arriving in Madrid, he again meets Martha Gellhorn, now a correspondent covering the Civil War in Spain for *Collier's*. She is a splendid woman, though ruthlessly competitive and totally without scruples as a correspondent. This meeting in Madrid proves fatal to Ernest's Catholic marriage. The two of them pool their efforts as journalists, and not long after, begin living together. In a heroic attempt to save her marriage, Pauline comes to Paris in December and Ernest joins her there. He spends the Christmas holidays with her, but their relationship is very strained and Ernest is bent on returning to Spain as quickly as posssible.

During this second trip to Spain, he visits the Aragon front, where Belchite has just won a great victory. He then goes to Catalonia and is present, later, when the plans for capturing Teruel are drawn up. He likes inspecting the front lines, and immediately understands the battle tactics employed. In December of 1937 he rushes to the front lines in Teruel, where it is freezing cold, wearing only a light summer suit (according to a number of correspondents who were there; see Ilya Ehrenburg), though he is equipped with a flask of whisky in each pocket. His room in the Hotel Florida is one of the few places in Madrid where his friends can be sure of finding something to eat and drink. He goes hungry more than once during the Spanish War, however.

In Madrid, in the winter of 1937–38, he begins writing *The Fifth Column*, his only work for the theater, which is a total failure when it is later staged in New York.

1938   After a visit to Paris, he returns to Spain in January and covers the capture of Teruel (January 8), along with Herbert Matthews, Tom Delmer, and the photographer Robert Capa, who becomes famous during the Spanish War and is later killed in Indochina.

He returns shortly thereafter to the United States and Key West to see Pauline, but he has changed a great deal and is now much more taciturn and withdrawn.

He returns to Spain in March and remains there until May. In his absence, Teruel has been lost by the Loyalists (February 22). Immediately after arriving, he covers the first battle of the Ebro and goes on to Valencia, Tortosa, and Lérida. In May he returns to Paris, and from there goes back to New York and Key West. He spends the summer in Montana with Pauline and the children, but at the end of August he goes back to Spain via Paris. He arrives in time to cover the great Ebro offensive, which goes on until November. Realizing that the Republican cause is lost after the retreat from the Ebro and the disasters on the Catalonian front, he leaves Spain in November, deeply disappointed and depressed. This has been his fifth and last visit to Spain since the beginning of the Civil War.

1939   He settles permanently in Cuba and begins writing *For Whom the Bell Tolls*.

1940   He buys a country estate outside Havana, called the Finca La Vigía, which is to be his home base until shortly before his death.

Scribner's publishes *For Whom the Bell Tolls*, by far his most successful book thus far. The first press run is 75,000 copies. Nine weeks later, the book has sold 180,000 copies, and a year and a half later, 500,000 copies will have been sold.

In the fall, Paramount acquires the film rights to the book for $150,000 a fabulous sum at the time. Hemingway demands that the roles of María and Robert Jordan be played by Ingrid Bergman and Gary Cooper. He has met the latter some time before, and Cooper later becomes one of his dearest and closest friends.

In November he and Pauline are divorced, and two weeks later he marries Martha Gellhorn.

1941   In the spring both he and Martha get assignments to visit the Orient as correspondents. During their extensive travels in the Far East they visit Indochina, China, and the Philippines.

The two of them return to Havana in July, and when President Roosevelt succeeds in getting a law passed by Congress allowing merchant ships to be armed, Ernest conceives the idea of arming the *Pilar* to go out chasing German submarines. The Chief of Naval Intelligence approves, and Hemingway assembles a crew and outfits the *Pilar* with machine guns for submarine-patrol duty.

1944   In May he is named chief war correspondent for *Collier's* and goes to London, where preparations for the Allied Armies' invasion of Normandy are under way. Shortly after arriving in London, he has a car accident and has to have fifty-seven stitches taken in his scalp. He is reported dead, for the first time, by press services throughout the world.

Before he has fully recovered, he slips out of the clinic and flies over the enemy lines on a reconnaissance mission. He has the stitches in his scalp removed before his wounds have healed, and on June 5 he embarks with the American Fourth Infantry Division, commanded by General R. O. Barton, to cover the establishment of the Allied bridgehead in Normandy. Bored by his passive role as a war correspondent, he takes active part in flights over the enemy lines and ground operations. He flies over the launching pads of the German V rockets and organizes a small but well-equipped combat group of his own. On one occasion, his band of irregulars manages to get sixty miles ahead of the advancing army troops, and he arrives in Paris with his contingent before General Leclerc's troops reach the city. He and his men have skirmishes with the Germans in the streets of Paris and "liberate" the Hotel Ritz, where he sets up headquarters. All this vastly irritates General Leclerc, who orders an official inquiry, since, as a correspondent, Ernest is prohibited from bearing arms and participating in combat operations.

He has met Mary Welsh, a *Time* writer, in London. Moreover, his relations with Martha Gellhorn, his third wife, have become more and more strained, for Martha lives her own life and is frequently away on assignments, and what little time they have together is spent quarreling and criticizing each other.

Mary is now also living at the Ritz in Paris. His third marriage, from this point on, is a marriage in name only. Mary, a svelte, intelligent, dignified woman, is with him constantly.

The investigation of his conduct as a correspondent, begun by General Leclerc, continues, but all the men in his band of irregulars swear that Ernest himself did not engage in combat. Their testimony, and his personal merits, save him from having his credentials withdrawn.

During his stay in Paris after Liberation, he catches pneumonia and is forced to stay in bed for several days. Among his visitors are Picasso, Sartre, and Simone de Beauvoir. His room at the Ritz is a popular meeting place for writers, correspondents, artists, and political figures.

1945   He returns to La Vigía, in Havana, and his two passions: writing and fishing. In December his divorce from Martha becomes final. This third marriage has been a disaster, and he often misses Pauline, whom he describes as "the best wife a man could ever hope to have."

1946   He marries Mary Welsh in March, and continues to write in Havana.

1947   He remains in Havana, writing, fishing, attending boxing matches and cockfights (and also raising fighting cocks at La Vigía), but begins to feel homesick for Europe.

1948   He cannot resist returning to Europe, and at the end of the year begins getting ready for a trip to Italy.

1949   He and Mary ski at Cortina d'Ampezzo in January and February, and then spend the entire spring in Venice (Mary has broken her foot skiing).

        During a duck hunt near Venice, he is hit in the eye by cartridge wadding. The wound becomes infected, and he nearly loses his sight in that eye. The doctors treat it with penicillin and manage to save it, but his vision in that eye is permanently impaired. He begins writing Across the River and into the Trees in Italy.

        He returns to Cuba in the summer, but in the fall he goes back to Europe, visiting Paris and northern Italy. He continues to work very hard on Across the River.

1950   At the beginning of the year he is still in northern Italy. He returns to Cuba later in the year, and in September Scribner's brings out Across the River and into the Trees. The book receives universally unfavorable reviews, and for many years he refuses to allow it to be translated in Europe.

1952   The September 8 issue of Life contains the first installment of his novella The Old Man and the Sea, the remainder of which appears in later issues, in serial form. The work is an enormous success, earning him both good reviews and wide popular readership. Scribner's publishes it in book form shortly thereafter. After the failure of Across the River, the success of The Old Man and the Sea spikes the rumors that Hemingway is "washed up."

1953   This year marks his return to Spain after fifteen years, a time
        that, as he himself reports, "was like being in jail except that I
        was locked out; not locked in." "I had never expected to be al-
        lowed to return to the country that I loved more than any other
        except my own," he is later to write.

        Thus when he crosses the frontier and passes through the border-
        control station of the Guardia Civil with no difficulty at all, in
        July 1953, it seems to him "too good to be true." He promised not
        to come back to Spain as long as any of his Spanish friends are
        still in prison, but by 1953 they have all been released. He and a
        group of friends head for the fiesta of San Fermín in his Lancia,
        driven by his Italian chauffeur, Adamo. Meeting all his old cronies
        in Pamplona (among them Juanito Quintana and "Uncle Ma-
        tías"), revisiting all his old haunts (the Casa Marceliano, the
        Choko Bar), fishing in the Irati again, and going on picnics in the
        woods nearby is like reliving his youth and the exciting days when
        he was writing *The Sun Also Rises*. On this visit, he stays at the
        Hotel Lecumberri, on the outskirts of Pamplona.

        He sees Ordóñez perform in the bullring for the first time, and
        is his guest at the Hotel Yoldi.

        In the fall he goes on another African safari. Pauline's death early
        in the year has greatly depressed him, and it is as if he is trying
        to relive the unforgettable days of 1931, first in Spain and then
        in Africa, this time with Mary. After bagging several lions and
        other game in East Africa, he and Mary board a plane one day to
        see Victoria Falls from the air. A flock of ibises crosses the plane's
        path, and in order to avoid them the pilot makes a sharp turn.
        The plane hits a telephone line and crashes. The next day,
        search planes spot the wreckage but see no signs of survivors. For
        the second time, the world press services report that Hemingway is
        dead, and this time more than twenty-four hours go by before the
        news is proved false. Ernest, Mary, and the pilot are picked up by
        a passing river boat near the scene of the accident and are taken
        to Butiaba suffering from serious injuries. They board another
        plane, for Nairobi, which crashes and burns as it takes off. This sec-
        ond plane accident is even more serious than the first, and Ernest
        suffers head injuries and burns, and has bruises all over his body.

        During this year, he begins to reap the fruits of the enormous
        success of *The Old Man and the Sea*. In May he is awarded
        the Pulitzer Prize for Literature and in August the Italian Book-
        sellers' Annual Prize; still more prizes are to come.

1954   On January 28, having partially recovered from their injuries, he and Mary finally arrive in Nairobi, and go from there to Europe. Ernest convalesces in Venice and goes to Madrid in May for the San Isidro bullfights. He registers at the Hotel Palace and immediately visits his friend Dr. Medinaveitia, who puts him on a strict diet. Almost every morning, he starts the day by visiting the Prado Museum.

He attends the San Isidro *corridas* and again is impressed by Ordóñez. Early in June he returns to Italy in his Lancia and embarks for Havana on the *Morosini*.

On his fifty-fifth birthday he is awarded the Order of Carlos Manuel de Céspedes by the Cuban Government. In October he wins the Nobel Prize. He claims that the injuries he has incurred in the plane crashes in Africa prevent him from going to Stockholm to accept the award personally, but the real reason is that he hates ceremonies and formal dress and having to speak in public.

In March he also receives the Annual Prize of the American Academy of Arts and Letters.

1955   The enormous amount of publicity he receives after being awarded the Nobel Prize makes him even more depressed and irritable. At one point, he goes into total seclusion in Key West for a period of about ten days. His time is spent fishing and writing. He does not visit Spain this summer, and remains quite dispirited and uninterested in bullfighting until the following year, when he comes to Spain to see Ordóñez fight at Zaragoza.

1956   He arrives in Spain via Paris at the end of September and sees Ordóñez and Curro Girón fight in Logroño. He then attends the *feria* in Zaragoza, where he sees Ordóñez fight again, and goes from there to the Escorial, this time putting up at the Hotel Felipe II. The moment he sets foot in Spain and starts going to bullfights, he feels perfectly fine and begins to look like a new man. He tours the countryside around the Escorial, reliving war scenes as he visits the battlefields with friends, and even shows them "the bridge in *For Whom the Bell Tolls*," though of course the bridge exists only in his imagination. This year he remains in Spain throughout the fall and part of the winter, not leaving the country until shortly before Christmas. On October 9 he visits Pío Baroja, who is dying, and on the thirtieth he attends Baroja's funeral, in the non-Catholic cemetery in Madrid.

He stays on at the Hotel Felipe II in the Escorial, but at lunch-time and dinnertime he often visits Madrid, where his two favorite haunts are the Cervecería Alemana on the Plaza de Santa Ana, and the Callejón de la Ternera.

His health improves enormously in the pure air of the Escorial, and Mary, who has been under treatment for anemia, also feels much better almost the moment she sets foot in Spain. Dr. Medinaveitia nonetheless keeps insisting that Ernest must restrict his drinking to a minimum, a single glass of wine at mealtime and only one whisky a day. Ernest finds it very hard to follow the doctor's orders, despite Mary's watchful eye.

1957   His health and family problems prevent him from coming to Spain. The Batista regime in Cuba, under strong attack by Fidel Castro's forces, is reaching the point of collapse, and Ernest is definitely on the side of the rebels in the Sierra Maestra. He is the victim of a number of unpleasant incidents on this account.

The film version of *The Old Man and the Sea* is being shot in Cuba, and Ernest demands that the film crew photograph a real duel with a swordfish, not a fake one. He supervises the filming of the fishing sequences and will not be satisfied until they have shots of the biggest swordfish ever caught. In order to get them, the film crew is obliged to go to the Pacific, and the cost of the film eventually mounts to sixty million dollars. This project keeps him occupied the entire summer of 1958.

Life under Batista's dictatorship becomes more and more uncom-fortable. Murders, looting, illegal searches, and all sorts of vio-lence are the order of the day. Despite the fact that Ernest is a distinguished foreigner, he is not immune to outrages perpetrated by the dictator's minions. One night in April, soldiers from Ba-tista's army who are searching for two young fugitives knock on the door at La Vigía and get Ernest out of bed to question him. Ernest's favorite dog, his most loyal companion, who is very old and almost blind, barks furiously at the intruders, who bash his head in with the butt of a rifle, before Ernest's very eyes. This episode upsets Ernest so much that from this time on he begins to spend most of the year in Ketchum, Idaho, near Sun Valley. In 1959, he buys a house in Ketchum by telephone, the retreat where he is to end his own life two years later. At first he is very excited and enthusiastic about Fidel Castro's victory in Cuba, but the re-gime eventually proves a great disappointment to him.

1959 This is another of Ernest's great years in Spain, a vintage year like 1925 or 1931. He says later that the 1959 season has been one of the happiest times in his life. But as almost always with Ernest, the enormous excitement and enthusiasm of this "dangerous summer" is followed by one of the greatest letdowns of his life. He and Mary board the *Constitution* in New York and arrive in Algeciras early in May. A car is waiting there to take them to La Cónsula, his friend Bill Davis's estate near Málaga. He remains at La Cónsula, writing, swimming in the pool, and walking in the garden, seldom leaving the estate except for an occasional night on the town with friends in Málaga. On May 13 he leaves for Madrid and the San Isidro *corridas*, the beginning of his tireless tour of all the principal bullrings in Spain, following Ordóñez about and hoping for the sake of his art to witness some sort of ultimate bloody apocalypse. He collects photographs and takes notes for *The Dangerous Summer* in Madrid, Sevilla, Córdoba, Ronda, Algeciras, Aranjuez, Valencia, Alicante, Zaragoza, Burgos, Barcelona, Vitoria, and Bilbao, and soon begins to feel as though he is reliving the good old days, that time in his life when he was at the height of his physical and creative powers.

On May 30, in Aranjuez, he takes a young girl who has been run over by a motor scooter to the hospital and is convinced that the accident is a bad omen. And that same afternoon, Ordóñez is gored by the second bull of the day. Ernest goes back to La Cónsula to rest, and Ordóñez joins him there to recuperate.

The fiesta of San Fermín in Pamplona this year, spent singing and dancing in the streets and drinking in his old haunts (the Casa Marceliano, the Choko Bar, the Kutz Bar), causes Ernest to remark, "Everything's better now than in the days of *The Sun Also Rises*."

In Madrid he stays at the Hotel Suecia and again visits the Prado Museum early in the morning almost every day.

On July 21 Mary gives a huge party at Davis's estate to celebrate Ernest's sixtieth birthday. During the evening, Ordóñez puts a lighted cigarette in his mouth and Ernest shoots it out seven times in a row with a rifle, the butt growing shorter and shorter each time.

During the *feria* at Murcia (from the tenth to the fourteenth of September), a pickpocket lifts Ernest's silver money clip with nine thousand pesetas in it as Ernest is signing autographs in the horse enclosure at the bullring. The money clip, with an engraving of

Saint Christopher on it, is a gift from his son Patrick. Ernest puts ads in several papers announcing that the thief can keep the money but begging that he return the money clip because it is of great sentimental value. A few days later the clip is returned to Ordóñez's dressing room. As a reward for the thief's generous gesture and the help the Madrid papers have given him, Hemingway announces that for the next five years he will award an annual prize of five hundred dollars for the best article on bullfighting by a Spanish author.

In September he receives word from *Literaturnaya Gazeta*, in Moscow, that he will be an honored guest if he comes to Russia with President Eisenhower. Ernest answers that he has lost none of his possessions in Russia and prefers to stay in Spain and attend bullfights. In November he returns to Cuba.

1960   He arrives in Spain on August 5 and goes directly to his friend Bill Davis's *finca* in Churriana. Since he is still working on *The Dangerous Summer*, he does his best to remain incognito so that newsmen will not know he is there. The news gets out that he is in Spain, however, and reporters prowl all through the stands in the ring at Málaga looking for him. A number of them mistake Mr. Vanderford, a sort of double of Hemingway's who is also an American with a beard and a great bullfight fan, for Ernest. Ernest watches the *corridas* in Málaga from a cheap seat in the sun so that the reporters and the crowd will not spot him.

On August 8 a Swedish wire service sends out the following bulletin reporting Ernest's death: "The American writer Ernest Hemingway, the Nobel Prize laureate, has died suddenly in the village of Churriana, outside Málaga, where he was spending a few days with his friend Mr. Davis." The bulletin is picked up by news services all over the world, and Ernest is obliged to telephone Mary immediately from Málaga to reassure her. This is the third time that there have been false reports of his death.

That same day, Ernest leaves La Cónsula for Madrid with his friend Bill Davis. They arrive in Madrid on August 9, after having spent the night at the Parador in Manzanares. In the capital he again stays at the Hotel Suecia and continues revising *The Dangerous Summer* and collecting and selecting photographs. He is very worried about what he has written and begins to have tremendous doubts as to whether he has been fair or not, suspecting that he has gone too far.

On August 18 he visits the offices of the daily *Pueblo* and delivers a check for five hundred dollars for the Hemingway Prize. The terms of the prize, which is to be awarded in October, are announced.

Installments of *The Dangerous Summer* come out in the U.S. edition of *Life* on September 5, 12, and 19. Hemingway receives advance proofs shortly before this in Madrid, and is convinced that he has been unfair. He begins to suffer a pathological depression from which he is never to recover. He shuts himself up in his hotel room, refusing to go out or to see anyone. He even refuses to attend bullfights. He spends hours making pointless corrections that will never reach the printers in time. He is beside himself with anxiety about *The Dangerous Summer*, as proved for instance by the telegram he sends the editors of *Life* from Idaho on October 21, which they publish in the Spanish edition: COMPLETELY UN-JUST TO END ARTICLE WITHOUT MENTIONING GREAT EFFORTS DOM-INGUIN TO MEND HIS REPUTATION. SEPTEMBER–OCTOBER 1960 HE FOUGHT WITH GREAT SUCCESS FIRST-CLASS BULLS IN MOST CORRIDAS, WITH RECORD ATTENDANCE MADRID, BARCELONA, ETC.

When he realizes that he has been the victim of his own naïveté and that even Ordóñez wants to have nothing more to do with the whole business, he begins to behave very erratically; he is irritated by the slightest thing, falls into prolonged, brooding silences, and shows all the signs of a severe persecution mania. Nonetheless, like a person unable to leave the scene of his final downfall, he refuses to leave Spain. His friends and his secretary, a young Irish girl he met the year before during the fiesta at Pamplona, attempt to persuade him to return to the United States. But several times he cancels the plane reservations he has made under the name of his friend Bill Davis.

They finally manage to get him to take a plane to New York early in October, and he goes to Idaho, where the hunting season is in full swing. But even hunting seems to have no appeal for him. His depression becomes more and more severe, and in December he enters the Mayo Clinic, in Rochester, Minnesota, registering under the name of his doctor. The reporters are told that he is suffering from hypertension, a kidney ailment, and diabetes; the clinic does not reveal that he is really there primarily for electroshock treatment.

On December 21, the first Hemingway Prize is awarded to Alfonso Martínez Berganza for an article entitled "El Desolladero"—"The Skinner."

1961   In January the doctors decide that he has recovered, and he leaves the Mayo Clinic. He goes on several hunting trips, and more importantly, tries to resume work on his book *A Moveable Feast.* But his capacity for work is greatly diminished. He weighs only 167 pounds, though his normal weight is approximately 220 pounds.

He attempts to kill himself twice during the month of April, and is taken back to the Mayo Clinic. In May he undergoes further electroshock treatments but obsessively insists that he must leave the clinic. Late in June he manages to persuade the doctors that he is well enough to go home, and they release him. He returns to Ketchum on June 30, and that night he has dinner with Mary and his friend George Brown and seems very happy to be back home. After dinner he and Mary sing a favorite song of theirs. On the following day he takes a long walk with Brown, and in the afternoon he walks over to visit his friend Chuck Atkinson, the owner of a motel about half a mile away, whom he has known since 1941. He has dinner with Mary again that night, and except for being a little tired, appears to be his normal self. The following morning, July 2, while Mary is still sleeping, he gets out his favorite shotgun, leans the butt on the floor, puts the double barrel in his mouth, and pulls both triggers.

A few days before, he sent a telegram to Pamplona, canceling his hotel reservation and his reserved seat in the bullring. On the seventh, the opening day of the fiesta of San Fermín, he is buried in the Catholic cemetery in Ketchum. On the eleventh, his friends Juanito Quintana, Antonio Ordóñez, "Uncle Matías," Orson Welles, the mayor of Pamplona, and others attend a requiem mass for him in the Chapel of San Fermín.

Ordóñez promises that he will put up the money for the Hemingway Prize for the announced five-year period. In 1962 the prize is awarded to Pedro de Lorenzo. But this is the last year that entries for the award are solicited.